QUANTICO

Semper Progredi,
Always Forward

THE
DONNING COMPANY
PUBLISHERS

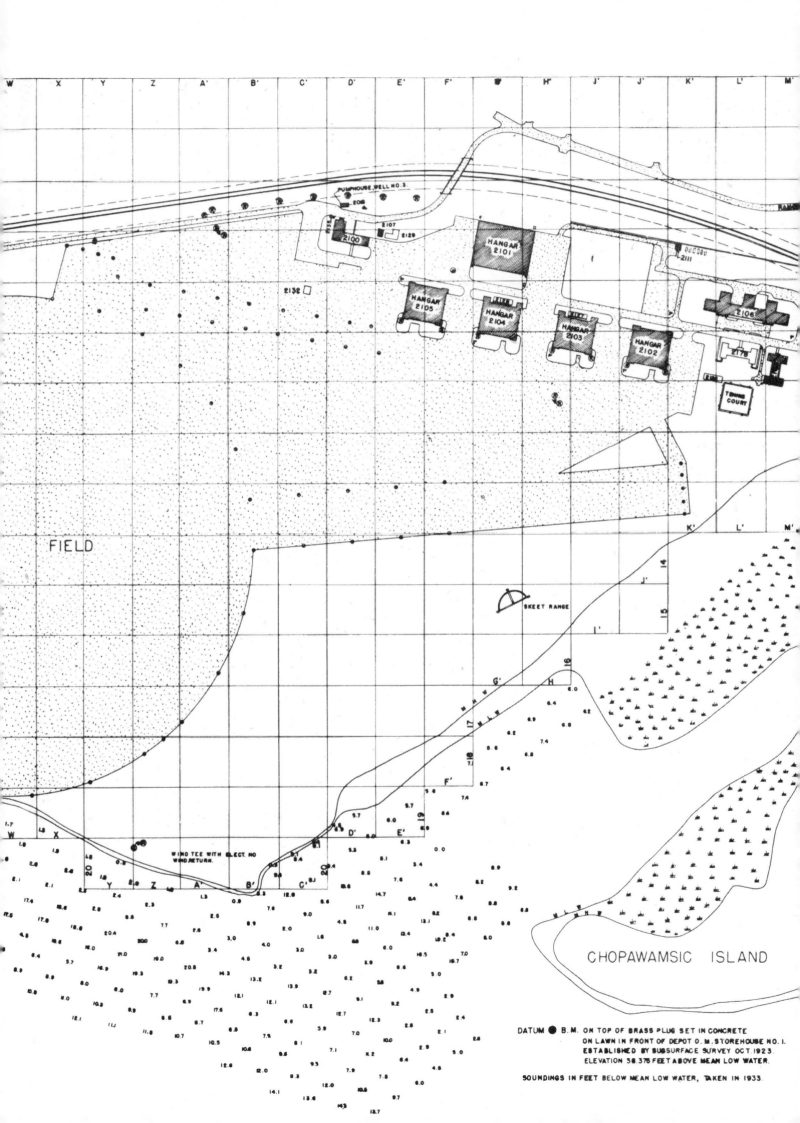

Quantico
Semper Progredi,
Always Forward

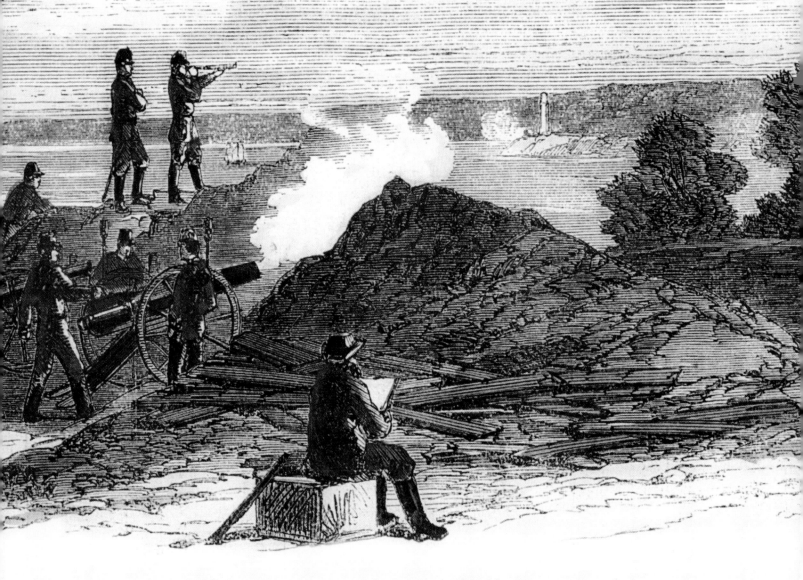

Bradley E. Gernand & Michelle A. Krowl

Courtesy Library of Congress, Prints and Photographs Division, PAN US Military–Camps, no. 5 (F size)

Copyright © 2004 by Bradley E. Gernand and Michelle A. Krowl

All rights reserved, including the right to reproduce this work in any form whatso-
ever without permission in writing from the publisher, except for brief passages in
connection with a review. For information, please write:

The Donning Company Publishers
184 Business Park Drive, Suite 206
Virginia Beach, Virginia 23462

Steve Mull, General Manager
Barbara B. Buchanan, Office Manager
Richard A. Horwege, Senior Editor
Cassie Perry, Graphic Designer
Stephanie Danko, Imaging Artist
Mary Ellen Wheeler, Proofreader
Scott Rule, Director of Marketing
Travis Gallup, Marketing Coordinator
Ann Cordray, Project Research Coordinator

Dennis Walton, Project Director

Library of Congress Cataloging-in-Publication Data

Gernand, Bradley E., 1964–
        Quantico : semper progredi, always forward / by Bradley E. Gernand and
Michelle A. Krowl.
            p. cm.
        Includes bibliographical references and index.
        ISBN 1-57864-268-X (hard cover : alk. paper)
        1. FBI Academy—History. 2. Quantico (Va.)—History. 3. Marine Corps Base
Quantico (Va.)—History. I. Krowl, Michelle A. II. Title.

        F234.Q36G47 2004
        975.5'2732—dc22

                                                                2004009927

Printed in the United States of America by Walsworth Publishing Company

Front cover:
Union batteries firning on Evansport,
*   author's collection (top)*
Inventory, Maurice Evans Papers,
*   Virginia Historical Society (left)*
Sketch of battery, Samuel Sidney Gause
*   Papers, courtesy of Dr. Edward L.*
*   Thackston, Nashville, Tennessee*
*   (right)*

Back cover:
Sgt. Maj. Jiggs, Marine Corps Historical
*   Center (top)*
Map, courtesy of Dr. Edward L.
*   Thackston, Nashville, Tennessee*
*   (middle)*
Receipt, Maurice Evans Papers, Virginia
*   Historical Society (bottom)*

Front and back endsheet maps, courtesy of
*   Captain Thomas W. Turner (Ret.)*

CONTENTS

Map of Quantico, courtesy Captain Thomas W. Turner (Ret.)
Devil Dogs in the Making, *base archive*
"Sergeant Jiggs," *courtesy Marine Corps Historical Center*

Suzie said to me one day long ago
"Honey, please don't join the Co' [Corps]

All they do is fuss'n fight
and they look kinda weird with those 'high and tights.'

They got poor table manners, and they're so rude.
They got a warped sense of humor, and they're so crude."

I said, "Suzie, let me tell you what I'll do
I'll join the Corps for a year or two."

So I packed up my trash and headed for the plane
and I went to the place where they make Marines.

Quantico was the name of the place.
The first thing I saw was a drill instructor's face.

He had razor creases and a Smokey Bear
Mountain climbin' privates everywhere.

Now Suzie said, "It's me or the Corps,
I can't take this life no more."

So I looked at her with a big ole' grin;
I haven't seen Suzie since I don't know when.

—Marching cadence chanted at Quantico[1]

INTRODUCTION
AND ACKNOWLEDGMENTS

An Old History in a New Museum

When the official title of the Marine base at Quantico changed to the Marines Corps Development and Education Command in 1968, the command appropriated as its motto *Semper Progredi*, the Latin phrase for "Always Forward," which had served as General John A. Lejeune's personal philosophy decades earlier.[2] Although the base has simplified its name in the ensuing years to Marine Corps Base Quantico (MCB Quantico), the Marine Corps commands on base, and the other government agencies with facilities within MCB Quantico's borders, continue to strive for forward movement in their educational, research, and development missions. Quantico is more than the military base and FBI Academy, however. Quantico is also an independent community which predates the base, but has since added the distinction of being "the town that cannot grow," being surrounded on all sides by MCB Quantico and the Potomac River. But the authors feel that *Semper Progredi* describes both Quanticos, always moving forward, while not forsaking their respective pasts.

The present volume was written to document and celebrate the remarkable history shared by the town and military base at Quantico, on the eve of construction of the new National Museum of the Marine Corps and Heritage Center, to be built just outside MCB Quantico's boundaries. MCB Quantico has hosted a museum in various incarnations since the 1940s, when Quantico crewmen began collecting, restoring and displaying the best specimens of Marine aviation. Now, for the first

time, artifacts telling the whole story of the Marine Corps will occupy a splendid facility devoted solely to the celebration of Marine Corps history. The authors hope that this book will complement that story by highlighting the history of Quantico and the people who have called Quantico home for either short tours of duty or their entire lives.

The Marine Corps Heritage Foundation, and the authors, would like to thank the following people, without whose assistance and support this book could not have been written: Lieutenant General Ron Christmas, president, Marine Corps Heritage Foundation; Mitchel P. Raftelis, mayor, Town of Quantico; Lena M. Kaljot of the Marine Corps Historical Center; Winnona Savoy-Rogiers and the staff of the Marine Corps University Research Archives; Kathleen Krowl, Karen Needles, B. J. Omanson, Susan Reyburn, Dr. Edward L. Thackston and, of course, the loyal and dedicated members of the Marine Corps Heritage Foundation, and Marines and former Marines everywhere, to whom we say—

Semper Fidelis

CHAPTER I

SETTLEMENT

1500s–1860

TO CIVIL WAR

In the Beginning

The making of a good land, like the making of a good Marine, is an arduous process. Quantico's first peoples believed in a creation myth in which a benevolent supreme being created the land we know today, bringing "the People" to live in it.

Whether by divine intervention or vulcanism, dramatic violence shaped and formed Quantico as it exists today. The underlying rock was formed in massive explosions of energy over 500 million years ago. Between 250 and 400 million years ago it was forcibly intruded by molten rock, forming the present geological base. Quantico became a flat alluvial terrace near a wide, shallow river flowing from the Appalachian mountain range to the west.[3]

Following the demise of the long-ago river, erosion sculpted the face of the Quantico we know today—winding, narrow, flat-bottomed valleys between gravel-capped hills, descending gently toward the Potomac River. The end of the last Ice Age—just a geological moment ago—left Quantico's fertile black soil covered by game-rich forests and fish-filled streams.

"By the Large Stream"

While the "first" Americans likely arrived on the continent between twelve and twenty thousand years ago, archeological evidence suggests that the Quantico area initially was inhabited a mere eight thousand years ago. Indigenous peoples gathered in groups beside local streams, and established winter camps from which the men would hunt and fish.

These true "First Families of Virginia" left behind spear points and arrowheads as a record of their tenure on the land.

In the beginning, these nomadic early settlers moved about the hills and valleys of the coastal plain and Piedmont regions. But by the time European colonists established settlements, the Virginian Indians had established a highly struc-

Powhatan, chief of an Indian confederacy which included the territory of present-day Quantico, in 1607. Smith, Generall Historie of Virginia.

Native American projectiles, including spear points, unearthed from a variety of sites throughout the Occoquan River valley. Prehistoric Indians were nomads, and the makers of these tools likely hunted or fished at Quantico. Courtesy Michael Johnson.

tured and organized civilization, which extended to the area now known as Quantico.

The Indians who inhabited Quantico were Algonquian-speaking members of the Powhatan confederacy, which extended from the Virginia Peninsula to the upper Potomac River region. The Powhatans' regional political district of Chicacoan included the Potomac River Valley. Opposite Quantico, on the Maryland side of the river, lived the Nacotchtanks, Piscataways, Pamunkeys, Nanjemoys, Potapacos, and Yaocomacos. On the Virginia side were the Tauxenents, Patawoomekes, Matchotics, Chicacoans, and Wicocomocos. The Indians used the rivers and streams as transportation routes blazing through the wilderness, connecting settlements and villages with prime hunting grounds and fishing areas. *Potomac*, a Powhatan word meaning "the Gathering Place," was then, as it

remains today, the area's most important waterway. *Quantico*, the Indian word for "by the large stream" or "by the long stream," served as a local landmark due to the distinctive mouth of Quantico Creek. A competing legend claims *Quantico* actually meant "place of dancing," but the traditional "by the large stream" interpretation seems more geographically plausible, if less festive.[4]

In from the Virginian Sea

Enter the Europeans. After establishing a permanent settlement at St. Augustine in 1565, the Spanish sought to extend the province of Florida northward and sailed up the Potomac River about 1571. Having landed just south of Quantico, in the vicinity of Aquia Creek, the explorers evaluated the land while the Jesuit priests set about converting the local Indians. Failing to appreciate the imperialistic

Spaniards, their religion, or the inference that their own religion was somehow less legitimate, the Indians killed all but one of the Iberian interlopers. Spain did not come again.[5]

But England did. After unsuccessful attempts to colonize sites in North Carolina, the English established its first permanent settlement at Jamestown, Virginia, in 1607. The next year, the infamous Captain John Smith left Jamestown to explore the Potomac River Valley just off the "Virginian Sea," as the Chesapeake Bay was then known. Smith's ships reached the Potomac's navigational fall line at Little Falls, just above present-day Georgetown, in Washington, D.C. Ever the explorer, Smith noted the native flora and fauna, and mapped his voyage up the Potomac. In 1624, he published an account of his adventures in Jamestown and the Potomac River Valley, which included the map depicting several of Quantico's distinctive geographic features.

Smith's *Generall Historie of Virginia* also recounted his contact with Powhatan, the chief of the Indian empire that bore his name. A contemporary sketch shows Captain Smith lying prostrate on the floor of Powhatan's dwelling, while Powhatan's daughter Pocahontas begged "King Powhatan" to spare the Englishman's life. While this scene would suggest the Indians held the upper hand in their relations with the English, this would not be the case for long. Not only did the English bring with them hopes for wealth and prosperity, they also brought European diseases and weapons, both of which contributed to the reduction of local Indian populations. After a few scattered rebellions, most Powhatan Indians decided to either adopt English ways and adapt to the new environment, or move elsewhere in the region. By 1700, the former Powhatan nation was under European control, and the inhabitants therein coexisted in relative peace.[6]

Potomac River below Little Falls, circa 1800. The falls were considered by the colonists and Native Americans who preceded them to be the region's most important and defining characteristic. Their location meant Quantico was near the head of Potomac River navigation—an enviable spot. Courtesy National Archives.

"The Woods Do Swarm. . . ."

Land-hungry Englishmen quickly ascended the Potomac for settlement and trade. Henry Fleet exchanged goods with Iroquois Indians from the north at Little Falls in about 1630. Noting a plentiful supply of sturgeon, he enthused breathlessly, "as for deer, buffaloes, bears, and turkeys, the woods do swarm with them and the soil is extremely fertile."

Inspired by reports like Fleet's, wealthier colonists established large plantations at choice locations along the Potomac and its tributaries. Yeomen soon followed, obtaining long-term leases from the vast land grant created in 1649 by King Charles II.[7]

The granting of property rights created the need for borders and boundaries, and the Potomac River served as an excellent demarcation line between the colonies of Maryland and Virginia. The royal land grant gave Maryland control and ownership of the Potomac, which a United States Supreme Court ruling later clarified by setting Virginia's border at the low watermark along its shore. Thus, the waters of Charles County, Maryland, lap at the foot of Quantico's town pier, and on the shore of the town park.

The establishment of boundaries encouraged even more land patents, settlements, and farms. In 1654, Nicholas Martiau secured the patent to a large 2,000-acre tract north of Little Creek, while an even larger 5,211-acre patent swallowed up the land south of Little Creek in 1657. Those familiar with modern-day Quantico may recognize Little Creek as the stream bordering Fuller Road, the main access road to the Marine base. By 1686, English colonists from London and Yorkshire had established a settle-

ment at Chopawamsic; one of the first communities in the Quantico area.[8]

Another early settlement at Quantico itself was the Dipple Plantation, established sometime in the late 1600s or early 1700s. The plantation house stood on the south bank of Chopawamsic Creek until the 1950s, when the Marine Corps demolished it to expand its air operations facilities. Quantico's proximity to Maryland further contributed to its settlement, as dissatisfied colonists from across the Potomac crossed the river to establish themselves in Virginia. By 1647 Giles Brent, for example, had moved to Virginia, after having married a Piscataway Indian princess named Kittamaquad.

Dipple Plantation, shown here in a rather curious state of preservation, was built next to the river in the late 1600s or early 1700s, overlooking what is now the heart of the Marine base. The plantation house was likely demolished around 1955. At the time this aerial photo was taken it must have been Virginia's only plantation home guarded by antiaircraft guns. Courtesy Marine Corps Historical Center.

"Land Travelers in Virginia," published in 1894. Quantico and its environs was settled by colonists such as these, shown fording a creek in the wilds of Virginia. One settler carries an implement used for hacking a trail. Rivers and creeks, traversed with ships and canoes, offered the easiest transportation. The region, astride Aquia, Chopawamsic, and Quantico Creeks and the Occoquan and Potomac Rivers, was particularly accessible for colonization. Lossing, Our Country.

Giles Brent and his family established several plantations in the Aquia area, including "Peace," "Retirement," and "Woodstock." The Brents may have owned property in the Quantico area as well, since George Brent's will bequeaths to his daughter Maria "my plantation at Quanticoe bought of Richard Rechlein, being three hundred acres." Another female Brent married Reverend Alexander Scott of Overwharton Parish (which included Quantico), who once owned the Dipple Plantation.[9]

Brent's descendants would eventually secure the land south of Little Creek, and were responsible for establishing Brent's Village, or Aquia, to the south of Quantico. A wharf was built sometime after 1680, and Aquia developed into a major tobacco port. It also developed a reputation as somewhat of a "party town" on the trade routes with whisky selling for sixty-cents a gallon and "horse races, cock fights, and a variety of other sporting events" providing entertainment. Perhaps this explains the need for Aquia Episcopal Church, built in the 1750s?[10]

To the north of Quantico, Thomas Burbage patented land on the Occoquan River in 1653, although a later resident, George Mason IV, would make it famous as "Gunston Hall." The Lee family could also trace its ownership of the "Leesylvania" property to the 1650s through Laetitia Lee, daughter of the tract's owner Councillor Henry Corbin. Although "Stratford Hall" in Westmoreland County prides itself on being the home of the Lees, "Leesylvania" would produce some equally famous Virginia Lees, such as Henry "Light-Horse Harry" Lee.[11]

Scottish tobacco factors and merchants established nearby Dumfries sometime between 1686 and 1696, naming it for a town in Scotland located near Glasgow on the Clyde River. As was the case elsewhere in Virginia, the cultivation, processing, and sale of tobacco fueled the economy of Dumfries and the surrounding region, especially after the area's first tobacco warehouse was built in 1713.

Native Americans occupying the Quantico region departed quietly as the colonists began encroaching upon the lands which they hunted, fished, and farmed. The unfortunate state of relations between Indians and colonists depicted here was never the case at Quantico, despite what generations of American schoolchildren learned through textbook images such as this one. Elsewhere in Virginia it was a different story. Lossing, Our Country.

Left: Scenes such as these were well known to the residents of colonial-era Quantico, whose regional economy was centered around growing and marketing tobacco. This overdependence on one agricultural staple caused Dumfries to go into decline when other nearby ports, such as Alexandria, began diversifying their economies. Shown here are the barns and methods used in curing the plant. Courtesy Library of Congress. LC–USZ62–72333

Above: A tobacco rolling road. Colonial settlers at Quantico used Indian trails as the basis for their roads. By the 1740s they were important routes for the shipment of tobacco to market. Since tobacco was shipped, or rolled, in large cylindrical casks, or hogsheads, such roads came to be called rolling roads, leading to large warehouses and a port on Quantico Creek. Painting by Carl Rakeman, courtesy Federal Highway Administration.

Cured tobacco would be packed in barrels (called hogsheads) and transported to depots at Dumfries, where agents inspected the tobacco and prepared it for shipping abroad. The tobacco would be loaded on to small-draft vessels at Dumfries, taken down Quantico Creek to the Potomac River, and then transferred to seagoing vessels. Imported goods would go back to Dumfries in the same manner.[12]

Wealth from the tobacco and merchant trade allowed the residents of Dumfries to finance warehouses, build beautiful homes, and transform the town into the economic and cultural hub of Prince William County. An act passed by the Virginia House of Burgesses in 1749 incorporated sixty acres as the Town of Dumfries, and the town's boundaries expanded again in 1759 and 1761, as the population expanded. The town's trustees, all men of wealth and prominence, clearly wanted to build a permanent and respectable city, as evidenced by prohibitions on fire hazards like wooden chimneys and the raising of pigs within town limits. During its heyday, Dumfries boasted a bank, a newspaper, schools, warehouses, fine stores, and even a Jockey Club. And as if foreshadowing the Marine heritage yet to come, Scottish merchant Alexander Henderson built a substantial (and still standing) home in Dumfries. His grandson, Archibald, would later become the fifth commandant of the Marine Corps.[13]

Infrastructure

Local government in Virginia has historically taken place primarily on the county level. Once it passed from Indian control in the Chicacoan district in 1645, Quantico was first part of the vast

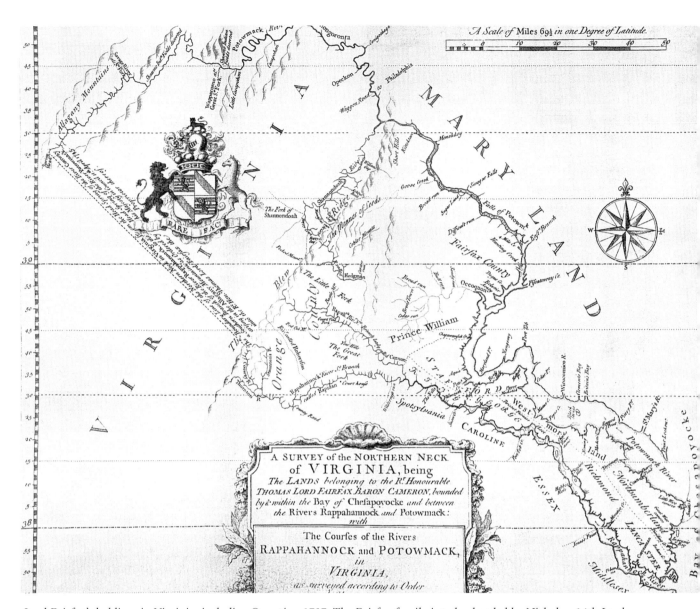

Lord Fairfax's holdings in Virginia, including Quantico, 1737. The Fairfax family is today headed by Nicholas, 14th Lord Fairfax, in Great Britain. George Washington, a Quantico neighbor, was a friend of the colonial-era Fairfaxes. John Warner, 1737. Courtesy Library of Congress.

Northumberland County, which included everything between the Potomac and Rappahannock Rivers. Westmoreland County broke off from Northumberland in 1653, and in 1664 Stafford County was carved from Westmoreland. Finally, Quantico found a permanent jurisdiction in Prince William County, which was formed from sections of Stafford and King George Counties in 1730. Prince William, named for George II's son William Augustus, would lose its northern territory with the formation of Fairfax County in 1742, while Fauquier County would take a section of western

Prince William in 1769. After the Fairfax subdivision, the Prince William County Courthouse moved from Woodbridge to a site on Cedar Run inside the present Marine base. Built on a rectangular plan with a sharply pitched roof, the single-story courthouse most likely resembled the one at King William, to Quantico's south. In addition to the courthouse, businesses, private homes, taverns, and other judicial offices formed the small community. Cedar Run, however, proved to be too far off the beaten trail (both literally and figuratively), and in 1762 the court seat transferred to Dumfries. The

Cedar Run Courthouse and its village subsequently fell into ruin. A stone marker now commemorating the spot is thought to be built from the courthouse's foundation stones.[14] (The current county seat is Manassas.)

With towns and courthouses came the need for roads—and those in the Quantico area were deplorable. The King's Highway, a postal road linking royal capitals at Williamsburg and Boston, passed through the Quantico area along the same general route as today's U.S. Route 1, but the segment between Fredericksburg and Dumfries was particularly infamous due to the terrible state of its bridges—if and when they existed.[15]

The Quantico Road was laid out in 1731. The road linked warehouses, local streams, and rivers, and when connected to the Potomac Path, provided access to the sites of both the first and second Prince William County Courthouses. Although presumably in better condition today, much of the historic Quantico Road lies within the boundaries of the Marine base. The Quantico Road eventually extended all the way across the Blue Ridge Mountains into the Shenandoah Valley. The tentacles of commerce were binding Quantico into the greater British world, and the reign of King George III promised to be a prosperous and locally peaceful one.[16]

Or did it?

The American Revolution

Britain was not the only colonial power in North America, of course, and when French colonists began to infiltrate the Ohio River Valley in the 1750s, Britain took offense. Virginians especially held an interest in French settlement as Virginia's western "border" then extended far into the

Although difficult to see, this map, produced in 1612, was the first to show the definitive geographical features of the Quantico region, in addition to showing the names of its native inhabitants. Smith, True Travels.

Northwest Territory. While the residents of Quantico *per se* may not have been much affected by French claims in Ohio, some of their neighbors were. To contest French claims, the British dispatched troops led by General Edward Braddock and a young Lieutenant Colonel George Washington, a familiar figure in the Dumfries-Quantico area. Braddock's army, which included Virginia regiments, passed through Prince William County in 1755 on its way to meet the enemy out west. Alas, Braddock's campaign was not a smashing success in that Braddock was killed, Washington took command, and the British were defeated. This campaign, however, served as a prelude to the confusingly named French and Indian War (so named because the French allied with the Indians to combat the British), fought between 1756 and 1763. The British ultimately won this round, which discouraged further foreign intervention in the American colonies and gained Canada for Britain in the

George Washington of Mount Vernon. Before he was president of an upstart republic, he was a gifted officer in His Majesty's Army and lived a few estates upriver from Quantico, with which he was very familiar. This was the Washington family's favorite likeness of its patriarch. Courtesy Mount Vernon Ladies' Association.

Below: George Mason of Gunston Hall. Mason, a guiding light of the American Revolution, provided many of the concepts from which James Madison drew the United States Constitution. Mason, like George Washington, was a neighbor to Quantico and knew it well. Courtesy Board of Regents, Gunston Hall Plantation.

process. It also provided American soldiers with experience in fighting with British regulars on their native soil . . . knowledge they would employ much sooner than expected.[17]

Other ramifications of the French and Indian War (also known as the Seven Years' War) did affect all the colonies in America. After years of a sort of benign neglect and a modicum of colonial independence, the war renewed Britain's attention to the colonies. Realizing that adequately defending its colonial outposts was expensive, Parliament decided that the colonies should contribute financially to their own defense, and enacted a series of wildly unpopular taxation schemes. Beginning with the Sugar Act in 1764, progressing to the Stamp Act of 1765, and finally the Townshend Duties in 1767, the colonists found themselves subjected to levies they found increasingly objectionable. The power to tax, after all, is the power to destroy. Having been accustomed to being taxed by their own colonial legislatures, Americans protested that Parliament's new taxes constituted illegal "external" levies, which were particularly obnoxious considering that the colonies had no official representatives in Parliament. Officials in London countered

that as part of the British Empire, America's interests were represented by Parliament as a whole. Few colonists agreed to the idea of "virtual representation." Repeals of the Stamp Act and most of the Townshend Duties (with the exception of a tax on tea) won a temporary reprieve in hostilities, but the Parliament blundered by enforcing the tea tax in 1773. Colonists resisted tea importations, and residents of Boston rebelled by dumping the tea into the harbor in the famous Boston Tea Party. Americans thought Parliament had gone too far. Parliament thought the same of the colonies, and in March 1774 it closed the port of Boston and restricted the Massachusetts government in retaliation. Hoping to isolate the Massachusetts malcontents, Parliament inadvertently started a revolution instead.[18]

Word of Britain's actions quickly traveled throughout the colonies, and like residents elsewhere, many Virginians sympathized with Bostonians and feared that their own rights and liberties could meet a similar fate. Several communities issued "Resolves," or point-by-point rebuttals again British actions, each beginning with "*Resolved*—That. . . ." Fredericksburg, to the south of Quantico, issued the first resolves, and

Dumfries followed on June 6 with its own set of resolves. George Washington and George Mason, Quantico's neighbors to the north, helped draft the "Fairfax Resolves." These resolutions did not confine themselves to trade matters, but also contested infringements by London on the colonists' civil rights. Even before issuing its resolves, the committee at Dumfries left no doubt as to which side of the issue it supported. "We . . . are fully determined to join our fellow Subjects in every Measure to avert the fatal Consequences to us and our posterity from principles so destructive to American liberty, & have not the least Doubt, but we shall be heartily joined by every Individual of the Community."[19]

At the Dumfries meeting in June, the citizens elected Henry Lee and Foushee Tebbs to represent them at the Virginia Convention scheduled to meet in Williamsburg on August 1, 1774. In the meantime, a county committee of safety was formed. In November, the county organized a separate minutemen militia called the Independent Company of Prince William County, captained by William Grayson.[20]

The first Continental Congress met in Philadelphia in September 1774, and after actual hostilities commenced in Lexington and Concord in April 1774, and at the Battle of Bunker Hill in June 1775, Congress appointed Virginia's own George Washington to command the Continental Army. Until 1778, most of the physical fighting of the war would take place in the North, and after that year campaigns in the South commenced in South Carolina and Georgia. Not until 1781 would Virginia see real military action, apart from supplying troops to the Continental Army.

But all was not completely quiet in Virginia, or Prince William County. When the despised royal governor, Lord Dunmore, ordered the confiscation of gunpowder from the magazine in Williamsburg in April 1775, outraged Virginians resisted. Leading the protest was Patrick Henry, who just a month

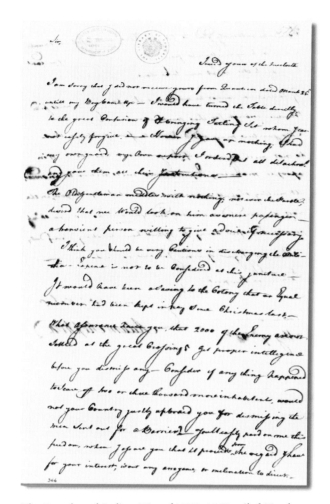

The French and Indian War of 1756–1763 roiled North America, pitting Great Britain and its colonies, including Virginia, against the French and their Indian allies. This letter indicates George Washington and the British army were encamped at Quantico in March of 1756, during a lull in fighting. Hamilton, Letters to Washington.

before had stunned the second Virginia Convention in Richmond with his rousing "Give me liberty, or give me death!" oration. As a result, Dunmore fled Virginia to the safety of British warships in June. Virginia further contributed to the course of liberty in 1776 by supplying Thomas Jefferson, the author of the Declaration of Independence, and Richard Henry Lee, who introduced the resolution for independence before the Continental Congress. On the military front, Prince William's own Henry "Light-Horse Harry" Lee had joined the local militia by 1776, destined to make a name for himself as one of Washington's favorite cavalry commanders. William

The Apollo Room, Raleigh Tavern, Williamsburg. Lord Dunmore, royal governor of Virginia, dissolved the colony's legislature when its revolutionary and reformist fervor became apparent. The councilors, some of them from the Quantico area, promptly defied royal edict, reconvening in the Apollo Room to decide the colony's fate in the revolutionary movement. Their decision that day, for proactive change, altered history. Lossing, Pictorial Field Book of the Revolution.

Grayson of Dumfries became one of Washington's aide-de-camps in August 1776.[21]

Prince William County failed to furnish a great battlefield of the Revolutionary War, but its soil was trodden upon in the war effort. The Marquis de Lafayette, the young Frenchman fighting on behalf of the revolutionary forces, led part of the Continental Army on the King's Highway through Prince William en route from New York to the James River in April 1781. The cavalry and baggage wagons of the combined French and American armies would travel over the same road in September, ultimately on their way to Yorktown and the end of the Revolution. Shifting his base of operations south also gave General Washington a rare opportunity to visit Mount Vernon, from which he wrote Henry Lee about military matters and requested transportation for the Count de Rochambeau and the Chevalier de Chastellux, who were apparently in Dumfries at the time. General

Nathanael Greene, passing through Quantico in 1783, halted for the night in Dumfries when his coach needed repair. He may have been distracted by the unscheduled stop, or annoyed, as his only observation about Dumfries was its location on a creek emptying into the Potomac.[22]

Not surprisingly, given its location on the Potomac River, Prince William and the Quantico area achieved a bit more distinction for naval operations. The Commonwealth of Virginia used Quantico Creek as a major operational base for its new seventy-two vessel navy, serving the Virginia State Marines. The Virginia Navy harassed the Royal Navy more than actively engaging it in equal warfare. Quantico became a supply and equipment depot for the fledgling navy, and the creek's broad and sheltered estuary provided anchorage for many smaller ships. In July 1776, Lord Dunmore sent a fleet up the Potomac River searching for rebel ships and supplies. The royal fleet landed at Aquia Creek just below Quantico, burned the beautiful home of revolutionary landowner William Brent, and then sailed past Quantico to the mouth of the Occoquan River. The British threatened to return again in April 1781, intending to sail up Quantico Creek to burn the town of Dumfries. Colonel Henry Lee caught wind of this rumor, and local militias were raised to track and report the British threat that never materialized.[23]

For most of the Revolutionary War, however, Quantico rarely played a notable role other than as navy anchorage and host to the many soldiers passing up or down the former King's Highway through the present military reservation. For most Prince Williamites, life went on as the British empire crumbled in the American colonies.

Dumfries did, however, contribute one further participant in creating the legend of George

Washington and the Revolutionary War. After marrying a Dumfries girl in 1795, Parson Mason L. Weems made the town his home. Parson Weems, you may remember, wrote a popular book about Washington, perpetuating the myth of his chopping down a cherry tree and not being able to tell a lie.[24]

Royal Colony to Commonwealth

With the end of British rule over the American colonies, the colonies went about establishing themselves as independent states and as a united nation. The Commonwealth of Virginia received a new state constitution in 1776, and the Virginia General Assembly officially abolished the proprietary status of the Northern Neck, which had been established in 1649. The tradition of allotting two representatives per county to House of Delegates continued, and Cuthbert Bullitt and Jesse Ewell served as Prince William's first representatives, while Colonel Henry Lee represented the county in the state senate.

The United States government as a whole struggled to determine the shape the government should take, and the principles under which it should be governed. After delegates from Virginia and Maryland met in 1785 and 1786, to work out interstate trade agreements, representatives from all the former colonies (except Rhode Island) sent representatives to Philadelphia in 1787 to forge a new

constitution to replace the flawed Articles of Confederation. None of the Virginia representatives hailed from Prince William, but the state was ably served by George Washington, George Mason, James Madison, and John Blair. While the resulting bicameral legislature and balance of executive, legislative, and judicial powers are familiar to us today, the ideas in the Constitution proved controversial to those who feared tyranny by a central government. The promise of a Bill of Rights and a brilliant propaganda campaign by the Constitution's supporters helped secure ratification of the Constitution in 1788. After a close vote (eighty-nine to seventy-nine), Virginia was the tenth state to ratify the Constitution, although interestingly the delegates from Prince William County voted against ratification during Virginia's convention. A provision in Article I, Section 8 of the Constitution would eventually exert a lasting influence over Quantico and Northern Virginia as a whole. It gave Congress the power to control a district "not exceeding ten miles square" which would serve as "the seat of government of the United States." In 1800, the federal government took up residence in the District of Columbia, and became Quantico's neighbor on the banks of the Potomac approximately thirty miles to the north.[25]

Engravings from the Revolution, circa 1775. Virginians from the Quantico area were important conspirators of the American Revolution. George Washington, whose home was near Quantico, led colonial armies. This sepulchral device, a skull and crossbones and crown hovering over the Cap of Liberty, suggested "all was death and destruction between the Crown and liberty." So it seemed to Virginians, who forced Lord Dunmore, their royal governor to flee. Lossing, Pictorial Field Book of the Revolution.

Colonial recruitment poster, circa 1776, showing the manual of arms designed to encourage young men to rally to the cause. Courtesy George Washington's Office Museum.

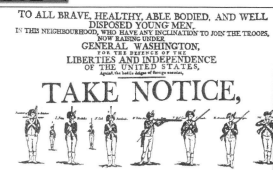

With the establishment of the United States federal government, the states sent their first representatives to Congress. Two men well known in Prince William County, Richard Henry Lee and William Grayson, served as Virginia's first senators in the United States Senate. Grayson, for whom Virginia's Grayson County is named, also had the distinction of insisting that a clause prohibiting slavery be included in the Northwest Ordinance of 1787, which governed the land north of the Ohio River and east of the Mississippi River during the territorial phase. After the Revolution, General Washington also appreciated Grayson's knowledge of foliage in the Quantico area, asking Grayson to furnish him shoots of the yew or hemlock trees "that grows on the Margin of Quantico Creek" to plant at Mount Vernon.[26]

The Downfall of Dumfries

Thanks to Mother Nature and the vagaries of trade, the good times enjoyed at Dumfries before the American Revolution would not last. By the end of the Revolution, Quantico Creek had silted so seriously from agricultural runoff that it became increasingly difficult for any vessels to reach the docks at Dumfries, thereby making vital trade nearly impossible. By the 1740s a canal had been dug along the northern banks of Quantico Creek to facilitate shipping, and from 1795 to 1834, the Quantico Company dredged and cleared the creek channel for the same end. But all for naught. The Revolutionary War furthered the decline in the tobacco market as European merchants, cut off from their supply in Virginia, looked to other colonial products, like sugar in the West Indies. Furthermore, the economy's dependence on tobacco failed to take into account the soil-depleting nature of the crop, which quickly drains the soil of nutrients and makes it unfit for further tobacco cultivation.[27]

Merchants decided to build tobacco warehouses at the mouth of Quantico Creek in 1787, creating a

George Washington, commanding general of the rebelling colonies' Continental Army. The general passed through the Quantico area repeatedly traveling to and from his farms along the Potomac. Painting by Charles Willson Peale, courtesy Library of Congress. LC–USZ62–96753

town on the north bank called Newport to host them. Yet another town, Carrborough, appeared on the south bank in 1788, and at least one warehouse was built to complement those at Newport. Among the trustees of Carrborough were Cuthbert Bullitt and William Grayson. But with Dumfries already sliding into decline and the tobacco industry beginning to wane, the new warehouses closed within five years, and the new towns they supported withered and died. Without another cash crop to rely on, and having not adequately diversified its economy with other products, the decline of trade along Quantico

Creek forced the economic and social life of the Potomac River Valley to move elsewhere, such as larger ports farther up the Potomac like Alexandria and Georgetown. By 1840 the pronounced decline of Dumfries prompted a visitor to lament that "Dumfries itself, once the mart of that part of Virginia, the scene of gaiety and fashion . . . is now in ruins . . . desolation reigns around." Once Dumfries lost its seats as the regional judicial district to Haymarket in 1803, and the county seat to Brentsville in 1822, even the town's judicial and administrative functions were stripped bare.[28]

The War of 1812

Yet another war between France and Britain caused Britain to impose naval blockades around European ports, severely impeding trade by neutral nations like the United States. The British Navy also asserted the right to search ships for "deserters," and impressed these men into service. Inevitably, American seamen were among the impressed. Economic embargos imposed by the Jefferson and Madison administrations failed. Relations between the upstart American republic and its former colonial master, never good, once again erupted into open warfare in June 1812.

As had been the case in the Revolutionary War, the key military engagements took place elsewhere, primarily on the Great Lakes and in Canada, with a memorable battle undertaken by Andrew Jackson in New Orleans after the war technically had ended. But the War of 1812 would be lodged in American memory for the British campaign up the Potomac River and against Washington, D.C. In August 1814 the Royal Navy ascended the Potomac, anchoring for a night off Quantico, in clear view of observers on Rising Hill. Many of the spectators were from Dumfries, which expected to be attacked, a silted Quantico Creek and navigational woes notwithstanding. For Rising Hill's audience, it was a night they would not soon forget. A torrential (locals said

providential) gale discouraged the British, sparing the town. After mauling plantations at the mouth of Quantico Creek, the enemy fleet hauled up anchor, sailing farther upstream to the young city of Washington, D.C., which the British army captured after defeating ragtag Americans at the ill-fated Battle of Bladensburg—the "Bladensburg races," as dispirited Americans called it.

President James Madison, his cabinet, and the government fled in panic. Important state documents were taken into Virginia's interior, and the president, searching for his wife, headed out of the city on chaotic roads filled with frightened refugees. Dolley Madison had refused to leave the White House, waiting for her husband's return. She finally dispatched one last, quick note to her sister: "Mr.

Revolutionary firebrand Richard Henry Lee served as a member and president of the Continental Congress, and sponsored the resolution which became the Declaration of Independence. Despite having large landholdings in Prince William County, he lived on a leased estate, Chantilly, in Virginia's then-remote Northern Neck. Painting by Charles Willson Peale, courtesy Library of Congress. LC–USZ62–92331

23

Henry "Light Horse Harry " Lee III. Lee won the admiration of George Washington during the Revolution and earned his moniker by proving to be good with cavalry. Leesylvania, his birthplace at Freestone Point, just upriver from Quantico, is now a state park. Engraving by J. F. Prudhomme, courtesy Library of Congress. LC–USZ61–1190

Madison comes not. May God protect him! Two messengers, covered with dust, come to bid me fly." And fly she did, though not before ordering that the oil portrait of George Washington be unscrewed from the wall, cut from its frame, and sent into the interior for safekeeping.

Mordecai Booth, a messenger from the Washington Navy Yard, soon dashed to the White House, which stood dark and quiet. He yanked the bell-pull at the front door, eventually realizing to his horror that no one remained to answer his summons. "The Metropolis of the Country," he later recounted, "was abandoned to its horrid fate." Booth then rode to the Capitol, where the newly arriving British fired upon him, prompting him to leave the city in haste.

The British entered the deserted Capitol and its empty legislative chamber and, mocking American democracy, held an "election" to determine the building's fate. The British army voted to burn it, whereupon the soldiers piled books, documents, and draperies into a large pile and set it ablaze. They then torched the White House and many of the public buildings in the city.

Booth, who by that time had reached the hills overlooking Washington across the river, stood with other witnesses in sick and numbed dismay, helplessly watching the capital go up in flames. The conflagration in Washington—its burning ships, storehouses, government buildings, and homes—could be seen for miles in all directions. Worried residents in Baltimore heard no news about the attack, but the glow from Washington literally had been their fire bell in the night. "We only know from the light during the night that the city was on fire," David Winchester of Baltimore wrote the next morning. Nearby Quantico residents must have lived through much the same anxiety as the fires lit up the night skies along the upper Potomac.

The chaos and disorder engulfing the region also set fire to wild rumors of slave insurrection, a constant fear in slaveholding communities. As with most rumors, no one knew how widespread the revolt was supposed to be, or whether it was approaching in earnest. But it frightened everyone alike, both slave and free, for the violence and destruction it portended. Quantico area landowners, whose plantations depended on slave populations, felt particularly vulnerable to attack. The rumor proved untrue, but it unsettled nerves already stretched beyond the breaking point.

With the destruction of Washington fresh in their minds, on August 29 the panicked citizens of Alexandria decided to surrender their town to the departing British, rather than suffer the same fate as the capital. The ever-observant Mordecai Booth, rode to a prominent hill in Alexandria, from which he was treated to the vile sight of the Union Jack

District of Columbia boundary stone. Each marker read "Jurisdiction of the United States" on the District side of the stone, and "Virginia" (or "Maryland") on the other. In 1790 Congress chose a site just upriver from Quantico for the new national capital. This decision was to be pivotal to Quantico's future, though none could yet know it. Courtesy Mary Riley Styles Public Library.

flying above Washington and the British plundering Alexandria's warehouses for supplies.

The Americans were powerless to prevent the British from accomplishing whatever they wished, and the enemy eventually moved off on its own accord, its powerful fleet sailing down the Potomac to other battles—and into history.[29]

The war wound down to something of a stalemate, as both the United States and Britain agreed in the December 1814 Treaty of Ghent to return captured territory, and Canada remained part of the British empire.[30] But many historians call the War of 1812 America's *second* war of independence as America's "victory" in repelling the British con-

firmed the survival of the young republic. It also brought to the fore military heroes who would exert further influence in the future, such as the wily Andrew Jackson, William Henry Harrison (the hero of Tippecanoe), and Virginian Winfield Scott. More ominously, the burning of Washington also created the lasting image of enemy forces sailing up the Potomac to lay siege on the nation's capital; an impression etched into the minds of many subsequent wartime leaders.

Prince William between the Wars

Having weathered yet another threatened British invasion, Prince William and Quantico settled back to enjoy whatever peace and prosperity they could find. Declining tobacco fortunes and the rise of cotton cultivation in the Deep South, and the opening up of new lands in the Louisiana Purchase territory, may have contributed to the decrease in the county's total population after the War of 1812. From over eleven thousand residents counted on the 1810 federal census, Prince William's population only reached eighty-five hundred by 1860. While the white population hovered steadily around five thousand persons, the slave population in Prince William decreased by half, from over five thousand in 1810 to only twenty-three hundred in 1860.[31] This shift might suggest that some planters left the county and took their slaves with them, but the population statistics likely suggest a change in agricultural focus among Prince William planters. As tobacco yields declined, many farmers probably changed their crops to wheat and corn, neither of which required the large labor forces tobacco demanded. Field drawings made in 1861 by Samuel S. Gause clearly show cornfields and pastures among the marshes and piney woods along Quantico Creek and the Potomac River. With a surplus of slave laborers in the county, and plantations elsewhere in the South clamoring for more, some Prince William slaveowners may have turned from selling tobacco to selling slaves. But after Nat Turner's violent slave rebellion in Southampton County in 1831, and the murder of a Woodbridge man by his slave woman in 1850, questions about the presence and fate of slavery certainly occupied the minds of Prince Williamites, especially as the issue became an increasingly volatile one during the antebellum period.[32]

Whereas Dumfries languished by 1835, Brentsville was poised to become a thriving community. It boasted stores, taverns, churches, a school, bible and temperance societies, as well as three attorneys and three physicians. Up the river at Occoquan, a cotton manufacturing plant, flour, grist, saw, and plaster mills, herring and shad fisheries put the village "in a flourishing condition." Dumfries, however, appeared to have reoriented its economy slightly to take advantage of the overland routes through the town. In 1835 it counted the usual churches and taverns, but also two saddlers and two blacksmith shops. When the Potomac River froze during the winter, the mail between Washington, D.C., and New Orleans "is carried through this town." Unfortunately, the roads had not improved much from the colonial days, leading to the observation that the road between Fredericksburg and

America's second war of independence with Great Britain, the War of 1812, was traumatic for Quantico. The British fleet sailed up the Potomac, anchoring briefly off Quantico before proceeding to Washington, D.C., which it burned. The enormous conflagration lit the sky at Quantico that terrible night. Courtesy Library of Congress. LC–USZ62–1939

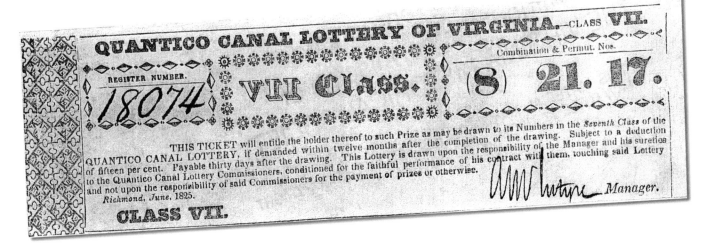

Alexandria "is in a worse condition than perhaps any in the middle States, so utterly impassable at times that the mail cannot travel." On the bright side, the mouth of Quantico Creek was proclaimed "the best winter harbor on the Potomac," since the river remained passable at this point.[33]

By the 1850s, the wave of the transportation future ceased to be simple roads like King's Highway, but rather railroads. The Manassas Gap Railroad and the Orange and Alexandria Railroads arrived in Prince William County in the early 1850s, allowing for faster and more reliable transportation of people and goods in the area. Private enterprise primarily constructed railroads in this era, rather than governments, and were thus particularly susceptible to economic downturns, such as the Panic of 1857, which halted construction on several projects. The railroads were also undertaken on a local scale, meaning that they were often built for the purpose of getting products to markets or ports, and did not necessarily form a national network. Furthermore, until track gauges became standardized, trains designed for one gauge of track could not be transferred to lines using a different gauge. Despite these early bumps in the road, the railroads helped transform how Americans got from place to place, and in Prince William the presence of the railroad would soon determine the contour of the Civil War. Although Quantico itself would not receive rail service until after the Civil War.[34]

The Stage Is Set

Whatever peace and tranquility enjoyed in Quantico and Prince William County between the wars would be shattered by John Brown's raid on Harpers Ferry (then still part of Virginia) in October 1859. Although an unsuccessful raid in terms of inciting slave rebellions in the South, Brown's actions crystallized the sectional resentments simmering throughout the 1850s. The white South was outraged, and saw the raid as confirmation that Northerners meant to undermine its way of life. Brown's subsequent trial and execution failed to mollify the South, and when "black Republican" Abraham Lincoln won the presidency in 1860, South Carolina and other states in the Deep South seceded from the Union. And another war was on.

Above: Several attempts have been made to keep Quantico Creek open for navigation. The early attempts, such as this one, a lottery from the 1820s, were private commercial affairs; later ones were undertaken by the U.S. Army Corps of Engineers. The battle was and is unending. Barbour Family Papers, Virginia Historical Society.

CHAPTER II

THE WAR

BETWEEN THE STATES

1861–1865

The secession of South Carolina from the United States in December 1860, followed by other states in the Deep South, did not foreordain that Virginia would follow suit. While deeply concerned about the issues of slavery, states' rights, and the South's influence in the federal government and the nation at large, Virginia contemplated her response longer than her firebrand sisters to the south. Virginia held a state secession convention in February 1861, but because a majority of the delegates favored remaining in the Union, the convention postponed making a final decision until the results of a peace conference held in Washington, D.C., became known. It is perhaps indicative of the stronger feelings of Prince William County that Eppa Hunton, a secessionist delegate, was elected over a Union man. The failure of the peace conference weakened Virginia's unionistic resolve, and after President Lincoln's call for seventy-five thousand men to quell the rebellion begun with the firing on Fort Sumter in Charleston harbor in April, Virginia chose to cast her fate with the new Confederacy. On April 17 the Virginia convention drafted an ordinance of secession, and on May 23 Virginia voters ratified it. In an instant, Quantico was located not in the United States of America, but the Confederate States of America. Of perhaps more immediate importance to the area was the moving of the Confederate capital from Montgomery, Alabama, to Richmond, Virginia; a mere one hundred miles from Washington, and thus a natural military objective for Union troops.[35]

The first major land battle of the war occurred in July 1861 near Manassas, a railroad junction connecting the Manassas Gap and Orange and Alexandria Railroads. While the first Battle of Manassas (or Bull Run, as it became known in the North) proved a chaotic battle between two green and untested armies, the Confederate victory gave the South an early psychological edge over the North. The South's victory, made possible by the last-minute arrival via railroad of troops from the Shenandoah, suggested how critical railroads would be in terms of supply lines.[36]

The Evanses of Evansport

By 1861, present-day Quantico had acquired the name Evansport, after one of the families who settled there. Samuel Evans, the patriarch of the family, was born in Pennsylvania in 1816, but by the time of the Civil War, he had established himself in Prince William County. Evans listed his occupation as "farmer" on the 1860 census, but he may have also owned a fishing wharf and steam mill on the waterfront, and likely operated a ferry service as well. By 1860 the household consisted of Samuel, Mary A., Maurice, Henry C., and a nine-year-old African-American girl named Jane Williams. Regardless of his primary occupation, Samuel Evans did fairly well for himself, and according to a September 1861 appraisal of his Evansport property, the value of his barns, dwelling house, outbuildings, crops, orchard, and assorted other non-land assets totaled nearly $8,000.

Unfortunately, the likely reason for the appraisal is that Confederate forces had taken over his property to erect batteries along the Potomac.[37]

Samuel's twenty-two-year-old son Maurice sided with the Confederacy, and in April 1861 joined the Prince William Cavalry, which became Company A of the famed 4th Virginia Cavalry. Maurice Evans never rose above the rank of private during the war, but he did have the distinction of serving as a scout for J. E. B. (James Ewell Brown) Stuart, under whose command the 4th Virginia ultimately fell. Given that the 4th did some raiding and skirmishing in the Dumfries area during the war, Evans' knowledge of the vicinity probably came in handy. Alas, young Maurice must not have had the swiftest horse or he experienced a run of bad luck in 1863. He was captured by Union forces at Elk Run in March, exchanged in April, recaptured in Dumfries in June, and exchanged yet again on Christmas Day, 1863, after having enjoyed Yankee hospitality in Old Capitol Prison in Washington, and Point Lookout Prison in Maryland. To his credit, Maurice survived the war, having only suffered a wounded hand in 1862. When the war ended, Evans took an oath of allegiance to the United States, and after the war managed a Richmond business called Evans, Porter and Company, which for a few months in 1865 ran a small postal agency called the Magic Letter Express. Evans did not abandon his interest in the Confederacy, however, and later joined the Virginia Division of the Army of Northern Virginia and evidently hung on to the old flag of his cavalry company. By 1913 Evans had moved to Guiney, in Caroline County, Virginia, apparently having never returned to live at Evansport. Samuel Evans died in 1893, and his son Maurice died in 1915.[38]

Embattled Evansport

The railroad never completely supplanted water routes in Virginia, which explains why Confederate forces first began looking at Quantico in June 1861. General P. G. T. (Pierre Gustave Toutant) Beauregard suggested to a subordinate in Stafford

The Confederate military closed the Potomac River to shipping after war's outbreak to isolate Washington, the Union capital. This engraving shows the USS Seminole *and USS* Pocahontas *engaging Southern batteries at Quantico, then called Evansport. The Union Navy attempted repeatedly to neutralize the batteries and open the river to traffic. Guerney,* Harper's Pictorial History of the Great Rebellion.

County that he explore the possibility of erecting batteries in Brentsville, which would forestall an advance on Beauregard's position in Manassas from "any force of the enemy attempting to land at Quantico Creek or even at Aquia Creek." Beauregard further recommended that a telegraph station be installed immediately at Camp Chopawamsic, near Evansport, to facilitate communication with their respective headquarters and Richmond.[39] As it turned out, the Union took an overland route from Washington to meet Beauregard's troops at Manassas, and his fears of a water invasion did not materialize.

Confederate forces, however, realized the strategic importance of Evansport and the area around Quantico, Chopawamsic, and Aquia Creeks as both supply depots for their own troops, and for blockading the Potomac River from use by the Union military and commercial shipping. Evansport seemed an ideal location for river batteries as the Potomac River narrows at that point, and scouts had a clear view of approaches from both the north and the south. Depending on the speed of the vessel and the weather conditions, a Union ship could potentially be under fire for at least an hour from a battery at Evansport. The proximity of Rising Hill also meant that fortifications could be erected close to the river, and again four hundred feet above, effectively doubling the firepower from this location. Furthermore, Evansport's road connections to Fredericksburg and Manassas were considered optimal, although the conditions of those roads would prove far less satisfactory than anticipated. General Robert E. Lee concurred on Evansport's strategic worth in August 1861, and ordered the erection of batteries there. When taken in connection with other strategic

THE REBEL BATTERIES ON THE LOWER POTOMAC

Fac Simile of a Plan of the Batteries and Encampments on the Lower Potomac Up in the Rebel Camp by Our Troops.

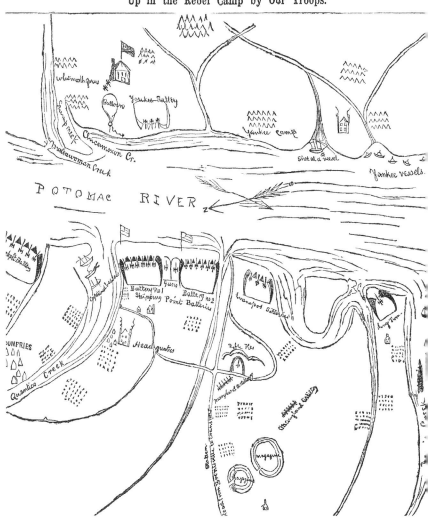

Quantico's importance early in the war was revealed by the intensive press coverage of events there. This front-page map, published in the New York Herald *on March 17, 1862, shows Chopawamsic and Quantico Creeks. The presence of Confederate Marylanders at Quantico must have seemed bittersweet for those soldiers, who fled their Union-occupied but Southern-leaning state to join the Confederate army in Virginia.*

points in the vicinity at Freestone Point, Cockpit Point, Possum Nose, Shipping Point, and those on Chopawamsic Creek, the Confederate defenses on the lower Potomac looked formidable. Nearby Aquia proved its value primarily as a supply depot, since it boasted access to both the Potomac River and a railroad line into the interior.[40]

A fair number of Confederates had already taken up a position at Evansport, which the Union realized in June after a reconnaissance party from the USS *Reliance* discovered small boats being used to ferry men and supplies from Maryland, and observed soldiers along the beach at Evansport. Naval commanders would also hear about fortifications in the process of being erected at Evansport when a Confederate deserter from an Arkansas regiment crossed the river into Maryland and told Union officers there what he knew about the fortifications and the number of men garrisoning them. But little was done to really fortify Evansport until September, when Confederates installed a battery of five guns, including a rifled thirty-pounder, at Freestone Point. (Freestone Point currently forms the northwestern tip of Leesylvania State Park, to the north of Quantico.)[41]

Union military minds quickly recognized their dilemma on the Potomac: the Confederates could build as many batteries as they wished, without the Union being able to stop them unless it arranged for twenty heavy guns on Maryland's Indian Head, with fifty along the Maryland shore opposite Cockpit Point and Evansport. This was considered prohibitively expensive, both in terms of guns and men. "I would wait until the disposition and ability of the enemy seriously to molest the navigation is more fully developed before commencing," Chief Engineer General J. G. Barnard suggested. His suggestion was accepted, and indeed it would be mere days before the Confederates were able to "molest" navigation successfully. By October 9, 1861, the *New York Times*, interested in rebel movements outside Washington like the rest of the country, reported rebel campfires

at Evansport and for three miles up and down river. The guns were in place.[42]

The Potomac Flotilla

Beyond merely countering Confederate batteries, the Union Navy recognized the importance of maintaining a presence on the Potomac for its own interests. Just days after President Lincoln authorized a naval blockade of the Confederate coast in April 1861, Commander James H. Ward proposed to Secretary of the Navy Gideon Welles the assembly of a "light flying force with a view to service in the Chesapeake and its tributaries; to interrupt the enemy's communications; assuredly keep open our own; drive from those waters every hostile bottom; threaten all the points of a shoreline accessible to such a force exceeding one thousand miles in extent; protect loyal citizens; convoy, tow, transport troops or intelligence with dispatch; be generally useful; threaten at all points, and to attack at any desired or important one." Impressive goals indeed, but ones

Maurice Evans of Evansport, a loyal Confederate cavalryman who was, among other things, a scout for the famous "JEB" Stuart, had to sign a loyalty oath to the Union-backed restored state government of Virginia before regaining his freedom. It must have been a bitter pill to swallow. Maurice Evans Papers, Virginia Historical Society, Richmond, Virginia.

"Confederate Batteries at Evansport," modern Quantico. This engraving shows the extensive system of fortifications linking Confederate batteries in and near the present town. Guerney, Harper's History of the Great Rebellion.

to which Secretary Welles assented. The new "Potomac Flotilla" began with just three ships: the *Thomas Freeborn*, a side-wheel steamer carrying two thirty-two-pounders; and the small screw vessels the *Resolute* and the *Reliance*, each supplied with twenty-four-pound howitzers. Eventually the USS *Pawnee* and *Anacostia* would join Ward's "humble armada."[43]

While technically under the auspices of the Atlantic Blockading Squadron, the Potomac Flotilla operated quite independently, and concentrated its efforts in the upper Chesapeake Bay and along the Potomac. For several days at the end of May and beginning of June, 1861, the Flotilla set its sights on Confederate guns at Aquia Creek, with negligible damage done to either side. In late June Commander Ward decided to take out Confederate guns and troops farther down the Potomac at Mathias Point. During skirmishing from the *Thomas Freeborn* with the rebels on shore, Ward received a fatal abdominal wound, making him the first Union Navy officer to die during the war.

Although the commander was dead, his brainchild, the Potomac Flotilla, would continue to harass rebel batteries on the lower Potomac for months.[44]

"Schooner ahoy!"

Under its new commander, Captain Thomas T. Craven, the Potomac Flotilla achieved a spectacular success right in Evansport. In October 1861, crews from the USS *Union*, USS *Rescue*, and USS *Resolute* spied the Confederate schooner CSS *Martha Washington* anchored in the mouth of Quantico Creek. Employing a bit of guerrilla warfare, Lieutenant A. D. Harrell of the *Union* commanded a party of sailors who entered the creek under cover of darkness, boarded the ship, and set fire to a pile of furniture in a cabin. By starting the fire below deck, Harrell hoped to have time to leave the *Martha Washington* before attracting attention. Unfortunately, an overeager Union sailor set fire to a sail on deck, causing Confederate sentries to note their presence. "Schooner ahoy!" came the challenge which, when not answered, was followed by a volley of gunfire. "Ah! you damned Yankees, we have you now!" the Confederates yelled, along with other "opprobrious epithets." But the "light from the burning schooner" guided Harrell's men safely back to their own ships, and into history.[45]

The destruction of the *Martha Washington* became national news, and was especially welcome in the North at a time when few victories had been won and the Army of the Potomac remained stalled outside of Washington. Newspapers like the *New York Herald* published Lieutenant Harrell's reports of the incident, and the *Saturday Evening Post* included an engraving of the "beautiful conflagration." Harrell was hailed as a hero, and Secretary Welles effused that "the successful result under great disadvantages, without loss of life, demonstrates the daring intrepidity of the Navy, which only requires a field whereupon to prove the quality of those who serve under its banners."[46]

And perhaps for the first time in the war, United States Marines participated in operations off the coast of Quantico. In August 1861, two hundred Marines were attached to the Potomac Flotilla to aid the Navy in identifying Confederate sympathizers and seizing their arms.[47]

"Varmints"

The Potomac Flotilla was not through testing the Confederate batteries along the Potomac, nor making national news for having done so. A few days after destroying the *Martha Washington*, the USS *Seminole* reported a damaging engagement with Evansport's batteries. On the morning of October 15, the USS *Pocohontas* passed Evansport without challenge, even after having fired on the rebel batteries. Thinking the coast was clear, the *Seminole* followed at a "majestically slow" speed. This time the Confederates revealed themselves on the shore, cutting away the trees which had previously masked their location. The Confederate batteries opened fully, striking the unfortunate steamer eleven times. While still within range, the *Seminole* returned fire, getting off twenty shots to the thirty or thirty-five lobbed at it from shore. Some balls passed completely through the ship. Its captain, Commander Gillis, reported his ship "suffered severely," but his crew escaped largely without injury.

"Several persons were scratched by the splinters" falling from the damaged railing, Gillis conceded.[48]

"Did you hear the row?" the *Seminole*'s commander asked Captain Craven in an unofficial

Confederate battery at Possum Nose, near modern Cockpit Point. Note the Stars and Bars, the southern flag, waving proudly from the tall pole. Wright, Official and Illustrated War Record.

A gunboat of the Union Navy's Potomac Flotilla illuminating Confederate batteries at Evansport (Quantico) with a calcium light. Technological advancements, or their application to warfare, marked the Civil War as the first war of the modern era. Leslie's Illustrated Weekly, *issue date unknown.*

report. "It continued about forty minutes, as the 'old wagon' moved leisurely down the river." Gillis explained, off the record, that after the *Pocahontas* "stirred up the party" on shore, she "[left] us to do battle with the Dixie boys." The "'varmints' shot away our mizzenmast and mizzen," as well as their mainstays, some railing, and hammock nettings.[49] The "varmints" kept shooting during the next few days—at the USS *Pawnee*, USS *Columbia*, USS *Resolute*, USS *Reliance*, USS *Release*, USS *Susquehanna* and the USS *Murray*, as well as several civilian vessels.

Log books from ships assigned to the Potomac Flotilla confirm that Confederate batteries around Evansport remained very active in their firing in October and November 1861. The log of the USS *E.B. Hale*, for example, records almost a daily barrage:

> *October 16*—At 4:40 a.m. U.S.S. *Pawnee* passed down with two boats in tow. When the boats were down toward Shipping Point the battery opened fire upon them. Kept on till 6:25; twenty-seven shots were fired.
>
> *October 17*—At 6 a.m. sixteen shots were fired from the battery, Shipping Point, and fifteen at 8:25.
>
> *October 18*—From 1:45 till 12:10 midnight:

Fourteen shots were fired from the rebel battery toward the U.S.S. *Columbia*, which passed us during the time up river. From 1:57 to 2:20 a.m. six shots were fired from the battery. . . .

> *October 19*—At 12:40 a.m. six shots were fired from the rebel battery. At 2:10 three shots were fired; at 9 seventeen shots fired. At 10 a.m. commenced firing, continuing until 10:55; in that time fired 152 shots from the rebel battery toward the towboat *Resolute*. . . .[50]

And the list goes on and on. For residents living within earshot, the frequent early morning cannonading must have been as disturbing to their sleep as it was to their nerves!

"Amusing themselves by firing"

"Since the engagement [between the Confederates and the *Seminole*] the rebels have been amusing themselves by firing at a small schooner which is at this time out of reach of his [*sic*] guns," reported Captain Craven in October 1861. If newspaper reports from camps near Budd's Ferry on the Maryland side of the Potomac accurately recorded the expertise of rebel artillery trials, "amusing them-

Union warships repeatedly challenged Confederate batteries at Evansport. This attempt to force passage by the USS Pensacola, shown here, made the national press. Harper's Weekly, *February 1, 1862.*

Engraving, "Schooners running the Evansport (Quantico) and Shipping Point Batteries." Events at Quantico also made international headlines. Illustrated London News, *December 7, 1861.*

———————

selves" was all the Confederate gunners seemed to be doing with their weapons. Since log books from Union ships in the Potomac Flotilla failed to mention any significant damage to the ships being fired upon, perhaps reports of artillery inaccuracy were themselves accurate. "This morning the rebels at Evansport . . . again opened their batteries upon a small schooner, with the same brilliant effect which has characterized all their former experiments," the *New York Times* reported. "Not a shot struck her, or came within a range to create any apprehensions as to her safety. They do not seem to improve in the least," it continued, "notwithstanding their daily practice." The *Times* reported that even the seamen being fired upon got caught up in the thrill of the Confederates' abysmal firing record. Given that shells thrown from Evansport widely missed their mark, "the three or four men on board the schooner seemed to enjoy the excitement they occasioned among the rebel batteries, for they leaped up, and swinging their caps, gave lusty Union cheers at every discharge of the enemy's guns."[51]

To be fair, many of the Confederate troops assigned to artillery pieces in the Evansport area had not been trained for field duty. Although the batter-

ies were under the control of the Confederate Navy, ordinary infantry soldiers manned the guns. When soldiers with a bit more experience in shelling took over the guns at Evansport, Federals across the river took notice. Even the *New York Times* had to admit that when better gunners manned Confederate artillery pieces, "the firing from the rebel batteries is now very good, especially from the one located on the classic locality known as Possum Nose. It has become a very formidable battery."[52]

By December the Confederate artillerists had either truly advanced their skills, or they had at least perfected the bravado necessary to suggest they had. On December 11 a gunner at Shipping Point used his pair of "lusty lungs" to bellow at the men of the 11th Massachusetts Infantry, on the Maryland shore, much questionable language and even worse opinions of the North, and informed them that while he did not have the pleasure of knowing them, he would entertain them with his skill and mastery in firing his weapons. This he did, much to their alarm.

One is tempted to think that the Confederates at Evansport may have let one ship through the Potomac blockade on purpose. The schooner *Susquehannah*, which set sail from Alexandria, carried a load of guano as her cargo. The rebel batteries at Quantico Creek fired four times at the ship, and though the shells "came in unpleasant proximity to the vessel," perhaps Confederate gunners thought the alternative would be even more unpleasant. Given that guano is composed of bird dung used as agricultural fertilizer, perhaps a ship full of flaming guano was more than a Confederate kill was worth?[53]

"From the Lower Potomac"

The quality of the action along the Potomac in the fall of 1861 failed to dissuade Northern newspapers from reporting on it, and papers like the *New York Herald* and *New York Times* had reporters with the Potomac Flotilla to record the day's events (or

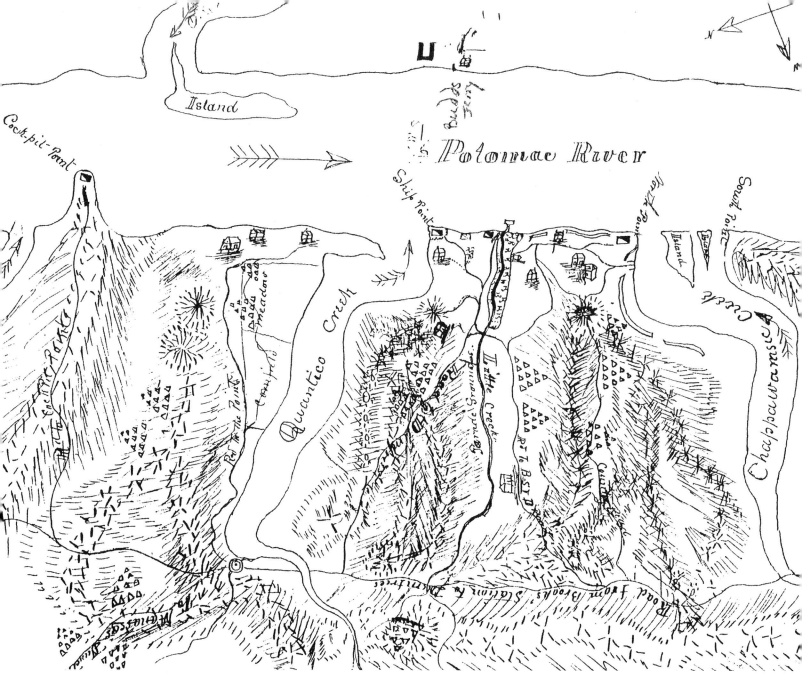

This map, drawn by a soldier of the 1st Arkansas Infantry—one of several regiments from across the Southern states fortifying Quantico—shows a close-up view of the fortifications at Shipping Point and Cockpit Point. Samuel Sidney Gause papers, courtesy of Dr. Edward L. Thackston, Nashville, Tennessee.

nonevents, as the case may be). A *Herald* reporter had the ear of Captain Craven, who allowed him to read Lieutenant Harrell's report on the burning of the *Martha Washington,* and the scene when Craven read Secretary Welles' effusive congratulations to all the men who participated in the raid.[54]

In November a reporter for the *New York Times* told his readers about an incident involving an "infernal machine." According to Union soldiers on the Maryland shore, a small boat bearing Confederate soldiers exited Quantico Creek, nearing the Maryland shore while flying a white flag of truce. When fairly near it released a barrel with something attached to it—an "infernal machine," it was supposed. As crude naval land mines, or "torpedoes" as they were known, "infernal machines" were metal devices filled with explosive powder and attached to barrels as flotation devices. This was not the first time the Confederates had used "infernal machines" to booby trap the Potomac in the Quantico vicinity. The July 22, 1861, issue of the *New York Illustrated News* featured a remarkable sketch by Alfred R. Waud of a Confederate "infernal machine" discovered by the Potomac Flotilla off the coast of Aquia. Waud's sketch depicted the above- and below-river image of the machine, in which a metal torpedo made from an oil tank was suspended from a wooden barrel floating on the surface of the water. At night, or to the untrained eye, the barrels would just appear as debris in the river, thereby masking their deadly intentions. Crews from the *Freeborn*, *Pawnee*, and *Resolute* discovered two devices off Aquia on July 12. One machine struck the *Resolute*, but sank after being detached from its buoy, and before doing any damage. The other was successfully defused by dipping its India rubber-coated fuse in water. Crews hauled the five-foot-long machine onto the *Pawnee*, and found that the iron device was "filled with all sorts of destructive elements, designed to blow the Potomac Squadron to atoms." "The machine looks devilish," the *New York Times* observed. Since the "infernal machine" found off the coast of Quantico in November apparently failed to do much of anything but attract attention, the incident proved a mere curiosity.[55]

By far the most protracted "nonevent" to capture the imagination of the Northern reading public was the nightly forays of the Confederate steamer the *George Page*. For weeks Northern newspapers almost daily printed a line or two about the *Page*, a steamer which had been captured in Alexandria by Confederate forces in 1861 and renamed the CSS *City of Richmond*. But like the CSS *Virginia* which remained famous as the *Merrimac*, the *City of Richmond* was forever known as the *George Page*. Names notwithstanding, the *Page* anchored in Quantico and Chopawamsic Creeks, and would harass Union ships and fortifications after dark, and scurry back to its hiding place before being discovered. Aside from this, the *Page* did little else, but her minor movements were duly reported. "The rebel steamer *Page* ran aground in the Quantico Creek," the *New York Herald* helpfully contributed on October 31. "The rebel steamer *George Page* is still cooped up in Quantico Creek, but has worked her way sufficiently far in to be out of sight from the

Above: Shipping Point battery, at the mouth of Quantico Creek. Leslie, American Soldier in the Civil War.

Right: Confederate ingenuity, described as "infernal machines" by its intended victim, the Union, were loosed in the Potomac River at Quantico by the Southern navy. The machines, an early prototype of anti-ship mines, are shown here floating near Aquia Creek, just downriver from Quantico. The USS Freeborn, *foreground, and USS* Pawnee, *background, were among the intended targets. Drawing by Alfred R. Waud, Library of Congress. LC–USZ62–6209*

Union soldiers encamped on the Maryland shore opposite Quantico made several daring attempts to burn Confederate ships, like the CSS Martha Washington *(shown here), moored in Quantico Creek. This lithograph from the* Saturday Evening Post *of November 16, 1861, depicts a nocturnal Union raid into the channel of the creek—right under proverbial Confederate noses—which destroyed Southern shipping and embarrassed the Confederate government.*

Maryland shore," the *New York Times* added on November 2. Not much had changed by November 13. "The Confederate steamer *George Page* still harbors in Quantico Creek, and may be seen from Budd's Ferry." A correspondent to the *Philadelphia Inquirer* commented that the *Page* could be a formidable threat if she came out of hiding, to which the *New York Times* countered that with each attempt the rebels returned her "with most commendable alacrity." Not scintillating reading, to be sure, but it kept readers informed of "Affairs on the Lower Potomac."[56]

A Mental Block

Regardless of the extent of actual damage inflicted on the Potomac Flotilla and other vessels which

attempted to outrun the Confederate batteries, the true measure of the success of the Confederate blockade on the Potomac was the psychological toll it took on the Union for five months. Official Union military correspondence repeatedly pointed to the threat of Confederate guns in rerouting supplies and halting military transport along the river. "So long as that battery stands at Shipping Point and Evansport the navigation of the Potomac will effectively be closed," reported Captain Thomas Craven of the Potomac Flotilla. "To attempt to reduce it with the vessels under my command would be vanity." Craven recommended that until something could be done about the rebel batteries, "there shall be no more transportation of Government stores upon the river." After the firing on the *Seminole*,

Admiral John A. Dahlgren at the Washington Navy Yard hesitated to send troops down the Potomac. "The *Pawnee* is just about to start," Dahlgren telegraphed Secretary Welles, "but as she is so filled by the troops that the effect of shot or shell might be very fatal."[57]

Northern newspapers also lamented the situation near Washington. "The Potomac appears at last to have been effectually closed by the rebels to all except our vessels of war—all merchant craft being afraid to run the gauntlet of their batteries," reported the *New York Times* on October 18.[58]

The Confederate blockade of the Potomac also created unexpected strains for those in Washington. With ships prohibited from traveling the Potomac, troops and supplies were rerouted to Baltimore or Annapolis, and then transported to Washington via rail. The extra freight stretched the Baltimore and Ohio Railroad's limits to its capacity, and in response the Union government began intensive efforts to expand the B&O's single track into Washington by installing long sidings at short intervals, and switches in every direction served by the station houses. Secretary of the Navy Gideon Welles largely blamed General George B. McClellan for the debacle on the river, recording in his diary in 1862 that McClellan's "hesitating course" in responding to the erection of Confederate batteries "had shaken my confidence in his efficiency and reliability," an opinion which he expressed to President Lincoln and the cabinet. While McClellan's subsequent actions (and lack thereof) in the field shook the confidence of many government officials, that he allowed "the closing of the only avenue from the National Capital to the ocean" won him little sympathy within the Lincoln administration. Thus, for the five months of what one former Confederate

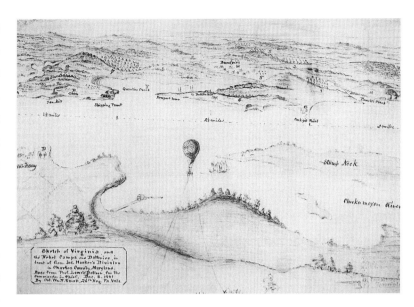

Colonel William F. Small of the 26th Pennsylvania Volunteer Regiment drew this birds-eye view of Confederate fortifications at Quantico after riding in a Union observation balloon over Maryland. The flight provided valuable intelligence to federal authorities—but did not help them reopen the Potomac. Courtesy National Archives.

later called "the virtual blockade of Washington," the influence of the rebel batteries in and around Quantico extended much farther than their effective firing range.[59]

Hailing Distance

Union observers in Maryland watched Confederate positions intently through spyglasses, divining details which they forwarded to Washington. "Just about Quantico Creek is a camp on the other side of the hill, probably of light artillery or cavalry, judging from the number of horses which feed over the hill and the appearance of the men who watch them," reported the Union intelligence forces. The Union also observed ten distinct lines of campfires between Quantico and Chopawamsic Creeks. The number and nature of the Confederate defenses, however, remained to be determined.

On November 10, 1861, a Massachusetts soldier rowed across the river below Chopawamsic Creek, and, hailing one of the regiments patrolling there, learned it was the 4th Alabama Infantry.[60]

Unbeknownst to the Union, the Confederate Army had garrisoned the Evansport and nearby batteries with fourteen regiments from several Southern states:

4th Alabama Infantry (Camp Law, near Dumfries; picketed at Evansport)

1st Arkansas Infantry (Camp Holmes at Evansport Batteries Nos. 1 and 2)

2nd Arkansas Infantry (Camp Holmes at Evansport)

2nd Florida Infantry (Evansport Battery No. 1 at Shipping Point)

35th Georgia Infantry (Camp French near Evansport)

2nd Battalion Maryland Cavalry (Evansport)

1st North Carolina Infantry (Aquia Creek)

6th North Carolina Infantry (Camp Fisher near Dumfries; picketed at Evansport)

15th North Carolina Infantry (Camp Dave Curran near Evansport)

22nd North Carolina Infantry (Camp Holmes at Evansport, and at Battery No. 2)

2nd Tennessee Infantry, "Robinson's Infantry" (Evansport Battery No. 1 at Shipping Point)

1st Texas Infantry (Camp Quantico near Dumfries)

4th Virginia Cavalry

30th Virginia Infantry (Evansport Battery No. 1 at Shipping Point)

49th Virginia Infantry, the "Quantico Guards" (Dumfries)

Confederates at Evansport captured drunken Union soldiers who had set out in a small boat from the Maryland shore that took them up

---

Raids by Confederate cavalry officer James Ewell Brown Stuart at Dumfries, Occoquan, and in the Quantico vicinity during the Civil War caused Union forces a great deal of consternation. Library of Congress. LC–DIG–cwpb–07546

Chopawamsic Creek. The Union men were apparently sober enough to identify where they reported seeing several of the regiments named above. Some members of the Confederate regiments had brought their slaves with them, and the Union captives noted that this was true for Georgians particularly.[61]

Mud Marches

Those soldiers with slaves may have found camp life in Evansport more tolerable, but even manservants could do little to ameliorate the effects of the weather. Perhaps used to consistently warmer temperatures and drier humidity than what they found in Virginia, Texans seemed particularly annoyed by the winter climate. Private Robert Gaston complained that "it rained a great deal so much that the pegs of our tents pulled up & a great many fell down. . . . When we get wet, we have to wait until it quits raining before we can dry our clothes." He also noted that picket duty was particularly onerous when the soldiers had to stand guard in the cold night air, without any "spark of fire" to warm them. A chaplain from a Texas regiment would also recall conditions with which Quantico Marines in future

would sympathize: "There was but little of interest in our quarters, except rain, sleet, snow and mud, with which we were blessed in abundance." Unfortunately for the Texans, several false reports of Union advances gave them marching orders through the wet, muddy roads surrounding Quantico.[62]

A Visit from the "Goddess of Liberty"

The Union army frequently employed balloon observation tactics during the Civil War, thanks in large part to Professor Thaddeus S. C. Lowe, a self-proclaimed civilian "aeronaut" who lent his expertise to the Union war effort. Made of silk and featuring an image of the "Goddess of Liberty" on it, Lowe's balloon "The Constitution" was capable of holding nineteen thousand feet of gas generated by an "apparatus" located in a boat moored below the balloon. Floating far above the river, Lowe reconnoitered rebel positions, and at night he could see campfires stretching down the roads between Brentsville and Occoquan. "The Constitution" occasionally served as an irresistible target for Confederate artillerists, who, predictably, missed. But so common a sight was Lowe's balloon on the lower Potomac that official and amateur mapmakers alike included it as a local landmark on the Maryland shore. Military commanders came to depend on balloon reports. In February 1862, for example, General Joseph Hooker relied on Lowe's observations to confirm the feasibility of his battle plans. The infamous General Daniel Sickles, who commanded part of Hooker's division along the Potomac, not only used Lowe's observations, he made some of his own when he ascended in the balloon with Lowe in November 1861. But for a man whose career already included being censured for having brought a prostitute into the New York State Assembly chambers, killing his wife's lover within view of the White House, and having escaped a murder rap with the first successful "temporary insanity" defense, ascending in a balloon was all in a day's work for this colorful character (who would continue to court danger and scandal in the years to come).[63]

Hatching Plots

As the first winter of the war continued and the Evansport Confederates continued to prevent commercial shipping along the Potomac, Union General Joseph Hooker began plotting and scheming to end the outrage by invading the Virginia shore. He first proposed to bombard the Confederate batteries with fifty guns placed on the Maryland side of the river, but his artillery experts shot down this idea as being impractical for the range of the available guns. Then Hooker thought four thousand of his infantry could be landed at various points on the Virginia shoreline to storm the batteries and disable the guns. Another two regiments would land near Cockpit Point, take out those batteries, ford Quantico Creek, and rendezvous in Aquia. This ambitious plan was quietly abandoned as well. The high-banked and deep-flowing Quantico and Chopawamsic Creeks complicated his plans; especially considering Quantico Creek could not be forded below Dumfries.[64]

In the meantime, rebel firing from the new battery at Possum Nose and existing batteries damaged or thwarted Union military shipping in January and February 1862, when the USS *Harriet Lane*, USS *Baltimore*, USS *Jacob Bell*, USS *Pensacola*, and several smaller transports were fired upon, and the *Harriet Lane* hit. Each episode only hardened Hooker's resolve.[65]

...and Then They Were Gone

After months of embarrassing and commercially isolating the Union capital, the Confederates at Evansport disappeared—almost overnight.

For months Confederate authorities feared that Union General George McClellan had a new campaign planned for the spring, and worried that their river and inland positions in Prince William County were not suitably defendable. Agreeing that the best offense would be a good defense, General Joseph E. Johnston ordered his troops to move to stronger positions along the Rappahannock River. Johnston anticipated that bad roads and winter mud would slow his progress, particularly in terms of moving heavy artillery. Also complicating these maneuvers was the sheer mass of materiel to be moved, particularly at Manassas. "For what would prove to be the one and only time in four years of war," historian Stephen Sears observed, "the army's much-maligned commissary department had outdone itself." If the batteries at Evansport did not share in this bounty of provisions, their removal from the Potomac would be hindered by an overwhelmed transportation network elsewhere. As the end of February and the beginning of March 1862 rolled around, Johnston's patrols reported "unusual activity" on the Maryland side of the river. Apprehensive that the Yankees might try landing on the Potomac, Johnston accelerated the speed of his evacuation, ordering his troops to take whatever they could carry and destroy the rest. This order included the batteries along the Potomac near Evansport.[66]

What Johnston was hearing were preparations for McClellan's massive transport of Union troops to the confluence of the York and James Rivers to undertake his Peninsula Campaign in the spring. After rejecting proposals to meet the enemy at Manassas by effecting a water landing on the Occoquan River, McClellan determined to land his forces at Urbanna and capture Richmond from that approach. Ironically, Johnston's move to a better defensive position on the Rappahannock River negated the utility of McClellan's landing at Urbanna, and forced him to go farther south to Fort Monroe. However, Johnston's evacuation from the Potomac aided McClellan in being able to take his troops straight down the Potomac, without either rerouting them to Annapolis or taking the effort to disable the Confederate guns on the Potomac.[67]

March 7 to 9 witnessed Confederates on the Potomac setting fire to their batteries, and sabotaging the guns left behind. Suspecting that explosions and smoke across the river were not just smoke screens for further movements, the Potomac Flotilla shelled the Confederate batteries for over an hour, with no response. On March 9, Lieutenant R. H. Wyman telegraphed Secretary of the Navy Gideon Welles to confirm that Confederates had abandoned the Cockpit and Shipping Point batteries, and fires at Evansport suggested the same situation there as well.[68] Landing parties then went ashore, finding to their astonishment the fortifications deserted. As one newspaper reporter put it, "The enemy had *vamoosed the ranch*, to use a California phrase."[69]

Because the fortifications were supplied with so much heavy artillery and ammunition, and the evacuation was carried out with such great haste, the Confederates had to leave behind much of their supplies and equipment. Not wanting the Yankees to profit any further from their retreat, Confederates "fired everything at the Evansport batteries." They set fire to magazines and gun carriages, loaded cannons for bursting, and spiked other guns. In some cases Union soldiers extinguished fires before they damaged the guns, and saved stores of ammunition. Aside from the weaponry, there remained in camp tents, clothing, private and official documents, fresh beef for the day, and other detritus of camp life. Luckily for the landing parties the Confederates in their haste had forgotten to remove their flagpoles, which facilitated running up the "Stars and Stripes" as evidence that the Union had finally taken the Potomac batteries.[70]

By a nice coincidence, March 9, 1862, also saw the one and only battle between the famed ironclads *Monitor* and *Virginia* (nee *Merrimac*) in Hampton Roads. Although the battle was technically a draw, the North breathed a collective sigh of relief knowing the *Monitor* was more than a match for the dreaded *Merrimac*, which would not, as was feared,

These Union soldiers, men of the 1ˢᵗ Massachusetts Volunteer Infantry encamped at Budd's Ferry, Maryland, across the river from Quantico, fired frequently on Confederate encampments along the Quantico shoreline, causing damage and disrupting operations. Drawing by Alfred R. Waud, Library of Congress. LC–USZ62–14899

sail up the Potomac and lay siege to Washington. March 9 would not, however, prove to be the best day for the Confederate Navy.

Finally able to see the garrisons in person, Lieutenant Wyman discovered them to be "of a much more formidable nature than I had supposed, and great labor has been expended in their construction." He also observed with some surprise that "the guns are of the best description, mostly United States guns; one an English rifle gun." At the batteries on Cockpit Point, the Union found four heavy guns, and booby-trapped ammunition magazines. Shipping Point's guns included one weighing 9,068 pounds, a long 32-pounder weighing 6,200 pounds, a six-inch rifled pivot gun, a destroyed six-inch rifled gun, six long 42-pounders, and a seven-and-half-inch rifled gun weighing 10,759 pounds. Evansport's guns were similar, one of which—a giant Tredegar gun—was found in fragments. Although a *New York Times* correspondent reported that at least one of the guns found at the Shipping Point battery was actually a log painted to resemble a gun. These so-called "Quaker guns" had held off the Yankees elsewhere in Virginia, so why not along the Potomac

too? The soldiers who discovered the gun laughed at having been duped, but declared, "All their armament might as well have been composed of the same material, so far as effectiveness was concerned."[71]

And newspaper readers in the North would no doubt be delighted to learn that the Confederates had set fire to the pesky *George Page*, which burned to the water's edge. Assistant Secretary of the Navy Gustavus A. Fox led a party of ladies and gentlemen to view the Shipping Point batteries later in the month, and the group salvaged bits of wood and iron from the *Page* to take home as souvenirs.[72]

A Lesser Role

After the Confederates abandoned their fortifications along the Potomac, the Potomac Flotilla still maintained a presence in the area, albeit a largely reduced one without an enemy to engage. Ships in the Flotilla mainly patrolled the river to keep it open for communications to and from Washington, and discouraged illicit trade across the river. But with the Union in control of both sides of the river, Evansport lost its strategic value. Aquia, on the other hand, had served the Confederacy well as a supply station, and would continue to do so under a Yankee master.[73]

Beginning just days after the evacuation, however, residents in Evansport would be witness to one of the greatest naval transport movements in history. McClellan's spring campaign, the one troubling enough to Joe Johnston to move his troops farther south, finally got underway. Convinced that he could take Richmond by a flanking movement up the Peninsula from Fort Monroe and Newport News, McClellan assembled in Washington and Alexandria an armada of four hundred vessels, on which he proposed to move down the Chesapeake Bay over one hundred thousand men, twenty-five thousand animals, and hundreds to thousands of wagons, artillery pieces and other military accoutrement necessary to a campaign of this size. For nearly a month a steady procession of ships of all description sailed past Evansport on their way to rendezvous on the Peninsula. Elisha Hunt Rhodes remarked that his transport ship, the steamer *John Brooks*, was "gaily decorated with flags, and it looks more like a pleasure excursion than an army looking for the enemy." Regardless of their national allegiances, such a flotilla in their midst must have been quite a sight for residents along the Potomac.[74]

Little did they know, but with the waters of the Potomac clear for sailing, President Abraham Lincoln began sailing by Evansport en route to observe military installations on the Peninsula, or meet with his generals or envoys at peace conferences. Although the closest point of embarkation for Lincoln was army headquarters at Aquia, the proximity of the Potomac would lure many a future president to enjoy the waters near Quantico Creek.[75]

Affairs again became volatile during December 1862. While much of the Confederate Army was

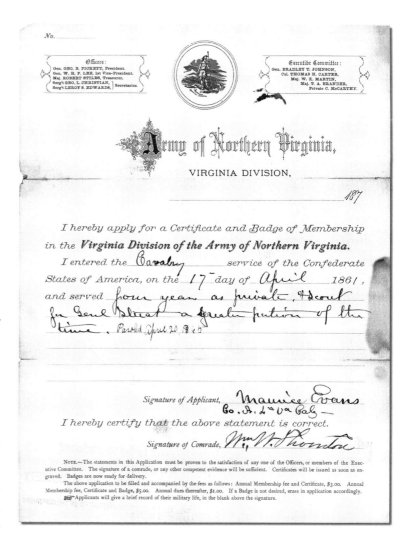

The South never died, at least not in the hearts of those who served her. Maurice Evans of Evansport remained proud of his service as a Confederate cavalryman long after the war's end, and belonged to the "Army of Northern Virginia," a brotherhood for those who served in the original, long after returning to the quiet shores of Quantico Creek. Maurice Evans Papers, Virginia Historical Society, Richmond, Virginia.

in nearby Fredericksburg, large numbers of Confederate soldiers and sympathizers began crossing the Potomac nightly from Maryland to Virginia, landing between Quantico and Chopawamsic Creeks, supporting efforts underway nearby. General J. E. B. Stuart also thought he would harass Union troops in the area, who had gone into winter quarters following their disastrous defeat at the Battle of Fredericksburg, in hopes of forcing the Federals out of northern Virginia. From Culpeper County, General Wade Hampton of South Carolina brought over five hundred men for a surprise raid on Union forces in Dumfries, successfully capturing men and materiel. Hampton repeated the action on the banks of the Occoquan. With a force of eighteen hundred cavalrymen behind them, Stuart, Hampton, and Fitzhugh and William H. "Rooney" Lee (Robert E. Lee's nephew and son, respectively) invaded Dumfries again on December 27. Stuart's commanders first took different objectives to maximize their efficiency, and then combined forces at Burke Station. With characteristic audacity, Stuart then telegraphed Union Quartermaster General Montgomery C. Meigs to criticize the inferior quality of mules pulling the wagons he captured. On December 27 and 29, noisy skirmishes occurred on Quantico Creek, followed shortly by a larger one, when a large group of the 2nd Virginia Cavalry made contact with Union regiments, capturing twenty-five horses, four pistols, twelve saddles, six sabers, and thirty prisoners.[76]

The steep banks of Chopawamsic and Quantico Creeks continued to confound military maneuvers, trapping columns on opposite sides while temporary bridges were built to replace those washed out by heavy rains. The heavy rains also had the perverse effect of rendering the roads almost unusable, causing large numbers of troops to encamp along the banks of the Chopawamsic in late January. Heavy rains also interfered with telegraphic communications, as Union Secretary of War Edwin M. Stanton was to discover. The Telegraph Road forded Quantico Creek, and in an April 1863 note to President Lincoln, Stanton explained that "telegraphic communication is broken by the flood in Quantico."[77]

Yet, for most of 1862 and 1863, Evansport remained out of the fray. Major battles would be fought in the region at Manassas (again), Fredericksburg, Spotsylvania, Chancellorsville, and the Wilderness. But not being a significant port or located on a railroad line, Evansport was largely off the beaten path for the military campaigns which

ravaged much of Virginia. Only the brief return of General J. E. B. Stuart in early 1864 brought troops back to Dumfries and Quantico Creek. During one engagement Stuart captured twenty-two men and several supply wagons; in another the Confederates captured fifty Union prisoners, although losing twelve soldiers and three horses. But limited skirmishes like these could not compare with daily cannonading of the Potomac Flotilla, and perhaps the residents of Evansport preferred it that way.

Apart from the military turmoil which had upset the balance of life in Prince William County, it appears that once the Confederate Army left the area, civilian government collapsed behind them. While the transfer of property had already ceased with the opening of the war, county court stopped on about the very day of the Confederate withdrawal from Evansport.[78]

With Malice Toward None

Almost exactly four years and six hundred thousand lives after it began, the Civil War effectively ended with Robert E. Lee's surrender to Ulysses S. Grant in Appomattox Court House on April 9, 1865. The war and the Emancipation Proclamation had resolved the question of slavery (and the Thirteenth Amendment would codify that solution), and "union" had triumphed over "states rights" and "secession" once and for all. But just as peace appeared on the horizon, the assassination of Abraham Lincoln convulsed the nation anew, and redefined what the postwar world look like. For Quantico, however, having lived under Union rule for the last two and a half years of the war helped ease its transition into Reconstruction. What Quantico would make of itself in the postwar world remained to be seen.

CHAPTER III

SLIPPING THE SURLY BONDS OF EARTH

Reconstruction

Unlike many other Virginia communities, the Quantico area likely entered the Reconstruction era with relatively little upheaval. After the Confederate evacuation of the batteries on the lower Potomac in March 1862, this section of Prince William County came under Union rule for the duration of the war. Having escaped being the site of any major battles, and only having scattered infrastructure at the beginning of the war, Quantico also escaped much of the physical damage suffered by communities between Washington and Richmond. Still, the Reconstruction era brought changes to the region. The 1870 federal census for Prince William showed that the county had lost over 1,000 residents in the previous decade. The figure certainly would have been higher had a census been taken immediately after the war. Some of that loss is attributable to the death of Prince William County soldiers during the war, but the vast majority of emigrants from Prince William were former slaves. Slaves in Northern Virginia and near Union military installations began escaping almost as soon as the war began, and with the Union Army and freedom in the North so close to Prince William, many blacks must have

Aviation experiments on the Potomac River off Quantico set the stage for the Wright brothers' triumph at Kitty Hawk several years later. Here flight pioneer Samuel Langley, secretary of the Smithsonian Institution, writes Alexander Graham Bell, who observed. These experiments earned Quantico an important place in the history of science. Courtesy Library of Congress.

sought their freedom elsewhere. Prince William's losses were small, however, compared to the Commonwealth's overall population loss of 370,000 residents between 1860 and 1870.[79]

Perhaps the combination of a relatively small African-American population and the years of wartime military rule helped to quell the racial tensions that characterized other Virginia communities and much of the lower South during the turbulence

SMITHSONIAN INSTITUTION.
Washington, U.S.A.

May 4, 1896.

My dear Mr. Bell:

I expect to take the 4.25 P.M. train (Sixth Street Station) to-morrow for Quantico, and to spend the night there, hoping to make the trial in the morning.

I am bound to say in advance that the prospects are not good for success, but if you will take the chance of a fruitless journey, I shall be delighted to have you come. May I expect to meet you at the station?

Very truly yours,

of Reconstruction. The Bureau of Refugees, Freedmen and Abandoned Lands (a.k.a. The Freedmen's Bureau) operated many branch offices throughout Virginia during the early years of Reconstruction, but it does not seem to have maintained one in Prince William County. Thus, any black residents of the Quantico area who encountered labor, domestic, or racial disputes requiring outside intervention would have had to travel to either the Fredericksburg or Fairfax County offices for Bureau assistance.[80]

Everyone in Prince William County, however, faced a change of authority after the war when all of Virginia (except Fairfax County) was designated the Military Department of Virginia in June 1865, and put under the control of Union General Alfred H. Terry. In a reorganization two years later, Virginia became part of Military District No. 1, headed by General John M. Schofield. All of the former Confederate states had been placed under military rule both to keep law and order, and to provide some level of administration while Congress and President Andrew Johnson quarreled over the terms under which these states would be allowed back in the Union. Compared with other more truculent and violent parts of the South, Virginia's tenure under military rule proceeded peacefully and civilian government was restored in January 1870. By that time Virginia had already formulated a new constitution which gave county-level control of government to boards of supervisors (rather than county courts), created New England–style townships to serve as magisterial districts, and established a tax-supported public education system.[81]

Still, evidence of the war abounded in postwar Prince William as houses and places of worship had been destroyed or used by the military, crops likewise destroyed or confiscated, and families struggling to rebound from the economic and social disruption of war. With this in mind, they set out to rebuild.

[Printer's No., 1356.

41st CONGRESS,
3d SESSION.

H. R. 2948.

IN THE HOUSE OF REPRESENTATIVES.

FEBRUARY 6, 1871.

Read twice, referred to the Committee on Commerce, and ordered to be printed.

Mr. BOOKER, on leave, introduced the following bill:

A BILL

Making an appropriation for the improvement of the mouth of Quantico Bay, Virginia.

1   *Be it enacted by the Senate and House of Representa-*
2   *tives of the United States of America in Congress assembled,*
3   That there be, and is hereby, appropriated, to be paid out of
4   any money in the Treasury not otherwise appropriated, to be
5   expended under the direction and superintendence of the
6   Secretary of War, for the purpose of improving the mouth
7   of Quantico Bay, Virginia, the sum of thirty-five thousand
8   dollars.

The government's first real interest in improving Quantico occurred in 1870. Quantico Creek, whose silting since colonial times rendered the creek unnavigable and doomed the port of Dumfries, was dredged by army engineers to deepen its channel and allow additional uses. Courtesy Library of Congress.

The first order of business seems to have been establishing infrastructure that would lure business and industry to the area, and Quantico (then still known as Evansport) appeared an ideal candidate for development. Quantico always had its proximity to the Potomac River and water transportation routes in its favor, and in 1872 the Richmond, Fredericksburg and Potomac (RF&P) Railroad extending north from Richmond and the Alexandria and Washington Railroad south from Alexandria finally met in Quantico.[82] "There can be a sufficient amount of water power obtained here to run a thousand looms," the *Prince William Advocate* reported while the road was still under construction. The paper added the prediction that the railroad would attract good and industrious people

A POPULAR RESORT.

QUANTICO.

BATH HOUSES, BATHING SUITS, TOWELS, FISHING, CRABBING, SAILING, MUSIC, AND DANCING ON BOAT AND GROUNDS.

The magnificent steamer, the EXCELSIOR, first-class in every respect, licensed to carry 1,500 people. Daily (except Sunday) at 9:30 A. M. and 3:30 P. M., from 7th st. wharf. Refreshments of all kinds on the boat at city prices. No tickets sold to improper characters. Adults 50c.: children 25c. au11—3w

TO QUANTICO ON PALACE STEAMER Excelsior. H. M. S. Pinafore and Billee Taylor will be sung in full by a chorus of 20 ladies and gentlemen. Tickets 50c. August 25. au 9—d&S7t

---

Steamers plied the waters of the Potomac daily by the 1880s, many of them exclusively for pleasure-seekers. And many of the pleasure-seekers came to Quantico. This ad from a Washington newspaper was similar to those printed in all the city's daily newspapers. Washington Post, *August 21, 1881.*

---

who would rediscover the area's former prosperity. The RF&P Railroad served Quantico for nearly a century. In the meantime, the railroad built a wharf at Shipping Point, erected bridges over Quantico Creek, and attracted workers to the abandoned townsite of Carrborough. The workers' tents and the hum of activity reminded local residents of the excitement of the batteries along the Potomac during the war.[83] Except, thankfully, without being shot at from across the river.

Anticipating a postwar economic boom, developers bought tracts of land around Quantico on which to erect villages and lure industry. As early as 1869 a company purchased the Evansport tract with the intention of establishing a community of 150 families which would supplant Dumfries as a commercial hub. Quantico particularly attracted New Yorkers looking for postwar investments. Dr. Anson Bangs saw Quantico's potential as both a riparian resort and commercial center, and in 1872 the Virginia Assembly awarded a charter to the Potomac Land Improvement Company to prepare a site between Quantico and Chopawamsic Creeks for

a new city. "An enterprising gentleman from New York, Dr. Bangs is starting a town at Quantico," the *State Journal* reported, "which combines the advantages of river navigation with those of the railroad." As envisioned by Bangs and his investors, a wharf along the river would welcome guests to a resort, while a railroad linking Quantico with West Virginia would bring coal to the area for transport via shipping or other railroad lines. In 1873, what is now Quantico was incorporated as the town of Potomac, one of three towns incorporated in Prince William County in 1873 and 1874. Potomac included most of the land between the creeks, and extended westward to the Telegraph Road, which is generally the boundary of current Route 1. Of the three newly incorporated towns, Manassas succeeded, as did Occoquan, but as had happened several times before, a town located at Quantico failed to live up to expectations. The county revoked Potomac's charter in 1894, and shipped its records to the county seat in Manassas. Interestingly, a town at Potomac would be chartered again in 1896, and local historians have never located documents suggesting that the second charter was ever revoked. Thus, the possibility exists that the Town of Potomac and the Town of Quantico exist simultaneously on the same tract of land.[84]

While Dr. Bangs' grand plans fizzled, elements of his vision did come to fruition. In the 1880s the Landsburgh brothers, owners of Washington's Landsburgh Department Store, built a resort hotel at Potomac, and named it the Bangs Hotel, presumably in honor of Dr. Bangs. Built on the west side of the railroad, the hotel survived until 1910. The Potomac Steamboat Company furthered the concept of Potomac as both a business and pleasure destination. In 1880 the company began running twice-daily trips between Washington and Quantico on its luxury steamer *Excelsior*. A railroad track on the top of the steamer transported railroad cars from Shepherd's Landing (across the Potomac from Alexandria) to Quantico, where they were offloaded to connect with established train routes. But judging from advertisement descriptions of the *Excelsior*, passengers below deck would never imagine the ship had an industrial purpose. The 230-foot-long steamer boasted a "beautiful grand salon, elaborately furnished with immense full-length mirrors, chairs of black walnut, cushioned with wine-colored velvet. A rich moquet carpet will soften the tramp of the heaviest feet." Passengers would also find a sumptuous dining hall, state rooms, smoking rooms, parlors for ladies and gentlemen, and "water in every room." In keeping with the racial segregation of this era, "colored men and women" would find their own sitting rooms on the lower deck. With all these features, can anyone wonder why the ship cost $200,000? With a travel time from Washington to Quantico of only one hour and forty minutes, the *Excelsior* could transport its

industrial cargo in a speedy fashion, while also providing an appealing river cruise to its passengers.[85]

Even when the town of Potomac failed to achieve success as a resort and industrial center, Quantico's natural resources continued to provide a livelihood for local residents. In 1882 the Quantico fishery made news in *Scientific American* for having provided the Fish Commission in Washington with "extensive shipments of young shad and herring." Although the article indicated that the fishery had just closed to follow the shad up river, the Quantico fishery still provided three million shad and sixty million herring, which were used to stock waterways in the West, South Carolina, and elsewhere in Virginia. Lumber also provided a source of revenue as abundant pine and other timber could be harvested in Prince William, and transported to the wharves at Quantico for transportation via the river or railroad. At least some "cooperage" products left Quantico bound for Cuba and Puerto Rico.[86]

Although the cash crops marketed at Quantico may have changed a bit since the colonial days, one problem associated with agriculture remained

Quantico Hotel as it appeared in 1918 was part of a resort founded by the Quantico Company, owner of the acreage later to be leased to Marines as a training base in World War I. The building, on Rising Hill overlooking the town of Quantico, served the Marines in a variety of purposes before being torn down as a safety hazard in 1968. Courtesy Marine Corps Historical Center.

Hotel Drusilla, at what was quaintly known as "Quantico Junction," or Triangle. Conveniently and pleasantly situated, boasting large windows for air circulation and sleeping porches for hot summer evenings, it would be overwhelmed by the area's burgeoning needs after creation of the Marine base in World War I. But those heady days were still in the future. Courtesy base archive.

constant: silt. Extensive silting in Quantico Creek had long since prohibited Dumfries from using the creek for commercial navigation, and by the 1880s silting threatened the creek farther down towards Quantico. Secretary of War Robert Todd Lincoln transmitted a report to the United States Senate in 1884, which included engineering studies of Quantico Creek and recommendations for its improvement. Engineer S. T. Abert concluded that the creek above Dodge's Landing was too full to warrant the expense of dredging, and that continued agricultural runoff would require still more dredging in the future. The bar accumulating at the mouth of Quantico Creek was a different story. The wharves at Quantico attracted enough commercial and recreational activity to make it a viable port if the silt was removed, and since it was "said to be the only safe ice-harbor on the Potomac River," public necessity would be served with its improvement. So while marshes formed on the creek closer to Dumfries, Abert recommended the government spend $33,000 to improve the harbor at Quantico. In the same report, Abert estimated the population of "Potomac City" to be about 250 people.[87]

Up the Possum's Nose, and a Paradise on the Potomac

While Potomac City was on the verge of losing its charter, more optimistic souls tried their luck just up the river at Possum's Nose. The Barrow Company laid out the town of Barrow in 1890, at what the *Washington Post* described as "the confluence of Quantico Creek and the Potomac River." While this initially sounds like Possum Point, the *Post* also helpfully described the land as having "the shape of an opossum's nose, and has been called by this name for years," which suggests the site was Possum's Nose instead. Regardless, the Barrow Company had big plans to develop "a busy, manufacturing village" with blast furnaces capable of producing two hundred tons of steel, rolling mills for

Shown here in an architect's rendering, the new Quantico Hotel was luxurious beyond local belief, with private restrooms in every sleeping room. Washington Post, *May 7, 1916.*

processing the steel, a charcoal and chemical plant, shipyard, marine railways and drydocks, and machine shops. The company's lands also boasted nine hundred acres of "the best timber land in the county," veins of "fine quality" iron ore, and spectacular views up and down the Potomac River. Yes, Barrow would have been quite an industrial giant . . . had anything happened on the site. By 1893 the Barrow Company sold the property and its dreams for Possum's Nose ended. The new owner opened a pyrite mine, connected to Quantico Creek by rail, employing a large number of hands.[88]

Another landowner south of Potomac City appealed to a different sort of investor when selling his land. George L. Horn, who either owned the land or acted as the real estate agent, placed an advertisement in *Forest and Stream* in 1891, hoping to sell 700 acres of "Fine Stafford Co. Virginia Property" located on the Potomac River and Chopawamsic Creek, just a mile and a half south of the Quantico railroad station. According to the advertisement, 250 of those acres were under cultivation, but the rest included pine, chestnut, elm, cedar and fruit trees, was "thoroughly stocked" with the standard farm animals and agricultural implements. Even "the competent Jersey farmer" would remain if the new owner so desired.

The property came with a fully furnished, eleven-room brick house, and views of the Potomac for fifteen miles each way. Having described this idyllic location to readers of *Forest and Stream*, Horn sensibly suggested that the property "would make an elegant game preserve, as there are on it quantities of Quail, Snip, Woodcock, Turkeys, Ducks, Rail, etc., with plenty of fishing in season." Unfortunately for the curious among us, Horn did not include the asking price in his advertisement. Because the advertisement does not specify the boundaries of the property, it is not clear if this tract was part of the old Dipple Plantation, or if it included the land on Chopawamsic Island that the Metropolitan Club of Washington, D.C., later operated as a retreat. The house was described as a Queen Anne style–dwelling, which either rules out the Dipple Plantation house, or suggests it underwent massive renovations.[89]

A Spate of Deaths

The Potomac River and the railroad did not just attract investors to Quantico; they inadvertently brought trouble along as well. After the Civil War, and especially at the turn-of-the-century, local newspapers began reporting on drownings and railroad accidents plaguing the Quantico area. A correspondent from Dumfries alerted the *Alexandria Gazette* to the unfortunate death of a sailor on a schooner docked near Quantico in 1871. The man had been ill, and it was surmised that he accidentally walked overboard in his fevered condition. He cried out for help, but strong currents pulled him into the Potomac River where he presumably drowned. Unlike the sailor of 1871, whose body was never found, a body found floating near Quantico in 1892 was presumed to be yet another sailor lost overboard in the Potomac. But not being able to identify the body, authorities buried him just above the high-water mark on the beach. William Stepper of Washington, D.C., drowned in Quantico Creek a

year later, after having gotten caught in a squall while rowing in the creek, leaving his family "in destitute circumstances." A gale at Quantico in 1899 caught the schooner *Three Buzzards*, capsizing the ship and catching its captain in the wreckage as it went down. While the other two "buzzards" of the crew survived, Captain Brown presumably drowned and was never found. The Potomac claimed yet another life in 1910, that of Washington stockbroker Maurice Joyce, whose boat capsized as he tried to land at Quantico. Although his yacht was in the river nearby, he apparently sank too quickly to be rescued by his friends on board.[90]

The railroad proved slightly less mercurial, but no less destructive in whom it claimed. A young boy riding the rails from North Carolina slipped while trying to move from one car to another, and fell between the bumpers and onto the track. The train mangled the youth's legs, and he did not survive an operation to amputate them. Frederick Thierault proved luckier the next year when he slipped on the train tracks at Quantico: there was no train coming at the time and he only broke his arm in what the *Washington Post* dubbed a "painful mishap."

It wasn't Paris, but Triangle, the little settlement near what is now Quantico's main gate, was a veritable seat of civilization for local residents before World War I. The Hotel Drusilla is visible above the crossroads. Courtesy base archive.

R. Lucian Cornell, a track hand on the RF&P Railroad, was less fortunate in 1910. He stepped back from one track to avoid a passenger train, only to be fatally struck by a freight train presumably coming the other direction. William Butler supplied perhaps the most unusual train mishap at Quantico in the process of committing suicide in 1896. Butler slit his throat with a piece of tin, and tried to finish the job by throwing himself on the railroad tracks at Quantico. The engineer of an oncoming train spotted Butler in time to stop and pick up the unconscious man. But Butler was a determined fellow, and jumped out of the moving train when he regained consciousness. After yet another rescue, a "slightly bruised" and certainly confused Butler was handed over to his mother in Richmond.[91]

Thus, in an era before life preservers and railroad safety precautions, too many visitors to Quantico would demonstrate time and again with tragic results why these precautions would be developed in the future.

The Great Train Robbery

A daring train robbery could have easily added to the list of railroad fatalities in Quantico, had not quick-thinking railroad employees saved the day. On October 12, 1894, seven masked gunmen held up a northbound express RF&P train between Brooke Station and Wide Water near Aquia Creek. Two of the robbers ordered the engineer to stop the train on the tracks, while the others relieved the Adams Express car of an estimated $180,000. The Express agent reported that although one robber looked like a farmer, "he seemed thoroughly to understand his business," and used a stick of dynamite to blow an opening into the car. He ordered the

agent to open the safe, and took bundles of cash. Having secured the loot, the robbers ordered the engineer and fireman to uncouple the engine from the train. The men escaped on the engine, leaving the frightened passengers stranded on the track. Witnesses observed the engine slowly move ahead for a mile, then stop for a moment, before gathering tremendous steam as it barreled off in the direction of Quantico. Apparently the ruffians had slowed the engine in order to make their escape, and sent the abandoned locomotive northwards at full throttle.

The station manager at Wide Water recognized that "something was wrong" (perhaps the runaway engine tipped him off?), and telegraphed a warning to Quantico. Once the engine was sighted in Quantico, yardmen at the station threw a switch, sending the runaway engine plowing into freight cars along a side track. The engine overturned in the collision, "panting not unlike an infuriated beast until it 'died,'" while the freight cars were reduced to "kindling wood." This action likely saved many lives as an Atlantic special passenger car was sitting on the main track at Quantico, and would have been crushed by the speeding locomotive.

The rescued, but much-delayed Express train finally reached Washington at 1:17 a.m., after having left Fredericksburg at 9 p.m. the night before. Shaken passengers told newspaper reporters that

Several audacious train robbers, stopping a northbound express outside Quantico station in 1894, stole money from the vault car before departing in haste. The locomotive they loosed at full speed narrowly avoided ramming a crowded passenger train on Quantico's siding, creating what would have been one of the nation's worst railroad accidents. Shown here is George Carter, one of the train robbers. Washington Post, *October 14, 1894.*

they had expected to be robbed of their valuables, and one man confessed to have hidden his money in his shoe. But all concurred that the train's conductor had been "cool and collected" throughout the whole ordeal, and had protected his passengers "as brave as a lion" against the possibility of assault by the armed men.

"The Aquia Creek train robbery will pass into criminal history as one of the most daring and cleverly planned hold-ups on record," one newspaper proclaimed. "So carefully were all the details arranged that the robbers had many hours in which to divide their booty and get well away before officers and detectives could be started after them." The press speculated that George Carter, a former resident of Stafford County, but more recently a resident of Sing Sing prison, was the leader of the gang. Carter also had experience as a locomotive engineer. Whether Carter was the ringleader or not, it appears that Charles J. Searcy and Charles Morganfield were the only ones convicted of the crime. Interestingly, the same page of the October 13, 1894 *Washington Post* which carried the news of the daring robbery near Quantico, also featured a story about a train robbery in Sacramento, California, that occurred the night before. As was the case in Virginia, the Sacramento robbers targeted the express car, escaped on the engine, and after abandoning the engine, let it steam ahead alone. (Fortunately the engine ran out of steam before doing any damage down the line.) Coincidence? Or perhaps evidence of the desperate economic times created nationwide by the Panic of

1893. The year 1894 saw one out of five workers unemployed, and perhaps these men decided that desperate times called for desperate measures. One of the robbers, Charles A. Morganfield, must have been very desperate, as he sustained injuries while jumping from another train in Cincinnati the very next month.[92]

A "Lucky Day" for the Ducks

Quantico's native flora and fauna convinced many investors of the area's potential as a pleasure and nature resort, and those charms proved equally enticing to the nation's chief executives as well.

THE PRESIDENT FINDS SOME DUCKS WAITING FOR HIM AT HOME.

Stephen Grover Cleveland—also known, somewhat strangely, as "Uncle Jumbo"—was the first American president to engage in recreational pursuits at Quantico. Cleveland established a tradition which continues today. An avid duck hunter, Cleveland found himself satirized by at least one editorial cartoonist for hunting Quantico ducks while important public business waited. Courtesy Library of Congress. LC–USZ62–70718

Beginning with Grover Cleveland in the 1890s, day trips down the Potomac to Quantico provided relief from the pressures of office, and a chance to enjoy some recreation as well. On several occasions from January to March 1896, President Cleveland boarded the lighthouse tender *Maple* in Washington for duck-hunting excursions to Quantico, where the ducks were reported to be "plentiful." Guests of Colonel Webster Waller, whose duck feeding grounds and blinds were said to be "the best along the Potomac River," Cleveland and his party bagged thirteen ducks on his January trip. The *Washington Post* noted Cleveland was obliged to leave after bringing down the last of his unlucky numbered catch, making it a very "lucky day" for the rest of the ducks.

Until the president returned the next month, that is. This time the president and his guests carried the idea of being "blind" to a new level to guard their privacy on the trip. Seeing Cleveland starting up the gangplank at Stevenson's wharf in Washington, a *Post* reporter inquired as to the names of his guests. The president merely grabbed his gun and boarded the ship. As the guests began arriving at the wharf, the reporter asked one for the names in the party. "I don't know them," the man replied. "Will you favor me with your name," the intrepid reporter asked. "Egad, I don't know that either," came the improbable answer! In a last, desperate attempt, the reporter appealed to the president's secretary for the names, eliciting the same "I don't know them, sir" answer. "That settled it," the reporter wrote in exasperation, "for if the Secretary does not know the names of the guests, and one of the guests does not know his own name, it is not likely that the American public will know them." Perhaps in retribution for the president's truculence, the party returned with only seven birds, after not surprisingly finding the ducks "wary." And the *Post* reporter made a better killing by discovering upon their return that the president's "secretary" had actually been a White House steward and the

Teddy Roosevelt, one of America's most colorful presidents, was an avid outdoorsman who took advantage of Quantico's proximity to Washington to visit and hunt its abundant game. In one such adventure, he invited himself to dine in the humble home of a local African American, who coached him in how to hunt properly—a visit neither were soon to forget. George Grantham Bain photo, courtesy Library of Congress. LC–USZ62–23232

man who did not know his own name was Attorney General Judson Harmon.

The *Post* also cleared up a mystery about Quantico as well. In reporting about Cleveland's adventures the *Post* described the picturesque scene surrounding Colonel Waller's elegant home of "Clifton," about four miles south of Quantico. The idyllic image painted by reporters was meant for "the uninitiated who only know Quantico as a tiresome little station at the southern terminus of the Pennsylvania Railroad." A qualified compliment, indeed.[93]

A Persistent President

Quantico also would prove to be neutral political ground for vacationing presidents, with Democrats such as Cleveland finding as much pleasure at the place as a thorough Republican like Theodore Roosevelt. An avid hunter and naturalist, President Roosevelt attempted to enjoy the duck-hunting delights of the Quantico environs for himself in November 1901, having sailed from Washington on the government yacht *Sylph*. After rain canceled his first hunt, the president took refuge on Chopawamsic Island, where the Metropolitan Club of Washington maintained a clubhouse. He dined and returned to the capital. The next month Mrs. Roosevelt, who had been present on the previous trip, took the children to visit the clubhouse on Chopawamsic Island, while the president remained in Washington to attend to his official duties. Following in his father's footsteps, however, young Theodore Jr. took advantage of the excellent blinds and did a little duck hunting of his own, bringing home several geese and ducks.[94]

Eventually the president's schedule coincided with suitable weather and Roosevelt explored Quantico to the fullest, with humorous results. After a period of duck-hunting on the water, the president decided to try his hand on land. Tired and hungry after their expedition, Roosevelt and his companion Dr. Rixey started for the government ship *Dolphin,* when the president spied a rustic log cabin nestled just at the edge of the woods, a thin blue trail of smoke emerging from its chimney. The president decided he would like an old-time southern "snack."

"Dr. Rixey," he said to his friend, "If there is anything in that cabin to eat, I intend to have it. Let's try our luck over there." And so he did. They knocked on the cabin door and it was opened by "a venerable negro." The man, apologizing for being "pow'ful pore," nonetheless took pleasure in sharing with them a sumptuous, if greasy southern-fried meal of corn "dodgers," bacon, ham, and fried eggs. Roosevelt pronounced the food quite good, and he and Dr. Rixey amazed their host by eating "like two schoolboys." When the president discovered the man had a good deal of buttermilk, he sent word to the *Dolphin* for the entire party to come ashore "for a regular buttermilk feast."

After overhearing the presidential party talk about wild turkeys, the man volunteered that there were many nearby. Always a man of action, Roosevelt immediately followed the old man to the blinds he had constructed in the woods. The man instructed the president to hold his fire when the first bird came into view, as the rest of the flock would soon follow, thereby increasing Roosevelt's chances of hitting more than one turkey. "Hol' on,

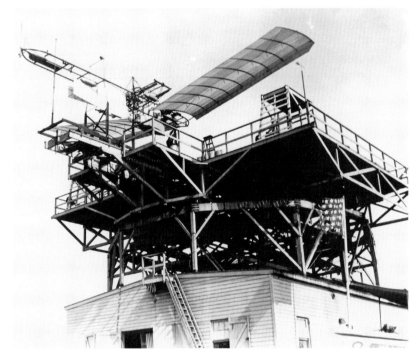

Professor Samuel Langley's pioneering aerial experiments off Chopawamsic Island brought the Wright brothers' more famous victory much closer to hand. This gossamer-light, but heavier-than-air machine, was launched from this houseboat. Alexander Graham Bell is believed to have taken this photo. Courtesy Library of Congress. LC–USZ62–107785

w'ite man, doan shoot jes' yet!" he whispered to the president. But Roosevelt's enthusiasm got the better of his patience, and he shot at the first bird he saw. Unfortunately for Roosevelt, "Mr. Wild Turkey was simply blown all to smithereens."

"Unm-m-mumphnh, now see what yo done!" the man declared. "Now yo done ruin't yo tuhkey-huntin'." The man's foresight and directness in the matter of wild turkeys impressed the president. After enquiring into the man's economic situation, he asked him if he had ever thought about working for the government. "Now yo' shoutin' in earnes', man," the man exclaimed, before asking Roosevelt if he was "one ob dem guv'ment 'ploys." Barely able to keep a straight face at the question, the president answered that he was, and in fact had "more bosses than all the rest." But after discovering that the old man had always wanted a job with the Government Printing Office, Roosevelt quietly arranged for a job for his new friend, who rewarded the president's trust by becoming one of the printing office's most valued and trusted employees. Not a bad return for an investment of fried eggs and some buttermilk.[95]

Quantico Sails into Aviation History

Until the twentieth century, Chopawamsic Island at Quantico was located in the middle of the Chopawamsic Creek estuary, where it emptied into the Potomac River. Construction of Turner Field forced the Marine Corps to reroute the creek to the south side of the airfield, thus changing the creek's topography in the name of aviation.

But in its original state of nature, Chopawamsic Island had already lent itself to aviation history once before. Interested in pioneering manned flight, Professor Samuel P. Langley, secretary of the Smithsonian Institution, wished to perfect flight by heavier-than-air machines. Langley determined that

Alexander Graham Bell, today remembered for perfecting the telephone, was a renaissance man responsible for forwarding other scientific advancements, including manned flight. In this letter Bell tells Mabel Hubbard Bell of his visit to Quantico to participate in flight experiments—"all successful," he wrote. Courtesy Library of Congress.

Alexander Graham Bell, the bearded gentleman at center, visited Quantico on several occasions to witness important aviation experiments taking place. Bell is shown here with several aviation pioneers—from left are Glenn H. Curtiss, J. A. Douglas McCurdy, Frederick W. "Casey" Baldwin, and Thomas E. Selfridge. Curtiss founded a major airplane-manufacturing firm; McCurdy later piloted the first manned airplane flight in the British Empire—at Bell's Canadian vacation home; and, in 1908, Selfridge became he world's first aviation fatality. Courtesy Library of Congress. LC–G9–Z1–137, 247–A

With the winds off Chopawamsic Island to guide them, the scientists in Professor Samuel Langley's flight study managed to successfully launch this aircraft from the deck of this houseboat. After flying several hundred feet, it spiraled gently to the surface of the river. Alexander Graham Bell photo, courtesy Library of Congress. LC–USZ62–19652

Chopawamsic Island represented the first suitable flight testing area down the Potomac from Washington, as the river widened considerably just south of the island and the winds gusted more than those closer to the capital. Establishing himself on a scow between the island and the mainland, the location so well suited Langley's purposes that he would return to this same spot for future aeronautical testing.

Langley was not the only scientific pioneer to attend the aviation trials at Chopawamsic. Traveling in the same scientific and social circles in Washington, Langley befriended Alexander Graham Bell, remembered today for his work in perfecting the telephone and telegraph. But Bell was a renaissance man of wide-ranging interests. He studied the science of genetics, attempting to determine the cause of deafness, a condition which afflicted his

mother and his wife. And he dabbled in flight experiments using intricate and huge kites at his vacation home in windy Nova Scotia. Langley and Bell spoke frequently on the professor's experiments at Chopawamsic Island, and Bell occasionally made the trip by boat to witness them. He was present on May 6, 1896, for what proved a very successful test of Langley's "aeroplane." Steam-powered and made of metal, the pilotless airplane set its own trajectory according to the winds. The plane weighed about twenty-five pounds and measured about fourteen feet from wingtip to wingtip.

Langley's experimental plane took off from a platform about twenty feet above the water, heading directly into the wind. It began a series of slow, lazy spirals upward to the height of about one hundred feet when its fuel exhausted itself and the flying machine—instead of plummeting—settled gently onto the river's surface, where it lay floating. A second test proved similar to the first, except the "aerodrome" passed over the wooded promontory, at least twenty or thirty feet above the treetops. Its flight was for at least a minute and a half, and took it over the course of at least a half mile. Bell's charts of the flight show Chopawamsic Island's distinctive shape, familiar even now though its setting has changed.

Bell, his scientific mind aroused, returned to Chopawamsic Island on November 28, 1896, to witness the flight of a similar flying machine. This one flew faster and farther than its predecessor. "We may live to see airships a common sight, but habit has not dulled the edge of wonder," Bell wrote of his experience. "A 'flying machine,' so long a type for ridicule," he observed, "has really flown; it has demonstrated its practicability in the only satisfactory way—by actually flying, and by doing this again and again."

Bell proved utterly prescient in another observation by predicting that flying machines would be developed to forward the "arts of war" before being applied to those of peace. And he predicted that flying machines, once perfected and with human pilots, would change the course of warfare by making national defense that much more difficult, saying "we may hope that this will hasten rather than retard the coming of the day when war shall cease."[96]

Quantico Cows under Siege

By 1912 Professor Langley's airplanes were not the only objects flying across the Potomac River. The naval proving grounds at Indian Head, Maryland, lay right across the river from Quantico, and occasionally the 14-inch guns fired errant projectiles which landed in Quantico. While thankfully no civilians were injured, the shells ploughed up the earth where they hit, and sometimes the cows of Quantico literally got caught in the crossfire when the proving grounds tried to prove itself. "In vain

Professor Samuel Langley's flight crew gathering their aircraft off the surface of the river. The craft delighted all by flying, under its own power, several hundred feet above the Quantico headland before settling onto the river. Courtesy Library of Congress. LC–USZ62–77351

does one search the pages of history," a *Washington Post* editorial protested, "for a parallel to the insidious and unprovoked siege of Quantico." Pointing out that neither the peaceful Quanticans nor their equally pacific cows had done anything to provoke such violence, the *Post* asked: "Does the United States think it can turn 14-inch shells, weighing 1,000 pounds, on the cows of Quantico without hearing from the owners thereof?" Little did the good citizens of Quantico, or their cows, know that within a few short years it would be the Marines, and not the Navy, who would turn their world upside down.[97]

A group of mischievous young boys had to claim responsibility for at least one of the shellings near the turn-of-the-century. Frank McInteer, who

had lived in Quantico since the 1880s, remembered that Civil War cannons proved too tempting to the lads to just leave alone. "One of those cannons was lying on top of a hill back in 1896, I think it was," McInteer later told *The Leatherneck* magazine. "Anyway, it was left behind by the Confederates; just layin' there collecting rust. So, on the 4th of July, a couple of kids loaded it with gunpowder, pushed a log down the muzzle and lit 'er up. That dang log flew all the way across town and came to rest in the middle of a house roof down along the river." McInteer would not admit to being one of the "pranksters," although he seemed to know a little too much about the incident not to have been involved. In any event, at least the cows escaped harm in this round of shelling, or rather "logging."

And the apparently still-operable cannon went on to guard the entrance of the Quantico Hotel, which would later become Waller Hall.[98]

Building Boom at Quantico

An article in the February 22, 1916 edition of the *Washington Post* carried the fantastic heading of "Building Boom Opens at Quantico: Magic City Expected in the Wake of Steel Plant and Brick Works." Perhaps the residents of Quantico read this headline with a mixture of optimism and healthy skepticism. After all, over the years they had seen one company after another try to turn Quantico into the next big industrial hub, and seen those same enterprises fail every time. Longtime residents might have even remembered the succession of

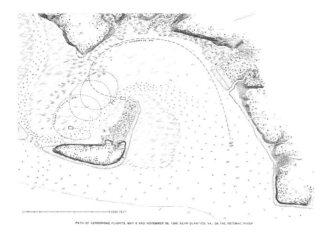

PATH OF AERODROME FLIGHTS, MAY 6 AND NOVEMBER 28, 1896, NEAR QUANTICO, VA., ON THE POTOMAC RIVER

A fascinated Alexander Graham Bell and Smithsonian Institution director Samuel Pierpont Langley watched as Langley's aircraft, "Aerodrome No. 5," took off from the cove of Chopawamsic Island and, under its own mechanical power, spiraled through the sky, settling to a graceful, gentle landing on the river at the island's inland tip. This chart also shows the path of "Aerodrome No. 6," which skirted Quantico's shoreline for a similarly graceful river landing. Courtesy Library of Congress. LC–USZ62–102678

names attached to each new venture: Newport, Carrborough, Evansport, Potomac City. The names did not last much longer than the developers' hopes. But the Quantico Improvement Company ignored history and began construction on an industrial center it promised would be "another Hopewell, where thousands of people will find profitable employment and where millions of dollars will be invested in all sorts of improvements." Surveyors marked the locations of the steel manufacturing plant, brick works, hundreds of workers' cottages, power plants, and even the projected $20,000 hotel. "Dirt will begin to fly by March 1," the *Post* projected. But unlike similar projects, such as Barrow, this development scheme inspired a real estate boom in the Quantico area as others wanted to invest in the prosperity the Quantico Improvement Company's plans were sure to bring.[99]

"Quantico Is Made Over. Old Town Becomes an Industrial Center Over Night," the *Post* reported in April. This time it seemed like the dreams might just become reality as the bank, power plant, hotel, and residential area were under construction, and the streets were being surveyed and graded for improvements. Because of the proximity of the electric plant, some of the older houses received electricity for the first time, and the streets were lit at night. Even a pyrite mine up the creek towards Dumfries had been reopened to work at full blast. For those looking for a bit of recreation, Quantico offered a bathing beach on the banks of the

Potomac, good views, a healthful atmosphere, a clubhouse, and a proposed dance pavilion.[100]

The industrial city coalesced into the Quantico shipyards, located on Shipping Point. The shipyards quickly contracted enough work to remain open for at least a year, and it intended to build ocean freighters, tankers, and passenger liners in the future, with U.S. Navy contracts hopefully to follow.

"Quantico Booming; The Industrial City of Tidewater Virginia" proclaimed a section of *Quantico Times* of July 14, 1916. An advertisement

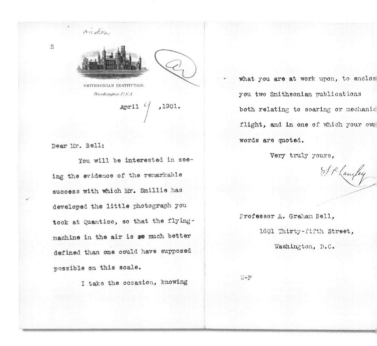

Professor Samuel Langley writes Alexander Graham Bell that his photograph of flight experiments at Quantico—published here—turned out nicely. Langley, using the lexicon of the day, refers to airplanes as "flying machines" and their accomplishment as "soaring" or "mechanical flight." Courtesy Library of Congress.

placed by the Quantico Company in the same issue offered 25-by-110-foot lots in town, or "villa sites" ranging from five to ten acres. "Property in Quantico is growing more valuable every minute," the advertisement promised. "So will prices of the Quantico lots." Such advertisements and promises of a prospering town worked magic, and a photograph published in the May 21, 1916 edition of the *Washington Post* proved the phenomenon. The image showed a crowd at the docks at Quantico, identified in the caption as "only part of one of the throngs that attended recent auction sales of lots in Quantico, Va."[101]

All indications suggested that Quantico might really be on the verge of something big and lasting this time.

From the Halls of Montezuma, to the Shores of Quantico

And it was. But the lasting influence over Quantico would not prove to be the Quantico Improvement Company, but rather the United States Marine Corps.

What would later be known as World War I had broken out in Europe in 1914. The United States initially maintained a neutral position in the international conflict, but Germany's increasingly belligerent use of submarines against the Allies and neutral nations, and its ruthless sinking of the passenger ship *Lusitania*, drew the United States into the war on the Allied side. Hoping a victory in this war would make the world "safe for democracy," President Woodrow Wilson broke off diplomatic relations with Germany in February 1917, and on April 6, 1917, Congress declared war on Germany. Another war was on, and this one would have a far-reaching impact on the little town of Quantico.

Advertised somewhat optimistically as one of the largest shipyards in the Western Hemisphere, Quantico Shipyard, shown here in 1916, built wooden freight ships for use on the Potomac River and Chesapeake Bay. The yard closed in 1920, taking Quantico's hopes of being the "New Industrial City" with it. Courtesy base archive.

CHAPTER IV

THE WAR TO END ALL WARS 1917–1918

"It is a fearful thing to lead this great peaceful people into war, into the most terrible and disastrous of all wars," President Wilson admitted to Congress in April 1917, when seeking its permission to declare war on Germany. "But the right is more precious than peace, and we shall fight for the things we have always carried closest to our hearts."[102] Having heard of the horrors of the war in Europe for the nearly three years it had already been raging, Wilson knew this would be a war unlike previous conflicts the United States had entered, and could change the country in unexpected ways.

If the residents of the village at Quantico thought about the impending war in terms of their own lives, they probably worried about the young men they knew going off to war, or perhaps the financial toll waging war could exact on the nation, or fortified themselves to endure hardships on behalf of rights considered "more precious than peace." Little did Quanticans know that "The War to End All Wars" would permanently alter the landscape of their little hamlet.

In the years leading up to World War I, the Marine Corps had been developing an "Advanced Base Force" component, based on Admiral George Dewey's conclusion that the "Marines would be best adapted and most available for immediate and sudden call for use in defending any advanced base." The peacetime Advanced Base Force supported two 1,250-man regiments, one in Philadelphia and the other near San Francisco, and participated in limited operations in Mexico and the Caribbean.

The wartime strength of the force was estimated at 5,000 troops. But the United States' possible entry into the European war immediately prompted revisions in estimated troop strength in 1916, and the opening of new recruiting depots at Parris Island, South Carolina, and San Diego, California. By the middle of 1916, the Marine Corps boasted 11,000 officers and troops, with authorization to increase the rolls to 18,000 in the event of an emergency. Even with the "leisurely pace" of recruiting, the Marine Corps quickly discovered that its traditional East Coast facilities could not handle the influx of new recruits. With the Navy expanding as well, the Marines could no longer rely on training their recruits at naval stations. The Marines needed their own base, preferably one which could house the East Coast branch of the Advanced Base Force. The search for a suitable location had barely begun when President Wilson authorized an increase in Marine strength to 18,000 men in March 1917.[103]

On April 6, the same day the president committed the United States to war, Major General George Barnett, Commandant of the Marine Corps, established a board charged with finding a new East Coast training site for the Marines. Barnett and the board had specific criteria in mind: the site needed to be accessible by railroad and waterways; it needed to have a terrain varied enough to be suitable for target ranges and a variety of training exercises; and it needed to be able to accommodate seventy-five hundred men.[104] After visiting a few locations in the Washington, D.C. area, the board

The Evening Star.

WASHINGTON, D. C., FRIDAY, APRIL 6, 1917—TWENTY-SIX PAGES.

No. 29,645.   ONE CENT.

U. S. AT WAR WITH GERMANY; PRESIDENT SIGNS RESOLUTION

EXECUTIVE IN PROCLAMATION CALLS ON ALL CITIZENS AND OFFICERS TO SUPPORT NATION

Germany's Challenge to World Formally Is Accepted by United States in Defense of Humanity.

Navy Department Summons All Naval Militia and Reserves and Coast Guard Becomes Part of Fighting Force.

The war resolution was signed by the President at 1:11 o'clock this afternoon.

The President also signed a proclamation declaring a state of war between the United States and Germany. In the proclamation he called upon all officers of the United States to exercise their duties and appealed to all American citizens to give support to all measures of the government.

All the naval militia and naval reserves were called to the colors with the President's signing of the war resolution.

WAR FORMALLY RECOGNIZED

COAST GUARD PASSES TO NAVY

ALLIED WITH TEN OTHER COUNTRIES

HUNDRED MILLION SPECIAL WAR FUND VOTED BY SENATE

Upper House Quickly Adds Big Sum to General Deficiency Bill.

TO BE USED BY PRESIDENT FOR DEFENSE OF NATION

Additional Money Also Provided for Secret Service and Department of Justice

House Committees at Work Devising Ways for Raising Big Fund for Financing War

PRESIDENT PROCLAIMS WAR BETWEEN U.S. AND GERMANY CALLING CITIZENS TO COLORS

The President's war proclamation is as follows:

GERMANY IGNORES PRESIDENT'S SPEECH

But Imperial Reply May Be Made if It Be Sent to Neutrals.

EDITORIAL ATTACKS BITTER

GERMAN VESSELS IN ALL U.S. PORTS ARE TAKEN OVER

Authorities Act Promptly After Passage of War Resolution by House.

FOR STEAMERS' SAFETY; NOT FOR CONFISCATION

Crews of Teuton Ships Are Put Under the Care of Immigration Officials

Congress's declaration of war against the German Empire galvanized the country and the Marine Corps, which within hours of the declaration began looking for ground near Washington—Quantico was soon selected—on which to train recruits bound for the war. Nineteen seventeen would prove the most pivotal year in Quantico's history. Evening Star, April 6, 1917.

rejected most of them. But on April 17, 1917, the board made its way to Quantico, and fate or destiny was about to take over.

The Quantico Company, which had begun with high hopes of transforming Quantico into an industrial and recreational paradise, had yet to realize its vision and had overextended itself in the process. The company owned more land than it could use, but found it difficult to sell at a reasonable price. Barnett's board must have reported favorably on what they had seen at Quantico as Barnett's assistant, Brigadier General John Lejeune, seemed impressed with its potential. "I think we have about made arrangements here for a very fine place for a temporary training ground on the Potomac at Quantico," Lejeune wrote General Littleton Waller a few days later. "It has very good water facilities and also some public utilities which we can use. . . . There will be ample ground at this place for both military and infantry combat firing." The board agreed wholeheartedly with Lejeune's assessment, and reported to General Barnett that they "believed that the site at Quantico fulfills all requirements of a concentration and training camp for the Marine Corps, and has all the requirements for a permanent post, except that it is not on deep water." With a favorable recommendation in hand and the need to move quickly, the government negotiated a lease with the Quantico Company for fifty-three hundred acres. Quantico was on its way.[105]

"The Outlook Was Not Pretty"

With the pressure on, the Navy Department geared up to complete the new base at Quantico in six short weeks. First, authorities needed to determine where to build the camp itself, and Barnett convened yet another board to choose building sites. General Lejeune must not have actually seen Quantico before he wrote his enthusiastic letter to

Navy Secretary Josephus Daniels, shown here, was an ardent supporter of the Marines training at Quantico, and visited them many times—along with his wife, whose visits the Marines particularly enjoyed. According to legend, the term "Cup of Joe" dates from Josephus Daniels' proscription against the use of alcohol in the fleet, causing sailors to take up coffee instead. Copyright Scherer Studio, courtesy Library of Congress. LC–USZ62–107582

General Waller, otherwise this second board would not have been so surprised by what it found:

An inspection between south and northbound trains showed a few sleepy houses along a dusty street which ended at a small wharf. The hills beyond were covered with pine and a tangle of underbrush. Two hundred laborers were cutting a road through the forest (now Barnett Avenue). To the left of the settlement was a swampy pond, and a rutted wagon trail led to a cornfield. The entire area was roughly segmented by three creeks that meandered down from the hills and fanned out into the marshes bordering the Potomac. The outlook was not pretty—a primitive corduroy road, connecting with the outside world, red clay, quagmires, and five thousand acres in the camp.[106]

But just as Rome was not built in a day, improvement at Quantico would come in time, and the board chose sites on which the work of encampments would begin.

To house the estimated five thousand recruits on their way to Quantico for training, the Navy decided to erect wooden barracks rather than tents as a cost- and time-saving measure. Counter-intuitively, wooden barracks were discovered to be cheaper and easier to obtain than tents. With the base scheduled to open on May 14, however, the first recruits to arrive at Quantico on May 18 were by necessity housed in tents until barracks could be erected. In those beginning days almost everything was temporary, including the commanding officer, Major Charles Campbell. Campbell commanded Quantico for only eleven days before Major Julius Turrill took command. Turrill himself would soon turn Quantico over to Colonel Albertus Catlin when he left for Philadelphia with his battalion of the 5th Regiment, Advanced Base Force.[107]

A City Is Built

"A few weeks ago Quantico was a village, with a Post Office, a water tank, half a dozen stores, a church or two, and about 200 inhabitants," the *New York Times* observed in October 1917. "And then came the 'Soldiers of the Sea'. . . . Today everything is changed." Breathtaking both in speed and scope, within months of opening Quantico's camp, con-

This busy train platform was Marine trainees' first view of Quantico during the war. Trains ran every few hours and were Quantico's only reliable link with the outside world, aside from ships. Wartime necessity drove the federal government to fully nationalize the railroads during the war. Courtesy base archive.

Quantico Shipyard, as seen during 1919 when operating at full capacity. The yard never gained the Navy business it hoped to receive, and the war wrecked its chances to build ocean-going passenger liners. Courtesy base archive.

struction could accommodate seven thousand recruits. While the town itself could claim a fair number of public utilities from its improvement by the Quantico Company, the Marine base had to create its infrastructure literally from the ground up. After clearing construction sites, a virtual city arose from the wilderness. Numerous nearby wells pumped water into concrete holding tanks, which then supplied the base. Electricity wired into the camp supplied its lighting needs. Construction of the barracks supposedly took sanitation needs into account, but on this score theory failed to translate into reality at the start. Three weeks after the first recruits arrived, no garbage disposal or sewage systems had been put into place, which quickly became an odorous, not to mention unhealthy, problem as the camp faced its first hot Virginia summer. The Marines first tried field incinerators, then trash pits. When the incinerators failed and the trash pits filled faster than new ones could be dug, camp authorities resorted to loading the refuse on barges and dumping it downriver. This proved an equally untenable

solution, and only the construction of a huge hillside incinerator could keep Quantico clean.[108]

The barracks themselves consisted of wooden dormitories capable of accommodating seventy-five to one hundred men. Companies had their own mess halls, kitchens, and showering and toilet facilities. The cantonment as a whole comprised 350 buildings, but those were divided among infantry, artillery, and officers' schools. As work on the base progressed, an icehouse, laundry, gymnasium, post library, and other nonessential, but most welcome facilities, were added to the overall plan. In the meantime, the base boasted a YMCA building and an auditorium capable of seating 2,000 men. Not forgetting the ladies, the YWCA constructed a hostess house for friends and families visiting the base, and for use by the men themselves.[109]

One structure on the base did not have to be built from scratch, and in fact predated the base itself. Located on Rising Hill and dating from the 1880s, the Quantico Hotel had been constructed when developers still anticipated Quantico's success as a resort town. When this dream failed and the Marines moved in, the Corps quickly appropriated the building as officers' quarters. The Quantico Hotel became "Waller Hall" in 1918, in acknowledgement of Major Littleton Waller's heroic service on the island of Samar in the Philippines in 1901. Generations of Marines appreciated the charm of Waller Hall until structural failures led to the building's demolition in 1968.[110]

"A Military Center of First-Rate Importance"

"From a lazy Virginia town to a military center of first-rate importance has been the transformation of Quantico," proclaimed the *Washington Post* in July 1917. While the *Post* may have overstated Quantico's transformation slightly, its prediction that the base would receive thousands of troops certainly came to pass during the war. One historian of the Marine Corps during World War I estimated that one thousand officers and forty thousand Marines ultimately passed through Quantico on their way to other assignments between May 1917 and November 1918.[111]

Until accommodations could be made at Quantico, officers initially received training at Mare Island or San Diego in California, Parris Island, South Carolina, or at the Marine Corps Rifle Range at Winthrop, Maryland. After the first group of over three hundred officers arrived at Quantico in July 1917 and the Officers' Training School in Norfolk closed, the Officers' Training Camp of Instruction opened at Quantico. During their three-month course, these new lieutenants studied weapons, tactics, and leadership skills before departing for the Western Front. The officers in training followed a schedule likely familiar to many of their successors: "reveille 0545, physical drill 0600, breakfast 0630, drill 0730–0930, inspection of quarters 1145, dinner 1200, drill 1300–1430, 1500–1600, supper 1800, study 1900–2100, taps 2200." The prebreakfast drill sounded like a leisurely half-mile run through the streets at Quantico, but the unsettled state of infrastructure on base made it more of "an obstacle course" than we can appreciate today.[112]

As early as July 1917, the Chesapeake and Potomac Steamboat Company put its steamer *St. John's* on a twice-daily schedule between

Raw land, newly incorporated into the rapidly expanding training camp, provided the somewhat unpleasant view greeting newly arriving Marines. Fields and forests now hosted the infrastructure of a small city. Courtesy base archive.

The River Styx, the stream shown here at the entrance to the Quantico encampment, was bridged not by Charon's unhappy ferry but by this sturdy wooden span. The gully was later filled. Courtesy base archive.

Washington, D.C., and Quantico to handle the wave of regular recruits. Likewise, the Southern Railway ran additional trains between the capital and the camp. After just three weeks, Quantico boasted a population of one thousand men. By the end of September the base built for seven thousand men had already filled to six thousand, and by mid-October the *New York Times* reported finding ten thousand men at Quantico.[113]

The camp population fluctuated, of course, as new recruits arrived and "veterans" shipped out to other assignments. As exciting as it was for the men embarking on what they hoped would be a "great adventure," as former President Theodore Roosevelt called the war, every regimental departure left the men remaining at Quantico anxious, envious, and heartbroken with waiting. "Unit after unit entrained and departed for the mysterious land where battles raged and between which and us there seemed to be an impenetrable curtain hung," remembered General John A. Lejeune, who was himself desperate

Trench warfare proved one of the chief characteristics of World War I. This trench system, dug by Quantico trainees, shows the planning which went into the construction of each. Courtesy base archive.

for an overseas assignment. "Always at six o'clock in the morning the detachments left. What bleak, cold, wintry mornings they were. . . . All of those left behind stood along the railway tracks and shouted three lusty cheers for their departing comrades, while the bands played until their instruments froze. As we turned away to resume our daily tasks, how heavy-hearted we were!"[114] Lejeune's chance to ship out finally came in May 1918.

State of the Art

From its beginning, Quantico developed a reputation for military training aimed at the latest developments in warfare. As befitting an officer training facility, the *New York Times* concluded that at Quantico, "their business in camp is a postgraduate course in the actual work of war." While trench warfare was certainly not a new technique in the annals of war, the extent and deadliness with which it came to characterize fighting on the Western Front demanded that Quantico Marines be ready to face it. To this end, a complete set of trenches was constructed about a mile away from the camp, where Marines could familiarize themselves with trench warfare, including the "wire entanglements" which proved so lethal to men sent over the top. The "maze" included trenches, bombproof cellars and dugouts, tunnels and communication passages, all on the advice of officers who had experienced the real thing in Europe. Camouflaged gun emplacements completed the scene. Although as the *Times* reporter noted, these trenches would never be "completed," since much of the training the Marines received in the trenches involved erecting them from start to finish. Every day the network of trenches at Quantico increased as new Marines learned how to build and fortify them.[115]

In true "postgraduate" style, Marines trained with the latest weapons as well. "At Quantico they react to the weapon of the moment," a newspaper reporter enthused. "Only a few months ago the Mills grenade was the popular weapon—now it's the bayonet." Again, like trenches, bayonets were certainly not new, but Quantico Marines practiced several new and different bayonet drills, should they find themselves in hand-to-hand combat on the front. Given that General John Pershing, commander of American forces in Europe, advocated shifting from trench warfare to "open warfare" by relying on rifles and bayonets, training with the primitive weapon was prudent indeed. Luckily for those Marines still developing their techniques, practice drills involved heavily padded and masked men, using guns outfitted with rubber bayonets at the end of which a button was placed. The opponents would charge each other at forty yards, and if the bayonet button touched any portion of the enemy's body, a "hit" was scored. Other drills used dummy opponents or involved practicing new thrusts adapted for the angles encountered in using bayonets in trenches. Marines' recollections confirm that bayonet practice formed part of their daily life at Quantico. "Between nearly every two tents, there are dummies for bayonet practice," James M. Sellers described, "and at all hours of the day enlisted men can be seen slaughtering these dummy Germans."[116]

Dummy trenches also helped Marines hone their skills at grenade throwing. Constructed of pine boards, dummy trenches featuring high parapets could be moved around the field. The idea behind the moveable trench targets was to accustom Marines to throwing grenades from their trenches into those of the enemy at a variety of angles and distances.[117]

Infantry and artillery ranges also supplied Marines with a chance to perfect their techniques. And although animal power would still provide a major portion of the military's transportation needs in Europe, at Quantico tractors pulled the heavy artillery as war became increasingly mechanized. Caterpillar tractors hauled the pieces onto the firing range, where officers learned to select their targets,

"TEUFEL HUNDEN" ON THE MARNE

Cartoonist Clifford Kennedy Berryman summed it up nicely with this reinterpretation of a popular U.S. Marines recruiting poster showing a German dachshund being chased by a "Teufel Hunden"—a "devil dog," as the Germans called the Marines after their performance at the Battle of the Marne. The Marines at Quantico identified particularly with, and were proud of, the hard-won battlefield moniker. (c) 1918. The Washington Post. *Reprinted with permission.*

compute the range, and order the weapon fired. When the big guns practiced, the sound of cannon fire could be heard in Fredericksburg. The smaller guns still relied on old-fashioned manpower, in this case two men pulling the gun carriage. Four guns and ten men comprised a platoon, and it was not unknown for these unfortunate men to be sent on hard marches in the surrounding hillsides.[118]

For the first time, radio and telephone technology would play a role in a global conflict, and the Marines responded to this by creating squads dedicated to this equipment. But since the technology was in its infancy, every company prudently maintained a signal squad which trained in flag and flashlight communication.[119]

This crop of Marines, however, would also have to learn skills from other branches of the military. Many of the Marines sent to France fought under the auspices of the American Expeditionary Force, which served under the United States Army. As such, AEF Marines had to also learn Army regulations, after having just gotten accustomed during basic training to Marine Corps rules.[120]

What no one could know during officer training was that once in France, the Marines would experience little trench warfare in comparison with their Allied counterparts. By the time the Marines arrived, General Pershing's desire to transform the war into one of "open" combat across battlefields had begun to take effect, and their experiences would be equally devastating, but above ground. Regardless of where they fought and whether or not they had trained for that particular type of warfare, Marines brought to the front a gusto and tenaciousness that impressed even the war-hardened Germans, who called the Marines *Teufel hunden.* This translates as "devil dogs," a nickname the Marines appropriated with pride.[121]

Wargaming in the sandbox, or "sand table," proved an effective means of training these infantry officers, and is one of the enduring innovations of World War I. Courtesy base archive.

First Impressions

Ordinary Marines, particularly those who arrived during the camp's early days of construction, frequently formed less enthusiastic opinions of Quantico when they first arrived. James M. Sellers was among the first officers transferred from the rifle range at Winthrop, Maryland. Sellers thought the community of Quantico resembled the rough mining towns he had seen in photographs. "There is one small street which constitutes the original town," he wrote.

> There are rows and rows of unpainted wooden shacks. . . . The small streets between are all cut up with rain wash, and we stumble over what is left of a former small forest, roots and stumps, and sewer excavations. There are always a pack of dogs and cats around Marine camps, and they always seem to be contented. Downtown there are little restaurants where we can get an egg sandwich for 50

cents. And there is also a dance hall where they charge 20 cents for a dance with one of the painted ladies brought to town for the purpose.[122]

Another of the early arrivals at Quantico was Gunnery Sergeant Frank Zissa, who had begun his service with the Marines during the Spanish-American War and had been sent to the Caribbean during the intervening years. "This is absolutely the worst kind of place they could have 'dumped' us off," Zissa confessed to his wife in May 1917.

> Our camp is right close to the few houses that compose the town and it is all most uninhabitable for dirt and dust flying about. The bedding and clothes are just literally covered with dust all the time. The place has been layed out for a town for many years but the town never materialized owing to the poor section of the country. The town is laid out

nicely but the streets of course are not paved and it can be easily imagined what amount of dirt and dust there is from the increased traffic since the arrival of a large contractors force who are constructing many temporary buildings for the Marine Corps.[123]

Given that the base was still under construction when Zissa first arrived, he probably saw Quantico at its worst. But while he highlighted the town's shortcomings, even then he could see promise. Reflecting on the effect the Marines were sure to have, Zissa predicted that Quantico would soon prosper, and confirmed in June that "this village is surely on the boom now. . . . Stores and stands of all kinds are in operation."[124]

Other Marines concurred with Sellers' and Zissa's disparagement of the town's appearance, but after long days of hard training, Quantico town began to exert a different allure. Those who fre-

quented some of Quantico's questionable restaurants remembered that it was not so much the food that brought them in, but rather that a Marine could "order what a fellow wanted without a threatening sergeant standing over, making one feel that his liberty, if not his very life, was at stake." They don't call it "liberty" for nothing.[125]

From One Extreme to the Other

Until the town and the base paved their streets and installed proper drainage systems, Quantico Marines would echo the same complaints raised by their Union and Confederate counterparts fifty years before: rain and mud. The week after Frank Zissa complained to his wife about the dust at Quantico, he wrote to update her on the weather. "We are sure having our troubles down here this week," he explained on May 29. "The week before it was dirt and dust but since Sunday lots of rain and, of course, plenty of mud to contend with." High

Quantico's wartime post exchange, shown here in 1918, was a busy place. Food rationing was the rule of the day, but consumer goods, such as cosmetics, toiletries, and entertainment items, continued to be churned out by America's factories—and sold here. Courtesy base archive.

winds had blown tents away, as well as the temporary kitchens, which lost cooking utensils to the mud and rushing waters. Fortunately for Zissa, he and his companions were able to rescue their provision tent, and "thereby did not lose a meal." (The dust had returned in force by June, however.) The first issue of the base newspaper poked fun at the soggy conditions editors knew every Quantico Marine encountered. "Quantico in the Indian tongue means 'slippery mud,' which every Marine concedes remarkably appropriate."[126]

The mud was said to be of "a slippery, red, gumbo-like variety." "Rumor had it," remembered Captain John Craige, "that after a hard rain these hay-wagons would frequently sink into holes in the street until only the horns of the oxen and the heads of the drivers were visible." Craige, noting the lack of road connections anywhere, continued, "A trip to Washington in wet weather was an adventure ranking with Admiral Byrd's dog-sled journey to the South Pole."[127]

Machine gun instruction, shown here in 1917, was an essential element of Quantico instruction. The use of machine guns, biplanes, tanks, and other new military technology was taught as Marines encountered and used all these in Europe. It was quite the war. Courtesy base archive.

In a certain regard, navigating the muck at Quantico proved excellent training for the field in France. James Draucker submitted a drawing to *The Leatherneck* magazine in 1978, illustrating the "duckboards" he and his comrades used in Camp Pontanezen in France during the war. As illustrated, the duckboards were essentially two parallel pieces of wood joined on the top by a series of shorter planks serving as steps; similar to a wooden sidewalk. By the time Draucker arrived in France, he was well versed in duckboards and mud, having trained at Quantico during rainy weather. "There was a main road into camp and across the railroad track into the village," Draucker recalled. "A concrete road went part way, ending just past the group of wooden barracks that were built in rows sideways up the hill. In rainy weather it was necessary to use the boards to get up and down the hill."[128]

Sometimes it was not just the mud that Marines had to beware of but standing water. Sarah McAllister submitted a photograph to the "Corps Album" section of a 1967 *Leatherneck* magazine. In this photo, two hardy Marines are shown carrying a wooden chest away from the tents in the background. So what is so unusual about this snapshot? The two hardy Marines are wading through almost waist-high water, after a flash-flood engulfed their tent camp during World War I! At least the two hardy Marines are smiling, apparently appreciating Mother Nature's perverse sense of humor.[129]

At the other extreme, cold winter weather turned everything to ice, including the Potomac River. The winter of 1917–1918 proved especially cold, and General Lejeune later remembered that the Potomac River froze over at Quantico, with humorous results. When rounds from the Naval Proving Ground across the river at Indian Head occasionally went astray, the river was so solidly frozen that the fourteen-inch shells would simply bounce along the ice over to Quantico. The men in camp would then walk across the ice to retrieve the shells, which would later appear as ornaments on company streets.[130]

While mud, floods, and ice proved uncomfortable and annoying to the men at Quantico, the presence of so much water in camp and in the nearby Chopawamsic Swamp did constitute at least one potential health hazard. Standing water provided an ideal breeding ground for mosquitoes, known carriers of malaria. Troops slept under mosquito netting when possible, while work crews tried to drain swamps and chemically spray insect breeding grounds. But these remedies only last for so long. Indeed, the mosquito menace at Quantico continued to be active well into the 1950s. Children who lived on base in that era still remember seeing trucks loaded with the chemical agent DDT patrolling the roads to wipe out mosquitoes in their larval stage.[131]

Commuters

Even before subdivisions in Prince William County became bedroom communities for people who worked in Washington, Quantico attracted commuters. Necessity forced some Marines into the commuter life. Given that the base at Quantico grew up from nothing, certain facilities could not meet the immediate demands of the military. Barracks for bachelor Marines took precedence simply because of the large numbers of men arriving at the base. Married officers who brought their families with them to Quantico had few residential options. If they could not rent a room at the Quantico Hotel or somewhere in Quantico town, they were forced to house their families in Fredericksburg,

> THE SECRETARY OF THE NAVY,
> WASHINGTON.
>
> 24th of December
> 1 9 1 9
>
> My dear General:
>
> I thank you very much for your letter of December 20th and particularly happy to know that you are going to start the schools, and I know that under your direction and Butler's you will be able to make these schools a blessing to all the men who enlist in the Marine Corps and to the Service and therefore to the country. I am gratified to learn from many sources of the splendid spirit at Quantico. One of these days I am going to come down and see you all.
>
> With warm regards and Christmas Greetings to you and yours, I am
>
> Sincerely yours,
>
> Josephus Daniels
>
> Maj.Gen. John A. Lejeune, USMC,
> Marine Barracks,
> Quantico, Virginia.

Many were interested, including Navy Secretary Josephus Daniels, in General John A. Lejeune's pioneering experiment to establish formal schools for Marines at Quantico; similar to those at West Point and Annapolis. The new Marine Corps Institute was a success, and continues today, as does Quantico's role in training. John A. Lejeune Papers, Library of Congress.

Alexandria, or even Washington, and commute to Quantico by train. The camp's commander, General Lejeune was himself a commuter Marine for much of his time at Quantico, while his family remained at home in Washington. Years later Lejeune would remember that the bitterly cold winter of 1917–1918 made his frequent commutes "very trying." The great irony of Lejeune's commuting woes is that his family stayed in their Washington home because a house for the commanding general was not built until after the war. When Lejeune returned to Quantico as its commander in 1920, his family moved to the newly finished commanding general's house in April—just in time to see Lejeune appointed Major General Commandant of the Marines in June. Until renovations on the Commandant's House at the Navy Yard could be completed, Lejeune and his family remained in Quantico and Lejeune once again commuted between Quantico and Washington.[132]

After becoming a second lieutenant, Frank Zissa decided to leave the base and live in nearby Fredericksburg, even though the quality of life on base and in the town of Quantico had improved dramatically since his arrival. Zissa may have thought taking a room in a private residence would make it easier for his wife to visit from Pennsylvania, but he soon gave up these arrangements after long waits for the train to Quantico made his commute intolerable. After a short stint living in town, Zissa ultimately ended up back in the barracks.[133]

Not all of Quantico's commuters came through by train, or had any connection to the Marine Corps. The old colonial "Quantico Road" morphed into the Washington-Richmond road over the years, eventually becoming part of present-day U.S. Route 1. Unfortunately, in the vicinity of Quantico and Chopawamsic Swamp, the quality of the road had not improved much since the colonial period. *The Washington Post* said this part of road was "acknowledged to be the worst piece of road in the United States by every one who has traversed it." The 2.5 miles from Quantico Creek to Chopawamsic Creek "which, has perhaps been a greater thorn in the sides of motorists touring North or South, than any other stretch in this country, no matter what its length, has been the cause of many motoring parties either not coming to Washington on their way South, going instead by the valley route or abandoning the trip altogether."

Imagine the unbounded joy of the motoring public when the *Post* announced in April 1917 that the "dreaded Chopawamsic Swamp" was gone, soon to be replaced by a new road and bridges across both creeks. Thanks for this project went to the

Semaphore signaling, demonstrated here by Quantico Marines in 1918, still had its place in modern combat. But not for long. The newfangled radio was soon to make swift impact. Courtesy base archive.

Although World War I was global, it never grew to involve much tropical island fighting, at least not by American forces. The Marines, however, chose to be prepared, hence this wicker gabion, used for transporting troops across islands they might someday encounter. Courtesy base archive.

fledgling American Automobile Association, which began a public subscription for funds and lobbied for federal money. As the road work neared completion, a *Post* reporter and an AAA representative decided to try the route for themselves, and set off in a Saxon six-cylinder touring car. As far as Occoquan the macadam road glided under them like a dream, but the unwise taking of a detour towards Dumfries taxed the Saxon Six's traction on hills and in mud. Detour aside, the reporter seemed pleased with the condition of the road, and concluded that once the final touches were applied to the road around Chopawamsic, the trip to Richmond would be "clear sailing."[134] The AAA representative or *Post* reporter could hardly imagine there would come a day when the Washington-Richmond road would be physically passable for any vehicle, but almost as horrendous a trip due to the volume of automobiles on the road!

The Quantico Leatherneck

The arrival of the Marines in Quantico also gave rise to a USMC institution still going strong today: *The Leatherneck*. The Corps produced very few publications prior to World War I, but that changed with

the enlargement of the Corps in 1917. Among the new recruits sent to Quantico was Corporal W. L. Foster, a reporter for the *Cincinnati Post* in civilian life. Foster approached the base commander, General Lejeune, with an idea for a camp newspaper. Lejeune agreed to the proposal, providing Foster produced it on his own time, and without government funds. The first issue was truly a cooperative effort. The YMCA provided office space and loaned the staff typewriters. Local businesses paid for advertisements, which provided the capital to get the paper up and running. Writing and producing the newspaper was the responsibility of the volunteer staff, which included men who had previously worked for the *Kansas City Star, Pittsburgh Gazette-Times,* and *Chicago News.* The *Quantico Leatherneck* first appeared on November 17, 1917. The four-page sheet cost two cents when first published, and featured articles of interest to Quantico Marines such as "Opening of New 'Y' Next Month Brings Great Joy," "Marines Want to Get in the Fray across the Pond," and "Interest Shown Here in Sport Events." Although Foster got the *Quantico Leatherneck* going, another newspaperman, Sergeant J. C. Smith took over as the paper's first editor. Under Smith's editorship, the *Quantico Leatherneck* appealed to readers as an informal report of news around the camp and local community, along with general Corps items of interest to Marines.[135]

The paper's name reflected both its location and pride in Marine Corps history. The "leatherneck" nickname may have derived from the leather neckbands Marines once wore, allegedly to protect themselves from being cut by enemy cutlasses. Or it

Hospital corpsmen. A naval hospital was established during the war and continues to this day. The horrors of trench warfare, with its mustard gas and high casualty rate, proved difficult for Quantico to teach. Courtesy base archive.

may have referred to the high collars on Marine uniforms. Whatever the reality behind the legend, the name became synonymous with "Marine," and served as a perfect title for the new publication. After forty-five issues, the journal's staff saw its potential to serve the entire Marines Corps, and changed the name and content accordingly. Since the October 24, 1918 issue *The Leatherneck* (no longer restricting itself to Quantico) has published features of interest to and about Marines stationed all over the globe. The paper continued to be published at Quantico until it moved with the Marine Corps Institute to Washington, D.C., in the 1920s. Not long after, the publication changed from its newspaper format to the recognizable magazine

style it maintains today. (The magazine would move back to Quantico in 1972, to be published by the Marine Corps Association.)[136]

"An Ideal Place for a Training Camp"

As 1917 ended, and the war continued into 1918, several great changes occurred at Quantico to seal its status as an important Marine Corps installation. Some businesses still held out hope for Quantico's development as a shipping center, or perhaps they counted on the Department of the Navy establishing a permanent presence in Quantico, which would give local shipbuilding concerns an advantage in contracts. In April 1917, the Potomac Shipbuilding Company assumed the interests of the International

Steel and Shipbuilding Company at Quantico, with the intention of establishing mills and factories for the production of ships and shipbuilding materials, securing patents for new technology, and dabbling in the real estate market. Whether or not, or for how long, the Potomac Shipbuilding Company succeeded in these endeavors is not known. But its promise was not enough to inspire the Quantico Company to continue with its operations. By the end of 1917, the company decided to approach the Marine Corps about a buyout of the land on which the base had been established. Given the time and money already expended on capital improvements to the site, the offer met a welcome reception with the Marines. The commandant selected a board to study the issue, and prepare a recommendation as to how much land the Marine Corps required at Quantico for its wartime activities and as an eventual East Coast base for the Advanced Base Force. The board included Quantico's commander, General Lejeune, who was certainly in a position to know the value of and potential military uses for the base. Not unexpectedly, the board reported favorably on the government's purchase of approximately five thousand acres at Quantico.[137]

The next step was to secure Congress' approval of the deal, and appropriate funds to secure the land. Secretary of the Navy Josephus Daniels, Marine Corps Commandant General Barnett, and General Lejeune testified before a subcommittee of the Committee of Naval Affairs in May 1918. General Barnett testified that the land at Quantico satisfied nearly every requirement for a base. The open space and hilly terrain supported both rifle and artillery practice, the latter of which required that gunners be able to shoot long distances, at high angles, and without being able to actually see their targets. Barnett stressed this point particularly, explaining that several members of Congress in the past had not appreciated the benefits of varied topography for artillery practice. Senator Martin, in

fact, had suggested that the level ground previously used for the Jamestown Tercentennial Exposition might suit the Marines even better than Quantico. "No; it would not be worth anything for our purposes at all," he told Martin. "Well, that is good, level land," the senator countered. "Yes; that would be very good for a parade ground," Barnett explained, "but I would not take it as a gift for our purposes." ("Senator Martin" was most likely Thomas S. Martin, who represented Virginia in the United States Senate between 1895 and 1920.) Barnett concluded to the subcommittee: "But this land at Quantico would be good for all purposes; there is the necessary land for parade functions, and the remainder of the land will be used, nearly all of it, for target practice, both infantry and artillery firing; and it is absolutely essential, under modern conditions of warfare that you should have the rough ground for artillery firing."

Quantico had more than its rugged topography on its side as far as the Marines were concerned. Several railroads served Quantico directly, which

Although no match for Germany's much-feared Big Bertha gun threatening Paris, this gun and many others like it were honed for the war effort at the new base. This photo shows a member of the 136th antiaircraft artillery. Courtesy base archive.

It doesn't look very appetizing, but the field mess kit was adequate, as demonstrated here. This photo appears to be taken near Quantico's main camp and not in the field. Courtesy Marine Corps Historical Center.

apart from normal transportation issues satisfied the Marines' need for moving troops to other embarkation points, such as Philadelphia. The Potomac River supplied Quantico with water access, although the depth of the water at the mouth of the Quantico Creek only measured twenty-two feet. But for the Marines' purposes, only shallower draft vessels would ever be required, making this objection negligible. Quantico's proximity to Washington also counted in its favor for administrative purposes, given that the headquarters of the Corps was just a short train ride north. Barnett explained that the site had previously been feared as malarial, but that adequate drainage had rectified the situation, and the climate was satisfactory otherwise. In short, Barnett made the case that Quantico offered everything the Marine Corps required in an East Coast base and would make "an ideal place for a training camp," not to mention the fact that the Corps had already staked a claim there.

From an economic standpoint, purchase of the base made good sense for the government. Under the current arrangement, the Marine Corps rented thirty-nine hundred acres from the Quantico Company for a yearly rental of $18,000. By 1918 the Corps only had authorization to rent the tract for one additional year at the same price. The Corps rented an additional twelve hundred acres from another party to provide a suitable firing range for artillery. Apart from the convenience of continuing to use this same land for training, the Corps had already expended more than two million dollars on the facilities erected at Quantico. Although much of that infrastructure could be collapsed and used elsewhere, as General Barnett pointed out, not all of the materials would be salvageable, and infrastructure such as the brick cold-storage plant, sewer systems, and roads could not be moved. Leasing the land put the fate of the base in limbo, and as such the Corps hesitated to make too many capital improvements to the site or erect anything but temporary structures. By the end of the subcommittee session, all present were in accord that it would be "good policy" to purchase Quantico for the Marines. All that remained in doubt was the purchase price.

The owners of the Quantico tracts, the Quantico Company and Dr. H. B. Hutchinson, initially sought $575,000 for both parcels. The secretary of the navy found these prices too high for land otherwise used as timber land, and the owners reduced the asking price to $525,000. Thomas Lyon, an attorney in Manassas, consulted with the Quantico Company and Dr. Hutchinson, and was able to commit them in writing to sell both tracts for the combined price of $475,000. The Quantico Company's parcel accounted for $375,000; Dr. Hutchison's, the remaining $100,000. The subcommittee agreed that $475,000 represented a fair price, and reported favorably to Congress. Congress approved the transaction, and President Wilson on July 1, 1918, signed legislation authorizing him to acquire the land as a permanent base of the United States Marine Corps.

The President did not issue his proclamation on the matter until November 4, so Secretary Daniels could not authorize the Marine Corps to officially take possession of the base until December 11, 1918. By that time the war had been over exactly a month, but the results remained the same. Quantico belonged to the Marines free and clear.[138]

Camp of Instruction

Even before the status of the Marines tenure at Quantico was resolved, the base's function as an "officers' camp of instruction" became more of a reality in 1918. The first class of six hundred officer candidates officially began instruction in April 1918. The men learned "infantry, drill, interior guard, bayonet, bombing (hand grenades), infantry tactics, military engineering, topography, administration, military law, gas warfare, sea duty, and marksmanship." Basically, all the skills an officer might encounter on active duty on the front. Given the breadth of the subjects covered, that the training was fast and furious should be no surprise, particularly since the course only lasted a few months. But the low failure rate among officer candidates attested to the quality of the men and their rigorous preparation.

Members of the 136th antiaircraft artillery are shown at Quantico with one of their weapons, used in downing biplanes and zeppelins. Courtesy base archive.

In May an "Overseas Depot" was established at Quantico for the purpose of training individuals and units for replacement service. Unlike the officers' schools, where all candidates learned the same skills together, men training in the Overseas Depot studied in specialized schools geared to skills such as infantry training, mining and sapping, and machine gun tactics. To an even higher degree than the standard field training, veterans fresh from service on the front acted as instructors in the Overseas Depot.

Instructors at Quantico did not neglect the medical arts, and medical personnel stationed at Quantico taught Marines basic lessons in sanitation, hygiene, first aid, and protecting oneself against chemical attacks. When they found time apart from their regular duties, doctors and corpsmen at Quantico trained in the field with the Marines, and Quantico ultimately provided approximately 750 corpsmen to the war effort in France.

Fitting for the place where Samuel P. Langley first tested his "flying machine," aviation training also found a home at Quantico. Having not yet built runways on base, airplane aviation would not be part of Quantico's functions for several more years, but balloon companies trained there to support heavy artillery movements. The Balloon Company was based just south of the encampment at Quantico, while seaplanes operated from the mouth of the Chopawamsic Creek, near where Langley had experimented with airplanes twenty years before. Although the company trained with artillerists in providing aerial reconnaissance information, the balloonists in this company never got the chance to put their skills into action on the front, and the whole unit disbanded in July 1919.[139]

That's Entertainment

Even though Marines undergoing training might only be at Quantico anywhere from a few weeks to a few months, their superiors recognized that the men needed entertainment and diversions.

Quantico's gymnasium was home to one of the country's most active cinemas, showing movies virtually every night of the week on the large screen shown here. The projection booth hangs from ceiling. Courtesy Mitchel P. Raftelis.

The fact that Quantico had its own "post athletic officer" suggested the importance of sports in keeping Quantico Marines both physically fit and engaged in activity. And recruitment in such a wide swath of the populace ensured at least a few players of professional caliber. By May 1918 the post baseball team could claim a roster filled with players who in civilian life had all played for either major or minor league ball clubs. The athletic officer, First Lieutenant (later Captain) Craige, planned to expand the number of baseball teams fielded at Quantico to forty. Quantico's proximity to the Potomac also encouraged water sports among the troops. All Marines at Quantico were taught to swim and row a boat. "We go in swimming every evening now—in fact it's a drill as all are required to learn," one Marine wrote his wife. "Everyone who does not know how is instructed until qualified to swim 100 yards." Although a requirement, one can imagine that swimming and rowing lessons must have been a welcome change for men used to spending all day drilling on an infantry or artillery field.[140]

Theatrics at Quantico also boasted a high level of quality as the post theatrical company claimed professional thespians and "talented amateurs." In April 1918, the men of the heavy artillery forces at Quantico staged an "elaborate theatrical production" called the "The Marine Review." This extravaganza featured two hundred Marines, and promised to be a mix of minstrel show and musical comedy. The production certainly could not have suffered from having a theater manager-director from Chicago directing their efforts, or a soloist from the Philadelphia Orchestra in charge of the music.[141]

Music represented one of the most frequently used means to entertain the troops. On July 27, 1918, the Marine Band traveled to Quantico from Washington to give a performance for the troops. One eighteen-year veteran of the Marine Corps wrote to his wife that it was the first time he had ever heard the band play. The band did not disappoint him, and he concluded the Marine Band "is the best in the country." The New York Symphony Orchestra played before an audience of five thousand at Quantico in April 1918. In between live performances, "canned music" could be heard on phonographs around the barracks.[142]

Visits from government dignitaries also provided occasions for merriment for the men. When the Secretary of the Navy Josephus Daniels paid one of many visits, the Marines put on a show with "all kinds of gun shooting, aeroplanes flying about and balloon ascensions." During a day of field exercises, members of Congress and invited guests got a first-hand look at the training Marines received at Quantico. As visitors approached the ranges, infantry fire announced their arrival. But what many did not see were the snipers the visitors had been specifically warned to look for. Recognizing that the visiting dignitaries had completely missed their presence, "privates grinning behind masks of green paint wearing weirdly camouflaged suits, stood up to disclose themselves, then merged into the background with the underbrush and proved their ability to travel yards without being seen." The men also demonstrated machine guns, aspects of trench warfare, heavy artillery, and tractors. The novelty of the weapons likely impressed the audience more than the men who trained at Quantico day in and day out, but the presence of seven thousand Marines all participating in wargames before an appreciative audience certainly added a festive flair to the day.[143]

Marines did not always wait for entertainment to come to them; frequently they went to it. With reliable train service from Quantico to Richmond and Washington and even Philadelphia, Marines on liberty could easily spend a weekend in a number of nearby cities. Washington took a special interest in Quantico, since the capital was the largest city nearby and proved an irresistible draw for Marines with time and money to spend. In fact, Washington stood to gain each time the govern-

ment increased troop strength at Quantico. Not only did Washington businesses provide much of the construction supplies used when Quantico expanded, but the additional Marines "on week-end passes practically always take the opportunity to visit Washington for outside diversion and amusement."[144]

The Grecian Formula

Another segment of the population with a keen interest in the Marines and how they spent their free time was the Greek community in Quantico town, many of whom had established restaurants and other businesses catering to a captive military clientele. Of all places in the United States, how did Quantico, Virginia, end up with such a substantial Greek presence? According to local history, Hopewell, Virginia, had attracted Greek immigrants with its industrial promise. One day, Harry Cokinides of Hopewell happened to be riding a train, and fell into conversation with someone from the federal government. The government representative asked Cokinides if he and his friends had any

General Lejeune's Christmas Message

EVERY Officer and every Enlisted Man at Quantico and their families and their friends have my best wishes for a Merry Christmas and a Happy New Year.

¶It is my aim to make Quantico nor only the most efficient military post in the world but also the happiest. I want to see it so developed and so administered that every man who serves here in the future will feel that his time has been usefully and pleasantly employed and that he has made himself both a highly trained Marine and a better and more useful citizen.

I ask each of you to join in this effort and to do all in your power to make this dream a reality.

JOHN A. LEJEUNE

Happy Marines: Marine Corps Commandant John A. Lejeune, sensitive to the mood of his Marines as Christmas 1917 approached, released this unusually heartfelt message to bolster spirits. John A. Lejeune Papers, Library of Congress.

America's first wartime Yuletide, that of 1917, was a sober affair—but that is belied by this cheerfully decorated enlisted men's mess hall. Note the propaganda posters on the back wall. Propaganda played a huge role in this war. Courtesy base archive.

money, because the government was about to establish a new Marine base at Quantico, and if they hurried with their investments, they would almost have an exclusive trade in the area. Cokinides took the hint and passed the word along to associates in Hopewell, many of whom did in fact move to Quantico to work at the base or set up stores, restaurants, and other businesses in the growing new town. Through wise investing and much hard work, many of the Greek families prospered, and in some cases their children or other family members continue to be active in Quantico Town today. Included in the first wave of Greek immigrants to Quantico were two Petes: Pete Raftelis and Pete Pandazides. Raftelis was one of the first to arrive, and initially followed his previous occupation as a

plumber, working at the burgeoning Marine base. In addition to his plumbing work, Raftelis opened the Star Café on Potomac Avenue, and attracted the patronage of Marines who came to town for a bite to eat. By the 1930s Raftelis turned his attention solely to running the restaurant with his wife. His young son, Mitchel, was given the responsibility of supervising the till. The other early Pete in Quantico was Pete Pandazides, who came from New York rather than Hopewell. Like Pete Raftelis, Pandazides became a restaurant owner and ran the A-1 Restaurant, in addition to other investments in the area. Thus, when John Craige later remembered that the first Marines in Quantico patronized "a restaurant presided over by Pete-the-Greek, a worthy destined to serve ham and eggs to hungry Marines for a score of years," he could have been remembering either Raftelis or Pandazides.[145]

"Skirt Marines"

One of the most famous recruiting posters of World War I featured a bob-haired girl in a modified Navy petty officer first class' uniform proclaiming, "Gee!! I Wish I Were a Man. I'd Join the Navy." The Marines had their own poster girl, however, and a copy of her poster hung in mess halls at Quantico. The Marines' woman was all "man," and decked out in full Marine sergeant's gear, complete with a sturdy knife in her hand. "If You Want To Fight," the poster declared, "Join the Marines." While certainly aimed at recruiting men for the Corps, the poster must have inspired some among the fairer sex as well. In August 1918, Secretary of the Navy Daniels authorized the enlistment of women in the Navy and Marine Corps Reserves. The Corps designated this group of over three hundred women as "Marine Reserve (F)," and while they did not fight alongside their male counterparts, the women went on other active duty between 1918 and 1919. (Daniels authorized "yeomanettes" in the Navy as well.)[146] By recruiting women to perform clerical duties, work in motor transport, or participate in war bond drives, the Marines freed up that many more men for combat, and gave the women a chance to demonstrate their patriotism in the war effort. The highest rank available in "Marine Reserve (F)" was that of sergeant, but most toiled at the rank of private. And unlike the outfitted woman in the recruiting poster, the women Marines (or "Marinettes," as people liked to call them) tended to accessorize their uniforms with ribbons and nonregulation footwear. Some of the women wore unauthorized "Sam Browne" belts not for any military purpose, but because "it made the uniform particularly stunning!" Who says patriotism can't be fashionable?

What was perhaps the most popular Marine recruiting poster of World War I may be seen on the far wall of the enlisted men's mess hall shown in the previous photo. It is reproduced here. Howard Chandler Christy, creator, courtesy Library of Congress. LC–USZ62–19932

But how do these women relate to Quantico? Almost forgotten in the annals of Quantico history are the visits by these so-called "Skirt Marines." The female Marines first visited Quantico in November 1918, just days after the armistice in Europe, but at a time when the Corps had reached its peak enrollment. Upon the women's arrival, Corporal Elizabeth Shoemaker heard one excited Marine yell out "Lady Hell Cats" as they marched by, presumably a complimentary title to match the male Marines' nickname of "Devil Dogs." But Shoemaker also remembered overhearing a less enthusiastic Leatherneck tell a friend, "This is a fallen outfit when they start enlisting skirts," hence the women's other nickname of "Skirt Marines."

The "Skirt Marines" arrived in Quantico on the train, and detrained to the post band's renditions of "Hail, Hail the Gang's All Here" and "How Do You Tame Wild Women?" *The Leatherneck* provided complete coverage of the visit, and informed its readers that:

> *The camp to a man was knocked cold.*
>
> *That's all there was to it. . . . They lined up in a column of two's and marched behind the band to the parade grounds where they watched the Officer Training Class men parade. They saluted colors and retreat. . . . Boys, they are just like any other girls in some respects, for they carry mirrors with Marine emblems on them, but they are regular Marines, for they are very proud of their personal appearance and carry their own powder.*
>
> *And how those Marine girls can dance!*
>
> *Everyone was proud of the Marine girls. They carried themselves like real soldiers, were good fellows and proved that they were ready to go anywhere and conduct themselves with honor to the Marine Corps.*[147]

The "Skirt Marines" obviously felt an equal attachment to the boys at Quantico as many of them traveled from Washington to Quantico each Friday to attend dances held on base. A goodly number of civilian girls did too, but as PFC Florence Gertler remembered later, "Every Marine girl was assured of all dances, even though some of the other girls might not." Semper fi!

As the military demobilized following the end of the war, the "Skirt Marines" disbanded as well. But Secretary Daniels inadvertently provided one last scene of hilarity for the girls. At a White House ceremony in the summer of 1919, Daniels praised the women for their service to the Marine Corps. But forgetting that they were women, in addition to being Marines, Daniels informed the women: "We will not forget you. As we embrace you in uniform today, we will embrace you without uniform tomorrow." Even the most solemn male Marines in attendance could not resist laughing at the secretary's suggestion of embracing the women out of their uniforms, and "all down the file of men standing at strict attention, the line broke, and everyone roared with laughter."[148]

"I Opened the Window, and In-flu-enza"

Proponents for the establishment of a permanent base at Quantico noted that except for the threat of malaria, the area boasted a healthy climate, and even these malarial tendencies could be controlled with drainage of local swamps. But in 1918, malaria represented the least of Quantico's health concerns.

Fresh air and exercise were considered essential to maintaining health, particularly during the outbreak in 1918 of the so-called Spanish Influenza. The virulent wartime flu, a global pandemic, attacked the young, usually the least likely to fall prey to a flu. Numerous Quantico Marines died. Courtesy base archive.

That spring, a mysterious outbreak of influenza occurred among troops stationed at Fort Riley, Kansas, but the disease seemed to have retreated as quickly as it attacked. The Fort Riley soldiers, however, unknowingly carried the virus with them as they and over a million other soldiers traveled east for transport to the European front lines. The virus soon proved more deadly than trench warfare, as tremendous numbers of soldiers on both sides fell victim to the disease. On the home-front, by merely breathing infected air soldiers carried the influenza virus from military base to military base, and helped spread the disease throughout the eastern half of the United States. Once the flu transferred to the civilian population, the disease knew no geographic boundaries.

The epidemic became known as the Spanish Flu. Various legends explained the origin of the name, but one historian of the epidemic has argued that because Spain remained neutral during World War I, it was therefore not subject to the same news censorship as nations engaged in hostilities. As a result, the press reported the spread of the disease in Spain more widely than anywhere else, leading the world to associate the disease with Spain.[149] Whatever its title, by the time the pandemic subsided over the winter, six hundred thousand Americans had died of influenza and another thirty million people succumbed worldwide.

Unlike previous incarnations of influenza, which struck the very young and the weak, this strain attacked healthy victims in the prime of life. One public health official later noticed that people between the ages of twenty-one and twenty-nine were the most vulnerable; just the right age of military enlistees being drafted for service in the Great War. Given that the first wave of illness spread among young soldiers crowded into military camps,

Quantico's rifle range machine shop, teaching the tricks of the trade to a newly mechanized infantry. Courtesy Marine Corps Historical Center.

it was only a matter of time before the new training facility at Quantico felt its effects.[150] September 13, 1918, later remembered as "Black Friday," saw the first case of the Spanish Flu at Quantico. Over the course of the next twenty-four hours, the camp hospital admitted an additional 130 patients. The next day, 233 men showed signs of the disease. Within two weeks of "Black Friday," an astonishing 1,300 Marines on the cantonment were ill, all on a base designed to accommodate 7,000 recruits. By the time the flu ran its course at Quantico, over 4,000 cases had been reported, with one very conservative estimate placing the death toll at 140 deaths.[151] This total does not include those Marines from Quantico who may have perished of the disease after they reached Europe, or indeed on the way to the front. Troop ships proved a perfect breeding ground for influenza: one infected soldier could condemn an entire boatload of otherwise healthy men.[152]

The illness struck the base at Quantico in a variety of ways. Poised to win a championship in the first section of the District Baseball Association, the Quantico Marines baseball team withdrew from the series in September on account of the players being in quarantine due to the flu outbreak on base. The aptly named War Risk team went on to win the title instead. The war also turned out to be safer for Brigadier General Charles A. Doyen than did the homefront. After having served as the first officer to command the first Marine regiment under General Pershing in France and having trained the Marines who checked the German advance before Paris, Doyen's ill health prompted his superiors to send him back to the United States to assume command at Quantico. Not long after his arrival at Quantico, Doyen contracted the Spanish Flu and died on October 6, 1918. The height of the flu epidemic hit the nation in October, and the Mays family bore witness to the devastation. On October 24, Benjamin F. Mays died at Quantico of the pneumonia he developed after a bout of the flu. One week later, his wife Audrey followed her husband to the grave, dying of the same influenza at the base hospital. The Mays left behind a four-year-old daughter. For this little girl, a popular jump-roping rhyme would have been heartbreaking: "I had a little bird, It's name was Enza. I opened the window, and in-flu-enza."[153]

SOLDIERS WANT BEAR CUB

Editor *Forest and Stream*:

I am writing to you in hopes that I may receive some information regarding the purchase of a cub bear, as I have read your magazine over and over but have not seen anything regarding such.

Our intention is to have this cub bear as a mascot for our company which is to embark for France in the near future.

Hoping you will furnish us with the information requested as soon as possible, I remain

Yours very respectfully,
CORPORAL JOHN TROFF,
83d Company, 6th Regiment,
"U. S. Marines," Quantico, Va.

This Marine's sentiment for a proper mascot was shared by General Smedley Darlington Butler, who provided one for Quantico in the 1920s: a bulldog, not a bear. Although, as it turned out, Butler's first mascot, Jiggs, a real "Mess Hall King," ended up eating almost as much as a bear. Forest and Stream, *October 1917.*

The Boys Come Home

And then it was over. In the eleventh hour, of the eleventh day, of the eleventh month of 1918, Germany signed an armistice ending the war that would shortly be remembered by Americans as "The War to End All Wars," or more succinctly, "The Great War." By the end of the war, Quantico alone had sent almost thirty thousand Marines to the American Expeditionary Forces in Europe, as well as additional men assigned to other international positions or naval duty ashore.[154] After having expended so much effort to get the boys ready for duty, the Marine Corps now faced the daunting challenge of demobilizing a large percentage of the seventy-five thousand Marines still on active duty just after the armistice.

One Marine from the Great War came home to Quantico in 1921, and never left. Artist Charles Peyre visited France with the intention of creating a statue honoring the U.S. Army for its service in the war. While in Paris, Peyre met Carl Millard, a Marine recuperating from wounds he received at Belleau Wood. Using Millard as his model, Peyre produced a strikingly realistic sculpture of an American serviceman . . . with a Marine Corps emblem on his helmet. While the Army had been willing to accept Marines into its ranks during the war, it refused to be represented by them in perpetuity, and refused to buy the statue. The Marines, on the other hand, were delighted by Peyre's creation, and raised donations among their ranks for the purchase of the statue by the Marine Corps. The statue, officially called *A Crusade for the Right*, came to Quantico after the war, where the Marines promptly dubbed him "Iron Mike." Ever since, "Iron Mike" has held a place of honor in front of the old administration building off Barnett Avenue, serving as both a reminder to Marines of their predecessors in World War I, and perhaps too the history of how the base at Quantico came into being as a result of that conflict.[155]

Above: Quantico as viewed from the range of hills framing its picturesque location along the Potomac. Confederate Civil War gun emplacements on these heights commanded excellent views of the river. Courtesy Mitchel P. Raftelis

Top: "Flying machines," or biplanes, shared the air with observation balloons during World War I, and a balloon company trained at Quantico through 1921. But America was moving into a bright and technological future, in which such low-tech approaches would not play a role. Courtesy Marine Corps Historical Center.

"Historic, Quaint Quantico"

The first issue of *The Quantico Leatherneck* recounted the scenes of triumph in the village's past and marked the arrival of the Marines:

> *HISTORIC, QUAINT QUANTICO IS AGAIN MILITARY CENTER.*
>
> *Quantico-land, where the hardy redmen fought and died, where the Union and Confederate forces met in mortal combat, where Langley flew his first model airplane on May 6, 1896—what thrills the name brings forth!*
>
> *As the years have gone by, you have marked great epochs in world history, but your greatest has come today. Upon your soil are training thousands of United States Marines, the first military body . . . in the greatest conflict this grey old earth has ever seen to make the world "safe for Democracy."*[156]

A sleepy village on the eve of the war, by the armistice Quantico town found itself abuzz with off-duty Marines and physically surrounded on all sides by the Marine base or the Potomac River. Yet everything in Quantico's history prepared the town for the Marines to leave and life to return to normal. The Indians had left. Union and Confederate forces had left after the Civil War. Langley and his airplanes had left. And just about every attempt at creating a town at Quantico had proved a disappointment, and investors were left in dismay. But having purchased the land and invested in infrastructure, the Marine Corps decided to stay. Indeed, Quantico's most notable epoch lay ahead, courtesy of the United States Marine Corps.

CHAPTER V

GROWING PAINS

1919–1940

Demobilization

Although most wars alter the societies that wage them in countless ways, American GIs came home to a world vastly changed from the one they had left in 1918. Monarchies, which had ruled Europe for centuries, finally had succumbed in the conflict, and a revolution in Russia introduced the world to a communist regime. New countries, such as Czechoslovakia, arose from the ashes of the Ottoman Empire. With traditional world leaders like Great Britain weakened by years of expensive and brutal combat, the United States emerged as an economically stronger nation, and a serious contender for a larger share of world power. But the horrors of trench warfare, the insidious physical effects of chemical attacks, the almost unimaginable

numbers of casualties, not to mention the domestic deaths caused by the influenza epidemic of 1918, left many Americans dazed by the cost of making the world "safe for democracy." While most people actively embraced a "return to normalcy," or as normal as life could be in the postwar period, some young, disenchanted Americans saw themselves as a "Lost Generation" whose youthful idealism had been crushed by global reality. While this disillusionment would give the world the literature of Ernest Hemingway and F. Scott Fitzgerald, the mental and spiritual toll on this generation would be high. The failure of the United States Senate to authorize America's membership in President Wilson's beloved League of Nations (a precursor to the United Nations) left additional questions as to how successful peace would be. The immediate concern for most Americans, however, was getting the boys who survived the war home from "over there."

As World War I came to an end, roughly two million American soldiers remained in Europe. Considering that the United States military could

Whatever was underway at Quantico? Navy Secretary Edwin Denby had reason to wonder. Secretary and Mrs. Denby are shown at the head of the column after coming by ship to inspect the base and see flight demonstrations. Quantico aviators were achieving national fame and setting flight endurance records. And Quantico was building a huge football coliseum for its team, one of the most newly visible in the country. The tough-minded Denby, flanked by Marine Corps Commandant John A. Lejeune and Quantico's legendary General Smedley Butler, was impressed. Major Roy Geiger, chief aviator, is also shown. Courtesy base archive.

When Quantico was given a permanent lease on life by authorities in Washington, who valued its proximity and its excellent record in World War I, the need for a larger railroad station became immediately evident. This two-story structure was built in 1919 and accommodated traffic until World War II prompted the need for a still larger station. Courtesy base archive.

From swords to ploughshares—a retired "big gun" from World War I, then still referred to as the "Great War," is shown in picturesque retirement in its own, nicely landscaped Quantico traffic circle. Note the perfectly sculpted box hedges, flowering plants, and planted trees. Courtesy Mitchel P. Raftelis.

only field three hundred thousand men at the outbreak of war, it is easy to see that orderly demobilization after the war would be almost as daunting a task as mobilizing America's entry into it. Despite the turmoil and confusion of the demobilization period, the Marine base at Quantico was not necessarily overrun by returning troops. Not all the Marines who passed through Quantico on their way to the front would come back through this base. A somewhat hastily assembled demobilization plan called for soldiers to be discharged at camps and demobilization centers near their homes. And while the men had usually gone to France in units, the government responded to public pressure by discharging individuals, even before disbanding their units.[157]

For those who remembered Quantico as the exciting, bustling military base it had been during the war, demobilization initially struck them as a somewhat depressing time. In October 1919, General John Lejeune returned to Quantico to assume command at the base. Recently returned from the Army's famed Second Division in France, Lejeune found the routine at Quantico dull . . . dull

. . . dull. He wrote to his sister that he had decided against continuing to commute daily from his home in Washington, as he had done during the war, and instead had taken a room at the former Quantico Hotel (better known as Waller Hall). But he did leave open the possibility of commuting for "there isn't much to do there [in Quantico], as there are very few men." He was even more candid in a letter written a week later about the challenges posed by a peacetime assignment at Quantico. "Quantico is very different from the wartime days," he confessed, "being dull by comparison." Perhaps he missed his family back in Washington; however, he felt confident that the completion of the commanding general's house on base would provide him contentment and give him "something to do."[158]

Lejeune's "Quantico Experiment"

What soon energized General Lejeune, and marked his lasting contribution to the function of Quantico within the Marine Corps, was his commitment to military preparedness and the role education would play in that goal. Lejeune himself was well educated by Marine standards, having graduated from Louisiana State University and the United States Naval Academy. But by commanding troops in France during the Great War, Lejeune gained first-hand knowledge of the military's failure to keep its officer corps well trained and ready to anticipate and respond to changes in warfare. With the introduction of chemical warfare and even more destructive weaponry in World War I, Lejeune recognized that all subsequent conflicts would be complicated affairs, requiring extensive understanding of new tactics and technology, as well as the traditional leadership skills.[159] With this in mind, Lejeune instituted an ambitious educational agenda. Almost twenty years later, Lejeune looked back on the early days of education at Quantico, and explained his philosophy:

> The military and naval professions are never static but are always changing, so it is mandatory that each officer of the Navy and Marine Corps continue to be a student in order to keep up with the rapid progress of his profession.
>
> This was one of the thoughts I had in mind when it fell to my lot to establish the Marine Corps Schools in Quantico for the advanced education of Marine officers, a short time after the termination of the World War. In so doing, I was convinced that advanced military and naval education was necessary for all Marine officers in order to keep abreast of the progress of the Army and the Navy of our own country and of the other nations as well.[160]

Lejeune quickly established Quantico's niche with specialty schools for Marine Corps officers, and this educational ideal far outlasted his brief service as Quantico's postwar commander.

Lejeune rounded up the few instructors remain-

John A. Lejeune, Quantico's commanding officer. Lejeune, in concert with Smedley Butler, did much to create for Quantico a unique education and training role. Expansion of that mission caused much new construction at Quantico in the 1920s. Courtesy base archive.

ing at Quantico after demobilization, and appropriated a building on Barnett Avenue in which to open the Marine Corps Officers Training School in the fall of 1919. While some traditional classes continued to be offered, all courses incorporated the lessons recently learned during the war to bring training in line with changes in warfare. Other specialty schools soon joined the educational roster at Quantico, including an infantry school, course for field officers, and the Basic School. While the names of some of the schools and courses changed as they reorganized under different administrative structures, their functions remained largely the same.[161]

While the schools at Quantico catered to the training of Marine Corps officers, General Lejeune's program did not overlook enlisted men. Lejeune understood two important facts about the enlisted class: that they needed some intellectual stimulation apart from their military training regimen, and that not all enlisted men would ultimately make the military their profession.

Anyone familiar with the training of Marines will admit that as a steady diet, more than two hours of purely military training a day will make an enlisted man muscle bound and cause him to grow stale, except in time of war under the attendant excitement. . . . Heretofore an enlistment in the regular service of the United States has been considered a waste of time unless a man intended to make it his life work and it certainly was, as far as preparing him for any duty in civil life. . . . Men who had professions or trades when they entered the Corps necessarily ceased to advance during the period of their enlistment, and a man who does not

continually advance goes backward; no man can stand still.[162]

To make the men more serviceable to the Marine Corps, and anticipating their eventual reentry into civilian life, Lejeune organized vocational schools to teach enlisted men useful trades. The first three vocational schools focused on automotive mechanics, music, and typewriting and shorthand. When the schools opened in January 1920, two hundred students enrolled. By the end of the first week of instruction, four hundred of the six hundred Marines stationed at Quantico had signed up for classes. Not surprisingly, the automotive school attracted the most students. So many men wanted to take the class that enrollment was capped at one hundred students, primarily because the garage facilities at Quantico could accommodate no more. But observers noted that could additional facilities be arranged, the class could easily double in size. Stenography also proved to be popular among the

Quantico's role as a training base was confirmed when the Marine Corps Institute was established there after World War I. The brilliantly successful institute, which formalized vocational training, began the armed forces' first and now oldest correspondence course. Courtesy base archive.

America's growing involvement in world affairs is suggested by this view of Quantico Marines studying foreign languages. This classroom was technologically advanced—the men are wearing headphones and listening to wax cylinder recordings. Note the wax cylinders on each desk. Courtesy base archive.

men, while classes in English grammar and elementary mathematics appealed to Marines who brought only a rudimentary education with them, and wanted to improve themselves. Courses in foreign languages advanced English-speaking Marines beyond their own native tongue.[163]

Lejeune anticipated that the educational opportunities open to Marines would be of great benefit to the Corps itself. By making the Corps attractive in terms of educational advancement as well as military training, Lejeune hoped that so many men would voluntarily join the Marines that recruiting offices would become obsolete. He proposed to publicize outside of the Corps the course offerings of the schools at Quantico, and even suggested that the schools' top students be sent to civilian universities at government expense to complete their educations, thereby enhancing the quality of the Marines' officer corps. But Lejeune also urged his

officer candidates to attend vocational classes, both to learn new skills and enhance their leadership abilities by mingling with the enlisted men.[164]

Despite its long association with the Marine Barracks in Washington, D.C., the Marine Corps Institute (MCI) got its start at Quantico in 1920. Charged with assisting Marines with furthering their educations wherever they may be, the MCI assumed charge of the vocational schools at Quantico, and instituted a series of correspondence schools for the benefit of Marines serving outside of Quantico. Practicality gave rise to the correspondence school when over six hundred students from the vocational schools shipped out to the Caribbean, but requested that they be allowed to continue their studies while on duty. While the automotive courses would have been a challenge to continue while onboard the USS *Henderson*, other classes offered by the vocational schools translated to a correspondence school–format, and in the process gained for MCI the honor of being the oldest correspondence school in the United States military. Unfortunately for Quantico, its physical ties to the MCI were severed almost as soon as they began. On the birthday of the Marine Corps (November 10) in 1920, MCI moved to the Marine Barracks, Washington, where it has remained ever since. Quantico's Marines remained intellectually connected to MCI, however, as specialty courses became available or men on maneuvers continued their education by enrolling in the correspondence courses offered by MCI.[165]

While training officers to be proactive in their thinking, and providing transferable skills to enlisted men might in retrospect seem like a natural progression in the Corps' development, and merely made Quantico a counterpart to Annapolis or West Point, the ideas behind forming the Marine Corps Education Center were quite a departure from traditional notions of what a Marine was supposed to do. Smedley Butler, Lejeune's successor at Quantico, recognized what had been done, as he explained in his own colorful way. The schools, Butler observed were "a revolution. It is something new. The old officers of the Marine Corps would turn over in their graves if they knew what we were doing because in the old days, they did nothing but soldier. We want to make this post and the whole Marine Corps a great university." Lejeune's and Butler's faith in education for furthering the goals of the Corps would certainly come to fruition, but it required overcoming prejudice even among Marines themselves before succeeding. In the early days of educational reform at Quantico, a cadre of self-styled "real Marines" would assemble each day to taunt the student Marines on their way to classes. The "real Marines" considered the schools "sissified nonsense" and "that damned education."[166]

By 1933 "that damned education" had become such a permanent fixture of the landscape at Quantico that the commandant of the Marine Corps suggested a revolutionary idea in his annual report to the secretary of the Navy. For years the Marine Corps had often been considered as something of a stepchild of the Army, and needed to find a niche of its own to ensure its uniqueness and survival as a separate branch of the military. Its niche would come in the form of advancing amphibious techniques (see next section). But Corps commanders also decided that uniqueness should find its way into instruction as well, and undertook a campaign of "Marine-izing" the curriculum. Amazingly, until 1933, Marine training had largely followed that of the Army, using its textbooks and equipment. The "Marine-izing" instituted at Quantico involved using data collected by the Marine Corps, and

A Marine Corps Institute instructor with his vocational students in a 1920 photo. The students appreciated the new institute: when many were sent to stabilize affairs in Latin America they asked for their instruction to continue aboard ship while en route. Courtesy base archive.

developing textbooks suited to the amphibious operations and small wars in which the Marines anticipated participating. Students examined the specific history of the Marine Corps for clues to how the mission of the Corps had evolved over time and where it was likely to go in the future. In short, the curriculum now focused exclusively on the function of the Marine Corps, and the techniques and equipment used by the Corps. By asserting its own institutional identity, the Corps contributed not only to its survival, but also to its honor as an independent military entity.[167]

Pete Ellis' Legacy: Amphibious Warfare

Learning new technologies was only part of the educational story at Quantico between the World Wars. Anticipating where wars would be fought in the future and how to respond to these trends complemented the technological side of instruction. Following World War I, Marine officials looked at the shift in world power centers, and Major Earl Hancock "Pete" Ellis recognized Japan's growing dominance in the Pacific. Almost predicting the island-hopping warfare of World War II, Ellis saw that Japan could use the series of smaller islands in the Pacific as a sort of "screen" protecting Japan itself from easy invasion. What Ellis observed while serving in the Philippines and the Asiatic Fleet convinced him that the United States and Japan would eventually come into conflict in the Pacific, and that it would be a war unlike any the United States had fought previously. To ensure that United States naval strategy would be ready for the challenge, he published *Advanced Base Operations in Micronesia* in 1921. Ellis' report provided a guide for using amphibious operations to secure enemy-held islands in order to challenge Japan directly. General Lejeune, who by this time commanded the entire Marine Corps, fully accepted Ellis' predictions and his plans to make the Marines combat-ready in the Pacific. However, in approving this new approach,

Lejeune understood that fighting an island war in the Pacific would require a whole new series of strategies, weapons, and skills than the Marines had employed in past conflicts, and he chose Quantico as the site for research and development into amphibious warfare. Thereafter, refinement of the "advanced base" concept of warfare would occupy an important position in Quantico's educational role. Ironically, Major Ellis would not live to see his predictions come to pass. Ellis died in 1923, while on a fact-finding mission to Micronesia.[168]

Again, the lessons of World War I came into play at Quantico. Traditional military minds discounted the efficacy of amphibious assaults against well-entrenched enemy positions, and pointed to the disastrous experience of the British at the Turkish peninsula of Gallipoli in 1915–1916 as evidence. But the Marine officials promoting the Advanced Base Force, including Lejeune and Colonel Robert Dunlap, turned that notion on its head, and advocated studying why and how the

Andres Pastoriza, ambassador of the Dominican Republic, visiting Quantico, is shown greeting Colonel Charles H. Lyman. The diplomat inspected the Marines, recently back from stabilizing affairs in his country. Courtesy Marine Corps Historical Center.

Marines from Quantico, under Smedley Butler's dynamic leadership and eye for flair, began yearly and highly publicized maneuvers on the sites of Civil War battles. President Warren Harding is shown visiting maneuvers underway in 1921 at The Wilderness in Virginia. The president is being greeted by Judge John T. Goolrick while the legend himself, General Butler, looks on. While at The Wilderness General Butler had Marines dig up Confederate General Stonewall Jackson's famous severed arm and then reinterred it, this time with a plaque. The battlefield manager was appalled. Courtesy base archive.

British attack on Gallipoli had failed to assess how such operations could succeed in the future. Dunlap, the commander of the Advanced Base Force at Quantico studied the battle intensively, determined where the British had gone wrong, and offered solutions for how to avoid the same mistakes in the Pacific.[169]

The new emphasis on amphibious warfare also helped to further distinguish the role of the Marine Corps in the United States military. Since the Marines had traditionally performed duties that overlapped those of both the Army and Navy, perfecting amphibious assault techniques gave the Marines a niche in securing advanced bases on enemy territory. Unlike the Army and Navy, amphibious warfare required the Marines to be fast and mobile, necessitating that men and materiel be immediately ready for any emergency. Quick mobilization would be key to Marine success. With this in mind, the Corps established complementary amphibious teams in San Diego to cover the West Coast, and at Quantico to cover the East Coast. To better reflect the mission, these forces were renamed the "Marine Corps Expeditionary Force" in 1923.[170]

While study of the problems of amphibious warfare primarily occupied Quantico's students in the classrooms, their academic coursework took a backseat in 1925 in favor of field experience. In the spring of that year nearly 750 instructors and students from Quantico participated in joint Army-Navy training sessions off the coast of Hawaii, designed to simulate a forty-two-thousand-man landing force. Not only did these types of exercises allow the Expeditionary Forces to put their classroom training to the test, but they suggested problems not previously considered, such as the landing craft necessary to transport men and machines onto enemy beaches, and the logistical complications of executing such maneuvers. Data collected in field experiments would soon find its way into the curriculum at Quantico.[171] Over the coming years the Marine Corps would continue to refine and revise its thinking on amphibious warfare, and would change the name of the force to reflect its evolving role. The continuance of the program and publication of multiple reports highlighting the status of amphibious warfare plans adopted by the Marine Corps only confirmed the Corps' commitment to the concept, and the educational priority it assumed for students at Quantico.

Step-by-Step

By the mid-1930s, officer training at Quantico had evolved into a logical progression of educational stages. New officers would begin their education at the Basic School, where they would learn their duties as officers. The instruction included administration, law, topography, command, infantry weapons, and tactics. All these subjects prepared junior officers for leadership roles in infantry units and assignments to battalion staff. Having graduated from the Basic School and completed several years of active service, Marine officers then enrolled in the Junior Course. Presumably these officers had mastered the basic skills, but were given a "refresher course" in administrative duties, maps and topography, infantry weapons, tactics, and the like. Students in the Junior Course then studied tactical operations and command and staff functions, operations of Marine units independent to and as part of naval forces, and securing and defending advanced bases. Officers could alternatively enroll in the Base Defense Weapons Course, which prepared officers for artillery service in the amphibious fleet.[172]

Completion of either of these intermediate courses would eventually lead to the Senior Course, which trained field grade officers, and captains moving up to the rank of major. Students in the Senior Course received advanced training in the traditional subjects of topography, tactics and techniques with regard to both land and naval warfare, as well as command and staff functions in a variety of organizations. The courses offered at Quantico were designed to train Marines for the level to which their military careers had progressed to that time, and for study at the Naval War College, which was considered the final step in a Marine's educa-tional career. Factoring in active service and the completion of correspondence courses between attending the schools at Quantico, the entire educational cycle could easily occupy the first two decades of a career-Marine's military service.[173]

"Old Gimlet Eye" Takes Quantico by Storm

While General John Lejeune served as the architect of Quantico's educational system, Quantico truly blossomed under the leadership of General Smedley Darlington Butler, who assumed command at Quantico after Lejeune became the commandant of the Marine Corps in 1920. Butler had earned quite a reputation before arriving at Quantico, and as one wag later noted, a Marine with the names "Smedley" and "Darlington" "would *have* to be a scrapper" to survive a thirty-three-year career in the Corps. Despite his Quaker upbringing, Butler enlisted in the Corps in 1898 at the age of seventeen, and received two Medals of Honor by the end of 1915. His service during World War I earned him both the Army and Navy Distinguished Service Medals and the French Order of the Black Star. Butler did not rest on his laurels, however, nor did he stand on too much ceremony with the men under his command. But Butler's habit of boring into Marines who had not lived up to his standards gave rise to the nickname "Old Gimlet Eye," a gimlet being a tool used to bore holes in wood. His tendency towards outspokenness

---

Above: Smedley Darlington Butler, Quantico's legendary three-time commanding officer. The charismatic, energetic, and unusual Butler, always conscious of the value of publicity to the Marine recruiting effort, built at Quantico a football team of national stature, and led Marines on Civil War reenactments which captured the public's imagination. Courtesy base archive.

Quantico's legendary commanding officer Smedley Darlington Butler, shown here circa 1910, was responsible for building the football stadium and establishing a nationally award-winning team. He was synonymous with the success of the base during its early years. Copyright G. G. Bain, courtesy Library of Congress. LC–USZ62–93375

would land him in hot water with military and government officials in the 1930s, but his reign at Quantico in the 1920s only added luster to his "colorful and tumultuous" career.[174]

Butler was fully committed to Lejeune's education program at Quantico, and the Marine Corps schools on base continued to thrive during Butler's tenure. Yet Butler understood that demobilization following World War I had caused the government to take a serious look at the role of the Marine Corps in the military, while at the same time the country's "return to normalcy" had led to a decreased interest in the military by the general public. Before the Corps found its specialization in amphibious operations, its survival as an independent force depended on making a name for itself wherever and whenever possible. In Smedley Butler, Quantico and the Corps found its greatest cheer-

leader and most accomplished public relations director. Officers who served under Butler remembered his mission of transforming Quantico into "the show place of the Corps" and that his "customary vigor" made the impossible possible.[175]

Whereas General Lejeune anticipated drawing quality recruits to the Marines with the promise of an excellent education, Butler added an athletic component to the package. The football program at Quantico began in 1919, even before Butler took over command of the base. But under Butler's direction, the program quickly courted men with proven athletic abilities, many of whom had played for college squads. Lieutenant Walter Brown came to Quantico in 1920 as an aviator, after having led the Marine Corps football team at Mare Island, California, to various championships. Brown's talent as a quarterback proved equally apparent at Quantico, getting the "Quantico Marines" team off to a victorious start in the 1920 season. Brown would certainly have led his team to many more successful seasons had he not been killed in a plane crash in 1921. As tragic as Brown's death was for the base and the team, the momentum of Quantico football led the Corps to seek out other talented players from posts around the world. Frank Goettge, who had played for Ohio State, arrived at Quantico fresh from duty in Haiti in 1921, and led the football team into its glory days in the 1920s. The lineup in the 1920s would also include recognizable names such as Swede Larson (formerly of the Navy's team), Harry Liversedge from the University of California, and the legendary dropkicker Johnny Groves.[176]

The secret to the football team's success, other than attracting talented players from throughout the Corps, was its traveling schedule. The team journeyed around the country playing other military teams and a host of university squads, including Georgetown, Vanderbilt, and Michigan State. The Marines brought their own players, their own crowds, their own mascot, their own band, and of course, the irrepressible Smedley Butler, who led cheers along the sidelines. The Marines made a splash wherever they went, and even included presidential cabinet members among the spectators in games played near Washington. The fact that General Butler's father, Thomas S. Butler, was a congressman and served on the Committee of Naval Affairs may have helped bring notable politicians to the games (not to mention giving the Corps friends in Congress). But the quality of sportsmanship exhibited by the Marine squad drew attention on its own, putting the team in the same league as West Point and Annapolis, "but with more color and better publicity," as some Quantico historians noted. Still, the Marine record of winning thirty-eight out of forty-two games in its first four seasons spoke for itself.[177]

The football team's success inspired the creation of other sports squads, although few achieved the national reputation enjoyed by the "Quantico Marines." The baseball team played exhibition matches against college teams like Holy Cross, the University of Virginia, and Brown University, on their way to and from spring training. As General A. A. Vandegrift would later remember, these games provided an enormous boost of morale at Quantico for very little cost to the Marines. "The men loved it," he recalled. Fewer Marines played polo than football or baseball, but that did not hinder the formation of a polo squad at Quantico in 1929. Marines who had served in Haiti and China picked up the sport, although their losing streak in the 1930 and 1931 seasons prompted *The Leatherneck* to compare the team's dedicated fans to a "well beloved child who strenuously voices his belief in Santa Claus," with about equal results. But having seemingly adopted the goal in 1930 to "lose to bigger and better teams," *The Leatherneck* commended the team on its stunning success on this score. "Lose they did, and how!" With experience came teamwork, however, and a slightly improved record in subsequent seasons.[178]

Lieutenant Walter Vernon Brown, star of Quantico's football team, lost his life in a tragic flying accident. Quantico named its Marine Flying Field in his honor and it was a fitting honor. The Leatherneck, *November 1936.*

Teams from Quantico did face challenges that college and university squads only dealt with under wartime conditions. As disturbances erupted in the Caribbean and in China in the 1920s and 1930s, or as the Marines were called out for training maneuvers, the athletic schedule at Quantico suffered accordingly. In 1927, for example, much of the summer athletic season was lost when turmoil in China prompted the Corps to detail eight hundred Quantico Marines overseas, seventy of whom were on athletic teams.[179]

The sports program at Quantico served a number of functions. The recreational aspect of sporting events for the morale of the men stationed at Quantico cannot be underestimated, and followed General Lejeune's philosophy that Marines could only drill so many hours a day without becoming "stale." In addition to educational endeavors, sports and recreation kept the men active and their spirits high, especially when their teams enjoyed winning seasons. Success on the field, furthermore, contributed to success in the recruiting depot as men increasingly viewed the Marines as an attractive military option. Perhaps more importantly, as the Marines traveled the country playing university teams, luring civilian crowds to watch the games, the Marine Corps became part of the nation's consciousness and kept the Corps in the public eye. Blessed with such good public relations, it was less likely that the Corps would be disbanded and absorbed into other branches of the military. And a winning team from Quantico kept Quantico's name in the news, ensuring continued support for the base as well.

"Butler's Colosseum"

The willingness of Marine sports teams to travel certainly brought the Marines valuable free publicity outside the vicinity of Quantico. General Butler, however, thought that the Marines should have their own facilities at Quantico, at which they could host visiting teams. A stadium at Quantico could also be put to other useful purposes, such as graduation ceremonies and other public events. The fact that no extra funding was available to build a stadium failed to impress the intrepid General Butler, who nevertheless set out to build what he envisioned as "the world's largest stadium," capable of seating thirty-three thousand spectators. Where there is a will, there is a way, and Smedley Butler never lacked will.[180]

Quantico's acclaim-winning football team playing the President's Cup game in 1925. Frank Goettge is shown intercepting a forward pass. The Marines defeated the Army, 20 to 0. The usual. The Leatherneck, *January 1936.*

A bunch of "damned foolishness," according to Navy Secretary Edwin Denby, referring to Quantico's controversial new football stadium. Designed to be the world's largest, when completed it was smaller than the largest— but still large. The stadium was built by the Marines, with no outside help, to save costs. Courtesy Marine Corps Historical Center.

Butler found a way by marshalling all the resources at his disposal. Labor, of course, posed no difficulty because Butler commanded a base full of hale and hearty Marines who could be put to work. Iron was salvaged from other Marine Corps bases closed after World War I, and Butler convinced the Richmond, Fredericksburg and Potomac Railroad Company that served Quantico to donate rails to reinforce the concrete bleachers. Likewise, area contractors agreed to donate the necessary sand and gravel. In fact, of the $5,000 Butler budgeted to spend on the stadium, most went to pay for the cement used for the stands and support structures.[181]

Had Butler chosen a more level site for what jokingly became known as "Butler's Colosseum," the project might have been completed sooner and with less blood, sweat and tears. The site ultimately chosen, however, was on a hillside above the intersection of Barnett Avenue and Henderson Road. Without much in the way of heavy machinery to move the tons of earth and rock excavated from the site, the determined Marines got to work. General Vandegrift began his career as an officer at Quantico in the 1920s, and later remembered the incredible effort required to transform a forest into a field:

My engineering forays in Nicaragua soon involved me in this task, an immense one since we had to excavate a large quantity of earth with old-fashioned steam shovels. Together with about 150 men from my battalion we worked some eighty days on the stadium.... A fitness report of mine detailed our accomplishment: "[We] moved 19,307 cubic yards of earth, 200 excavations for concrete pillars were dug. 197 pillars were poured, 30 rails were laid. 381 concrete slabs were placed. Concrete footer was poured for all stone walls laid this year. Grass seed was planted over the sanded field. And field was leveled from side to base wall."[182]

Marines' new love affair with "machines," as cars were called at the beginning of the Automobile Age, prompted the establishment of Quantico's first traffic signal—manually operated—at the corner of Barnett Avenue and First Street in 1920. Courtesy base archive.

Quantico's wooden buildings were erected hastily during World War I and with no regard to a dim and uncertain future. They didn't weather well once pressed into permanent service, and major upgrades ensued by the late 1920s. They appear in good condition in this photo, likely dating from the early 1920s. Courtesy base archive.

Quantico's post laundry, as shown during the 1920s, was an indispensable facet of life for the average Marine. Many of the women shown here were likely Quantico housewives for whom this was steady, reliable employment. Courtesy Mitchel P. Raftelis.

Routine military drills probably looked like a walk in the park in comparison to the labor expended on the stadium!

Butler also used the stadium construction to offer lessons in leadership. Butler worked on the stadium himself, as did his officers; no one was exempt from duty. One day General Butler came across a gunnery sergeant watching as other Marines worked on the stadium. When Butler asked what the man was doing, he replied, "I'm supervising the work." Butler gave him a hard stare. "You *were* supervising, Private." Butler showed more sympathy to members of the post band, who protested that performing hard labor on the stadium might damage their hands. "I understand and agree," Butler informed them. "But henceforth if a single man is working on this stadium there will be a band playing music to improve his morale." And henceforth if a single Marine labored on the project, the band played to cheer him on.[183]

Critics who lacked vision also lacked much enthusiasm for the project. The secretary of the Navy, to whom the Marines ultimately reported, called the stadium "Butler's Folly" and dismissed the construction as "damned foolishness." Some thought taxpayers' money could be better spent by having the Marines do something more useful than waste their efforts on a stadium that few people would ever use. But the "colosseum" continued, naysayers aside. Unlike a civilian project with a crew assigned to complete the job, construction on the stadium would be halted many times as training exercises and other military responsibilities took precedence over the labor supply. As a result, Butler's grand stadium would not finally be completed until after World War II, several years after Butler's death in 1940. Yet, as any Marine or civilian employee at Quantico who has ever jogged around the track or challenged themselves to run up the bleachers at Butler Stadium can attest, Smedley Butler's "colosseum" has served the base well.[184]

The Jiggs Dynasty

What is a winning football team without a charismatic mascot to cheer it on? Not the "Quantico Marines," to be sure. The Marines had appropriated the "Devil Dog" epithet bestowed on them by the Germans during World War I, and a famous Marine recruiting poster of the war depicted a bulldog representing the Marines as chasing a German dachshund. It had occurred to Butler during the war that a bulldog would be the perfect mascot for "Devil Dog" Marines, and in yet another flash of inspiration, General Butler in 1921 purchased for Quantico an English bulldog dubbed "Jiggs." "He was the best bulldog money could buy," Butler would recall fondly.[185]

Sergeant Major Jiggs, Quantico's new bulldog mascot. Jiggs, an enlistee, was promoted through the ranks—a very successful Marine indeed. A winning football team needed a mascot, and now it had one. Jiggs gave new meaning to the Marines' nickname—"Devil Dogs." Courtesy Marine Corps Historical Center.

Although Jiggs, whose birthname was the more regal King Bulwark, came from a prestigious lineage of English bulldogs, he enlisted in the Marine Corps at the rank of private, as any other new recruit would have done. General Butler himself signed Jiggs' enlistment papers. Having connections with the top brass, however, Jiggs rose through the ranks more quickly than any enlisted man could ever hope to, achieving the rank of sergeant major in 1925. Perhaps counting that time in dog years put him right on schedule? In any event, Sergeant Major Jiggs earned his stripes many times over during his term of service. Anywhere his Marines traveled, he went along to provide moral support. He went to football games, he went on maneuvers, he posed in airplanes; he generally did whatever the Corps asked him to do. Of Jiggs' participation at Marine sporting events, it was said that "he cheered for them, pulled for them, barked heavily over their victories, grit his teeth in the face of their defeat." Jiggs' presence heightened the morale of his troops, and attracted a fair amount of attention from civilians in the vicinity, which helped the Corps maintain its public profile. He even graced the cover of the January 3, 1925 edition of *The Leatherneck*. "Graced" may be too delicate a word to apply to Jiggs, though. The *New York Times* proclaimed Jiggs "no beauty," while the *Washington Post* recalled that "even in his babyhood, [he] was about as ugly as they came." The *Post* did concede that "with his service cap, tipped rakishly over his right eye, the brilliant brass of his collar shined to the burnishing point, chevrons and medals bedecking his blanket, old Jiggs cut quite a figure."[186] No matter how homely his mug or snazzy his dress, the Marines loved their scrappy mascot.

Alas, they loved him a little *too* much. Jiggs, still a dog after all, proved to be a bit of a scavenger and even more of a glutton. By July 1926 the seven-year-old pooch had grown to a stout seventy-five pounds, and "one mess kit too many" sent Jiggs to the hospital. During his service in the Corps, Jiggs learned most of the bugle calls regulating a Marine's day. He typically ignored reveille, but he never missed a call to chow. "Mess call for Jiggs," noted a

The ever-popular line of sports mascots known as Jiggs continues. This Jiggs is particularly urbane (note the pipe, a sign of refinement). Courtesy Marine Corps Historical Center.

national newspaper, "meant a bulging stomach." Jiggs' stomach bulged on a regular basis. After finishing his own meal, he would make the rounds of the kitchens in camp. The human Devil Dogs could not refuse him anything, and nearly killed him with kindness. Afflicted with "stomach trouble" at Quantico, Jiggs was flown to Bolling Field outside of Washington, D.C., and rushed to an animal clinic in the city. The veterinarian proclaimed Jiggs' ailment to be the result of a bit too much of the good life. "Jiggs ate too much," Dr. Locke explained to the *Washington Post*. "He has a lot of friends at Quantico and he probably fed from one mess kit too many." Dr. Locke assured the public that Jiggs would be fine and be home within a few days, much to the relief of the Quantico Marines worried about their canine companion. Jiggs failed to complete his scheduled convalescence at the dog hospital, for his Marines required his presence at a sporting event in Philadelphia. In what likely proved to be a bad omen for Jiggs' strict diet, he was sprung from the hospital, against doctor's orders, by the Marine athletic caterer.[187]

HEY STORK
BEAT IT!

U·S·MARINE
WANT YOU
for a
MASCOT
travel
adventure
comfort
BIG EATS

APPLICANTS.

Oh no! Jiggs was dead! Long live Jiggs! Who, or what, would replace him? The Marines, proud of their "Devil Dog" moniker, chose to stick with bulldogs. The hunt for "Jiggs II" was on. The Leatherneck, *March 1927; reprinted in* The Leatherneck, *July 1986.*

Early in January 1927, another attack of overeating sent Jiggs back to Dr. Locke's hospital in Washington. At first the doctor thought this attack no more serious than Jiggs' previous stomach ailments, but Jiggs slipped into critical condition several days later, prompting Dr. Locke to send for other consulting physicians. Despite their best efforts, Jiggs "died like a marine . . . without complaining or whimpering about his condition." It appeared that when his Marines stopped feeding him extra provisions, Jiggs went in search of his own midnight snacks, and likely ate something that prompted the second, fatal attack of gastritis.[188]

The normally stoic Marines were beside themselves with grief over the loss of their devoted friend. His body was transported to a Washington funeral home, where Jiggs was placed in a child-sized, satin-lined coffin, his collar and lead beside him. He was then airlifted back to Quantico, where his body lay in state. *The Washington Post* initially reported that hundreds of Marines were scheduled to stand at attention when Jiggs' casket was transferred to a caisson and draped with a Marine Corps flag, and taken to Butler Stadium on January 10 for burial at sunset. "While his body is being lowered into its grave," the *Post* announced, "a firing squad and a bugler will sound a soldier's final farewell." These plans went somewhat awry due to the huge number of admirers who wanted to pay their final respects to Jiggs, and his funeral was delayed as a result. Over eight hundred Marines, and many of their wives and children, filed past the "flower-embowered bier," some weeping openly. Jiggs was committed to the earth in Butler Stadium the next morning.[189] Naturally there was talk of erecting a monument to Jiggs, but if one was ever erected, it has since disappeared.

Jiggs, as it turned out, was the forefather of what would become a bulldog dynasty at Quantico. Not long after the passing of Jiggs I, boxing champion Gene Tunney, himself a former Marine, presented the Marine Corps with "Silent White Richards," a pedigreed bulldog better known as Jiggs II. Like his predecessor, Jiggs II enlisted in the Marine Corps as a private, and worked his way up the ranks, also ending his career as a sergeant major.[190]

Like Jiggs I, Jiggs II suffered anything on behalf of the Corps. Legend has it that in 1928 the "Quantico Marines" played the Navy's football team in the partially completed Butler Stadium. Unfortunately, the Marines were in the process of rebuilding their football team at the time, and the Navy had swabbed the decks with the Marine squad by halftime. As the Navy band played a triumphant "Anchors Away" during the halftime festivities, the drum major made the mistake of punting Sergeant Major Jiggs down the field. While perhaps Jiggs was willing to take the abuse, General Butler was not about to see both his team and his dog beaten by the Navy. When the spectacle reached the fifty-yard line, General Butler led his Marines in a spirited charge against the Navy men on the field. This resulted in "a good old fashioned riot," and earned General Butler a split lip for his trouble. Having instigated the brawl in the first place, the Navy band did its best to quell the melee by playing the "Star-Spangled Banner" in hopes that the servicemen would all cease fighting to stand at attention. It worked . . . sixteen choruses later. The Marines still lost the game and General Butler supposedly received a stern warning from Washington about contact sports, to which he jauntily responded to a friend, "It was almost worth it, watching a squad of charging Marines in action."[191] And the Marines satisfied the honor of Sergeant Major Jiggs II in the process.

Jiggs II also followed in his predecessor's footsteps in another unfortunate way. Jiggs II passed away in March 1937, another victim of canine overeating.[192]

About the same time Jiggs II arrived for duty at Quantico, "Private Pagett" (also spelled Paget and Padgett) made his debut. The death of Jiggs I made national headlines, and apparently international ones as well. The British Royal Marines heard of Jiggs' passing, and sent another pedigreed bulldog to the Quantico Marines in sympathy.

The saintly (if portly, were one to be churlish and say so) Jiggs, lying in state in his satin-lined coffin at Quantico, guarded by an honor detachment. Hundreds of Marines and their families visited to pay last respects to their beloved mascot bulldog, and Jiggs' passing was national news. From the scrapbook of PFC Charles William Raguse, courtesy B. J. Omanson via Scuttlebutt and Small Chow, Inc.

Private Pagett arrived in New York on the passenger liner *Leviathan*, where he was met by a squad of Marines and escorted to Quantico. At the base, he made the acquaintance of his mascot colleague, Jiggs II. While Pagett became the Marines' new mascot, Jiggs II retained his position as "athletic mascot" at Quantico, and the two dogs shared their duties peacefully.[193] At least until Private Pagett died in May 1928. In true Marine style, Pagett died of heat exhaustion after doing his duty in cheering on the Quantico baseball team in Lexington, Virginia. The unseasonable heat, combined with the excitement of the three-day trip, proved too much for Pagett, who collapsed upon returning to Quantico. While Private Pagett had made many friends in the short year he served at Quantico, he also left behind a somewhat checkered service record.

> *30 June 1927. Chasing a blonde stenographer down the hall. Transferred to barracks.*
> *25 July 1927. Attempting to incite a riot by quarreling with the Post Dog. Confined to Chains.*
> *12 August 1927. Biting the hand that fed him. Public Reprimand.*[194]

Following the death of Jiggs II in 1937, Quantico did not go without another mascot for long. The Bulldog Club of Philadelphia stepped into the breach and presented the Marine Corps with Jiggs III. Gene Tunney presented Jiggs III to the Marine Corps on behalf of the Bulldog Club, and General Smedley Butler (now retired) accepted the newest addition to the Jiggs dynasty. While his aristocratic pedigree marked Jiggs III as a blue-blood in the bulldog world, *The Leatherneck* assured its readers that "the new Jiggs has a scowl stern enough to scare the wits out of a pirate."[195]

Apparently Jiggs III's scowl could not ward off the Grim Reaper because by March 1939, Jiggs IV

had reported for duty. Jiggs IV performed well, achieving the rank of corporal in June 1940. At that time General Louis Little, commander at Quantico, complimented Jiggs on his exemplary service record and prudent saving policy. Jiggs had "performed his duties at this post in an outstanding manner," General Little reported. "He is thrifty, as evidenced by his record: Under deposit account—1 December, 1939, 1 turkey leg." Jiggs demonstrated his acquisitive habits again upon receiving his sergeant's stripes in August 1941. "He dug up an old bone he was hoarding against hard times and offered to share it with his shipmates."[196]

"Mother De Boo"

Beginning in 1929 Jiggs II had something of a human counterpart at Quantico. In that year General Butler created the position of "Official Hostess" at the base, and appointed Mrs. Katherine De Boo as Quantico's first hostess. Mrs. De Boo had come to Quantico with her husband in 1925, and

Back from the "banana wars": Marines returning from Nicaragua in 1933 are seen marching up Potomac Avenue from the docks. Waller Hall is visible on Rising Hill in the distance. Courtesy The Leatherneck.

Seaplane hangars at Quantico during the 1920s, of which one still survives. Courtesy Marine Corps Historical Center.

her home soon became something of a haven for homesick Marines. Mrs. De Boo's maternal presence earned her the nickname "Mother De Boo," and the men adopted her as their surrogate mother. Every Mother's Day found her inundated by cards and flowers from her boys around the world. She also helped to augment her extended family by playing matchmaker between marriageable Marines and eligible young women in Northern Virginia.

In 1929 General Butler decided to repay some of the hospitality the Marines had enjoyed in Baltimore when visiting for sporting events, by inviting a delegation of Baltimoreans to Quantico. "There is a bunch of damn women coming along to the post today. I want you to greet them at the barracks and look after them," General Butler said, by way of a request for assistance. "And I'm making you the Marine Corps hostess at Quantico." Thereafter, "Mother De Boo" greeted visitors to the base, participated in weddings, provided a shoulder to cry

on, helped get celebrities to visit the men on base, and generally gave whatever assistance the Marines required of her. And like Jiggs, Mother De Boo traveled with her boys to sporting events and even World's Fairs. Her nickname occasionally confused the uninitiated, however. According to legend, while Mrs. De Boo and Mrs. Smedley Butler chatted in the lobby of a hotel in which the Marine contingent was staying in 1930, the Marines passing by greeted Mrs. De Boo by calling her "Mother." The confused doorman finally could not contain his curiosity, and inquired if ALL the men were her boys. Without batting an eye, Mrs. De Boo confirmed that they were, prompting the doorman to exclaim, "What a remarkable woman!"

When this remarkable woman became gravely ill during World War II, she continued to write letters for wounded Marines, greet their parents, and offer a sympathetic shoulder. When her now very far-flung family of Marines heard about her illness,

Construction of Quantico's pier, at the river end of Potomac Avenue, is seen in this undated photo. The old Quantico Hotel, now Waller Hall, is seen on Rising Hill. Courtesy National Archives, Record Group 71.

they showered her with messages of goodwill from battlefields around the world. Mother De Boo died at Quantico in 1943.[197]

The Blue and Gray Return

General Butler had one more trick up his sleeve for getting his Marines in the news and the public eye. In addition to sporting matches and beloved bulldog mascots, Butler instituted annual maneuvers for the expeditionary forces at Quantico, during which the Marines would reenact famous battles of the Civil War. Unlike modern reenactors who take pride in outfitting themselves and fighting with as much authenticity as possible, Butler conceived of his Civil War maneuvers as a way to showcase new weaponry, give his men some practical field experience, and put on a good show for the public. The first maneuver in September 1921 saw the Marines stay relatively close to home by reenacting the 1864 Battle of the Wilderness. The detachment of Marines marched from Quantico to the Wilderness battlefield, where the troops were to camp until the beginning of October. While the men might be sleeping under the same skies as their Civil War counterparts, very little about the Marines' version of the battle would look familiar to either the Blue or the Gray. The exercises at the Wilderness included ground operations in conjunction with the air service, and night attacks by airplanes.[198]

General Butler later admitted disappointment with some of his troops on the march to the Wilderness. On the third day of marching, a motorcycle orderly caught up with General Butler, walking at the head of the column, to report that twenty stragglers refused to march in the heat. Catching a ride with the orderly to the rear of the column, Butler found the men resting under the shade of the trees, eating ice cream in the company of some girls. No hardened "Devil Dogs" were these lads! Butler's uniform lacked the stripes that would have identified him as an officer, and the new recruits did not recognize their commander. Realizing their ignorance, Butler offered to carry one man's pack and equipment, in addition to his own: a combined weight of seventy-five pounds. Butler informed the men that they were going to march that day, and told them if he could do it, so could they. He formed a column out of the stragglers, and led the march with a whistle. Soon Butler had the men whistling and singing along with him, and making good time in the process. At a rest stop, the men finally realized that the general himself had been leading their

march, although the skeptical among the group could not believe a general would carry a knapsack or march with the troops.

As the discussion of the marching habits of generals progressed, a group of distinguished visitors stopped for directions. They asked where they might find General Butler, not realizing they had already found him. The men in the car sought confirmation that they'd find Butler at the head of the column, riding a horse while making his men hoof it themselves. "Sure," Butler told them, "all the officers are up in front." The Marines found the situation absurdly amusing, and they all had a good time marching afterwards. Being nearly twenty years older than the enlisted men, Butler confessed that the march wore him out, but he refused to give in to show the men "that they could force themselves to

do things that would be necessary in war," like marching uncomfortable distances. And when word got out that the general had rounded up the stragglers himself, the Marines knew it would be no use trying to fall out in the future.[199]

Maneuvers near the Wilderness, attended by President Warren Harding, included an unusual event of historic importance. General Butler had heard that Stonewall Jackson's amputated left arm had been buried near Ellwood farmhouse in Chancellorsville in 1863. In one version of the story, Butler expressed disbelief that the arm was still there, and had it dug up to prove or disprove the legend. In another version of the story, a granite tombstone already honored the final resting place of the venerated arm. In both versions of the story, Butler did have the arm disinterred, confirmed its

Many historians believe World War II began in 1932, with Japan's invasion of China. Certainly world affairs after that date went rapidly from bad to worse. The military began reshaping itself for the war to come, including Quantico Marines on maneuvers in 1935. The world was still at peace—but only just. Courtesy base archive.

existence, had it placed in a metal box, and reburied the box with all proper honors, leaving behind a plaque to commemorate the occasion. The tombstone still marks the spot, but the National Park Service, which oversees the Chancellorsville battlefield, has since removed the plaque.[200]

Reenactments of other famous Civil War battles were yet to come: Gettysburg in 1922, New Market in 1923, and Antietam in 1924. All involved long marches for the troops, public parades and reviews in many towns along the route, visits by presidents and other dignitaries, and displays of new weapons being applied to old battles. The Marines reenacted Pickett's charge at Gettysburg, on the anniversary of the actual charge. Newspaper reports failed to mention whether or not the Marines were any more successful than the Confederates had been, but a demonstration the next day of how a modern attack against Little Round Top and Cemetery Ridge using twentieth century artillery, airplanes and tanks surely would have turned the tide for the Confederates in 1863.[201]

Maneuvers in 1923 took the Marines from Quantico to New Market, in the Shenandoah Valley, to recreate the famous 1864 battle pitting Union forces against cadets from the Virginia Military Institute. Remaining faithful to the players, the series of events, and the outcome of the battle, the Marines invited VMI cadets to represent the Confederacy, and the Marines took the Union role. Before the Marines left Quantico, officers from the expeditionary force typed up detailed instructions for each of the units in the field, to help faithfully choreograph the battle. One can imagine the chagrin of the reenactors of the 51st Virginia when they read their instructions. "When the RED POSITION is reached the FEDERAL fire will be intense. The 51st will become confused and falter." No self-respecting leatherneck wants to "become confused and falter" on purpose, especially when they read on to find that some men in the 51st then disobeyed their officers and fled. Perhaps had the men of the real 51st been supported by the "infantry, artillery, signal equipment, tanks, machine guns, chemical warfare apparatus, searchlights, aircraft, and trench mortars" taking part in the twentieth-century version of New Market, they might not have faltered and fled so quickly. Particularly if they had the option of watching a motion picture in the evening, as their modern counterparts did![202]

A young officer in 1923, General A. A. Vandegrift would vividly remember this maneuver forty years later. He particularly recalled that a cold, driving rain made the march rather miserable for twenty-eight of the thirty days in the field. After a particularly difficult day slogging through the mud and trying to free trapped Liberty trucks, Vandegrift overheard one of his men grumble, "Just to think of it—that my grandfather fought four and one-half years to keep this miserable state in the Union." The march also demonstrated the fund of practicality lodged in the lower ranks. When the troops reached a railroad trestle in the Blue Ridge Mountains, they discovered that a large boiler being transported for the purpose of providing hot water to visiting dignitaries, was two inches too tall to fit under the trestle. General Butler, his senior officers, and a group of engineers all studied the problem with very little success, until one of Vandegrift's corporals spat out the wad of tobacco he had been chewing and said, "Why the hell don't they let the air out of the tires?" The corporal's solution saved the day, and thereby proved a valuable lesson to all: "that all brains are not found in brass." Once at New Market, Vandegrift's troops represented the 68th Virginia Regiment, and after putting on a good show of it, his battalion headed back to camp. Along the way they encountered an automobile full of Confederate veterans returning home from the reenactment. "Son, that was a good fight," one of them told Vandegrift. "You did almost as well as we did." As Vandegrift began to thank the veteran for his generous praise, the man's comrade cut him short. "You know you're a liar, Jack—they did it a damn sight better."[203] Thus confirming that not all lessons are learned on the battlefield.

A boat landing party, in an undated photo. The Marine (far right) looking at the camera—one of the wettest, for whatever reason—appears to be enjoying himself. Courtesy Marine Corps Historical Center.

The 1924 maneuvers at Antietam would be the last of the series of Civil War battles refought by the Marines in the 1920s. By then the exercises had taken the Marines through their paces, allowed them to experience combat-like conditions, and as importantly, had given the Quantico Marines a national spotlight and provided both government authorities and the general public multiple opportunities to come out, enjoy a show, and see what the Marines could do. Probably more instrumental to the end of Civil War maneuvers was the leave of absence from the Marine Corps taken by General

Butler in 1924 to become the public safety director for the city of Philadelphia.[204]

The idea of reenacting Civil War battles would be briefly resurrected in the 1930s, and the Quantico Marines would participate in reenactments of the First Battle of Manassas and at Petersburg. The Manassas reenactment drew an estimated fifty thousand spectators. Many men found the Petersburg exercise a less than satisfactory experience because they again faced cadets from VMI, and the Marines were ordered to lose the battle, as they had had to do at the Manassas reen-

Potomac Avenue—with its new, postwar paean to America's wartime ally, France (see the New French Café)—was a bustling place. Courtesy National Archives, Record Group 71.

battles. The Quantico Marines between the World Wars were called out for active duty in China and the Caribbean, and to protect the mails domestically.

In 1921, the United States Post Office experienced a rash of domestic mail robberies and other instances of interference with mail distribution. The problem of stolen mail became so acute and so costly that the Post Office appealed to President Harding for assistance. In November, Harding commanded that the secretary of the Navy provide enough Marines to guard the mail, which resulted in over fifty officers and more than two thousand enlisted men from Quantico providing guard service for post offices, distribution centers, and mail trains. The Marines considered this a serious responsibility. "We armed our people with .45 automatic pistols, 12-gauge riot shotguns, and Thompson submachine guns," recalled General Vandegrift. "We publicized both their armament and Butler's personal orders, 'Come back with your shields or upon them.'" Secretary of the Navy Denby was even more graphic in his commands to the Marines: "There is no compromise in this battle with bandits," he assured the public. "If two marines, guarding a mail car, for example are suddenly covered by a robber, neither must hold up his hands, but both must begin shooting at once. One may get killed, but the other will get the robber and save the mail. When our men go as guards over the mail, that mail must be delivered or there must be a marine dead at the post of duty." The *New York Times* succinctly labeled Denby's message as "Mail or Dead Marine." Whether the Marines or their Tommy guns proved more threatening is not known, but the overall effect was to significantly decrease the incidences of postal disturbances, and

actment as well. "We are getting well fed up on always being licked by a passel of college kids," one Marine complained. "Why don't they fight Gettysburg over again? If they don't watch out we'll wade in and win one of these historic battles some time and change history all around."[205] Perhaps this accounts for the brevity in the experiment of fighting Civil War battles over again in the 1930s?

Real Maneuvers

Not all the maneuvers in which the Marines at Quantico participated involved reenacting Civil War by March 1922 the Quantico Marines were on their way home. Quantico Marines would be called out for mail duty again in October 1926, but as was the case earlier, their presence stabilized mail delivery by the end of the year.[206]

Quantico Marines received an even more interesting guard assignment in 1937. On May 6 the German dirigible *Hindenburg* burst into flames in mid-air, after a spark of unknown origin came in contact with the hydrogen responsible for making the ship "lighter than air." To the horror of the spectators gathered to watch the zeppelin land in Lakehurst, New Jersey, in an instant, the doomed ship became a free-falling inferno, eventually killing over thirty of the passengers and crew on board. In the aftermath of the disaster, two hundred

Marines from Quantico were sent to New Jersey to assist in crowd control as spectators flocked to the scene of the disaster, and to guard the remains of the airship.[207]

Two years later another two hundred Marines headed north, but this time for much more festive duties. During the 1939 World's Fair in New York, a group of 211 Marines from Quantico formed the U.S. Marine Corps Detachment at the fair. Even though what Winston Churchill would call "the gathering storm" loomed over Europe, America was enjoying the calm before the storm and celebrating its technological prowess. Because the Marine Corps detachment marched in parades, greeted dignitaries at official functions, and performed other ceremonial duties, the elite group assigned to the fair had

This view of Potomac Avenue, looking west toward Rising Hill, is particularly charming because of the car for sale. The owner has painted the price on the car! Courtesy National Archives, Record Group 71.

Automobiles were not the only mechanized transit available. This scene of Potomac Avenue shows a motorcycle with side-car leading a parade of marching Marines. Undated photo, courtesy base archive.

their records scrutinized for appearance, moral character, discipline, and reliability. Before leaving Quantico the men drilled for long hours in Butler Stadium, and then practiced another three hours every morning at Camp George Washington at the fair, all to hone their ability to drill without audible commands. But considering their maneuvers included performing the welcoming ceremonies for the king and queen of England, and representing the Marine Corps at large, perfection was the only option.[208]

More often, however, maneuvers by Marines at Quantico involved postings to hot spots in Latin America during the so-called "banana wars" of the 1920s, or to China. Throughout the 1920s, the Marine Corps had maintained a presence in China to protect American nationals from internal divisions among Chinese warlords. Although no large units from Quantico received assignments for duty in China, smaller detachments were periodically sent to supplement the units already there, or provide replacements for units sent elsewhere in the Pacific. By early 1927 trouble between diplomatic

missions in China and local warlords necessitated heightened Marine intervention. At the time General Butler remained on leave from the Marines in order to serve as Philadelphia' director of public safety, but left this post to command a brigade in China. Marines from Quantico took the train to San Diego, where the USS *Henderson* met them as their transport to China. Not among the troops on this occasion was Jiggs II, who authorities determined to be of greater value to the Corps by cheering on the Quantico baseball team in Philadelphia, rather than shipping out to China.[209]

Nicaragua proved to be an equally troubled nation in 1927, and Quantico Marines stationed in Guantanamo Bay, Cuba, were reassigned to Nicaragua. Following the Spanish-American War, the Marines had established a naval base at Guantanamo, which provided the Marines a convenient outpost for training maneuvers, and established a Marine presence in the Caribbean, the Panama Canal Zone, and elsewhere in Latin America. When a fragile political peace in Nicaragua collapsed in 1927, leading to a revolution, the Quantico-by-way-of-Guantanamo Marines moved in to maintain order until an acceptable government came to power in 1933. As *The Leatherneck* pointed out, however, the Marine presence in Nicaragua had extended much longer than six years and had involved a multiplicity of duties. "For nineteen of the last twenty years," the magazine reminded its readers in 1933, "the Marines have been guarding American life and property in Nicaragua; they have beaten off hundreds of bandit attacks, trained an army, supervised elections and restored peace to our sister republic." Many different Marine regiments ultimately saw service in Nicaragua before the last troops left in January 1933. In the meantime, a series of units comprised of Quantico Marines rotated through Cuba to serve six-month tours on the island nation.[210]

The USS Henderson, *seen here in 1925, was kept busy during that decade transporting Quantico Marines to and from hot spots throughout the Caribbean and Latin America. Courtesy Marine Corps Historical Center.*

The expeditions in the Caribbean and Latin America, apart from helping to stabilize the region, benefited the Marine Corps in a practical way. The maneuvers provided practical testing grounds for theories on amphibious assaults and principles of conducting small wars. These experiences were later analyzed at Quantico to determine what did and did not work in the field. These findings would become the basis for Marine Corps manuals and textbooks, such as *The Strategy and Tactics of Small Wars,* which would be updated and revised over the next two decades. The Marine Corps also staged its own amphibious maneuvers to study tactics and train troops under more controlled circumstances than actually invading foreign soil could provide. For some of the Marines detailed for training maneuvers, the expeditions must have felt more like a vacation than a duty. For the twelve hundred Quantico Marines who left Virginia for Puerto Rico in January 1938, the chance to participate in "two months of joint Army-Navy exercises in the pleasurable warmth of the tropics" must have sounded

much more appealing than a mid-Atlantic winter, even if they would have to storm beaches rather than lie on them.[211]

Maneuvers exacted a toll on Quantico, regardless of their practical benefit. As mentioned previously, the established sports teams on base could lose almost a whole season of play if too many members on the squad received orders to report elsewhere in the world. Similarly, in 1928 the professional schools at Quantico nearly ceased operation when the instructors were sent to the Caribbean to rectify a lack of experienced officers there.

And when the men left, they left "maneuver widows" behind them. While scenes of embarkation usually involved piers or railroad stations lined with honking cars and families waving to their departing Marines, the presence of wives and girlfriends assembled to say goodbye to the men also brought "a group of fluttering handkerchiefs, some tear-stained," as the women faced the prospect of many months on their own. Not surprisingly, the social scene at Quantico suffered tremendously when units went on maneuvers. When the First Marine Brigade left Quantico for maneuvers in January 1939, the *Washington Post* reported that the base settled in for "a quiet social schedule." Many "maneuver widows" took the opportunity to go on extended visits with their parents, or take their children on vacations, while others invited friends and relatives to Quantico to keep them company. Marine authorities recognized the psychological toll maneuvers took on the wives left behind, and the generals' wives would hold teas and other social functions for "maneuver widows" to provide them companionship and a social outlet.[212]

But as military families throughout history have experienced, there is nothing sweeter than the homecoming. When Marines stationed in Nicaragua returned to Quantico in 1933, the "enlisted men disembarked to be greeted by wives, kiddies, and sweethearts. The clicking of movie camera, the blare of the band and the surging crowd added the necessary color for a proper welcome to the returning boys." This scene would be repeated many times as maneuvers ended and the men came home in the 1920s and 1930s, although sometimes the uniforms and souvenirs provided clues as to

where the men had been. For the boys in Nicaragua, "campaign hats" and "crocodile bags" announced that they had been in the tropics.[213]

The USS *Henderson*

Regardless of where in the world the Quantico Marines went, one constant of their journey was that they were likely to get there on the USS *Henderson*. On her first voyage, the *Henderson* safely transported Marines from Quantico to France during World War I. The *Henderson* later picked up Marines in San Diego who had traveled by train from Quantico, and transported them to China to suppress warlord activity. It brought them home to Quantico from service in Nicaragua, and served as the backdrop for grand celebrations when the men disembarked. For the purpose of expeditionary training maneuvers in Hawaii in 1925, the *Henderson* acted as the stand-in for a whole fleet of ships, while the 750 Marines aboard pretended to be a more formidable force of 40,000.[214]

The USS *Henderson* (AP-1) was launched in Philadelphia in 1916, and her name honored Commandant Archibald Henderson, the fifth commandant of the Marine Corps, who had grown up near Quantico. Unlike the modified commercial

Going to Nicaragua: the Marine 5ᵗʰ Regiment is seen boarding the USS Henderson *at Quantico's pier in 1927. Courtesy Marine Corps Historical Center.*

Marines returning from Nicaragua aboard the USS Henderson *are treated to a rousing welcome at Quantico as the ship approaches the pier.* The Leatherneck, *February 1933.*

Another view, farther east, of Potomac Avenue. Courtesy National Archives, Record Group 71.

ships previously available to the Marines, the *Henderson* had been specially designed as a transport and landing vessel for expeditionary forces, and could comfortably accommodate both the men and their equipment. The 483-foot ship could carry over fifteen hundred men at a time, traveling at a maximum speed of fourteen knots. Over the course of her long military career "Ol' No. 1" took Marines all over the world, depositing them in France to fight at Belleau Wood in the Great War, servicing ports in Latin America during the "banana wars" of the 1920 and 1930s, and providing medical care for the wounded after horrific fighting at Iwo Jima in 1945. During all that time, Quantico became a frequent destination point for the *Henderson*, and

almost any photograph of men embarking or disembarking on the pier at Quantico shows the *Henderson* somewhere in the background.

By the time the United States entered World War II in 1941, the *Henderson* remained the only World War I–era troopship still in active duty, although her design and changes in amphibious landing techniques rendered her obsolete for landing troops in the Pacific theater. Accordingly, the *Henderson* was decommissioned in October 1943, and after an extensive overhaul at the Naval Supply Depot in Oakland, California, she set sail under the new name USS *Bountiful* (AH-9) to begin a new career as a Navy hospital ship in the Pacific. The Navy decommissioned the *Henderson-Bountiful* for the last time in 1946, and, somewhat callously, sold her for scrap. However, her yeoman service to the Marine Corps earned the ship the well-deserved title of "Transport of the Marines," and the men who appreciated her historic role in the Marine Corps salvaged the ship's bell, which now sounds watch at Henderson Hall in Arlington, Virginia.[215]

Building Booms

When Quantico first became a Marine Corps base in 1917, it occupied rented land and consisted of temporary wooden buildings. A couple of years later, the United States government bought the land for the Marines, but the transition to permanent infrastructure took a little longer to achieve. The YWCA opened a hostess house on base in 1919, and the Red Cross opened a convalescent house just a month later, but demonstrations of commitment by outside organizations was only the first step in providing the infrastructure a viable Marine Corps base would need. The first nod to permanency by the Marines themselves came in the early 1920s, with placing concrete foundations under all the wooden barracks left over from the war, and building officers' quarters with materials salvaged from extra barracks rendered obsolete by reductions in troop strength at Quantico. By using recycled materials and Marine labor, the new construction projects had cost the public next to nothing in tax dollars, and had given the structures an additional lease on life.[216]

The Marines put a good face on the situation at Quantico, and did the best they could with materials at their command. In 1924 General Dion Williams presided over the cornerstone laying ceremony for a new officers' club. While *The Leatherneck* was effusive over the merits of the new facility, it did highlight that only the "can-do" attitude of Marines made it possible. "The building of this magnificent clubhouse entirely by Marines is not alone a remarkable achievement from the construction point of view," *The Leatherneck* explained, "but when one considers that all the material used in its construction is either obtained or manufactured within the post limits, one is forced to admit it is indeed a wonderful monument to the resourcefulness of the U.S. Marines." With Butler Stadium still under construction using donated and salvaged materials and Marine labor, it's a wonder the men had any time left to soldier at all! That the building's construction required masonry, carpentry, electrical, and plumbing work, however, may have supported the vocational schools' mission to provide Marines with practical skills they could transfer to civilian life.[217]

But the officers' club was only one of many structures Quantico required, and even with the additional structural supports, the temporary buildings of the World War I era were not meant to last and became both eyesores and fire hazards. New, more permanent structures had to be built, both to replace buildings facing condemnation and to accommodate the increasing numbers of officers and enlisted men being sent to Quantico. As General Lejeune, commandant of the Corps, explained to the secretary of the Navy in 1924:

> *The housing situation . . . is in urgent need of remedy. The barracks and many other buildings are of wartime construction and have reached the stage of deterioration where they are practically beyond repair. . . . The labor of the Marine garrison has been utilized to the greatest extent possible, without interference with the necessary training, in performing maintenance work and certain new construction which has been urgently required. . . . It is believed, however, that unless appropriations are available to assist in the work of new construction that the task of keeping the post in suitable condition will exceed the capacity for accomplishment which the Marines of this post have demonstrated.[218]*

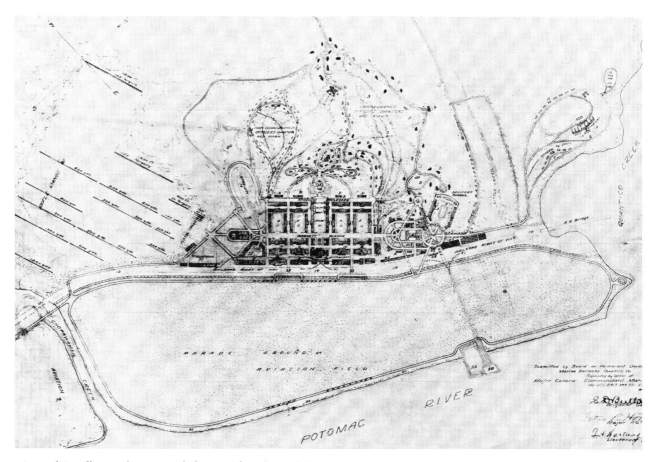

General Smedley Darlington Butler's intent for a beautiful Quantico never bore fruit, at least not as he hoped. Shown here is an architectural rendering of a proposed campus of beautiful symmetry fronting the Potomac River. The Marine Corps leadership was not willing to make such an investment, and Quantico lost the opportunity to rival West Point and Annapolis architecturally. Architectural Record, *June 1925.*

Proposed Quantico campus, view from Barnett Avenue of a quadrangle. Architectural Record, *June 1925.*

Lejeune would report the same conditions in his annual report the next year as well. The *Washington Post* concurred, arguing Marines on active duty at Quantico had a right to live in accommodations better than those which "just barely serve as human dwellings."[219]

Thinking more grandly than realistic budgets allowed, General Lejeune had convened a board in 1923 to study the development of Quantico as a permanent Marine base, and report on the steps needed to be taken to bring Quantico into the future. Among the board members was noted architect Glenn Brown, who submitted an article to the *Architectural Record* outlining the board's vision for Quantico. "The topography of the Marine Reservation," Brown explained, "gives an opportunity for a dignified and imposing installation of buildings and a picturesque and pleasing park treatment, allowing unexcelled views of beautifully wooded valleys and the broad Potomac River with the hills of Maryland and Virginia rising in the distance." Clearly, the planners envisioned not just a run-of-the-mill military installation at Quantico, but rather, an attractive, university campus-like setting combining both the practical and aesthetic. The plan allocated space for all the essential structures, like barracks and armories, but grouped them in such a way as to minimize the utilitarian functions the buildings performed. "The Barracks being the largest and most important group around which the Post rotates, have been given a decided individuality," Brown wrote. "Dignity is attained by grouping each Barrack or Regimental Unit on a large quadrangular court around which the porches form a continuous encircling colonnade." Taking a cue

from Virginia's colonial past and Quantico's proximity to Mount Vernon, the board chose a neo-Colonial or Georgian style of architecture for the new campus. This architectural style was both appropriate for the surroundings, and economical in its use of simple lines and plain materials. The plan called for new barracks, recreational facilities, an expanded administration building, parade ground, additional roadways, and the other supporting infrastructure required for keeping a base of several thousand men operating smoothly. Planners also proposed taking full advantage of the natural features of Quantico's location, and suggested installing parks and bridle paths in the wooded valleys surrounding the base, and damming the stream running under Butler Stadium to create a "lake in the woods" for canoeing in summer and ice skating in winter. In short, it was a grand plan for what the

Proposed Quantico campus, view from the post exchange to the chapel. Architectural Record, *June 1925.*

121

board anticipated would be a grand military and educational facility.[220]

And in fact, some grandeur had found a home at Quantico by 1921, establishing a precedent for the introduction of traditional Georgian architecture on base. Captain Phillips Brooks Robinson had been stationed at Quantico during the war, and recognized the need for a living area for Marines to be able to read and relax, or entertain guests. Before being called to staff duty, Robinson began sketching plans for the sort of space he envisioned. Robinson died in an automobile accident in Maryland in 1918, and his widow decided to install an impressive room at Quantico to honor her husband and his love of the Corps. The thirty-six-by-twenty-one-foot room boasted pine paneling, oak floors, a marble fireplace, recessed bookcases, maps, decorative light fixtures incorporating Marine Corps iconography, and a Palladian window framing a view of the Potomac. It resembled a proper gentleman's club in every way, and brought a ray of elegance to a base still comprised largely of decrepit wooden barracks.[221]

Had Brown's board been successful in bringing its comprehensive plan to fruition, the Quantico of today would look much differently. Although elements of the plan survived and many future building projects would employ Georgian architectural features, the Quantico plan as formulated died in the way many urban planning ventures fail: money, or rather lack thereof. In spite of urgent requests and the presentation of what a rehabilitated Quantico could be, Congress stymied every effort by failing to appropriate the necessary funding.

Until 1927. Unfortunately, an event in early 1927 only confirmed the urgency of the construction projects at Quantico. One of the temporary wooden buildings on base caught fire in February, as Quantico authorities had worried and warned would happen someday. Four people were trapped in the burning house, three of whom lost their lives immediately. Another woman nearly died of asphyxiation before escaping the inferno. The dead included Marine aviator Andrew Holderby and his five-year-old daughter Clotilde, and Eleanor Griffin, a Washington woman engaged to be married that June. Lieutenant Holderby's wife and other daughter had been staying with friends that night and escaped being caught in the fire. Tragically, firemen discovered from the positions of the bodies

Proposed Quantico campus, view from the chapel to the post exchange. Architectural Record, *June 1925.*

It took a tragic and lethal fire in 1927—such as this one from 1938, of the post exchange, the only one captured by camera—to spur Congress to replace Quantico's rickety World War I–era wooden buildings with substantial new ones. The Leatherneck, *December 1938.*

that the occupants of the house had attempted to flee, but the structure's single door caught fire and prevented escape.[222]

Just days after the deaths of Andrew and Clotilde Holderby and Eleanor Griffin, the House of Representatives approved an appropriations package for new construction at Quantico requested by the Marine Corps in 1926. The bill finally gave the secretary of the Navy the authority to begin construction of permanent facilities at Quantico, and called for dismantling World War I–era structures and replacing them with new barracks, apartment houses for officers, a power plant, storehouses, sidewalks, landscaping, and an electrical distribution system. Congress ultimately approved nearly $4 million in two appropriations to cover the cost of the new construction, even though estimates ran as high as $8 million.[223]

Recognizing the need to address the "wretched accommodations now there," once Congress appropriated funds for construction, housing projects at Quantico immediately jumped to the top of the priority list for the Bureau of Yards and Docks, the entity in charge of construction at Quantico. The first wave of building focused on erecting new barracks for the men on base, perhaps inspired by the Holderby-Griffin tragedy. The first group of Marines began moving into attractive brick barracks facing Barnett Avenue in 1929, and the entire series of barracks reached completion in 1932. One old-timer recalled that "the change from the old to the new quarters was almost like moving from an old East Side tenement to the Waldorf-Astoria!" By 1929 *The Leatherneck* magazine proudly proclaimed that "the low, green buildings that housed the famous wartime Marines are fast disappearing, and growing in their stead are modern structures of concrete and steel." The modern appointments the new barracks received provoked equal admiration, and it was said of the kitchen facilities that "if meals of exceptional quality are not produced in these kitchens, it will not be through lack of mechanical conveniences." The *Washington Post,* on the other hand, suggested that those Marines stuck with KP duty would be thrilled to discover that the "twin nightmares of this detail," potato peeling and dishwashing, had been eliminated thanks to the installation of mechanical peelers and dishwashing equipment. The men would also enjoy, for the first time, full-length lockers in which to hang their clothes.[224]

Whereas the barracks received the most attention, also under construction by the middle of 1929 were the central heating plant, a garage, motor transport repair shop, warehouses, roadways, and officers' apartment houses located in the hillside just above Butler Stadium. Although a garage simply could not hope to capture the public's imagination in the same way that "bean cart" serving

Construction of new barracks in January 1928. Congress voted funds for a series of new barracks after a tragic fire killed Marines in one of Quantico's rickety World War I–era buildings. These replacements, used today, were said to be fireproof and, finally, to provide the base with barracks worthy of men and mission. Courtesy National Archives, Record Group 71.

wagons in the mess hall could by promising to "distribute the food so swiftly that it will find itself on a hungry Marine's fork before it has half a chance to grow cold."[225]

Still, *The Leatherneck* could not help but express a little wistfulness at the fate of the wooden barracks, and that their decay and demolition heralded the end of an era in Quantico's history. "There is something touching in the passing of the old green, wooden barracks that housed the wartime Marines," the magazine's editors confessed. "Smothered in the dirt and ruin that a decade has heaped upon the floors of these old buildings are many little wooden plaques giving the name of the Marine who once slept in a certain bunk in that room. Then beneath the name is the age-old disposition of a soldier: 'Killed in Action, Blanc Mont, October 3, 1918.'" After shedding a tear for the past, *The Leatherneck* recognized that "the old must make room for the new; else there would be no progress"

and that "Phoenix-like, old Quantico is passing, and a newer one rises from the ashes to take its place."[226]

A second renovation boom hit Quantico in the late 1930s. By then construction had begun on the million-dollar medical dispensary at Shipping Point, a site of Confederate gun batteries during the Civil War. This facility would become the Naval Hospital, Quantico. Other building projects included expanding the post chapel, creating clubs and lounges for officers and noncommissioned officers, installing prefabricated housing for married noncommissioned officers, building sidewalks and parking lots, and erecting a post school for the children at Quantico. The officers' apartments were finally finished in 1937, and a year later an enlisted men's club, called "The Tavern," opened on base.[227]

The G-Men Cometh

Quantico's role in the Corps had also expanded since the Marines first arrived on the site, and the creation of specialized schools required appropriate infrastructure to support courses of instruction. As a result, the 1930s bore witness to the creation of new rifle and machine gun ranges and parade grounds. The establishment of this infrastructure also attracted the Federal Bureau of Investigation, who saw in Quantico an answer to their own training needs. For much of the 1930s, the FBI conducted their training exercises wherever they could in the metropolitan Washington, D.C. area, which clearly did not help the bureau in terms of concentrating their instruction efforts or having a reliable facility at which to train. By 1936, however, the FBI began to use firing range facilities at Quantico for target practice using pistols and submachine guns, and gas bombing exercises. The open spaces at the Marine base also allowed the bureau to train "rookie" G-men to "fire from moving cars, to shoot moving objects, and to make raids on 'hideout' houses." The FBI also used Quantico to stage other crimes for the sake of education, and "Oscar the dummy" met his maker over and over and over again on base to train law enforcement professionals how to read a murder scene and recognize clues identifying individual murder suspects. By 1938, bureau chief J. Edgar Hoover proposed to Congress that the FBI build its own speedway and target range at Quantico so that his G-men could "machine gun dummy mobsters while roaring along in automobiles at 70 miles an hour," after the Marine Corps advised him that as the Marines increasingly needed their own ranges for instruction and practice, the Justice Department might not be able to rely on USMC facilities as often as they had enjoyed in the past.[228]

Apparently the prospects of speedways and G-men with Tommy guns did not faze the Marines in

Interior of Quantico's new barracks in March 1929. Quantico's leadership was dissatisfied: the beds were too close together. But finally, in a major quality-of-life initiative, there would be enough lockers for the men—see background. Courtesy National Archives, Record Group 71.

the slightest, and in 1939 the Marine Corps invited the bureau to build its proposed academy at Quantico. Perhaps having an arsenal at its own disposal made the Corps and the FBI perfectly suited, if well-armed, neighbors. At Quantico the bureau found the same benefits the Marines had recognized twenty years earlier: proximity to Washington, good transportation networks in the vicinity, open space suitable for firing ranges, and the benefit of enjoying the infrastructure and support facilities put in place by the Marines. The FBI jumped at the chance of locating its academy at Quantico, construction began that fall, and the first agents began classes in the spring of 1940. The original FBI academy was housed in a three-story brick facility on Barnett Avenue, which for the first time allowed agents to "live, work and train together at one location."[229] The arrangement proved very satisfactory to the Marine Corps and the FBI, who still peacefully coexist as neighbors, although the FBI has since moved to a larger facility on the USMC reservation.

Those Daring Young Men in Their Flying Machines

Quantico's postwar building boom of the 1920s and 1930s certainly did not ignore the fledgling Marine aviation corps, although in many ways the aviation component at Quantico remained physically and organizationally separate from the rest of the base.

The Marine Flying Field in Miami, Florida, closed at the end of World War I, and the aviation units returning from France established their base at Quantico instead. The flyers had hoped to secure land north of Quantico, but the powers-that-be at Marine headquarters in Washington decreed that the airfield should be nearer the barracks. Thus, the Marines leased land south of Chopawamsic Creek on which to establish an airstrip. Two two-thousand-foot-long flying fields, creatively named Field No. 1 and Field No. 2 (later Brown Field), soon took shape near the railroad tracks. As was the case on the rest of the base at the time, if the Marines wanted any new infrastructure, they had to build it themselves, which resulted in the erection of two hangars, several barracks, storehouses, and a recreation facility. By 1920 the aviation fields south of

Indoor plumbing, not to mention heated washrooms, were more than many Marines had ever known at home. Quantico's new barracks must have seemed downright luxurious. Courtesy National Archives, Record Group 71.

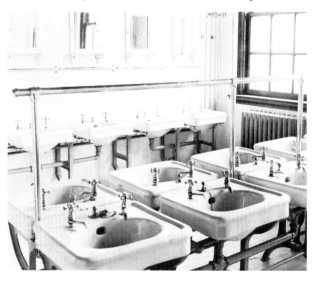

Quantico also supported thirteen officers and 157 enlisted men, who flew a host of different aircraft, from DeHavilland and Curtiss airplanes to observation balloons. The pilots who trained at Quantico became known for the records they set. In April 1921, Major Thomas C. Turner achieved notoriety by leading a demanding flight from Washington, D.C., to the Dominican Republic, which at the time counted as the longest flight ever undertaken. To modern eyes Turner's exploit was all the more notable for having been undertaken without any sort of navigation device in the plane or other guideposts along the way. The next year Major Roy Geiger broke time and distance records in flying from Quantico to Pensacola, Florida. In 1922 a record flight, not including two stops for refueling, took but nine hours, when flying at the "phenomenal" speed of 110 miles per hour. In 1923 Geiger and a party of aviators traveled to San Diego to pick up four Martin bombing planes scheduled to join the squadron at Quantico. While no speed records were set with this trip, cross-country flights were still something newsworthy. What did break a record in 1923 was when Captain Russell Presley flew from Quantico to Minneapolis, Minnesota, in the exceptional time of fourteen hours, forty-five minutes, particularly given that Presley flew a "standard military training plane."[230]

Quantico aviators honed their skills in practical maneuvers as well. In July 1921, two battleships, one captured from the Germans and one retired from the American Navy, were anchored off the coast of Virginia and bombed by practiced Quantico pilots. Apart from providing an excellent chance for target practice, the successful exercise bolstered Army General Billy Mitchell's confidence in the utility of aerial bombardments. Quantico aviators had to content themselves in 1925 with bombing buoys arranged in the shape of battleships, instead of actual ships in the Potomac River. The flyers bombed their targets from altitudes of six thousand and

Quantico's expansion required establishment of a post fire department in the 1920s. The base's World War I–era wooden buildings gave the fire engines more than one run for their money. Courtesy base archive.

three thousand feet, demonstrated parachute maneuvers and aerial machine gun assaults, and laid smoke screens. An unfortunate change in wind direction lessened the effectiveness of the smoke screen demonstration, but naval observers pronounced the exercise "impressive and satisfactory in results obtained" nonetheless.[231]

Progress in Quantico's flying program continued apace and soon included training reserve officers, night flying, transcontinental trips, and perfecting aerial support for ground forces. Interestingly, the Civil War reenactments of the 1920s and 1930s provided opportunities to practice the last skill, as aviation units went with the ground troops, lent aerial support, and ferried troops. For example, the four Martin bombers Geiger and his crew flew across country in 1923 provided transportation support for the 1923 and 1924 Civil War maneuvers. Not very accurate for the 1860s, but a

practical demonstration of the concept of air-ground cooperation nonetheless. General Smedley Butler, not surprisingly, thought the Marine aviators under his command could reach even higher heights if provided the right equipment, and informed his superior officers of the woeful inadequacy of the fleet at Quantico. Butler complained that one squadron lacked two airplanes to complete its strength, the planes in another squadron were obsolete, and the third squadron could only rely on one plane for anything more strenuous than "spraying mosquitoes."[232]

One can assume that General Butler's complaints were resolved in some satisfactory manner, since in 1930 work began on yet another airfield at Quantico. As the aircraft industry produced planes that were larger, heavier, and carried more equipment, Brown Field became as obsolete as some of the planes of which Butler complained. The

Sumptuous is one word for this new bachelor officers quarters at Quantico. Shown here is the Captain Phillips Brooks Robinson Memorial Room. Architectural rendering, 1921, courtesy National Archives, Record Group 71.

increased number of aviation accidents on the old field also raised concerns that its design hindered the safety of Marine aviators. With only two runways, fliers were at the mercy of the winds and had few options for the direction of takeoffs and landings.[233] Unfortunately, the site chosen for the new airfield was exceedingly impractical at the start. Planners chose a location on the mouth of Chopawamsic Creek that required dredging, filling, and rerouting the creek itself before the land stabilized enough to support aircraft traffic. If the plan did not sound simple, it was no easier to complete in reality. One of the Quantico aviators later recalled that:

> *They had trouble filling in the place and making the proper foundations for the hangars, and this was to plague us years later, when the concrete ramps fell through when we had heavier equipment . . . they put down piling after piling after piling as a foundation for the hangars. They put these pilings down and they just disappeared in the mud. I know one night as I understand it a bulldozer was left out in the field and it disappeared overnight. Just vanished.[234]*

While the equipment could possibly have been stolen overnight, the implication is clearly that Chopawamsic Creek took its revenge by swallowing the bulldozer whole. It's not nice to fool Mother Nature, but eventually she relented and the airfield was finally completed almost a decade after construction began.[235]

As this airstrip underwent construction, Quantico fielded Marine Fighting Squadron Nine-M (VF-9M), which author Jess Barrow has called "without doubt one of the most colorful squadrons in the history of Marine Aviation." Its former pilots put it more bluntly: "It was the best damn squadron we ever flew with during our Marine Corps careers!" Still based at the old Brown Field, the squadron, under the direction of Colonel Thomas C. Turner, traveled to scores of military and civilian aviation functions to promote Marine aviation and garner whatever publicity it could. As Smedley Butler did with football teams and Civil War reenactments, Turner gained support for his programs by taking his message directly to the American people by exhibiting his "aerobatic squadron," which

· LOUNGE ·
· BACHELOR OFFICERS QUARTERS ·
· QUANTICO · · VIRGINIA ·
· BUREAU OF YARDS & DOCKS ·

flew first under the leadership of Lieutenant Lawson "Sandy" Sanderson.

Sanderson operated under few official guidelines. "Just get the job done any way you can," he was told. "We don't want to know how you do it, just don't get caught!" A year later, his squad of "Rojo Diablos," or "Red Devils," had already won aviation awards with their six "hand-me-down" Curtiss F7C-1 "Seahawk" fighters. The more planes and pilots added to the squadron, the more impressive the show, and the more attention the squadron received. For its efforts, the Marine Corps awarded the squad twenty-eight new Boeing F4B-4 fighters in 1933, making the Red Devils "the largest and most modern fighting squadron in Marine Corps history." Emboldened by success, Sanderson decided to test what his men could do in formation. He received permission to field an eighteen-plane squadron in airshows, which required the planes to be specially marked for ease of identification by adjoining pilots. The pilots themselves had to know their aircraft so intimately that they could fly their planes by touch, their eyes never straying from the planes on either side of them. The squad had to fly in unison; together the results would be spectacular, but a single wrong move could be fatal. As Sanderson repeatedly told his pilots, "When you men leave this squadron, other flying will be easy."

In 1934, Captain Ford O. "Tex" Rogers assumed command of the squadron, and its first test under his leadership came at the National Air Races in Cleveland. Despite losing one plane in a forced landing, and having his crew pleasantly distracted by having to stay in a residential hotel for women after discovering that the squad's regular hotel reservations did not include room for the mechanics and crew chiefs, Rogers' VF-9M team performed flawlessly. Before a standing-room-only crowd the Red Devils took off and landed with all eighteen planes in formation, and in the air executed intersecting loops, loops through a figure eight, dive bombings, and a special maneuver called the "Squirrel Cage." At the end of the performance, the announcer declared, "There's just no way of outdoing the Marines!" These demonstrations led to invitations to appear all over the United States and Canada, and the Quantico Marine pilots became the "undisputed show squadron of Marine Aviation." And although the Marines' prowess threatened the egos of Navy pilots, the Navy realized that good publicity and congressional support for Marine aviation reflected well on the Navy too. With the darlings of Marine aviation located just thirty short miles from Washington, taking visiting dignitaries to see an impromptu air show was sure to impress, and score goodwill points for the Marine Corps.

Alas, Hitler's threatening presence in Europe and looming war clouds convinced the secretary of war in 1938 that all nonmilitary aviation should be curtailed in favor of allocating time and money on

Interior of Quantico's new bachelor officers quarters, circa 1929. Courtesy National Archives, Record Group 71.

Marine aviators from Quantico made national headlines in the 1920s with visionary and record-setting flights. Major Roy Geiger and his comrades are shown here after flying four heavy bombers from San Diego to Quantico—an endurance record. Courtesy Marine Corps Historical Center.

military preparations. The carefree era of the VF-9M was over, but not before securing for Quantico a lasting reputation in the annals of Marine Corps aviation.[236]

Of course, not all the flying done at Quantico broke time and distance records, or proved as glamorous as eighteen-plane formation takeoffs. In addition to the day-to-day military flying at the airstrips at Quantico, Marine pilots executed even less exciting missions. In 1926, military pilots from Quantico participated in aerial spraying maneuvers in an attempt to quash the local mosquito population. The DeHavilland plane used in the operation was jokingly dubbed the "mosquito louse" and sprayed a lethal (to mosquitoes) powdered concoction of paris green and soapstone over the marshes surrounding Chopawamsic and Quantico Creeks. While certainly not airshow-quality adventure, the pilots of the "mosquito louse" must have enjoyed wreaking havoc on their airborne enemies, knowing

that they "wrought terrible destruction among the mosquito population here."[237]

A decade later, Marine pilots flew missions of mercy on behalf of local wildlife, albeit a more endearing variety than mosquitoes. In the winter of 1936, ducks along the Potomac managed to strand themselves on the ice-bound river, and airplanes based at Quantico were loaded with five-pound paper sacks of grain, which were then tossed to the starving birds. During a two-day period in February, over a ton of grain was distributed by the Biological Survey in this manner. Having fed the ducks, the survey team then turned its attention to conducting a census of the duck population, which would then be used to calculate the number of ducks the hunters could bag during duck season! The poor birds were sitting ducks either way. But Quantico pilots would not participate in the aerial census-taking; that honor went to the Goodyear blimp. Apparently the airplanes and dropping grain bags had so frightened the ducks at Roaches Run that the survey determined the quieter, less threatening blimp would be better for a census operation.[238]

Aviation Disasters

Building a viable and indeed successful aviation corps at Quantico came with a steep price to pay. If airplane crashes can still happen today, even with the safety measures and technological advances we take for granted in aviation, obviously early aviators literally took their lives in their hands when they entered the cockpit. One of the first fatalities at Quantico was Lieutenant Walter V. Brown, the promising aviator and star football quarterback. Brown was scheduled to participate in the 1921 bombing exercises of the German and American battleships in the Chesapeake, but upon returning from a practice flight, he apparently became lost in foggy conditions. Brown missed the airfield and instead plowed into the Potomac River, a crash which killed Brown instantly. Other reports claimed

The variety of aviation tasks and experimentation assigned to Quantico's able aviators is demonstrated by this Martin MBT heavy bomber, used in aerial bombing experiments. Martin's corporate descendant is Lockheed-Martin. Courtesy Marine Corps Historical Center.

Brown's engine stalled, causing the plane to go into a tailspin before hitting the muddy banks of the Potomac near Colonial Beach. In May 1922, the blandly named airfields No. 1 and No. 2 gained distinction by being renamed "Brown Field" in honor of the young lieutenant who gave his life for Marine Corps aviation. At the same time that Brown Field gained its name, a bridge over Chopawamsic Creek was dedicated as Minnis Bridge, to honor the memory of Captain John A. Minnis. Captain Minnis had also met his fate in a disaster along the Potomac in 1921. While practicing with the Searchlight Battalion, Captain Minnis executed a sharp dive to avoid a searchlight beam. Observers noted that when Minnis came out of the dive, he appeared to lose control of his airplane, which crashed into the bank of Quantico Creek. His body was recovered from the wreckage, which was sadly near the Quantico Hotel, where Minnis' wife and infant daughter were staying. Appropriately, the causeway spanned by the Minnis Bridge would later be transformed into an airfield.[239]

Whereas drownings and railroad accidents dominated the local news in the late 1800s, airplane tragedies dominated the Quantico accident reports in the 1920s and 1930s. After three pilots died in an unfortunate mid-air collision four thousand feet over Quantico in 1922, the *Washington Post* noted that "Quantico has, within the last year, been the scene of three serious accidents, costing, in all, five lives." If the *Post*'s tally included Quantico pilots killed in accidents elsewhere, the death toll would have risen to seven by the end of 1922, after two Quantico fliers died in a crash in Baltimore. All was quiet at Quantico until 1924, when two more pilots died when their plane crashed in Garrisonville, Virginia, while on a practice flight. And the death toll would continue to climb in the 1930s.[240]

Colonel Thomas C. Turner, who as Major Turner had set distance-flying records in 1921, also gave his life and his legacy in the name of Marine aviation. In a tragic incident in Gonaives, Haiti, in 1931, Colonel Turner was riding in a Sikorsky RS-1 transport craft that encountered a bumpy landing along the beach.

Turner exited the plane to check for damage to the fuselage, and the pilot shut off the engines. Apparently the plane's propellers had not fully stopped rotating before Turner returned to the plane, and one of the propellers struck him, cutting off part of his jaw and skull in the process. Gravely injured but still conscious, Turner died in a Port-au-Prince hospital two days later. Turner was about to become the first Marine aviator promoted to the rank of brigadier general at the time. Death cheated him out of the richly deserved promotion, but the Marine Corps decided to honor Turner's memory by naming the new airfield under construction "Turner Field." Although the field would not be completed until several years later, a dedication ceremony affixed the name to the field in 1936.[241]

Quantico and Quantico

The story of Quantico is not just the story of the Marine Corps installation, although given that the Marines surrounded the Town of Quantico on three sides, and the Potomac River took care of the fourth border, the presence of the base certainly loomed large over the village. (Technically, the Corps even owned the strip of land along the Quantico waterfront, thus adding to the natural boundary provided by the Potomac.) But this situation gave Quantico a unique status as "the town that cannot grow."[242] For the most part, the Marine Corps and the town residents have been good neighbors, especially as the town came to depend upon the goodwill of the Marines for its economic livelihood, and the Marines enjoyed their liberty outside the confines of the base.

Brown Field No. 2, in 1937. Turner Field, under construction, is seen at top of photo. "The Browns" were named for Quantico football star Second Lieutenant Walter V. Brown, who was killed in a 1920 airplane crash. Courtesy National Archives, Record Group 71.

This aerial view is one of the best available showing Quantico in relation to the Potomac River and its tributaries. Newly rerouted Chopawamsic Creek, lower left, is shown emptying dislodged silt into the river. Its original channel met the river at Chopawamsic Island, north of the four hangars on the new, and still raw, Turner Field. Undated photo circa 1937, courtesy National Archives, Record Group 71.

After the end of World War I, residents of the village at first returned to the timber trade, fishing and mining operations, and shipping industry they had followed before the Great War and before the Marines came to town. After all, so many groups before the Marines had had visions of Quantico's potential, only to be disappointed by reality, leading to abandonment of the town. Once the government bought the installation, however, and troop strength crept up with the establishment of educational centers and the East Coast branch of the Advanced Base Force, Quantico realized that the Marines had suddenly become its most viable industry. Soon more businesses catering to the Marine trade sprang up, and the economic life of the town flourished. The Town of Quantico was incorporated in

1927, and elected its first mayor, A. E. McInteer, the same year.[243]

Quantico was unlike other company towns across America in that the company did not technically own the town or its establishments, and could only exercise varying degrees of moral and economic persuasion to affect what occurred beyond the boundaries of the base. Alas, businesses focusing on the needs and wants of young Marines did not always meet with the approval of base commanders, or the commandant of the Marine Corps. The conditions he found in Quantico in 1923 horrified General Lejeune, who labeled the town "an insanitary [*sic*] place and an abode of bootleggers and other undesirable persons." Earlier in the year two Marines had died of wood alcohol poisoning after a party, and subsequent investigation led to the discovery of a vial of cocaine in the barracks. While the town was not implicated in this incident, the suspicion of bootlegging activities certainly indicated an undesirable element among the local civilian population. Lejeune's solution to the problem, as if to make the company town comparison complete, was for the Marine Corps to simply purchase the town and add it to the base property. The Marines could then control what elements operated within the town limits. Congress failed to adopt Lejeune's plan, and the unsavory elements continued to operate undisturbed.[244]

Prohibition of alcohol had become the law of the land in 1920, when the National Prohibition Enforcement Act (or Volstead Act) criminalized the manufacture or sale of intoxicating beverages with a 0.5 or higher alcohol content. While prohibition was popular enough as an idea to codify it as the Eighteenth Amendment to the Constitution, the actual enforcement of laws relating to alcohol consumption proved nearly impossible to execute.[245] Bootleg liquor distribution carried the promise of big profits, and what better venue for selling illegal alcohol than in an unregulated town adjacent to a military installation filled with young, isolated men.

The indomitable General Smedley Butler agreed wholeheartedly with Lejeune's assessment of the bad influence the town of Quantico exerted over his Marines. When he returned to Quantico in 1929 for another tour as the base's commander, he recommitted himself to making the base "a model post," but that was unlikely to happen as long as disreputable merchants in the town continued to ply Marines with "bootleg poison." "Before I came," Butler remembered, "at

least seventy men were in the brig for drunkenness every day."[246] Instead of threatening to buy the town outright in order to effect change, Butler hit the town where it really hurt: its pocketbooks. Butler instituted a boycott of the town of Quantico by the base of Quantico.

In September 1929, Butler proclaimed the town of Quantico as off-limits to enlisted men, an order to be enforced by the military police. Only special details and those carrying passes would be allowed to venture into the village. Butler invoked the Marines' constitutional obligations in explaining his decision to the men. Propping his foot on a barracks porch railing, and resting his right elbow on his knee, Butler announced, "You birds took an oath some time ago to defend the Constitution. Don't let this news stun you, but the prohibition law is part of it. I understand that there is some difference of opinion among civilians concerning the right and wrong of prohibition," he continued. "Some of it got into camp, but those on the negative idea are in the

Aerial photos are a handy by-product of having aviators assigned to base. Quantico evolution has been cataloged from the air many times since the Age of Flight began. This photo dates from 1926.

135

brig. It's a closed question for the military, and as long as you wear those uniforms, don't get opinionated."[247] Case closed.

Respectable businesses in town, such as barbershops, restaurants, and drugstores, quickly found their trade diminished by 90 percent when Butler banned their regular customers. Three days into the boycott, townspeople were ready to give General Butler anything he wanted. Butler explained to the mayor and Town Council that he had no beef with the town or its residents, but he wanted the bootleg element run out of town, and to do that Quanticans had to stop tolerating their presence. The mayor in turn asked local businesses to report any suspicious activity in town, and to stop selling bottles and caps that might be used in the illegal distribution of alcohol.[248]

A couple days later, Mayor McInteer assured General Butler that the "big bootleggers" had left town. "What about the little ones?" Butler inquired. "We think they're all gone," McInteer replied. That was not the answer Butler wanted to hear, but he assured the mayor that when ALL the bootleggers had gone, he would personally lead the Marines on a parade through Quantico, and hoped "the boys buy a lot of extras to make up for our absence." When the town finished clearing out the bootleggers, it turned to evicting the "undesirables" as well, just to ensure the bootleggers would not return. Interestingly, all the "undesirables" were African Americans, and the mayor threatened to utilize vagrancy and nuisance laws against them if they did not leave of their own accord.[249]

By September 25, General Butler was completely satisfied with the town's transformation into a haven of clean living, and lifted the ban. True to his word, Butler invited Mayor McInteer to join him at the weekly review hour on base. When the mayor arrived, the Marines on the parade ground fell into formation, and proceeded to march behind the Marine Band on a parade route through town.

New French Restaurant
Fresh Clams   **Shrimp Salad**
Crab Meat Salad

On Potomac Avenue just
across the tracks   QUANTICO, VA.

Our Mocha Coffee   *Served Hot from the Pot*   *Goes to the Right Spot*
DEVIL DOG LUNCH
Next to Post Office, Quantico, Va.

Food of the Finest Quality

NICK'S NEW WAY
LUNCH
On "C" Street Left Side of Potomac Avenue,
One Block from Station
Coffee Like Mother's and "Good Eats"
6.30 a.m. to Midnight   QUANTICO, VA.

Quantico's business expansion along Potomac Avenue provided Marines a variety of eating places and shopping venues. The New French Restaurant was not the only choice now available. Hungry for a he-man's Marine-style lunch? Try the Devil Dog. The Leatherneck, *November 26, 1921.*

Upon returning to the parade grounds, the "fall out" order was given and the men "rushed pell-mell back across the railroad tracks." "Soda parlors, drugstores, restaurants, and poolrooms were soon filled with marines," noted the *Washington Post*, "and the cash registers began to click in picnic fashion." General Butler unfortunately missed the parade itself and the "carnival spirit" in town, as he had to leave the base immediately after the review.[250]

While it had been an anxious time for the business owners in town, and the Marines deprived of their favorite hangouts, the ban ultimately improved life for everyone but the bootleggers and "undesirables." Fewer Marines died of alcohol-related traffic accidents near the base, and the town took the opportunity to rid itself of its "less upstanding citizens," and literally cleaned up the town by clearing out alleys and vacant lots of debris and weeds. The truce between the town and General Butler was tested a few months later, however, when townsfolk complained that Butler's policy of stopping every car entering the base to search for alcohol was prompting shoppers to take their business elsewhere, hurting Quantico's retail trade in the process. It would take a few more years, but ultimately the Twenty-first Amendment to the Constitution resolved the problem once and for all. Americans finally realized the prohibition on alcohol was a losing proposition, and in 1933 repealed the earlier ban on booze. While the commanders at Quantico would still be justifiably concerned about alcohol use on base and in town, and consequent drinking-and-driving fatalities, the issue was no longer a constitutional one.[251]

With the "bootleggers and bums" run out of town, Quantico and Quantico settled into an era of peaceful, prosperous, and generally happy coexistence. The base appreciated the efforts of the town to provide a healthy environment in which the Marines could enjoy a little liberty, and the town prospered by ministering to the needs of the Corps.

The Great Depression

Quantico could also count its blessings with the proximity of the Marine Corps when the Great Depression hit the United States following the stock market crash in October 1929. The *Grapes of Wrath* and bread-line scenes most Americans associate with the Depression never occurred in Quantico, nor in most parts of Virginia. While the Depression certainly affected the lives of many Virginians, in comparison with other states, its impact was less severe and the effect of New Deal programs relatively minimal. Several factors account for Virginia's comparatively easy passage through the Depression. By 1930, Virginia as a state had diversified its economy enough between industry, agriculture, and business, that a hit to one section would not topple

Quantico's humble stores were more inviting than their architecture suggests—this one sold the highly popular Fussell's ice cream, made in what is now Arlington County by a local family whose descendants are still in the area and own the original machinery and—more important—highly coveted recipe. National Archives, Record Group 71.

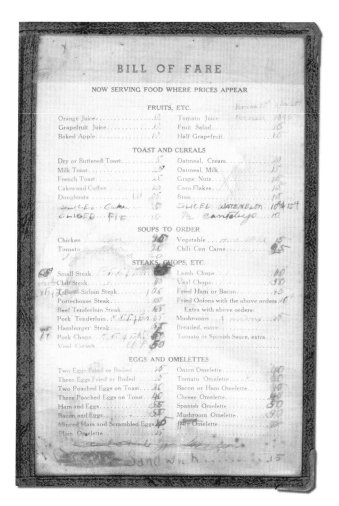

Pete Raftelis's popular Star Lunch Room, along Quantico's Potomac Avenue, fed many appreciative Marines during its day. Raftelis, the man in the tie standing by the table, offered an affordable menu, also shown here. Courtesy Mitchel P. Raftelis.

the whole economy. Despite a severe drought the first year of the Depression, Virginia farmers never experienced the Dust Bowl conditions of the Midwest, and could usually produce enough to feed themselves and their families, even if they did not always commercially profit from their labors. Furthermore, farmers and the poor, by virtue of their continuous poverty, were somewhat "depression proof" in that they had been poor before the Depression, and had already developed ways of coping with poverty. Virginia also maintained its reputation for fiscal conservatism in the 1930s, refusing to go into debt to supplement work relief and dole projects provided by the federal government. While this policy brought the state into conflict with Washington and some of its own suffering residents, Virginia's credit rating stayed high, few banks closed, and few of its residents relied directly on the dole since most of Virginia's projects focused on

work relief. Also, lacking a substantial middle class, which unemployment hit the hardest nationally, Virginia's unemployment figures remained low during the worst of the Depression. "The Virginia of 1939 was remarkably similar to that of ten years earlier," concluded historian Ronald Heinemann.[252]

The Depression and the New Deal did come to Quantico in several ways, however. Having the Marine Corps as neighbors assured the town that their businesses would survive since the troops would still get paid, and those men would still spend their pay in Quantico. Moreover, the installation at Quantico qualified for federally funded work-relief projects, primarily in the form of construction projects that continued the building boom Quantico began in the mid-1920s. The drought of 1930 did temporarily deplete the supply of both water and Marines in Quantico during the summer, however. In an effort to conserve water on base and in town until a larger capacity holding tank could be constructed, seven hundred Marines received special liberty for several days in August.[253]

The Civilian Conservation Corps (CCC) proved immensely popular in Virginia, because it combined ideas of self-help and work relief by employing young men to create new state parks, restore historic sites, work in national forests, and generally beautify the natural environment.[254] The closest CCC camp to Quantico was the 2349th Company, organized in nearby Joplin in 1935. The men assigned to this camp, nicknamed "Camp Fare-Thee-Well," worked on a creating a recreation area near Joplin. In addition to their prescribed duties, the young men at Joplin fielded successful athletic teams, took classes in vocational education, held dances, and published a camp newspaper. Reflecting the regional diversity of the men in Company 2349, the newspaper carried the name *Dixie Yankee*. They also interacted with the Marines at Quantico, and as thanks for being allowed to use the gymnasium at Quantico and the Marines' reserved balcony at the

The Great Depression caused economic suffering in the Quantico area. In 1933 the government began construction of the Chopawamsic Recreational Demonstration Area—the site of today's Prince William Forest National Park, adjacent to Quantico's military reservation. This local man, a Civilian Conservation Corps laborer at the site, must have felt quite lucky; jobs were scarce. Ironically, numerous area families, most of them poor, were uprooted by the government when it appropriated the lands. Courtesy Library of Congress. LC–USF3301–002325–M3

movies, the men of the 2349th sent a detail to Quantico to be put to work in whatever way the Marines could use them, which included landscaping and general cleanup.[255]

Prince William Forest Park also owes its development to the New Deal, as it was authorized as a National Park Service and Civilian Conservation Corps project in 1933. The park was originally called the Chopawamsic Recreational Demonstration Area, and was one of only three demonstration areas nationally to become a national park, rather than a state park. The government's reclamation of the fifteen thousand acres originally included in the park meant the displacement of hundreds of residents already living there. Since the land chosen for the park had been labeled as "agriculturally submarginal," the families toiling on the land were the least financially able to make a new start elsewhere. But this acreage has since flourished as a national park, and provides habitats for a profusion of plants and animals, both ordinary and endangered.[256]

Rest and Recreation

"Maybe you think Quantico is just an ordinary post where 'they ain't nothin' to do.' Well, buddy, you're all wrong. Quantico has things to amuse the Marines which any city of 10,000 inhabitants, let alone any service camp, would point out with pride." Perhaps "H. K." overstated the case of Quantico as an idyllic military resort in his "Bits O' Mud from Quantico" column in *The Leatherneck*, but entertainment and recreation could certainly occupy a great deal of a Marine's hours off duty if he chose to pursue any of the many diversions Quantico offered.[257]

From the base's very beginning, motion pictures provided a reliable source of quality entertainment for the troops. Before there were any buildings at the base capable of accommodating large crowds, outdoor screens erected near the corner of Broadway and Potomac Avenues allowed Marines to watch the latest celluloid shows under the stars. Once an early gymnasium was built, Marines could enjoy a succession of films, regardless of the time of year or the weather. The gym boasted a $25,000 organ, "bought and paid for in greater part by the enlisted personnel," to provide musical accompaniment to the silent features shown on the screen. On many nights a Marine with nothing else planned could spend an entire night in the gym, with a packed entertainment schedule before him. The program would begin with a concert from one of bands at the post, then move to "a high-grade comedy photoplay packed with laughs," followed by a sing-along of popular songs, and capped off by the featured movie. Unlike modern movie houses which show the same titles for weeks at a time, the "Palais de Cinema" in the Quantico gymnasium showed a different movie nearly every night. A typical schedule in late 1921 included *The Three Musketeers*, staring Douglas Fairbanks, *The Queen of Sheba*, *A Connecticut Yankee in King Arthur's Court*, and Rudyard Kipling's drama *Without Benefit of Clergy*. The opening films varied depending on the day of the week with Pathe newsreels on Sundays and Thursdays, Mack Sennett comedies on Tuesdays, Kiddie Komedies on Fridays, and Harold Lloyd, Buster Keaton, and Charlie Chaplin shorts on selected Wednesdays. And what did all this entertainment cost a Marine? Absolutely nothing. Marines and their families could enjoy the show for free. Well, the Marines and their guests might have to endure a pep talk by General Butler, who liked to address the men at the pictures, although his closest audience were the children who received the honor of sitting up front.[258]

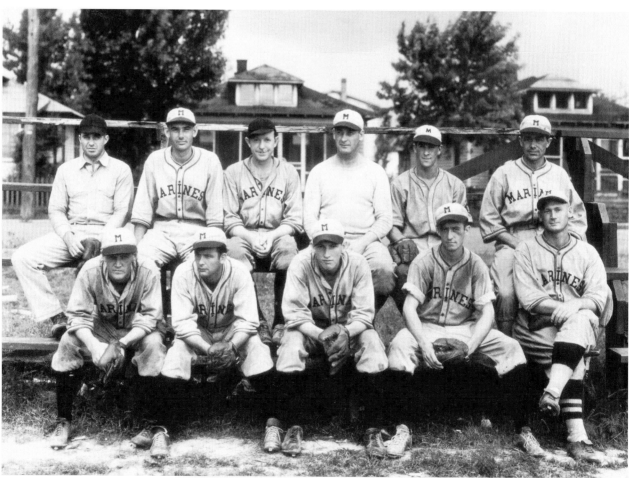

Baseball also established itself as a popular sport at Quantico, despite or perhaps because of the leadership's previous passion and backing for football. The team is shown at Freeny Field with the bungalows of the town's Fifth Avenue in the background. Courtesy base archive.

This close-up of Quantico's baseball team during the 1930s must have been taken at an away game—Quantico did not boast a stadium with seating such as that in the background of this photo. Courtesy Mitchel P. Raftelis.

Sometimes the tables were turned and the Marines at Quantico were *in* the movies, rather than just watching them. With the burgeoning film industry coming into its own just about the time World War I broke out in Europe, it was inevitable that new productions would from time to time focus on the Marines' participation in the Great War. What better place to re-create the trenches of France on film than at Quantico, which could offer film producers ready-made training trenches? One of the first motion pictures filmed on location at Quantico was *The Unbeliever*, a silent motion picture released in 1918. The film, the last produced by Edison Studios, enjoyed great box office success at the time, drawing 150,000 moviegoers in Detroit alone. Unfortunately life imitated art too closely in

this picture. Since it had been filmed at Quantico while the war was still underway, many of the Quantico Marines shown going "over the top" on film were then sent to France to go "over the top" for real. In fact, at least two of the Marines with roles in the film, Sergeant Moss Gill and Lieutenant James Rorke, later were seriously wounded during the war.[259]

Like all other Americans, the Marines at Quantico enjoyed listening to music and popular programs on the radio. But in the fall of 1938, Marines who tuned in late to a "Mercury Theater" broadcast might have thought they would be called out for a national emergency that very evening. On Sunday, October 30, 1938, Americans were stunned to hear a radio announcer declare that Martians had

141

invaded the Earth (specifically New Jersey), and were killing innocent people with heat rays. One "observer" described an attack to the radio audience: "I can make out a small beam of light against a mirror. What's that? There's a jet of flame springing from the mirror, and it leaps right at the advancing men. It strikes them head on! Good Lord, they're turning into flame!" By the end of the program, Americans understood that the U.S. Army had been called out to face the alien invaders, and New York City had been evacuated. And by the end of the program, a substantial part of the American population was in a complete panic.[260]

What was actually going on was a radio adaptation of H. G. Wells' book *The War of the Worlds*, being staged as a Halloween show on the "Mercury Theater" by the brilliant young writer-director-actor Orson Welles. The program began with an announcer explaining that it was a fictional story, but anyone who turned in after this disclaimer, or missed those occurring later in the broadcast, could easily think the world was coming to an end. Including impressionable young Marines at Quantico. On November 1, the *Washington Post* reported that "hard-boiled United States Marines wept and prayed in their barracks at Quantico, Va., in

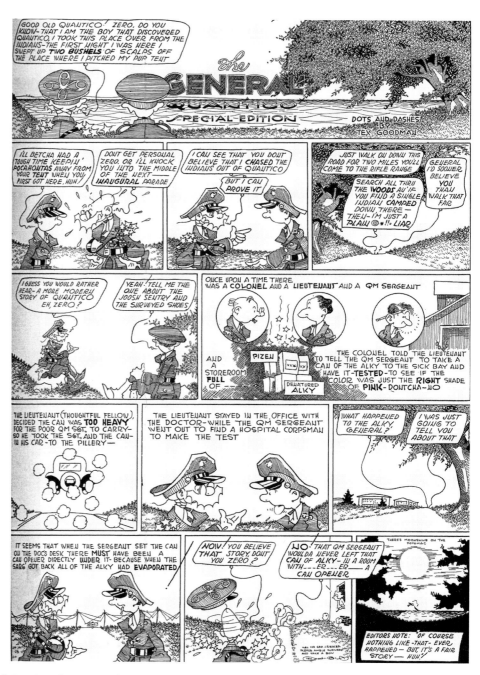

. . . Or did it happen? The Leatherneck, *May 1933.*

the wave of terror which swept the country." The *Post* received its intelligence from an anonymous Marine who had rushed back to Quantico from Washington, knowing that the Marines would be called out first in an emergency. At Quantico he found his frightened comrades complaining that "they didn't want to go to war in the winter," not to mention one involving Martians from outer space.[261]

This newspaper report created an even bigger furor at Quantico than had the initial broadcast.

Civic organizations in Quantico town have always been important to the town's life and heritage. Shown here are local Boy Scouts. Mitchel P. Raftelis, at right, would choose to make "Q-town" his lifelong home, and, over five decades later, become its mayor. Courtesy Mitchel P. Raftelis.

The "hard-boiled" Marines vigorously denied the report, and the base commander General James C. Breckinridge stated that his men understood perfectly that the show was just that . . . a show. In fact, the enlisted men claimed that only one radio at the barracks was tuned to "Mercury Theater," and those listening to the program showed "no sign of the slightest excitement." The men figured that the newspaper report had been planted by a Marine as an ill-conceived prank on his friends, but prank or not, the *Post* report raised the ire of one Quantico Marine to the point of writing a letter to the editor. "The way you print your papers, you will have the people of Washington thinking there is not a brave man left in the United States," he complained. "What you said in your paper about Quantico Marines weeping and praying was untrue. They don't pray and don't weep." The post chaplain may have disagreed with the assertion that real Marines did not pray, but the Quantico Marine expressed his conviction that the editor would not have the "guts"

to print his letter anyway. But the editor decided to prove him wrong, thus ending speculation about the backbone of the Marines at Quantico.[262]

Technology aside, Quantico Marines enjoyed old-fashioned pleasures as well. The gymnasium hosted boxing matches and basketball games, which the men who observed and participated in found enjoyable. In the summer and fall, baseball and football matches added to the sporting events available to the men at Quantico. Except when the troops left on maneuvers and the base took on a deserted look, Quantico rarely failed to offer a number of social opportunities to the men. Officers in particular joined the social whirl at Quantico. The Officers' Club hosted bimonthly dances on Friday evenings, and these events often included dinner parties prior to the dance itself. Social columns reprinted in the *Washington Post* noted a profusion of dinner parties and bridge club get-togethers attended by officers and their wives. Not to be outdone, the enlisted men at Quantico hosted their own monthly "hops" in the gaily decorated gymnasium, attracting "visitors of the fair sex from Washington, D.C., and the flower of Virginian femininity." *The Leatherneck* printed a photograph of one such hop held in 1933, which shows the men in their dress uniforms tripping the light fantastic with beauties in flowing dresses.[263]

Beginning in 1935 everyone at Quantico became well informed about the goings on in town and on base with the inauguration of the *Quantico Sentry* newspaper. The newspaper was conceived as a publication "for Marines by Marines and written with the dignity and traditions of the U.S. Marine Corps," even though the newspaper's first publisher was a woman, Mrs. Ruth Chambers Hamner. Mrs. Hamner came to the Marine Corps through her husband, Colonel George Hamner, a career Marine who served all over the United States and in Haiti. Her two sons and one of her daughters also followed their father into the Corps. While her husband was stationed at Quantico, it occurred to

Mrs. Hamner, the daughter of a newspaper man, that the Marine Corps deserved to have a first-class newspaper on base, and she secured permission from Commandant Russell to start one. "The general was enthusiastic," Mrs. Hamner later recalled. "He told me that it sounded like the best thing to happen to Quantico since the invention of the wheel!" With her friend Chaplain August Hohl on board, the two sketched out what the paper should look like and arranged for a publisher. Six months later, the first issue of the *Sentry* appeared on May 31, 1935. The paper quickly took off, and Hamner began to receive subscription orders from Marines around the world who had either served at Quantico or were interested in the content of the newspaper. This far-flung subscriber base inspired Mrs. Hamner to include sections devoted to the news from other posts, like San Diego and Parris Island. The *Sentry* was also unusual in being a completely civilian enterprise dependant largely on subscriptions and advertising for funding. This status gave the paper freedom from military restrictions,

and allowed the *Sentry* to report news in an honest and unbiased manner. In 1936, the paper was sold to Mrs. Clara Margaret Payne and Miss Daphne Dailey, who as "D. F. Dailey" served as a reporter, editor, and owner, without tipping off readers to the fact that she was a woman. The *Sentry* continued under civilian control until July 1944, when staff at Marine Barracks, Quantico, took over publication. Despite changes in ownership, the *Sentry* went on to become the Marine Corps' "oldest continuously published base newspaper," and one which continues to be published today.[264]

Hail to the Chief

Quantico's reputation, established during the 1890s, as a playground for presidents continued apace after the World War. President Warren G. Harding and a group of friends sailed to Quantico aboard the presidential yacht *Mayflower* on August 27, 1922. This may have been Harding's only visit to Quantico, as he suffered a fatal stroke the next year. Harding's successor, Calvin Coolidge, continued the tradition

The establishment in 1937 of Piney Echo, a Civilian Conservation Corps camp on the Quantico border, presaged major recreational facilities to come. The CCC planted Prince William Forest on what had been open fields. The Forest, now a beautiful national park, is adjacent to Quantico. Courtesy Prince William County Public Library.

Camp Piney Echo's men were allowed frequent use of Quantico's facilities, as their camp had none. This page from the Dixie Yankee, *the camp newspaper, reveals they were little different from Marines—see the cartoon in bottom left corner. Courtesy Prince William County Public Library.*

of presidential visits to the area, taking advantage of a lovely spring day in April 1924 for a cruise down the Potomac on the *Mayflower*. The presidential party enjoyed dinner on board the yacht before returning to Washington the same day. The Coolidges also decided to spend the afternoon of Easter Sunday 1924 cruising on the river, and anticipated going just as far as Quantico before heading home. The president and Mrs. Coolidge returned again twice in December, both times spending the night at anchor off Quantico.[265]

President Franklin D. Roosevelt, a devotee of all things nautical, not surprisingly followed his predecessors in planning river cruises to Quantico. Roosevelt, however, could not cruise on the *Mayflower*, which President Herbert Hoover had sold after determining that a presidential yacht was a luxury not worth the expense of maintaining. So the *Sequoia* took the *Mayflower*'s place during a weekend cruise to Quantico in May 1933. Instead of sailing to and from Quantico, however, Roosevelt took a drive to the Marine base, then boarded the *Sequoia* at Quantico. This unusual tour did allow the officers of the Marine barracks to see their president and have the honor of greeting him. According to locals, FDR would ride through town in an open touring car guarded by motorcycle policemen. In true Rooseveltian style, he would jauntily wave his signature cigarette holder to greet bystanders.[266]

Roosevelt returned in July for another weekend cruise, during which he promised to "catch a fish this time." Whether he was successful in this vow, the newspapers did not report, but once again the residents and Marines at Quantico cheered the president and his party as they boarded. Eleanor Roosevelt did not accompany her husband on most of these trips, but among the other familiar faces were Secretary Henry Wallace, advisor Louis Howe, and Roosevelt's dedicated secretary Missy LeHand. September 1933 found the president back again,

this time on the Astor family yacht, *Nourmahal*. FDR spent the final night of his trip at Quantico, after having visited George Washington's birthplace on the Northern Neck, and hooking a hundred-pound sea turtle. The president must not have had much luck on his previous fishing expeditions as the turtle catch "was cause for jubilation not only aboard the yacht but also on the accompanying destroyers, *Manley* and *Twiggs*."[267]

Yet more of the Roosevelt family appeared in Quantico in September 1933. After talking over possible military operations in Cuba with authorities at Quantico, FDR sailed off for an overnight fishing trip. However, his departure was delayed by his son, James. The young Roosevelt, a pilot, flew from Boston to Quantico to join his father and presidential advisor Harry Hopkins. Over the next several years, President Roosevelt would become a familiar face in the neighborhood of Quantico as he continued to take weekend cruises down the river. With the Great Depression still raging, the work of the president and architect of the New Deal was never done. But even when FDR composed speeches on board the *Sequoia* and attended to other governmental affairs, the change of scene and leisurely pace of cruising along the Potomac must have unburdened the president at least a little of the pressures of his office. These trips to Quantico often included close friends and advisors, people who invigorated the president and allowed him to relax. In 1937, however, Roosevelt came to Quantico to throw out the opening ball at a baseball game between newspapermen and members of Congress at the National Press Club's "annual frolic." As usual, FDR planned to drive to Quantico, and then board the *Sequoia* for the trip back to Washington. In honor of the occasion, the Marines scheduled a land and air demonstration. Unfortunately, Mother Nature had other ideas, and sent forth a torrential rainstorm just as the game was to get underway, drenching many of the visitors, including FDR.

Left: The presidential yacht Mayflower *berthed at Quantico's pier or just offshore many times before President Herbert Hoover sold the vessel as a cost-cutting measure.* Mayflower *bore a commendable pedigree: after serving in the Spanish-American War, she later served twice as Admiral Dewey's flagship. National Photo Company, courtesy Library of Congress. LC–USZ62–97440*

Despite the weather, a good time was had by all. To the refrain of "It Ain't Gonna Rain No More," provided by the Navy Band, the president boarded the *Sequoia* for a weekend trip, while other visitors enjoyed a Marine boxing match and buffet dinner on base.[268]

The Gathering Storm

In the decades following the end of the Great War, Quantico had been a busy place. Permanent structures made an imprint on the base. Smedley Butler's public relations campaigns of football games, bulldog mascots, and Civil War reenactments, in addition to fantastic Marine fliers, had kept the Marines active and in the public eye. Development of amphibious warfare tactics and participation in staged maneuvers, as well as police actions in China and Latin America, had kept the Marines in a state of military readiness. But despite the perpetual hum of activity and the growing pains at Quantico, it had been a period of peace for the Marines. But that was about to change.

The armistice agreement that ended World War I sowed the seeds for lingering resentments in Europe, particularly on the part of Germany, which felt humiliated by the terms of surrender in 1919. While America enjoyed "normalcy," conditions in Germany facilitated the rise of Adolf Hitler, who

President Franklin Delano Roosevelt, as he looked early during his lengthy presidency. A former assistant navy secretary, Roosevelt loved the water and all things nautical—including his voyages to Quantico. Pach Brothers photo, courtesy Library of Congress. LC–USZ62–90270

tapped a nerve of German nationalism by vowing to return the nation to a place of international honor. Italy had also fallen under the sway of Mussolini's "Brown Shirts," while Japan seemed to be fulfilling Pete Ellis' prophecy of achieving domination in the Pacific. All the pieces were in place for another global confrontation between democratic nations and totalitarian states.

CHAPTER VI

WORLD

1941–1945

WAR II

Igniting the Gigantic Boiler

As the New Year dawned, Americans certainly looked to the future with trepidation. War had been raging in Europe since 1939, and the isolationist policies the United States had been following since the end of World War I were becoming increasingly difficult to sustain. Hindered by neutrality acts, but wanting to aid Allied nations, President Franklin D. Roosevelt negotiated "cash-and-carry" and "lend-lease" arrangements in order to provide Allied nations with desperately needed materiel of war while still maintaining the façade of neutrality. The fall of France to the Germans in June 1940, however, disturbed America's confidence that the Allies would be able to contain Hitler's armies. Only the completely naïve convinced themselves that the United States could remain isolated indefinitely. President Roosevelt was certainly not among the naïve, and geared the military up for possible war by declaring a limited emergency in 1940. Taking a cue from the president, the Marine Corps slowly began preparing for war. The Corps increased its troop strength to thirty-four thousand men, and deferred many officers' retirements. Quantico received $1 million in emergency construction funds to improve its airstrips and build a post exchange. In February, the amphibious Fleet Marine Forces at Quantico and San Diego were redesignated as the 1st and 2nd Marine Divisions, and their aviation units likewise became the 1st and 2nd Marine Aircraft Wings.[269]

Still, life went on in Quantico, even if under the shadow of war. In August, Alma Carroll, an eighteen-year-old beauty queen from Los Angeles, won the title of "Miss America of National Defense." As part of her prize, Miss Carroll won a trip to Quantico to visit with the Marines there. One wonders whether Miss Carroll or the Marines themselves were the bigger winners in the pageant. Secretary of the Navy Frank Knox came to Quantico in November, just after the German navy sank two American ships. The secretary addressed a graduat-

"Air raid on Pearl Harbor—This is not drill" read the chilling and urgent Navy dispatch flashed to commands and fleet units from Hawaii as the Japanese surprise attack was underway. Quantico's copy of the flash has since been lost. This identical copy was received by the USS Ranger, *an aircraft carrier returning to Norfolk from sea patrol when the attack occurred. Courtesy Library of Congress.*

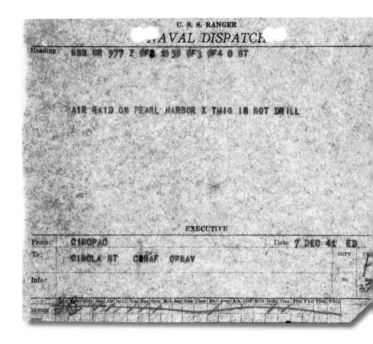

ing class, and advised the men that they lived in exciting times. "You are lucky to get a chance to play a man's part," he told them, clearly considering defensive hostilities to be inevitable. "For every one of you there is a hundred who want your place." But on that day, November 1, 1941, their military "place" remained in a peacetime military. As confirmation, the biggest news stories on the front page of the December 5th edition of the *Quantico Sentry* dealt with a horse show to take place in Quantico on December 6, available tickets for a Dramatic Club production, and a photograph of Colonel Pickett cutting a cake in honor of the Marine Corps birthday at the Officers' Club at Pearl Harbor.[270]

Quantico's quiet base commissary, shown in May 1941, was hopelessly inadequate for the crush of new customers who would soon be headed its way. Courtesy Marine Corps Historical Center.

Then on the morning of December 7, 1941, the Commander in Chief of the Pacific, the highest-ranking Navy officer in Hawaii, sent a brief dispatch to the primary commands and fleet units in the Navy. The two sentence fragments contained in this message would change the course of world history: "AIR RAID ON PEARL HARBOR [stop] THIS IS NOT DRILL." It did not take long for news of the attack to reach the mainland, prompting Secretary Knox to place a hurried phone call to President Roosevelt, interrupting a meeting between the president and Harry Hopkins. "Mr. President," Knox began, "it looks like the Japanese have attacked Pearl Harbor."[271]

After the president absorbed the news and met with military advisors, he drafted a message to Congress, in which he requested a declaration of war be issued against the Japanese. Just after noon, on December 8, Roosevelt addressed a joint session of Congress, beginning his message with a phrase which itself would outlive the age. "Yesterday, December 7, 1941—a date which will live in infamy—the United States of America was suddenly and deliberately attacked by naval and air forces of the Empire of Japan." In asking that Congress

declare war on Japan, Roosevelt reminded his listeners that "always will we remember the character of the onslaught against us. No matter how long it may take us to overcome this premeditated invasion, the American people in their righteous might will win through to absolute victory."[272] There was little doubt in anyone's mind that Japan had just brought the United States officially into World War II, and indeed, Congress immediately granted the declaration of war Roosevelt requested. Germany declared war against the United States several days later, and Roosevelt's congressional mandate was accordingly changed to include action against the Third Reich as well.

British Prime Minister Winston Churchill had reason to rejoice over these events. While certainly not pleased by the horrendous loss of American lives and materiel in Pearl Harbor, the British had been waging war against Germany since the fall of 1939, and America's declarations of war against Japan and Germany promised that American might would bolster the Allied war effort. The attack on Pearl Harbor brought forth to Churchill's mind an opinion Sir

Edward Grey had expressed about the United States three decades earlier. Grey compared the nation to "a gigantic boiler. Once the fire is lighted under it there is no limit to the power it can generate."[273]

Quantico Responds

"News of the Far Eastern assault struck Quantico Marines and the nation like a bombshell," the *Quantico Sentry* reported on December 12. "But after the first flurry of excitement subsided, this post began reacting to the dramatic situation with marked calmness." Acceptance was the word of the hour for those in Quantico, whose livelihoods, after all, depended on military preparedness. "I don't particularly enjoy the idea of going to war," conceded one noncommissioned officer. "I've been in a couple of them, and they are not pleasant. But this is my job." The wives of Quantico Marines displayed equal fortitude at the prospect of their own roles in the upcoming conflict. Mrs. Louis Little, the wife of Quantico's commander, steeled herself with experience. "During the last war I served with the American Red Cross overseas," she explained. "I would go back today if my services were needed." With the expansion of the Corps to over one hundred thousand men just weeks after Pearl Harbor, Marine wives also needed to prepare to send their husbands off to war.[274]

What the Marines needed first from their wives and civilian neighbors was cooperation. Uncertainty as to German and Japanese plans for invasion led to precautionary blackouts on both the East and West Coasts. Quantico's proximity to Washington and its importance as a military training center made it a prime target for the enemy, which prompted the initiation of many blackout drills during the war. One of the first came just days after Pearl Harbor, primarily as a trial run. Planes flew over Quantico for a twenty-minute period, and reported that some residents had forgotten to turn off their lights when they left home. Authorities suggested that each citizen be diligent about extinguishing all lights when not at home and "consider himself an air raid warden with a personal responsibility for the success of future blackouts." Future blackouts would be announced with whistle signals. After hearing the signal, street lights were to be extinguished, residents should turn off all lights visible from the outside, the movie theater (if in operation) would be evacuated with the minimum lights necessary for public safety, drivers should park their cars and extinguish the headlights, and Marines in the barracks would scatter around the base. Whistle signals of different duration would announce the "all clear" when appropriate.[275] Further modifications to these procedures were issued a week later and included orders that all

Shipping Point with its imposing Naval Hospital, and the town of Quantico in the background, shown here in 1941 before the outbreak of war, were quiet places—but not for long. Courtesy Mitchel P. Raftelis.

Left: The commissary provided an essential means of existence for Quantico's families during World War II. Shown here is Mrs. H. T. Nicholas, whose husband was serving abroad in the South Pacific. The Leatherneck, *March 1944.*

Bottom left: Commissary staff took their duties seriously. With consumer rationing in effect, proper inventory control was all the more important, as stocks could not be easily replenished. The Leatherneck, *March 1944.*

Below: Rationing was a necessary headache and pain for the commissary staff, as it was for consumers. Everything had to be paid for with ration coupons or money—the same as for families shopping at the commissary. The Leatherneck, *March 1944.*

lights visible from outside buildings would be extinguished after 11 p.m. These orders included the base and the town of Quantico. While the town was officially a distinct entity from the base, Quantico residents certainly did not object to military orders designed to protect them from enemy attack.

While even practice blackouts were serious affairs, some Marines took preparedness to a higher level than perhaps necessary. One unfortunate cook wore white trousers on the day of the drill. As he was on his way out of the building, the mess sergeant stopped him, telling him that he could not wear white clothing during a blackout. Alas, the cook's greens were still at the cleaners. So what is an order-obeying Marine to do under such circumstances? Why, throw on his overcoat and proceed outside . . . sans trousers of any sort![276] One can only hope his bare legs were less white than his trousers.

Defense officials held yet another blackout in the Washington, D.C. area in June 1942, including

Quantico in the blackout radius. Officials hypothesized that enemy planes would first drop bombs on Bluefield and Abingdon, Virginia, and might attack Washington on the way back to waiting aircraft carriers. Thus, the practice drill included a staggered warning system, with Washington receiving its warning after western Virginia. Officials encouraged the public to stay home during the all-night blackout, both to test the efficiency of home equipment and to avoid having too many curious folks going outside "to see the blackout." Automobiles were permitted on the roads only in cases of emergency and if equipped with special "blackout driving lights."[277] Thankfully, the feared enemy attack never came, and all the blackout measures remained practice runs.

Quantico did experience another kind of blackout very early in the war, but a communications blackout rather than an electrical one. Late in December 1941, Captain James P. Berkeley, director of Quantico's communications system, received a

Tent cities were erected at Quantico to handle the new wartime arrivals. This one featured wooden walkways called duckboards. The camp commander's tent is behind the sentry. Courtesy base archive.

mysterious order to shut down all telephone and telegraph communication between Quantico and the outside world. Heightening the mystery, Virginia state police closed parts of Route 1. Four hours later, Quantico emerged from its communication blackout to discover that Prime Minister Winston Churchill had arrived in Washington to confer with President Roosevelt about the war. Only then did Quantico discover it had been designated as Churchill's secret alternative arrival point, had something prevented his landing in Washington.

This would not be the last time Quantico served as a safe alternative to Washington, or indeed a meeting place in its own right. Its geographic proximity to Washington, always a selling point where Quantico was concerned, made it a close and feasible alternative. Gasoline rationing during the war also made Quantico an attractive location, as did its military presence and experience with blackout drills.[278]

"Nothing Is Impossible"

While the war may have been a new conflict (or perhaps a series of old conflicts under a new name), Quantico's primary role in the war remained a traditional one: education. That established function would, however, include new schools for new circumstances, and operate at warp speed. The Marines in training at Quantico may have enjoyed the comforts of home compared to their comrades stationed elsewhere in the world, but they understood the importance of refining their understanding of amphibious warfare and operated under the assumption that "nothing is impossible." The schools at Quantico would put this philosophy to the test during World War II, training fifteen thousand second lieutenants and twenty thousand additional officers for service before the end of the war.[279]

As the needs of the Marine Corps shifted over the war years, the schools and specialized units at Quantico came and went accordingly. In January 1942, a battalion of the 5th Marines was detached from the 1st Marine Division to train at Quantico as the 1st Separate Battalion. Successful British and Chinese guerrilla forces convinced the Corps that its amphibious forces would benefit by having Marine commandos at the ready, and the 1st Separate Battalion, renamed the 1st Raider Battalion, studied landings and raids behind enemy lines before being shipped off to Guadalcanal in 1942.[280]

A little less daring, but no less necessary to the Corps, the School of Quartermaster Administration opened in February 1942 with a beginning class of two hundred enlisted men and thirty officers. Graduates of this school were trained as supply specialists, challenged with ensuring the smooth operation of supply lines. Apparently the specialists did their job superbly, as this school closed before the end of the war.[281]

One of the more interesting schools developed at Quantico during World War II was the Marine

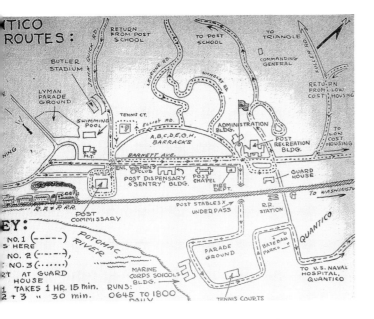

Marines Hold First Evening Mass at Quantico

Rules of the Catholic church providing that celebration of mass be confined to the morning hours have been relaxed for members of the Army, Navy and Marine Corps so that mass may be said at any time during the day until 7:30 in the evening.

Relaxation of the church rules prohibiting celebration of mass after noon was requested by Archbishop Francis J. Spellman, head of the Army and Navy Diocese, to whom it was pointed out that under present rules servicemen called to duty in the early morning hours have little oportunity to maintain a close contact with their religion.

Under the new ruling by Archbishop Spellman, mass was celebrated June 15 at the Marine Corps Base at Quantico by Lt. Paul J. Redmond, O.P., Post chaplain, at 6:00 P. M.—believed to be the first evening mass ever said within the territorial limits of the United States. Mass will be celebrated at the base on Mondays and Fridays at this hour for the remainder of the war. Though the mass is said primarily for members of the arm—

(Continued on Page 8)

(Official U.S.M.C. Photographs)

Above: Quantico's burgeoning population, whose automobiles were grounded by tire and gas rationing, used a popular base-wide bus system for transit to and from Quantico's many points. Quantico Sentry, April 19, 1945.

Right: Catholicism got surprisingly short shrift at Quantico, as throughout the military, during World War II. Masses were not celebrated until June 1942. These poor-quality newspaper photos show the first mass at Quantico, in which many of the men pictured passed up supper in order to be present. Quantico Sentry, June 26, 1942.

Corps Photographic Section, whose mission was literally to "Tell it to the Marines" by creating instructional films used to train officers and enlisted men all over the world. This unit produced pictures which "show realistically and describe understandably the very same methods which other Marines have used to save their own lives or to snuff out the lives of the enemies of our country, which amounts to the same thing in the long run." Other films updated Marines on changes in tactics and weapons, or anticipated problems Marines might encounter in the future, and visually demonstrated means of handling these situations. The unit filmed on location when possible, typically eschewing stunt men or set props, with the philosophy that if a Marine knew he was viewing a real Marine in action, he would be more confident that "if the other fellow can do it, he can do it too." With the introduction of training films, some observers estimated that the training time for certain combat subjects could be reduced by two-thirds, a crucial savings in time as men were needed overseas. The professional quality of these films came as no accident, since the Marines filled the unit with Hollywood veterans who had worked for some of the biggest studios in the film industry. Even the Walt Disney Studios provided animators to create animated training films and other illustrative materials for the Marines. Quantico served as the main distribution center for films produced by the Photographic Section and other branches of the military, making sure that the film libraries of Marine bases around the world had the instructional materials they needed to train their men. The Still Camera and Film Strip Section also came under the jurisdiction of the Photographic Section, and had the critical job of training combat photographers.[282]

Those Marines dealing with ammunition and the firing of it were not lost in the educational whirl. The Ordnance School opened in April 1942, with

Live machine gun bullets enliven Quantico's blitz course experience for this new Marine officer in 1942. The experience was prelude to what Marines would find in countless European and South Pacific battles. Courtesy National Archives, Record Group 127.

the purpose of demonstrating the capabilities of artillery and teaching students how to keep artillery operational under the most challenging conditions. Maintenance responsibilities included "artillery weapons, antiaircraft guns, fire control directors, range finders, gasoline-electric power plants, gyrostabilized guns in light tanks," just to name a few. While it seems obvious that to "keep 'em firing" in the field, someone needed the expertise to service weapons, the Ordnance School initially got underway thanks to the labors of individuals who literally begged and borrowed enough textbooks and equip-

ment from throughout the armed services to start their own school of instruction from scratch. Artillery officers variously trained at Quantico with the Marine Corps Schools Training Battalion or the Field Artillery Training Battalion. By 1944, training artillery officers had become the third largest program, superceded only by officer candidate training and the Reserve Officer Course.[283]

Although the Basic School became one of the schools most associated with Quantico, during the war it physically operated in Philadelphia, where it had moved in 1923 from lack of space at Quantico.

It did, however, remain under Quantico's intellectual control during this period. Quantico did offer a number of other officer training schools including the Officer Candidates Class, Platoon Leaders Class, and Reserve Officers Class. These schools concentrated on producing skilled junior officers, which the Corps needed in abundance during the war. Higher level officers who had mastered the basic skills were largely left to advance their education in the field. Skilled instructors were simply too valuable in the field to be spared for the classrooms, and the senior schools were all but closed during the war.[284]

Nor did Quantico forget that Marines could be "Devil Dogs" in the most literal sense. In January 1943, the Marine Corps Dog School opened at Quantico with a beginning class of fourteen Dobermans. For two months these "students" received training in scouting and security duties, before being transferred to a site near Camp Lejeune.[285] While this school might have sounded a little far-fetched, dogs proved their worth over and over again during the war, for their excellent sense of smell and direction in scouting out enemy territory, and for the companionship they provided their human comrades.

Despite the fact that most battles in World War II would be fully mechanized affairs, military preparedness at Quantico anticipated circumstances where only beasts of burden would do, and accordingly the post stables became part of the Marines training program. Students from Artillery and Staff Command Schools received equestrian training designed to acquaint them with the care, packing and riding of horses, and the vagaries of animal transport. Sergeant Adolph Rocheleau, in charge of the stables, pronounced himself pleased with the men he had trained, commenting that "some of them wouldn't make bad stable hands, either!"[286]

Marine officers were not the only ones who advanced their educations at Quantico during World War II, however. Wars might reduce crime on the homefront, but they do not eliminate it, so the FBI continued to train agents at its academy at Quantico. Included in the regimen of instruction were lessons in disarming criminals, the care and handling of Tommy guns, recognizing incendiary devices, and reconstructing accident scenes for evidence of sabotage.[287] Other students had to remain satisfied with just learning their A-B-C's, especially since they were not old enough for the military or the FBI. While their fathers trained as officers, Marine children attended the Post School during the war. While some derided the school as "a cheese box on a hill" because of its temporary building design, the Post School faced the challenge of educating children from kindergarten to high school age, and hailing from every state in the nation. In addition to the normal classroom facilities, the Post

Propaganda played a major role in World War II, and this powerful poster, considered shocking, resonated particularly with sailors and Marines. It doubtless adorned walls at Quantico, where loose lips—which would soon be riding Navy transports—remained sealed. Courtesy Northwestern University.

Singer Kate Smith, famous during the war for her stirring and patriotic rendition of "God Bless America," visited Quantico in 1942 to show her support for the clearly delighted Marines. Courtesy National Archives, Record Group 127.

School boasted "a modern yet homelike library, a music studio, art studio, photographic laboratory" and technological teaching aids such as movie projectors and microphones for diagnostic work in speech. A school board oversaw the operation of the facility, which was accredited by the State Board of Education in Virginia. This accreditation proved crucial to Marine children for it meant their education at the Post School would be transferable to any school in the United States, an important factor when almost half the children in the school would transfer with their families each year. While the age range and turnover rate in the student body made education at the Post School a challenge for teachers and students alike, "the pleasant school environment, the happy relationship between teachers and pupils indicate the quality of the work to be expected."[288] In this regard, children living in the Town of Quantico had a less chaotic educational experience. As residents of Prince William County, they attended classes operated by the county, rather than the Marine Corps.

Experimental Aviation

Being the center of research and development for Marine Corps education and equipment, Quantico had opened new schools even prior to America's entrance into the war. In June 1941, the Barrage Balloon Training School had organized at Quantico to explore the efficacy of barrage ballooning in modern warfare. The use of balloons in war was certainly not a new idea, but strategists still saw utility in the use of balloons in air defense. Several officers trained at the Navy's facility in New Jersey, and returned to Quantico to instruct their troops. Unfortunately, an initial lack of balloons kept the would-be balloonists grounded, occupied with research instead. Only after the school moved to New River, North Carolina, in September 1942 did the squadrons become fully activated. The New River facility would eventually become Camp Lejeune.[289]

Similarly, aviators at Quantico experimented with parachuting, and formed the 1st Parachute Battalion. The Marine Corps had seen both the Germans and the U.S. Army make strides in parachute techniques, and decided to add it to its research and development roster. As with the balloonists, training first occurred in New Jersey, where the parachutists practiced tower jumps. More training would occur at Quantico before the men were allowed to dive from moving aircraft. A company of parachutists organized at Quantico in May 1941, and was nearly two-thirds complete before it too relocated to New River in September. This group eventually participated in the Guadalcanal campaign in the Pacific Theater. To add insult to injury, however, that same September Quantico also lost its Aviation Specialist School to New

Most Marines would have given their eyeteeth to swoon over the visit by heartthrob Gladys Swarthout, but Jiggs the mascot appears in complete control, with no salivating evident. The Leatherneck, *July 1946.*

Dances at the enlisted men's club were popular wartime entertainment. The Leatherneck, *March 1944.*

River, although in this case a lack of space at Quantico prompted the move.[290]

The first months of the war saw the creation at Quantico of the Aviation Ground Officers School (later renamed the Marine Air-Infantry School), with the purpose of training aviators and ground officers in coordinated air-amphibious operation strategies. Over a hundred of the pilots who trained at this school achieved "ace" status during the war. In furthering aerial support of ground troops, in this case the infantry, the first Marine Observation Squadron (VMO-1) organized at Quantico in 1943 to train ground troops as airborne artillery spotters. Six such squadrons would ultimately participate in the Pacific Theater during the war, and all of them received their training at Quantico.[291]

World War II would prove a blow to Quantico's aviation program generally, however. In December 1941 Quantico had been redesignated Marine Corps Air Station, Quantico, but the opening of additional air stations and the outbreak of war drained squadrons away from Quantico. Thereafter, the air station became largely a training station for aviators, and a repair facility for their aircraft. The tactical squadrons would make their home bases elsewhere. Furthermore, once the 1st Marine Aircraft Wing decamped for the Pacific, aviation training at Quantico then focused on individual pilots, rather than whole units. Old Field No. 1 became home to a new aircraft overhaul and repair facility, although the building itself reflected its wartime construction. With steel in short supply, wood beams made up the back of the structure. Mixed-material construction aside, the facility worked on F4U Corsairs, SB2C Helldivers, Mitchell PBJ bombers, and F6F Hellcats.[292]

"Laboratory of Life and Death"

"Laboratory of Life and Death" was the title *The Leatherneck* bestowed on the Marine Corps Equipment Board (MCEB) based at Quantico. While the label grabbed the reader's attention, the idea behind it was not far off the mark. The board moved from Washington to Quantico in the 1930s and began working on solutions to some of the Corps' most vexing equipment problems, such as amphibious landing craft that would offer the ramp lengths necessary for landing troops, while also stable enough to withstand punishing surf. In the early days, before "Marine-ization" of the Corps, the Marines relied on equipment developed by the Army and Navy for their own particular use, which did not always correspond to what the Marines required. Eventually the MCEB recruited top-flight scientists and engineers to serve on the board, and made great strides in developing equipment suited for modern Marine warfare. Furthermore, before quartermasters requisitioned any untested and unproven supplies, the MCEB conducted its own

These happy Marines and their dates are shown enjoying the enlisted men's club. The women are drinking Cola-Cola. The club was crowded almost every evening, particularly during the weekly dance. The Leatherneck, *March 1944.*

tests for the reliability and suitability of new products. Rubber boats would be subjected to trial runs in the Potomac for seaworthiness, machine guns would be fired day after day to test for long-term failures, rifles would be filled with sand or water to determine if they could perform under adverse climatic conditions, mock combat drills would test the durability of knives and bayonets, and even hammocks were tested for their ability to keep out weather and insects while still being lightweight enough for a typical pack. The open space, varied terrain, proximity to water, and military training presence made Quantico a perfect venue for the work of the MCEB. In 1944 the MCEB moved into a sixteen-thousand-square-foot facility near the docks at Quantico, allowing it to consolidate its administrative and experimental functions into one structure, rather than the scattered offices and Quonset huts which previously housed the board.[293]

Guadalcanal in Virginia

As spacious as the Quantico reservation might have seemed at the beginning of 1941, it became clear within a year after America entered the war that the existing training facilities on base could not accom-

modate the extra schools, their additional students, and the accompanying training needs. The Corps purchased an additional fifty thousand acres of land west of Route 1 in 1942, adding significantly to the reservation. The new tract became known as the "Guadalcanal Area," in honor of the bloody, but ultimately successful Marine amphibious campaign in the Pacific. The new training areas in Quantico's Guadalcanal proved exceptionally useful for artillery exercises, and abandoned structures on the land endured repeated attacks and artillery obliterations as officers experimented with what their equipment could do.[294]

While the additional thousands of acres came as a blessing to the Marine Corps, the deal was a curse to the families evicted from the land. The affected tracts in Prince William, Stafford, and Fauquier Counties had been labeled as "submarginal, sparsely settled and wooded areas," and the government promised to pay the property owners fair value for their land, and help relocate farmers and their livestock and equipment. Few people questioned the necessity of providing wartime training facilities for the Marines, or the speed in which the transfer was executed, but lost in the equation was the psychological toll taken on the nearly two thousand residents uprooted in the name of national security. Descendants of the original families later explained how distressing the forced evacuation was. The Arrington family had lived in the community of David since the late nineteenth century, and the town took its name from that of Arthur David Arrington, who worked as the local postmaster, a storekeeper, and lumber merchant. Since the Marines moved with such speed, there was little time for the Arringtons to move the contents of their home or family farm. "The crops weren't even harvested," A. D. Arrington's son recalled. "We had to just leave them in the field. They gave us two weeks to move a building or tear it down for materials if we wanted them." Most of the Arringtons' furniture was sold at auction, and the Marines slaughtered the hogs not sold at a Warrenton stockyard. The King family suffered similar hardships in Stafford Springs. The government condemned their property, but only gave them $1,700 for it. George N. King recalled that the government failed to pay the family for months, and that in the meantime it cost them $2,500 to buy a new homestead on loan. Even more painful for the Kings than the loss of their property was the uncertainty of what became of their ancestors buried on the land. Although the

What Prince William County residents thought when the federal government annexed their communities to expand Quantico is now little remembered. But the ever-present fear of German submarines entering the Chesapeake Bay and Potomac River served as a very local reminder of greater war needs. Miss Hetty Evans, postmaster of Onville, is shown during the 1930s. Hers was one of the communities which the government closed in 1942 to enlarge the base; Camp Barrett was later built on the site. Courtesy base archive.

Marines vowed to give first priority to removing burial grounds from firing zones, family members claiming the over fifteen hundred affected remains, including those of the King family, were never completely satisfied that all the deceased were moved with the necessary diligence or reverence. The subsequent discovery of over one hundred grave sites in the Guadalcanal Area reinforced this concern.

On the other hand, Eunice Smith Nashwinter remembered that her family coped quite well when the Marines moved in. Although her father had been in the lumber business and the loss of public domain forest hurt him economically, he still donated part of a disputed acre in Cromwell to the Marines with the remark, "Oh well, it ain't much. Let 'em have it." Eunice recognized that having a Marine base across the street could be lucrative, and she built a store for her parents to run. The family ran the Eunice M. Smith's Store until it closed in the 1950s, and developed close relationships with the Marines who patronized the store. "Mothers and fathers would write my parents and thank them for taking care of their children," Mrs. Nashwinter remembered, concluding that the Marines "were just a nice bunch of people." Happily, at least some of the families affected by Quantico's expansion saw lemonade among the lemons.[295]

The Never-Ending Need for Housing

While the Guadalcanal deal alleviated the growing pains the Marines experienced professionally, there was always the issue of base housing for Marine families. This problem arose before America entered the war, and only got worse as more Marines came to Quantico. In late 1940 came the promise of alleviating a perpetual housing shortage for families in Quantico with the erection of prefabricated steel houses made in Alabama. The houses contained separate apartments for two families, each suite included a living room, kitchenette and dining room, two bedrooms, and a bathroom. The houses

Many solid homes, like this one built in 1891 at Stafford Store, were emptied of their owners and residents when the government expanded Quantico's military reservation in 1942. Communities like this one included now-forgotten settlements at Rogers Corner, Garrison's Corner, David, and Boswell's Store. Courtesy base archive.

constructed at Quantico would be assembled on concrete slabs and featured asbestos shingles applied over an insulation board, rather than the usual steel wall panels. The benefit of steel housing derived from the savings in price over traditional building materials, the speed with which they could be assembled, and that they could be disassembled and moved if and when the structures were no longer needed. Fifty steel homes were completed at Quantico in 1941.[296]

The Marines at Quantico further benefited when the Navy's powder plant at Indian Head, Maryland, discovered in November 1941 that it had built 186 more prefabricated houses than necessary, and transferred them to Quantico. Luckily, Congress had just approved a defense housing project on a site in the Aquia district of Stafford, just to the south of the base. But with congressional funds for defense housing projects exhausted, the prefabricated houses would be able to occupy the site without significant extra costs to the govern-

ment.[297] While the powder plant may have regretted losing the extra housing once it went on a wartime footing, the additional housing certainly proved a godsend to Marine families.

Affordable housing was in short supply during the war as was confirmed by the imposition of rent controls under the Emergency Price Control Act. Landlords in Quantico violated these controls at their own peril, however, and sometimes got caught in the process. Tenants of a property owned by Harry Cokinides (one of Quantico's founders) sued their landlord for $650. The suit charged that Cokinides had overcharged the residents of a property on Fourth Street in Quantico and that he "unlawfully and knowingly filed with the Office of Price Administration a false rent registration statement" regarding the property. Judge Lacy Compton agreed with the three tenants involved, and ruled in their favor in April 1944.[298]

In one case, however, local residents cheered the demolition of a piece of architecture on base. In 1943 a 210-foot-tall powerhouse smokestack was slated for demolition, much to the delight of pilots who had navigated around it for a decade. Spectators took bets on when the smokestack would fall, after workers cut portions of the tower's base to weaken the structure. The smokestack fell just where it was supposed to . . . only three hours behind schedule. No word on who won the bet.[299]

"Restfulness and Tranquility" at the New Naval Hospital

Housing was not the only welcome structural addition to the base at Quantico in the 1940s. Beginning in July 1941, Marines and their families had access to the new Naval Hospital, Quantico, built on the site of former Confederate batteries at Shipping Point. Before construction of the hospital, the site had been, according to the *Quantico Sentry*, "an eyesore of muddy roads, abandoned shipways and half completed hulls." Instead, the hospital gave the

Above: Chopawamsic School, with its distinctive cupola, shown here in 1941, lost its students after the area was depopulated by the government, and fell into ruin. Courtesy base archive.

Top: One of the many prosperous homesteads emptied by the government during its huge confiscation of private land during World War II. The area became known as the Guadalcanal Area. Courtesy base archive.

forty-acre site an attractive three-story Georgian building constructed of limestone, granite, and red-brick, which offered sunlit spaces, cross-ventilation, and flower beds between the wings of the hospital. The whole site lent "an invaluable air of restfulness and tranquility" for patients and visitors alike. If a case presented to the Post Dispensary required further treatment, the patient would be transferred to the Naval Hospital, treated for his specific condition and provided a full physical examination to identify any other potential medical conditions. "Those who have sons or daughters on duty at Quantico need have no misgivings as to the quality of medical treatment they will receive should they be taken sick or meet with an accident," the *Sentry* assured the parents among its readers. "Professional skill is of the highest and physical equipment of the best" at the new, up-to-date hospital. While the Naval Hospital at Quantico existed to serve the Marine Corps, it also accepted patients from other branches of the military, retired military, students at the FBI academy, and civil service employees on the base who needed the specialized care available at the hospital, which was the only facility between Alexandria and Fredericksburg equipped to handle civilian emergency situations as well. Additionally, the hospital provided out-patient services to Marine dependants, which eased the minds of men serving overseas, knowing that their wives and children back in Quantico had access to quality health care. The Naval Hospital also offered departments of dentistry, psychiatry, and physiotherapy to take care of patients with these special needs.[300]

Women Reservists: "We are Marines First and Women Second"

Included in the round of wartime construction at Quantico were barracks for female Marines, signifying that women had entered the Corps to stay. In 1942, the Corps received permission to form a Marine Corps Women's Reserve. Similar to the Marinettes of World War I, the operating philosophy behind the Women's Reserve was that by filling clerical, transportation, communication, and mechanical jobs with qualified women, the men who would have normally occupied those positions would be freed for combat duty. Unlike their World War I counterparts, however, the women Marines of World War II were fully enlisted into the Corps, and

Rosie the Riveter became a famous character during World War II, when women entered heavy industry for the first time to replace men away at war. These women, among the first to attend Quantico's ordnance school, position a depth charge underneath an airplane in 1944. Courtesy National Archives, Record Group 127.

truly served as Marines. By the end of World War II, over twenty thousand women had filled the ranks of the Women's Reserve, a number of whom completed their training at Quantico.

The first four women arrived at Quantico in November 1943, and within a year the number of women Marines on base had risen to almost one thousand. The *Quantico Sentry* reported with admiration in substituting female Marines in place of men, "this change in personnel is being effected without sacrificing efficiency or slowing up performance." A woman scheduled to assume a duty first "understudied" her male counterpart to learn the nuances of the job, thus ensuring a seamless transition when the task became hers alone. Women Marines served in at least sixty different capacities at Quantico, with their biggest success coming in taking over many duties at the Post Exchange.

In expectation that the number of women Marines at Quantico would double, red brick barracks were constructed between the town and family hospital for the women's use. Perhaps in concession to the femininity of the occupants, the lounge areas resembled "a large family hotel" with wicker settees, and offered radios, checkerboards, and reading material with which to occupy their own time, or entertain guests. Like male Marines, women were allowed liberty in Quantico town and around the base, and in fact followed most of the same regulations as their male counterparts.

"Here at Quantico, the Women's Reserve is an unqualified success," the *Sentry* enthused. "They had demonstrated their ability and willingness to assume unhesitatingly and cheerfully perform the varied and responsible tasks formerly done by male Marines, many of whom already have been relieved and are in the combat areas. In addition, they maintain a smart appearance and a snappy bearing, and scrupulously observe the military courtesies."[301]

Contributions to the War Effort

The Second World War affected the American homefront in a myriad of ways, but probably few communities faced the war on such a daily basis as did the small town of Quantico. Surrounded on three sides by the Marine base, town residents and other civilians worked intimately with the Marines and Marine dependants in their midst to do whatever they could to contribute to the war effort. H. Ewing Wall, president of the First National Bank of Quantico, had the opportunity to help just days after the attack at Pearl Harbor. When NBC's Blue Network broadcast a "This Nation at War" episode in 1943 focused on wartime banking, it sent one of its announcers to Quantico to investigate. Mr. Wall assured the announcer that his bank tried to provide the Marines the type of services they would find in any small town community, such as cashing their checks, arranging automobile loans, or selling war bonds. Although the bank typically opened and closed eight hundred accounts per month, the bank maintained a surprisingly consistent clientele, even when their customers were fighting overseas. But

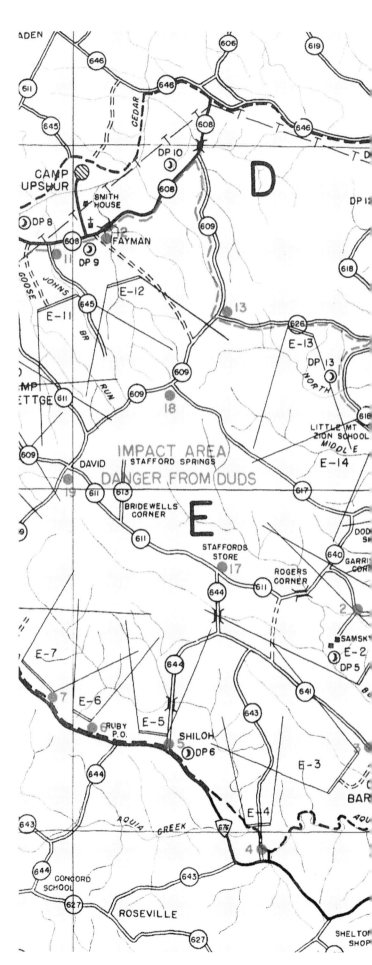

Map used by Marine trainees in 1948 showing some of the communities deserted in 1942 for annexation to the base. By the date of this map several had already disappeared, including Onville—Camp Barrett is there instead. Courtesy Captain Thomas W. Turner (Ret.)

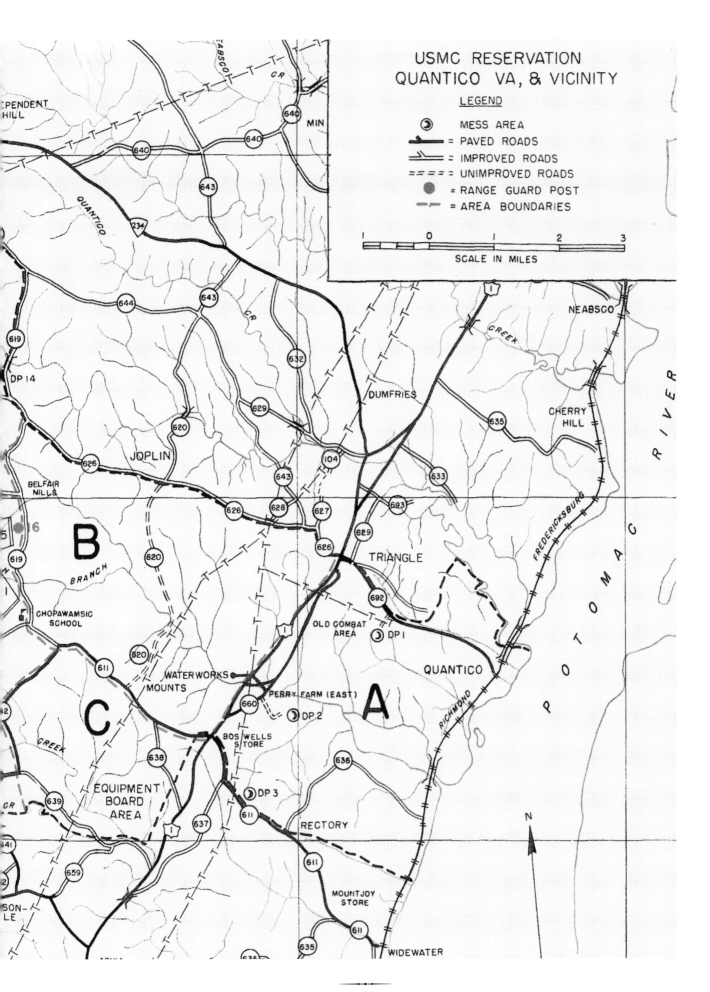

USMC RESERVATION
QUANTICO VA, & VICINITY

LEGEND

◐ = MESS AREA
━ = PAVED ROADS
═ = IMPROVED ROADS
= = = = = UNIMPROVED ROADS
● = RANGE GUARD POST
━ ━ ━ = AREA BOUNDARIES

SCALE IN MILES

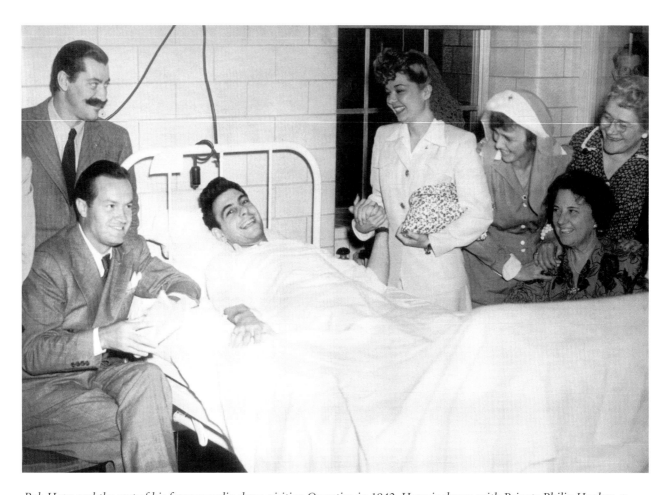

Bob Hope and the cast of his famous radio show, visiting Quantico in 1942. Hope is shown with Private Philip Hughes, a patient at the Naval Hospital, who appears to feel much better with the lovely Frances Langford holding his hand. Hope was beloved by generations of troops for always remembering the men in uniform, and performing for them near combat zones when no one else would do so. Katherine "Mother" De Boo looks on at right. Courtesy Marine Corps Historical Center.

Mr. Wall recalled that having Marine customers did provide some unusual challenges. Not long after Pearl Harbor, some of the Marines at Quantico discovered they were being shipped out immediately, and that they would need to withdraw some money before they left. Unfortunately, it was a Sunday, the bank was closed, and the vault at the bank operated on a time lock. Rather than allow the men to go off to war without change in their pockets, Mr. Wall talked to business owners on Potomac Avenue, explaining that the men needed $6,000. "Every merchant I approached," Wall remembered, "said that if it was for the Marines, I could take everything." By pooling the resources of the Quantico business community, the Marines got their money in the nick of time.

The same broadcast also told the story of Hugh F. Deakins, a Marine quartermaster clerk who facilitated one of the bank's biggest days. During his thirty-five years of military service, Deakins had left much of his back pay "on the books," but when he received a promotion to the rank of warrant officer, he had to retrieve the money. "Did it come to very much?" the announcer inquired. "It came to $21,269," Deakins replied. "Did you say $21,269!" the announcer exclaimed. "And twenty-nine cents," Deakins corrected. When asked what he had done with such a fabulous amount of money, Deakins answered that he had immediately walked down to the Quantico bank and purchased five $5,000 war bonds. "That's getting the situation well in hand," the announcer commented, complimenting Deakins on his practicality and patriotism. Not to mention his frugality over the previous three decades.[302]

Civilians and Marines alike made other donations to the war effort, just in a less financial way. The Red Cross frequently held blood drives on base, and usually surpassed its quota in each round. Throughout the war years the *Quantico Sentry* kept its readers informed as to how well their community had performed in each drive, although by 1945 the *Sentry* reported on an interesting development. With so many of Quantico's Marines having been stationed in the Pacific at one time or another over the years, more and more of them became disqualified as blood donors due to their exposure to malaria and other tropical diseases, in addition to the normal colds and common maladies endured by men in close quarters. While the Red Cross still exceeded its quota in an April 1945 drive, its local chairman decided that future appeals would target the wives of Marine personnel and other civilians with less well-traveled red blood cells.[303]

Even gardeners at Quantico got into the spirit of things by planting "victory gardens" to provide vegetables for their families, presumably so that more products of commercial agriculture could find their way to troops abroad. The "hundreds of new but zealous gardeners" kept Quantico's post forestry officer busy in the spring of 1943, but Captain Sebree offered advice on what to plant and how to fertilize it, and helped transform ornamental parks into productive vegetable patches. To help both the novice and experienced gardeners, the *Quantico Sentry* helpfully published an eight-page victory gardening guide produced by the Department of Agriculture. All involved hoped that Quantico gardeners would be able to "turn bayonets into spades" on behalf of the war effort.[304]

Production was only part of the solution to America's need to economize; rationing and recycling were the others. All of the United States came under rationing restrictions at one time or another

during the war, and Quantico was no exception. The products being rationed by the government by 1943 included gasoline, fuel oil, sugar, shoes, meat, and processed foods. Quantico residents received coupon books determining their individual or household allotments, and the *Sentry* published significant rationing dates. With sugar allotments in September, for example, stamps 15 and 16 continued to be valid until Halloween for five pounds of sugar for "home canning purposes." Housewives who needed more than that were welcome to apply to their local rationing boards for exemptions. Metal was in increasingly short supply for civilian use, and raw materials were directed to factories producing military materials. As a result, civilians had to make do in creative ways. Instead of issuing new license plates in 1943, the Commonwealth of Virginia decided to reuse the 1942 plates and just issue a small black metal tab for the rear license plate to indicate an automobile's registered status. Windshield stickers sufficed for the front of the car, thereby saving that much more metal. The state also participated in metal recycling drives to collect scrap metal that could be used in the war effort. Virginia ran contests to encourage as much recycling as possible, suggesting in advertisements that "Virginia's Scrap Can Lick the Jap!"[305]

The civilian world came to Quantico in the form of entertainers hoping to lighten the spirits of servicemen and improve morale generally. Popular singer Kate Smith, famous for her rousing renditions of "God Bless America," visited Quantico on at least two occasions in 1942 and 1943. Her March 1942 show at Quantico included the songs "Blues in the Night," "I Like to Make Music," and "A Soldier Dreams of You Tonight." Among her fellow performers was actor Randolph Scott, who gave a dramatic rendering of the "Ballad of Wake Island." At the conclusion of the show, Miss Smith led the audience in singing the Marine Hymn. Smith returned a year later, greeting the packed Post Theater with a cheerful "Hi-ya, Fellows," before bringing the house down with her "top-notch musical entertainment." This show held special significance for Quantico Marines as Smith introduced a new song, "What Makes a Marine." The words of the song were based on a poem written by Quantico-trained Private Paul Mills while on duty at Guadalcanal. Smith also brought her regular cast of characters, including comedian Henny Youngman.[306]

In 1944 Major Edward Bowes brought his "Original Amateur Hour" to Quantico for the second year in a row, both to salute and entertain the Marines, and to showcase local talent. The radio broadcast included eight singing acts, but the Marines cheered all of them with such enthusiasm that it was hard to declare a clear winner. The second half of the show offered more variety, including Private First Class Dan Albert playing a medley of Irish tunes on a flute he confessed to having won in a craps game a few weeks before. No doubt Quantico Marines appreciated even more an appearance by Carmen Amaya, a twenty-two-year-old "hailed as one of the greatest flamenco [dancers] of all time." Not surprisingly, the *Sentry* predicted "record attendance" at these shows. Even though they were "Marines first, women second," the female Marines at Quantico probably thrilled to hear the news that handsome movie star Tyrone Power was coming to town. Unfortunately for them, Private Power came to Quantico to attend Officers' Candidate School, rather than as the newest addition to the entertainment line-up.[307]

Of course, Quantico continued to offer its servicemen and women the traditional forms of recreation during the war as well. The air-conditioned movie theater offered affordable entertainment to the troops: free to anyone in uniform, and just a dime for dates. A museum at the recreation building recounted the glory days of Marines past, and next door a library held six thousand volumes for a reading Marine's pleasure. In the basement sixteen bowl-ing alleys, billiard and pool tables, a shuffleboard, and soda fountain provided casual diversions from drill and training. The officers and enlisted men both had clubs of their own where a cold beer or a dance with a pretty girl might be in order. To ensure that Quantico Marines had their dance cards filled, Washington's "Women's Battalion" sent five hundred of their members to the base for an outdoor dance in August 1942. The Women's Battalion was comprised of so-called "government girls" whose recreation hours consisted of traveling to local military bases and dancing with the troops. "They are doing one of the finest recreational jobs in town," observed Milo Christiansen, Washington's recreation superintendent. Doubtless the men at Quantico agreed. And if the men needed a more mature presence, there was always Mother De Boo to tell one's troubles to and receive some motherly advice in return. Or Jiggs IV, who restricted his advice to choosing new uniforms for the baseball team.[308]

Officials on base also recognized that the spiritual needs of Marines required special arrangements during wartime. In June 1942 the Catholic Church admitted that men serving in the military could not always attend mass in the mornings because of their duty schedules, and thus relaxed the rules temporarily, allowing evening masses to take place any time before 7:30 p.m. The first evening mass at Quantico was celebrated on June 15. Jewish Marines had reason to give thanks early in 1944 when Rabbi Philip Ritholtz of Alexandria began conducting Jewish services at Quantico.[309]

Civilians

While Quantico's primary role in the war was training men for combat, the base also served as the major source of employment for civilians in the area, and it was those civilian workers who helped keep the base operating smoothly. More than one thousand civilians held civil service jobs on the base, in addition to those who worked in the officers' mess and post exchange. Nearly 40 percent of the civilian labor at the post in 1943 were women, a percentage guaranteed to increase as more and more men were called for active duty. The varied occupations represented by civilians on base included mechanics, typists, plumbers, accounting clerks, librarians, messengers, sheet metal workers, draftsmen, stenographers, and patrolmen. Officials at Quantico realized that some of these craftsmen had skills in great demand by private industry elsewhere, and could have made significantly more money had they relocated to Norfolk or Philadelphia. But many of the civilians who worked on base also owned property in the area, and some even farmed their own land while also working as

machinists and metalworkers on the base. These individuals liked their Quantico lifestyles and found it advantageous to stay. While some of the civilian employees were residents of the town of Quantico, like the famous "Quantico Clipper" barber Joe Johnson, most Quantico residents owned or worked in local businesses which catered to the Marines. The bulk of civilian workers on base came from elsewhere in Prince William County.

The *Quantico Sentry* was particularly impressed by the civilian women staffing the Assembly and Repair Shop at the Air Station. Much as the Women's Reserve Marines took over men's positions to free them for combat duty, civilian women mastered traditionally male jobs as electricians, wood-

Victory over Japan! This scene is from the enlisted men's club, where all was joyous pandemonium. World War II was finally over. Quantico Sentry, *August 16, 1945.*

Informal billiards tournament, 1945. These Quantico Marines, who may have placed bets on the 8-ball, could be forgiven for wondering as well about their futures. The war was grinding to a close and the collapse of Imperial Japan was imminent. What would become of them? And the country and world? Courtesy base archive.

workers, welders, radio mechanics, and machinists, thereby stepping in to pick up the slack when men were called up by the selective service. This allowed the air station to continue to repair and overhaul aircraft needed by the Marine Corps. By 1943, over 70 percent of the civilians employed in the A & R Department were women, most of whom commuted from Fredericksburg every day.[310]

But what of Quantico Town residents? Apart from the obvious influences of having a large Marine base as a neighbor, Quantico residents lived their lives much as other Americans did. They ran businesses (albeit with an almost exclusively Marine clientele), visited friends and entertained guests, got married, raised children, and participated in local community organizations. A regular feature in the *Quantico Sentry* detailed the comings and goings of Quantico residents, and many entries read much as they would have in any other small town in America. Before visiting her sister in Tennessee in October 1943, Mrs. Ira Hill was the guest of honor

at a luncheon given in her honor by Mrs. Eastman Keyes of Dumfries. The Quantico PTA planned to hold its monthly meeting at the schoolhouse on October 13, and encouraged every one with an interest in children's issues to attend. The Bridge Club met at the home of Mrs. Dora Heyes, who served "lovely refreshments." The Quantico Town School undertook a "Triple Threat Campaign" of selling war bonds and stamps, and had by October raised over $2,000 for the war effort. Manuel Katsarelis, of the U.S. Navy, came home on an eight-day leave, much to the delight of his family. But like other American families, the Katsarelises spent much time worrying about their four sons serving in the military. In November 1943 Toni Katsarelis received the Air Medal with Oak Leaf cluster on behalf of his son, Army Staff Sergeant Peter A. Katsarelis. The younger Katsarelis had been listed as missing-in-action, but the family had recently received the good news that Peter was still alive, but being held as a prisoner-of-war in Germany.[311] Obviously not all Quantico boys grew up to be Marines.

Empires Collapsing

"I have a terrific pain in the back of my head," announced President Franklin Roosevelt on April 12, 1945, just before collapsing with a massive cerebral hemorrhage while vacationing in Warm Springs, Georgia. The president who had guided the United States through the Depression and the Second World War died within hours, leaving a grieving, worried country behind. No one knew what to expect from the new president, Harry S Truman, and in fact, Adolf Hitler briefly assumed that Roosevelt's death would help Germany reverse its fortunes in war. But it was too late for Germany, and for Hitler, who committed suicide at the end of April 1945.[312]

While Quantico certainly celebrated the fall of the Third Reich, civilians and military personnel in the area knew the country still faced a determined opponent in Japan. Given that most of the Marines fought in the Pacific, Quanticans were painfully aware that the war was far from over. But President Truman, initially described as "the little man from Missouri," also proved a worthy adversary, and in July 1945 the United States (with its allies the United Kingdom and China) issued an ultimatum to Japan: surrender unconditionally or face "prompt and utter destruction." The Japanese dismissed the ultimatum, and sealed its fate. On August 6 the first atomic bomb was dropped on Hiroshima, followed three days later by another bombing at Nagasaki. The Japanese surrendered on August 14, 1945.[313] The war was finally over.

Now Quantico could cut loose with abandon, and cut loose it did! Truman's announcement of Japan's surrender first prompted innocuous shouts of "Hooray—it's all over!" The volume of the celebrations increased as the news sunk in. Marines overwhelmed the telephone exchange as they rushed to call wives, mothers, anyone, to spread the good news. Crowds gathered around radios to listen to the celebrations in other parts of the country, while in their own backyard Marines and civilians poured into the streets and cafes in town. "Joy reigned supreme" in the Marines' clubs, manifesting itself in dancing and conga lines, not to mention frequent toasts with "amber suds." Over at the Hostess House the juke box went full tilt as people "jitterbugged themselves into near exhaustion." Amid the dancing and the backslapping, one Marine summed up the occasion for everyone, "Brother, this is it!"[314]

Demobilization

Then it was truly over. After the rush of celebration, the Marines and civilians of Quantico stepped back to reflect on the years of war and remember those

Quantico did. Courtesy Northwestern University.

who had not returned. And then they prepared themselves for demobilization. When the war ended, the Marine Corps had reached its peak strength of 485,000 men, and Quantico had likewise reached its peak of 10,000 new officers and specialists. By the end of the year that number dropped to 8,000, and would decline by almost half that by May 1946.

Quantico's role in the immediate postwar world would be to facilitate the demobilization of individual Marines, while continuing its educational responsibilities to men training to be officers in the Marine Corps. But at the same time the Corps lost men to demobilization, Quantico lost personnel, making the demobilization duties that much more challenging. Without directions for its peacetime role, and suffering from a "turbulent personnel situation," Quantico put any new education development on hold temporarily.[315]

Those in Quantico at the end of 1945 could not foresee what the future would hold for the base or the town. Nor could they see that as the hot war ended in 1945, a long, cold one was just beginning.

CHAPTER VII

INTO THE ATOMIC AGE

A New Symbol for the Corps

Each branch of the United States military pushed itself to the limits of its endurance and beyond during World War II, accumulating records of bravery and heroism perhaps never to be surpassed in any future war. For the Marine Corps, World War II would not only add new chapters in the annals of achievement, but also provided the Corps with a new symbol. Some of the bloodiest, most tenacious fighting of the war was done by Marines on the beaches of Iwo Jima in 1945, prompting Admiral Chester Nimitz to proclaim that "uncommon valor was a common virtue" on Iwo. When Associated Press photographer Joe Rosenthal's stunning photo-graph of the second American flag raising on Mount Suribachi hit the front page of newspapers around the world, it instantly became one of the most recognized images in history. The Marine Corps would also adopt the image as a visual representation of the values and history of the Corps.

Days after seeing Rosenthal's photograph, sculptor Felix deWeldon began working on progressively larger models of the scene, and the artist would eventually be chosen to execute a bronze likeness of the flag raising as the official United States Marine Corps War Memorial in Arlington, Virginia. Before the bronze statue was cast, deWeldon created a smaller limestone, cement and sand

"Sagging sausages" or "flying bananas," as these ungainly early helicopters were called by Marines, are shown during testing and deployment at Quantico in 1951. Helicopters were used extensively in Korea, in the war newly underway there. Courtesy National Archives, Record Group 127.

version, which went on display on Constitution Avenue in Washington, D.C., in November 1945. This copy came to Quantico in 1947, and after extensive restoration from weather damage, the statue was dedicated on November 10, 1951. During the dedication ceremony the original flag which flew over Mount Suribachi was raised on the statue's flagstaff, while General Keller Rockney intoned, "May this heroic statue stand not only to the glory of the men who fought on Iwo Jima, but also as an everlasting memorial to the glory of the United States Marines." The replica War Memorial statue still stands guard at the main entrance to Quantico, and like its sibling in Arlington, is more commonly known as the "Iwo Jima Memorial."[316]

The Marines entered the postwar world with a special veneration for items associated with the bravery displayed on Iwo Jima, and an increased interest in the Corps' history. The three flags ultimately flown on Iwo Jima were transferred to the museum at Quantico in 1945, but occasionally left the base to be displayed at Marine Corps functions, such as a 1949 reunion of the Fifth Marine Division, a division which had been instrumental in securing the island in 1945.[317]

While the Corps had maintained a museum at Quantico since the 1940s, the items displayed and the quality of the presentation had rarely warranted the title "museum." The serious effort at creating a real museum arose in 1958, and by 1960 the old post headquarters had been transformed into a showcase of Marine Corps history. By 1962 a small unit called the Marine Corps Exhibit Center toiled away in a corner of Larson Gymnasium, creating exhibits and displays dedicated to telling the Marine Corps' story.[318]

Quantico again fielded pigskin in 1946, after an absence of many years. The reborn team competed for another two decades, until budget cuts forced a permanent sayonara. Courtesy National Archives, Record Group 127.

"Feeling Its Way toward an Uncertain Tomorrow"

Interpreting where the Corps had been was much easier than divining where it would go in the Atomic Age, and just as it had after World War I, the Corps faced an identity crisis when yet again faced with threats of dissolution. The atomic bomb had changed everything, the "experts" said. The amphibious techniques of mass beach landings that had worked so brilliantly in the Pacific Theater would no longer be viable when the enemy could drop a single bomb on a concentrated fleet. And since the Corps had staked almost its entire raison d'etre on its skill in amphibious warfare, if that type of warfare had become obsolete, perhaps the Corps had too.[319]

But as was the case after the Great War, the Corps reinvented itself once again. Dire predictions of the end of amphibious warfare failed to impress Marine officials, but they recognized that the way the Marines engaged in amphibious assaults might have to change with the times. "I refused to share the atomic hysteria familiar to some ranking officers," General A. A. Vandegrift later confirmed. "The atomic bomb was not yet adapted for tactical employment, nor would this happen soon. Accordingly, I did not feel obliged to make a sudden, sharp change in our organizational profile. I did feel obliged to study the problem in all its complexity. For if we believed the basic mission of the Marine Corps would remain unchanged in an atomic age, we knew that the conditions surrounding this mission would change and change radically."[320]

Once again, Quantico rescued the Corps. Faced with concerns about the impact of atomic weapons, General Vandegrift convened a board at Quantico to study the issue, and determine the place of amphibious warfare in the future. The special board and the students at Quantico spent much of 1947 "groping toward the new technique of future war," determining which tried-and-true methods were likely to work again, and what technology would guide the Corps into the future. "Practically nothing was deemed too fanciful for consideration," Vandegrift admitted.[321]

"Flying Bananas" and "Sagging Sausages"

The fanciful solution to the Marines' problem turned out to be flying bananas. Actually, the solution to the problem was helicopters, but the unusual design of early models earned them the appetizing nicknames of "flying bananas" and "sagging sausages." What the special board ultimately recommended as the Marine Corps' conceptual model was "vertical envelopment," the key to which involved extensive use of helicopters. Although substantially unproven as machines of war, Marine intelligence saw the potential of using helicopters to ferry men and materiel from scattered positions in the rear to various points distributed along landing sites, rather than focusing their efforts on concentrated landing points. Air support provided by helicopters

Quantico's Potomac Avenue commercial spine is as healthy in this 1948 postwar photo as it was when pictured in the 1920s. The many arriving Korean War trainees doubtless helped. Courtesy base archive.

would also allow the Marines to avoid heavily defended beaches and penetrate interiors behind enemy lines.[322] The board's recommendations as to adopting both vertical envelopment and the use of helicopters convinced the powers-that-be, who approved the plan immediately.

Now all that remained to do was assemble a squadron of helicopters, determine how the machines operated, train pilots, train mechanics, devise new air traffic procedures, and figure out if the aircraft would actually do the job. Applying a "can do" spirit, Quantico got to work without delay. By December 1947, Marine Helicopter Squadron One (HMX-1) had been organized at Quantico under the leadership of Colonel Edward Dyer, with a grand total of nine pilots and zero helicopters. Considering that none of the pilots had ever flown a helicopter, HMX-1 was off to the proverbial "flying start." Two Sikorsky HO-35-1 helicopters arrived from the Navy in February 1948, soon to be followed by three additional Sikorskies, a Bell HTL-1, and a big Piasecki HRP-1, the infamous "flying banana" capable of carrying ten passengers at a speed of seventy-five miles per hour. By May 1948, HMX-1 was already participating in practice ship-to-shore maneuvers, and a year later the squadron impressed a group of visiting congressmen with amphibious landings, evacuation drills and "flying crane" lifts. "If the helicopter is accepted for regular use in the Marine Corps," *The Leatherneck* predicted in 1948, "it is very likely that they will become the workhorses of the Marine Air Corps."[323] And how!

The HMX-1 team put its training to the test sooner than anticipated when the Marines were ordered to Korea to halt North Korean communist forces advancing across the 38th parallel. During the long years of the Korean conflict, the Marine Corps proved the value of vertical envelopment concepts, and used helicopters to transport battalions of men and countless supplies to the front lines. Unlike the experience of World War II, the Marines could also use helicopters to evacuate wounded soldiers to medical facilities, and ultimately ten thousand Marines would be evacuated or rescued from behind enemy lines. Throughout the conflict, the HMX-1 crew at Quantico used the knowledge gained in Korea to assess changes in equipment, and to train new officers in helicopter technology.[324]

As the Marines' experience in Korea would confirm, the helicopter proved its worth a thousand times over and revolutionized how troops and materiel would be transported and landed in the future. And it again validated the prescience of the brain trust at Quantico.

A platoon leaders class is shown arriving on Quantico's train platform. Courtesy base archive.

After the Korean conflict, Quantico's helicopter squad assumed another integral, if unexpected role. While vacationing in Rhode Island in 1957, President Dwight D. Eisenhower discovered he needed to return to Washington immediately. An HMX-1 helicopter stationed in Rhode Island for emergencies ferried the president across Narragansett Bay to Air Force One, a historic journey, given that no American president had previously flown in a helicopter. But the safe and efficient service of the UH-34D convinced the government that one of HMX-1's new functions should be providing quick transportation for the president, his cabinet members, and other dignitaries. The Marine One tradition was born.[325]

"Marine One is the most recognized, yet least known helicopter in the Marine Corps," noted one reporter. As the HMX-1 squad at Quantico increasingly provided helicopter transportation for government figures over the coming years, the presidential helicopters in the unit would become a frequent backdrop for photo opportunities on the South Lawn of the White House and elsewhere. But the designation "Marine One" does not apply to a single helicopter, but rather whichever helicopter in the "white topped" presidential fleet is put into service on a given trip. The aircraft remain part of the HMX-1 at Quantico, which to this day takes seriously the "X" for "experimental" in its designation by continually testing and evaluating helicopter technology for the Marine Corps. But the pilots and crew of Marine One and HMX-1 would still find time to form personal relationships with their distinguished passengers. A particularly artistic member of HMX-1 sent a Christmas greeting adorned with an aviation cartoon to Caroline and John Kennedy, prompting their mother, First Lady Jacqueline Kennedy, to send a thank-you note to the HMX-1 commander in return.[326]

While the helicopter fleet at Quantico grabbed the headlines and ushered the Corps into a new aeronautical age, fixed-wing aircraft remained an important part of the air station at Quantico. Jets, specifically Douglas A-4D Skyhawks, first came to Quantico in early 1962, although short landing strips at Turner Field first had to be equipped with arresting gears to accommodate the supersonic craft. The conditions at Quantico, however, proved perfect for testing how small jets could be used at equally small airfields, thereby simulating the conditions pilots might encounter during combat in enemy nations, or on aircraft carriers. Recognizing that jets produced considerably more noise than the planes typically flown at Quantico, Marine spokesmen assured the public that the planes "are ours and not the enemy's."[327]

Jet landings at Quantico complemented a research and development program underway at Quantico in small airfield for tactical support,

After arriving at the train platform, these platoon leaders classmates, checking in for summer training, found their way to quarters. Left to right are Privates First Class Bob Gene Mathers, Jack N. Anderson, Dan L. Shavens, Kent Frizzel, and Kidd W. Reed. Courtesy Marine Corps Historical Center.

Women were a welcome new presence at Quantico during the Korean War era. Private First Class Latheldia Mattingly is seen here preparing for a date, 1950. The gender balance was tipped hugely in women's favor, making each popular. Courtesy National Archives, Record Group 127.

otherwise known as SATS. The SATS program created portable runways made of interlocking metal panels, measuring approximately two thousand by seventy-two feet, and employing arresting gears and catapults. These runways were designed to be easily constructed in combat areas for accommodating jet aircraft. One of the first was erected between Turner Field and the Potomac in 1961, and the experiments conducted at Quantico would later be applied in the field in Vietnam.[328]

Atomic Age Education: Back to Basic

Having determined the strategy that would continue to set the Marine Corps apart from the other branches of the military, Quantico set about reorganizing its educational structure and putting it on a peacetime footing. To solidify the key role played by education at Quantico, the Commanding General of

Marine Corps Barracks, Quantico, assumed a second title in 1946 as Commandant, Marine Corps Schools, suggesting that the operation of the schools had become a vital part in operating the base as a whole. This also allowed the base and the schools to share administrative staff, freeing school personnel to focus exclusively on education. To a certain extent the commander's dual titles became a moot point in 1948 when the name of the base itself changed from Marine Corps Barracks, Quantico, to Marine Corps School, further signifying that education would be Quantico's dominant role in the Corps. "The post is the intellectual and tactical center of the Corps," observed the *New York Times*, "as well as the keeper of its great traditions."[329]

Despite a clear understanding that Quantico would be the leading educational and research and development unit in the Corps, just how to achieve that mission was sometimes confusing. The years between World War II and Vietnam would witness a bewildering succession of schools and courses. In 1950 the Tactics and Techniques Board joined with the Equipment Board to form the Marine Corps Landing Force Development Center (which later became the Marine Corps Development Center), and the schools at Quantico came under one umbrella unit as the Education Center, all of which came under the jurisdiction of the Commandant, Marine Corps Schools. The Marine Corps School Training Battalion became the Schools Demonstration Troops. The Training and Test Regiment became the Officer Candidates School in 1963. The Junior and Senior Schools in 1964 morphed into the Amphibious Warfare School and the Command and Staff College, respectively, which were often mistaken for each other. With each name change came either slight or significant modifications in what was taught and the kinds of officers the school hoped to graduate.[330]

For the first time since the 1920s, The Basic School (TBS) physically returned to Quantico,

Women officer training candidates awaiting combat swimming instruction, 1950. Courtesy National Archives, Record Group 127.

although it would be on the move for a decade before settling into a permanent home. When it first came home to Quantico in 1946, it took up residence in the D Barracks on Barnett Avenue. The next year it moved to facilities at Brown Field at the Air Station. But because The Basic School had added the responsibility of training officer candidates, authorities felt it needed a larger training camp. Thus, training facilities in the Guadalcanal Area were constructed. The Corps had been using the Guadalcanal Area, or "The Guad" as later Marines would nickname it, since 1942, but the three individuals camps located in The Guad would not be ready until the 1950s. Camp Goettge and Camp Upshur were completed in 1950, followed by Camp Onville, later renamed Camp Barrett. Old-timers at Quantico would have remembered Frank Goettge as a star football player for the Quantico

Marines in the 1920s, but the naming of the camp paid tribute to his death during the Guadalcanal campaign. To be closer to training facilities, TBS moved from Brown Field to Camp Upshur in The Guad in 1955, but the school barely had time to unpack before being moved once again in 1958, this time to Camp Barrett, where it settled into the first permanent buildings specifically designed for The Basic School. The first two TBS buildings at Camp Barrett consisted of Heywood and O'Bannon Halls, with Ramer Hall to follow in 1963.[331]

After the outbreak of the Korean War, the training of junior officers assumed even greater importance. TBS responded by cutting its nine-month course first to twenty-one, then to seventeen weeks to meet the Corps' demand for men. Not surprisingly, it was during the Korean War that TBS graduated one of the largest classes in its history.

The 10th Special Basic Class that graduated in February 1952 included 889 lieutenants. A class which graduated the year before might have been a bit smaller, but produced a distinguished group of Marines. By 1979, the class of March 1951 had produced a lieutenant general, seven major generals, and two brigadier generals, who among them had earned three Silver Star Medals, eleven Legion of Merit awards, two Distinguished Flying Crosses, ten Bronze Star Medals, and two Purple Hearts. Not a bad record for a combined total of more than two hundred years of military service.[332]

Educationally speaking, the Korean conflict also helped keep Quantico's stables open. While the war may have been fought in the Jet Age, old-fashioned pack animals proved better adapted to the harsh terrain of Korea. Back at Quantico, officers could take a course in pack saddles and the use of horses in ammunition transportation.[333]

Unlike the aftermath of World War I, when the Marinettes returned to civilian life, women continued to fill the ranks of the Marine Corps after World War II, and the educational structure at Quantico adapted to meet their needs. After the Women's Armed Services Integration Act of 1948 allowed women to join the military as regular soldiers, Quantico instituted the Woman Officer Training Program under TBS in 1949. Like their male colleagues, the women learned their particular duties as second lieutenants, including drill, naval law, and administration. The women's equivalent of TBS was the Woman Officer Indoctrination Course, which was undertaken after the women graduated from college. This program underwent significant changes in 1962 when the Training Course became the Woman Officer Candidate Course, and the Indoctrination Course became the Woman Officer Basic Course. What's in a name? With the changes in titles, the curriculum and functions of the coursework more closely paralleled that taken by male officer candidates. Some of the women in the early classes thought enrolling in the Women Officer Training Program might teach them leadership skills and lead to a military career, while others admitted the summer course was "like going to camp and being paid for it." Yet like the male Marines, the women certainly learned military discipline, and to sing while they marched. While the men might have sounded off more traditional cadences, women in the class of 1957 "Marine-ized" the "Yellow Rose of Texas." "You

Quantico's burgeoning population during the Korean War prompted construction of more base housing, such as this at Thomason Park in 1951. Men, women, and families needed places to live. These new homes lasted fifty years, after which they were replaced by grander dwellings. Courtesy National Archives, Record Group 127.

Construction of Quantico's amazing new Lustron homes engendered such curiosity that a permanent guard was established on McCard Road, the entrance to the development. Private First Class Charles Roessler is shown keeping lookers-on at a distance. The homes were all metal, inside and out. The Leatherneck, *July 1949.*

ought to see us as we march. The finest ever seen. Our trousers full of starch, United States Marines. The DI likes our Drilling (Ha!). But, as we march along, the spit shine on our shoes is going, going, gone!"[334]

FBI and ABC

While the courses at Marine Corps Schools, Quantico, produced skilled officers of a military type, the FBI Academy at Quantico continued to train skilled officers of the law enforcement variety. By 1960, the academy at Quantico had graduated four thousand policemen, many of whom went on to head local police forces in the metropolitan Washington area. While the academy still taught its own agents, many of the men who went through academy courses were already police officers looking to enhance their skills. The academy students were taught in laboratories, in lectures, and in the field, the last of which included the famous "Hogan's Alley" and "Combat Village." Hogan's Alley replicated a typical street scene in which students had to decide what methods would best subdue a criminal element under various circumstances. Combat Village, on the other hand, consisted of a series of cinder-block houses "in which all sorts of nefarious schemes are hatched, enacted, and counter-attacked." Over the years, academy instructors perfected courses which would provide both practical experiences that police officers might encounter in their careers, and the theoretical grounding needed to solve these problems.[335]

The Post School on base faced its own set of challenges in the 1950s, all of which seemed to have been resolved amicably. While other public schools in Virginia would not even consider voluntarily integrating their classrooms, the Post School at Quantico quietly did just that in 1951. Fourteen-year-old Ethel Britt, the daughter of Master Sergeant Charles Britt, enrolled as the first African-American student at the Post School in January. Perhaps because the military had integrated in the

Mrs. Blanche Shul, a Marine wife, enjoying her new Lustron home on McCard Road, with its combination dishwasher/clothes washer. Mrs. Shul, like most Lustron occupants, must have had to figure out how to hang pictures on the metal walls (via screws inserted in vertical sealing strips). The Leatherneck, July 1949.

Above: Longtime Quantico restaurateurs Pete Raftelis, on left, and Pete Pandazides, at right, are shown in front of Pandazides' popular Potomac Avenue eatery, the A No. 1 Café prior to World War II. The restaurants operated by these men and their families contributed to the quality of life for many Quantico Marines. Courtesy Mitchel P. Raftelis.

late 1940s, or perhaps because the turnover rate at the Post School was always higher than that of a traditional school and the student body was always in flux, the arrival of Ethel Britt does not seem to have caused much commotion, or at least none that made headlines outside of Quantico. By the time of the Supreme Court's 1954 landmark school desegregation ruling in *Brown v. Board of Education*, the Post School at Quantico had been integrated for several years, presumably with other African-American students having followed in the path set by Miss Britt, thereby avoiding much of the tumult and confusion forced school desegregation caused in other jurisdictions.[336]

Of more immediate concern to the parents of all children educated at the Post School were threats in 1955 to close the high school and allow Prince William County schools to absorb Quantico students, just as they did students who lived in the town of Quantico. Because federal law stated that when the county school system could accommodate students from military schools, the latter had to close. Since Prince William County had just built a high school ten miles from Quantico that could accept the 119 military students, U.S. Education Commissioner Samuel Brownell alerted Congress that the high school at Quantico was in danger of elimination. Luckily, the school found friends in high places, including Representative Joseph Holt of California, a former Marine who had served under General G. C. Thomas, the Marine Corps education superintendent. General Thomas testified before Congress that because the children moved from post to post so frequently, the curriculum at the post high school was geared specifically to their educational needs, especially with regard to college entrance require-

ments. After much debate over the definition of "suitable" schooling and whether or not a public school could provide this to military children, the House Education and Labor Committee voted to amend the wording of the previous law in such a way that the post high school would remain open. The Post School dodged a bullet this time, but it would certainly not be the last time the base schools were threatened with closure.[337]

Battles Royal over Housing

It seemed that no matter how many barracks, apartments, and prefabricated houses were erected at Quantico, the issue of housing for military families kept coming to the fore. To alleviate the shortage, the government in 1948 opened the bidding process for construction of sixty homes for the families of officers and enlisted men at Quantico. Although

A veritable "Who's Who" of Quantico town VIPs gathered to inaugurate the new parking meters placed along Potomac Avenue in the early 1950s. Quantico's commanding officer Clifton B. Cates is shown feeding the first coin into a new meter. With him, from left, is Al Presti, owner of a dry-cleaning establishment; Hunt Moncure, the local Dodge automobile dealer; bank president H. Ewing Wall; town mayor "Sticks" Bourne; and town policeman John Adams. Courtesy Mitchel P. Raftelis.

This photo calls to mind the curious old tale of the cobbler's children—although Quantico cobbler Frank Mozza, shown here in 1947, is wearing shoes. The post cobbler shop repaired thousands of pairs of shoes. Courtesy National Archives, Record Group 127.

Television was still an infant technology in July 1952 when these Marines watched it in Daly Hall. Most of these men would not have come from homes with televisions; widespread distribution did not occur until the late 1950s. (Marines must have adjusted the adjacent heater, despite the sign forbidding them to do so. The knobs have been removed and are nowhere in sight. Some things never change!) Courtesy National Archives, Record Group 127.

steel homes had been assembled at Quantico in the early 1940s, this bidding competition would prove historic in pitting steel-construction homes against traditional wood structures, a fight the steel industry would ultimately win. The Lustron Corporation of Columbus, Ohio, submitted the lowest bid per square foot, and was ready to turn its assembly line over to the Quantico project immediately. The contract called for thirty three-bedroom and thirty two-bedroom homes, which were ultimately constructed in the Argonne Hills and Geiger Ridge sections of the base. The single-story, prefab-

ricated homes included standard features and room designs of the day: a single bathroom, a living room with attached dining space, and a utility room. On at least one level, however, they were a strange choice to house manly Marines. Although made of the same enameled steel panels as service stations, the homes came in a vibrant array of pastel colors, including surf blue, maize yellow, leaf green, and candy pink. Strong enough for a man, but made for a woman, perhaps? Men and women could appreciate that the steel homes were virtually maintenance-free and pictures could be hung on the walls with

Sergeant Jiggs, sixth in the noble line of succession of base mascot bulldogs, is shown teaching students a thing or two about scholarship. Courtesy National Archives, Record Group 127.

magnets rather than nails. Other Marines appreciated the pest-repellent nature of the Lustrons: "A termite coming on the front porch commits suicide—there's just nothing for him to chew on."[338]

As welcome an addition as the Lustron houses were, sixty units only began to address the housing needs of married Marines, many of whom lived in the town of Quantico by necessity. While the base and town generally sustained a spirit of mutual cooperation, a scandal arose in 1950 which brought back memories of General Lejeune's accusation of the town being "an insanitary place" harboring bootleggers. In 1950, Commander James Davis, USN, testified before the Virginia General Assembly of the "ruthlessness of property owners" and "appalling" housing conditions Marines found there, concluding that "the town of Quantico is a scab on the fair face of Virginia." The issue arose when a Virginia delegate proposed abolishing rent controls imposed during the housing shortages of World War II. Davis' investigation revealed that some Quantico property owners were already violating the spirit, if not the letter, of the law by renting substandard property at vastly inflated prices, while a shortage of agents prohibited authorities from actively enforcing the controls. Davis feared that lifting rent controls would aggravate the situation in Quantico, where Marines who lived off-post either had to settle for what they could get in town, or move considerably farther away. Some representatives thought it appropriate to leave the rent control issue to the localities to solve, or lift controls in parts of the state not including military centers like Quantico and Hampton Roads.[339]

What might have remained a legal issue to be resolved at the legislative level became a regional

Basic School, 1952. Courtesy National Archives, Record Group 127.

scandal when the *Washington Post* published in February 1950 an article which documented the third-world conditions under which the wives and children of some servicemen were forced to live in the town of Quantico. The John Manzutto family, for example, paid $34 a month (with utilities) to live in a converted chicken coop, with only a shared outdoor spigot for running water, a detached bathroom shared by eleven adults, and a cesspool prone to overflow. "I've seen better places on Okinawa," Corporal Manzutto complained to the *Post*. Other Marines told similar tales of woe.[340]

The *Post* article brought the conditions at Quantico to the attention of the House Armed Services Committee, which responded by adding a nearly $2.5 million project for an additional 150 units at Quantico to a larger military construction measure before Congress. Chairman Carl Vinson remarked at the time that he frequently disagreed

with the *Post*, "but I have to read it anyway. However, I want the record to show it was the *Post* which kicked into the open the Quantico situation." Unfortunately, this addition to the measure was deleted from the military appropriation, with the suggestion that the job instead be completed to Defense Department specifications by a private firm, which would then operate the development. By August 1950 a private builder had been chosen to construct Thomason Park, near the intersection of Fuller Road and Route 1.[341]

By September 1951 the housing situation at Quantico was again up for debate in Congress, as the Senate Armed Services Committee approved a $4 million appropriation for emergency housing at Quantico as the Corps prepared to expand its troop strength there. Meanwhile, the Virginia General Assembly revisited the rent control issue in 1952, threatening to lift controls on the three "critical

Some Basic School coursework is hands on, as these students who are making a diorama may attest. The human Colosseus at left holds a tiny warship. Courtesy National Archives, Record Group 127.

Jiggs: The Dynasty Continues

Another confirmed bachelor roamed the streets of Quantico in the postwar period: the ever-present Jiggs. As the Korean War came to a close, so did the reign of Jiggs V. On October 17, 1953, in conjunction with the Fredericksburg Dog Mart, Jiggs V formally retired from the Corps, and passed the torch to his successor, Jiggs VI. Jiggs V had enlisted in the Corps in November 1946, and achieved the rank of corporal two years later, after providing mascot leadership to the all-Navy championship Quantico basketball team. His promotion to sergeant was approved in 1952, but failing hearing and vision prompted his retirement a year later, after his commanding officers determined that his health problems would interfere with his official duties. Jiggs VI came to the Corps as a hearty one-year-old named "Mike," whose first day on the job did not bode well for a long reign. One newspaper report noted that the former "Mike" wore a "look of disinterest" while being enlisted, and indeed Jiggs VI only survived the Corps until late in 1955. The enlistment of Jiggs VII continued the tradition in 1955, and although he made sergeant in 1959, he carried a somewhat spotty record of AWOL charges. "Sharp counsel at 'captain's mast' saved him from conviction," the *Washington Post* noted. Jiggs VII died of a heart attack in 1960, and like so many of his predecessors, was buried in Butler Stadium, "scene of some of his maddest romps."[344]

The Buck Stopped Here

Another Quantico tradition which continued unabated during the Cold War era was presidential visits. President Harry Truman would prove to be a frequent visitor to Quantico, enjoying trips down the Potomac on the presidential yacht *Williamsburg*. Like his predecessor, Franklin D. Roosevelt, Truman combined official duties with a little rest and

defense" areas of the state exempted in the 1950 legislation, one of which included Quantico. Quantico survived this round of rent control as well, and received a "critical defense area" exemption from the lifting of federal rent controls in August 1953, which was then revoked that December. Presumably the national attention brought to the condition of rental properties in Quantico encouraged landlords to keep their properties in better repair in the future, and the addition of the Capehart housing project on the base in the early 1960s further eased the housing crunch for married enlisted men and officers.[342]

Accommodations for bachelor officers were not forgotten in the maelstrom over married Marine housing. Liversedge Hall opened as a BOQ for male and female residents in 1960, replacing the varied housing facilities scattered about the base. Liversedge Hall was appropriately named for a BOQ facility. In addition to making a name for himself as a Quantico football player in the 1920s, commanding a distinguished unit on Iwo Jima, and earning two Navy Crosses, Harry Liversedge was one of the few bachelors to become a brigadier general.[343]

President Harry S Truman, shown here in 1945, once visited Quantico after ordering the presidential yacht to dock at Quantico's pier so he could take an early morning "constitutional" (walk). The base commander learned, perhaps to his horror, of the unscheduled visit only after receiving reports of presidential "sightings." The flustered general managed to locate the president near the end of his walk, having enjoyed Quantico's picturesque scenery. Copyright Chase-Statler, courtesy Library of Congress. LC–USZ62–98170

relaxation on board. Appropriately, on one of Truman's first visits to Quantico in January 1946, he signed legislation authorizing $160 million for emergency housing for veterans, servicemen, and their families. Given that the weather was dreary and the Potomac provided ice and fog off the coast of Quantico, Truman probably did not mind staying on the *Williamsburg*, where he signed additional pieces of legislation and worked on his State of the Union address. But once his presidential responsibilities were out of the way, Truman and his guests enjoyed "a gay New Year's Eve stag party" to celebrate the New Year. Having assembled an improvised band, the merry party enjoyed singing along to standards like "Auld Lang Syne," "Deep in the Heart of Texas," and a tune the Marines on shore probably appreciated for its martial air, "The Caissons Go Rollin' Along."[345]

Truman made it to shore a month later, much to the embarrassment of Quantico's commander, General Phillip Torrey. The president again brought the *Williamsburg* to Quantico's shores, but being both an early riser and a diligent walker, Truman went ashore at 7:30 a.m. for a brisk walk around the base. However, no one thought to alert General Torrey, who was mortified that the president had

managed to get in two miles before the general "hot-footed down to the road where the President had been sighted" to do him the proper honors. Truman could outpace nearly everyone in Quantico. "Always glad to talk to you," one local remembered, "if you could keep up with him!"[346]

A trip to Quantico in April 1946 joined Truman with the man who would ultimately be his successor, Dwight Eisenhower. While still the General of the Army, Eisenhower met with Truman on the *Williamsburg* to discuss military concerns. Two years later, one of Truman's cruises turned into an impromptu rescue mission as crew from the *Williamsburg* saved three Marines whose boat had capsized during an episode of choppy water and strong gusts of wind on the Potomac. The president watched the rescue and proclaimed it "a job well done." Closer to home, Truman cheered the Quantico Marines football team when they played Virginia Tech in Alexandria in September 1949, explaining that as commander-in-chief his place was in the Marines' rooting section.[347]

Once Quantico developed its postwar conceptual plan of helicopter use, President Truman journeyed to the base to witness demonstrations of the new tactics and technology. One of his more memorable visits to a demonstration at Quantico occurred in June 1950. As the Corps angled for a bigger budget, Truman enjoyed "an impressive display" of the Marines' new helicopter fleet, and the ways in which helicopters and other modern technology would change amphibious warfare. After a demonstration in which a helicopter transported an old 75-millimeter howitzer near the observation stand, the president decided to take a look for himself. Truman had served with the Army in World War I, and the old artillery officer in him could not resist comparing weapons. "It's the same old gun I used to handle," Truman noted, "only mine had a longer barrel and wooden wheels that high," raising his hand to indicate about four feet. While the president inspected the gun, photographers asked him to look down the barrel as a nice photo op. "You don't look down the barrel, you look up it," the ever-practical president replied. "If you look down it, you might get your head shot off."[348]

President Eisenhower visited Quantico several times during his presidency, although Eisenhower would spend more time at the Camp David retreat in the Catoctin Mountains of Maryland. But when the president decided to stay the night at Quantico in July 1953, it almost precipitated a national crisis. Eisenhower had intended to return to Washington to update the nation on the truce ending the Korean War, but when he decided to tarry a bit longer at Quantico to attend Sunday church services and take in a round of golf with General Omar Bradley, his press secretary took pains to convince the news media that Eisenhower's decision did not signal any deterioration in the peace process. As his adminis-

The U.S. government has always been one of the largest film producers. These Marine students are shown cataloging the post's film library in 1952. Courtesy National Archives, Record Group 127.

Basic School students using manually fed punch cards to tabulate data in 1953. Punch cards, an annoying technology which was the bain of many an operator—were the precursor of today's desktop computers. Courtesy National Archives, Record Group 127.

tration later wound to an end, Eisenhower took his family on a long-weekend cruise down the Potomac, enjoying fishing, golfing, and spending time with his grandchildren. When the presidential cruiser *Barbara Anne* anchored off Quantico on its return to Washington, Eisenhower tried his hand at trap shooting. The president hit about half the clay pigeon targets, a record matched by the naval aide shooting with him.[349]

A Powerful Presence

In January 1954, several Marines at Quantico may have thought the base was being subjected to another "War of the Worlds" scare, or that they saw aliens en route to Roswell, New Mexico. Nineteen Marines reported seeing a "glowing red light which traveled at a slow rate of speed, and in some instances stood still, just over the treetops, making no sound." Officials suspected that the strange lights could have come from navigation lights from aircraft in the area, but depending on which way the men were looking, perhaps they mistook lights from one of Quantico's newest neighbors as an ominous alien presence?[350]

In 1946 the Virginia Electric and Power Company (VEPCO) announced plans to build a 60,000-kilowatt steam power plant at Possum Point, on the junction of the Potomac River and Quantico Creek. The station would be connected by power lines to Richmond, Alexandria, and Charlottesville, to respond to the power needs of the rapidly growing Northern Virginia area. The Possum Point plant, which carried a $10 million price tag, opened in 1948, but had already reached its capacity by 1953, prompting the construction of a $16 million addition, thereby adding 100,000 kilowatts to its supply. So great were the power needs in Northern Virginia that VEPCO announced in 1972 that it would expand the plant yet again, adding

another 845,000 kilowatts to the supply. In keeping with the increased environmental awareness of the time, the Possum Point plant would also be made more environmentally compliant in the construction process. Although the Possum Point plant primarily served the expanding suburbs of Northern Virginia, transmission lines from the plant eventually crossed the Potomac River to supply Southern Maryland as well. The station, with its tall steam-release towers, looms above Quantico town and has become one of the area's most visible landmarks.[351]

From "Rallyes" to Religion

In addition to stargazing and seeing strange lights in the sky, Quantico Marines continued to have a wealth of sports and recreational opportunities to occupy their leisure time. As always, America's favorite pastime of baseball attracted talented Marine players, and in 1948 the Quantico Devil Dogs took its second consecutive All-Navy

As the Korean conflict ground on, charity attempted to keep pace with the devastation. Private First Class Penny Wedemeyer is shown with the results of a clothes collection project which netted forty-four hundred pounds of donations. Courtesy National Archives, Record Group 127.

Community giving also included that of a very personal nature. These 1952 blood donors are doing their part for this vampire-a-thon—surprisingly cheerfully! Courtesy National Archives, Record Group 127.

championship title after a hard fight against the SubPac Sailors.[352] The championship had looked doubtful for the Marines the previous year, when they lost the first game to the Bluejackets of the Naval Training Center of San Diego, prompting an adaptation of "Casey at the Bat" in the NCO Club that night:

> Oh, somewhere in this favored land
>> the sun is shining bright
> The band is playing somewhere, and
>> somewhere hearts are light,
> And somewhere men are laughing,
>> and little children shout;
> But there is no joy in Quantico—
>> the mighty Marines struck out.[353]

But the mighty Marines had the last laugh by ultimately taking home the championship trophy. Beginning in the late 1950s, Quantico also hosted the Marine Corps School Relays, which in 1963 was held in conjunction with the Sixteenth Annual All-Marine Track and Field Championships. The relays attracted Marine and civilian participants, as well as thousands of spectators.[354] Football and boxing continued to be popular sports throughout the postwar period as well.

For those less inclined to participate in group sports, other recreational activities beckoned at Quantico. Sailors could take advantage of the Potomac and Quantico's marina facilities for a leisurely sail along the river. Heartier mariners participated in the annual Frostbite Regattas, which

Mail call! Reservists from Waterloo, Iowa, in training at Camp Barrett, eagerly reach for word from home. "Postmaster" is Joseph B. Sibert. June 1952 photo, courtesy National Archives, Record Group 127.

began in November 1953. Landlubbers could choose from a variety of special interest clubs to join, including the Quantico Sports Car Club, which held "rallyes" to test the skills of the cars and their drivers. At the end of a long day, there were always clubs on base, and after 1948 enlisted Marines at Quantico could enjoy a gorgeous new Enlisted Club, featuring attractive murals, tasteful furnishings, and a large dance floor. For the Marines' wives, there was always the rush of club activities and the social whirl of life on base.[355]

For a brief period from 1957 to 1958, Marines who felt like tempting Lady Luck had their chance off of Freestone Point, just north of Quantico. Although slot machines and sale of alcohol by the glass were illegal in Virginia at the time, the low-water mark of the Potomac River on the Virginia side marked the boundary between Maryland and Virginia, putting most of the Potomac under Maryland's jurisdiction. By operating a gambling boat just off the shore of a planned resort at Freestone Point, the establishment was technically located in Charles County, Maryland, in which gambling and liquor sales were legal. The governor of Virginia vigorously protested the intrusion, and the ship and its gambling became a cause célèbre among Maryland and Virginia politicians for several months in 1957. Governor McKeldin of Maryland even accused the ship of being a "waterborne highball haven" and a "drifting daiquiri dispensary." Ultimately the Maryland General Assembly outlawed these types of gambling ships operating in the Potomac, and in 1960 the Freestone Point resort was reopened as "a 'family-type' recreation area."[356]

Those needing divine intervention on behalf of their sports teams, or perhaps a place for quiet contemplation always had a post chapel at their disposal, and after 1957 the chapel offered lessons in Marine Corps history as well. From Quantico's beginning as a military installation, the structures housing the post chapel had been a varied lot, ranging between metal Quonset huts to more traditional clapboard buildings. The new chapel was dedicated in 1957, but it was soon decided that the windows in the chapel should commemorate in etched-glass different scenes from Corps history, portrayed using religious motifs. Marine aviator John Glenn's 1962 space orbit inspired the final panel, which includes words from Glenn's address before Congress: "As our knowledge of this universe increases, may God grant us the wisdom and guidance to use it wisely." Continuing the blending of religion and history, wooden deck planking from several World War II battleships and cruisers were fashioned into communion cup holders on the chapel's communion rail.[357]

Into the Future

Beginning in 1965, Marine families at Quantico probably found the chapel a more comforting presence than ever once the Marines landed in Vietnam. While the Vietnam War would prove a watershed event in United States history, Quantico itself weathered the conflict without too many dramatic changes. Quantico continued to focus on its educational agenda, and absorbed new officer candidates into its flexible training program. And as ever, what Marines experienced in the field would be translated into new courses of instruction back at Quantico.

But wherever the future led Marine officers, they could at least be sure of one thing: the campaign ribbons on their uniforms would be as straight as the creases of their trousers, thanks to a local Quantico tailor. In 1955 Alfred Bolognese, whose father had opened the familiar A. M. Bolognese and Sons outfitting shop in 1918, received patent No. 2,707,344. Noticing how difficult it was to keep the "fruit salad" of campaign ribbons in proper alignment on a uniform, Bolognese developed a frame on which individual bars could be arranged together and attached to uniforms as a single unit, rather than individual rows. Thanks to Quantico Town's own Alfred Bolognese, no longer would Marine officers have an excuse for allowing their ribbons to fall into "an unmilitary straggle."[358]

Word from home for Platoon Leaders Class candidate Carmen LaBianca amounted to a fifteen-foot love letter. Absence makes the heart grow fonder! 1953 photo courtesy National Archives, Record Group 127.

Romance flourished on base as women officer training candidates increased in number. Sandra L. Detwiler and John Coyne are shown on a date at the post exchange. Courtesy National Archives, Record Group 127.

Being a Quantico wife could be hard. Most recipes in this cookbook included options for "cooking in bulk." Families often entertained, either for enjoyment or to observe protocol. In bulk. Courtesy Virginia Historical Society, Richmond, Virginia.

A COOK'S TOUR OF QUANTICO

Martial arts have always been important Marine disciplines, and it was no surprise that Quantico fared well in the Middle Atlantic Boxing Tournament in the 1950s. Relishing victory, from left to right, are Eldridge Thompson, Mario DeSantis, Charles Baggett, and Tommy White. Courtesy National Archives, Record Group 127.

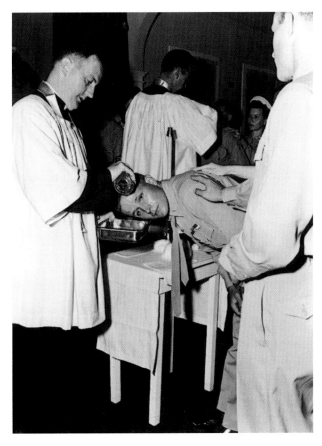

Above: Camp Barrett's chaplain and its Methodist choir rehearse for Sunday services in 1953. Courtesy National Archives, Record Group 127.

Right: It was a more religious age, and adherence to one's faith was widely practiced. Here Father Powell, base chaplain, baptizes a Marine. 1952 photo, courtesy National Archives, Record Group 127.

Considered a sport by many, bowling in the post's alley was both a popular pastime and an enjoyable competition. Undated photo courtesy National Archives, Record Group 127.

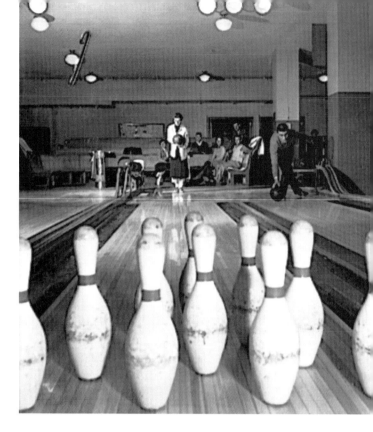

Equestrian activities played a role in the life of Quantico through the 1970s, when the stables burned. In this 1952 photo a young officer trainee performs a jump. Courtesy National Archives, Record Group 127.

The wonders of modern technology—mechanized infantries, etc.—did not remove entirely the need for horses in Korea, and Quantico's horse course continued. Horses also provided recreation. Courtesy base archive.

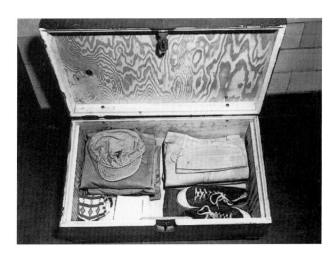

Discipline means dotting every "i" and crossing every "t." This included packing one's foot locker in the proper and approved manner—as demonstrated here. Courtesy National Archives, Record Group 127.

Submarines? At Quantico? These men test a troop-carrying sub, the USS Sea Lion, a standard World War II attack sub equipped with a special compartment on deck for carrying an amphibious landing vehicle or rubber boats. The sub would have been limited to surface trials. Courtesy National Archives, Record Group 127.

Marine trainees practice a 1952 embarkation run using a troop transport. The Potomac River was well suited to such surface warfare purposes. Courtesy National Archives, Record Group 127.

Left: Marines test-fire a 75-millimeter pack howitzer just after war's outbreak in Korea. The road in the background may have been a public road in the area claimed by the government during World War II; the cedar trees marked a former fence line. Courtesy base archive.

Right: Turner Field replaced the much smaller Brown Field No. 2 when it became too cramped to effectively support Marine aviation. This view looks due north along Turner's main runway. The newly rerouted Chopawamsic Creek is seen at bottom; previously it emptied into the river in the cove beyond the north end of the runway, at top of photo. Turner supported increasing aviation activities after World War II. Courtesy base archive.

High-altitude flying in the Jet Age required an oxygen mask and flight suit, modeled in 1949 by First Lieutenant Allen B. Phillips of Chippewa Falls, Wisconsin. Courtesy National Archives, Record Group 127.

The emblem of the Atomic Age (a mushroom cloud)? No. This is napalm set off by dynamite at Quantico in 1952. Napalm was one tool in the suite of weapons used by the military in Korea, and taught at Quantico. Courtesy National Archives, Record Group 127.

Several nations conducted Cold War biological weapons programs, and this trainee is practicing testing for biological contamination in one of Quantico's streams. Courtesy National Archives, Record Group 127.

Marching in formation, in an undated photo, courtesy of the base archive. As all good Marines know, marching in step is an art which must be learned.

This crashed airplane, fortunately, was a mock-up used by Quantico's firefighting school to teach trainees how to extinguish burning aircraft. Courtesy National Archives, Record Group 127.

President Dwight D. Eisenhower. An anxious country, awaiting word of an armistice in Korea, where a long and tiresome war was hopefully over, became concerned when the press reported the president staying longer than expected at Quantico, where he was visiting. The armistice was duly signed, and with only slight delay Eisenhower returned to Washington to announce it. New York Times *photo, courtesy Library of Congress. LC–USZ62–104961*

End of the war! "Korean Truce" screams the July 1953 headline in the Washington Post. *Salvatore P. Angerome of Brooklyn, New York, holds the newspaper; Walter J. Baker of Triangle stands behind. They and their many comrades were spared gruesome fighting. Courtesy National Archives, Record Group 127.*

Information played a greater role during the Cold War's fragile peace than it had during any previous peacetime. Quantico trained Marines in the various communication arts, several of which are represented on theses pages. All courtesy National Archives, Record Group 127.

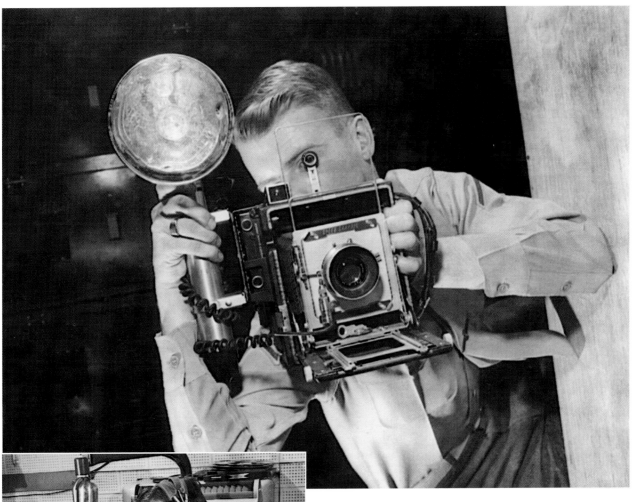

Below: Quantico's curious and angular geometry is shown in this 1954 aerial photo. Courtesy Marine Corps Historical Center.

Quonset huts, used so heavily during World War II, remained in use at Quantico even after the Korean conflict. This hut is a base chapel—note the little shrubs decorating the front entrance, making it more welcoming. Courtesy base archive.

Quonset huts were very functional, although slightly cramped, as seen in this photo. Note stove at center. Courtesy base archive.

Sometimes huts may become homes, as this Quonset hut at Camp Upshur shows, decked out for Christmas in 1954. There was much for which to be thankful during that post-war Yuletide. The fighting in Korea had stopped, and the country was at peace. Courtesy National Archives, Record Group 127.

Quantico's six-foot, four-inch, 240-pound Paul Ward, shown "crumpling" under a "savage" block thrown by sports commentator (and comedian) Mickey Rooney. The Leatherneck, *February 1961.*

Quantico devoted a sizeable building for the purpose of base chapel. This one, shown in 1954, was torn down in 1956. Courtesy National Archives, Record Group 127.

Integrating women into the Marine Corps proceeded fairly smoothly, at least at Quantico. Here women officer training candidates are being taught combat swimming "by a male instructor," as the caption prepared in 1955 offered helpfully. Courtesy National Archives, Record Group 127.

The town of Quantico's important and symbiotic relationship with the base is demonstrated by these military policemen escorting a post disbursement officer with money to the Quantico bank to make a payroll deposit. Courtesy Marine Corps Historical Center.

There is something slightly Greco-Roman about this photo—but then, the Marine Corps has always been infused with martial spirit, and Quantico's trainees have always been held to rigorous physical standards. 1956 photo, courtesy National Archives, Record Group 127.

Above: Sculptor Felix deWeldon, creator of the famous United States Marine Corps War Memorial overlooking Washington, D.C., also created a small-scale copy on display at Quantico. Here deWeldon monitors the statue's preparation in 1950. Courtesy National Archives, Record Group 127.

The "Man from Mount Suribachi," a depiction of Corporal Harlan H. Block, and a part of the Iwo Jima statue ensemble, is lowered into place at Quantico in 1954. Courtesy National Archives, Record Group 127.

Community outreach is and for many years has been a cheerfully observed practice at Quantico. Local Cub Scouts visit the post armory in this undated photo. *Courtesy National Archives, Record Group 127.*

Above: Marines march around Quantico's small-scale version of the Iwo Jima statue. *Courtesy National Archives, Record Group 127.*

Marching involves music, and music involves Marine bands. Quantico's music program meets high standards of excellence. *Courtesy National Archives, Record Group 127.*

Above: Aerial experimentation at Quantico, begun by civilians off the shoreline in 1895, has continued. YRON-1 helicopters, designed for aerial operations and courier duties, are shown being tested in 1959. *Courtesy Marine Corps Historical Center.*

Above: Giant jellyfish of the air—this view shows parachute riggers in the dry locker of the paraloft, or parachute loft, in 1957. Courtesy National Archives, Record Group 127.

Quantico's highly trained public safety employees aid and assist their civilian counterparts in Prince William and Stafford Counties, who benefit hugely from Quantico's presence. Courtesy Marine Corps Historical Center.

209

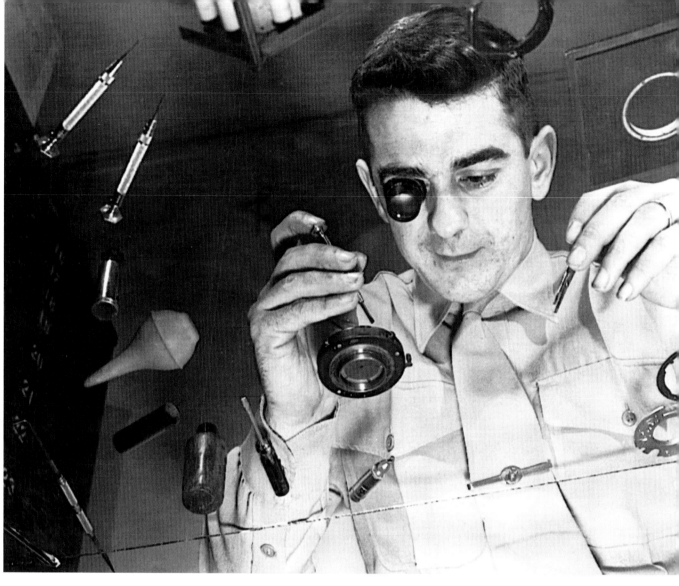

Training at Quantico concerned many things, from warfare to camera repair. Staff Sergeant John Kloczkowski is pictured "detail stripping" a camera shutter, 1957. Courtesy National Archives, Record Group 127.

Below: Basic School students learning the functions of a recoilless rifle during Quantico maneuvers in 1954. Courtesy base archive.

Above: Quantico infantrymen encountering a strangely pale but lantern-jawed enemy, 1957. Courtesy National Archives, Record Group 127.

Biological contamination was an ever-present aspect of warfare, particularly with several nations actively developing programs. Quantico Marines are shown checking a suspicious mist for the presence of chemical agents. None were found—this time. Courtesy National Archives, Record Group 127.

Above: Marines model the six different types of camouflage uniforms approved for use in 1957. Courtesy National Archives, Record Group 127.

It was the Jet Age, Information Age, and Atomic Age all rolled into one big unhappy tangle. This Marine is equipped with a filter mask—though his uncovered hands would not be protected from chemicals or toxins. Welcome to the Cold War. Courtesy base archive.

Jesus fed the five thousand with a single loaf of bread, but feeding the multitude at Quantico involves a different process. Here Walter Zuczek and Robert B. Smith prepare a meal in a post kitchen. Above, a butcher prepares a hind quarter for a roast beef. *Courtesy National Archives, Record Group 127.*

Marines drilling in formation in an undated photo, courtesy of the base archive.

Trainees abandoning the Basic School campus at Camp Upshur for a new one at Camp Barrett, 1958. Many Marines now arrived on base in their own vehicles, not by train. In the economic boom following World War II, almost all of them, by 1958, could and did own a car. Courtesy National Archives, Record Group 127.

Below: Home sweet home—if home happens to include bare concrete-block walls. This room was comfortable enough, as it included carpeting and was air-cooled. Undated photo, courtesy base archive.

Above: It may seem cold and institutional now, but this Quantico building, opening in 1965, followed the Space Age architectural style of the day. Courtesy base archive.

One of Quantico's most important tenants is the Federal Bureau of Investigation training academy, shown here during an undated dining-in. What about this photo may seem strange to the contemporary eye? Note the special agent training class is all white and all male. The serving staff is all black. The FBI now recruits officers of both genders and all ethnic origins. *Courtesy National Archives, Record Group 65.*

Above: Special agents receiving instruction in the nomen-clature and operation of the Thompson submachine gun at the FBI Academy's original building on Barnett Avenue. *Courtesy National Archives, Record Group 65.*

Before the National Transportation Safety Board assumed responsibility for investigating airplane crashes, the FBI performed this vital role. Here its special agents examine a simulated crash site in the woods near Quantico, photographing it and analyzing it for clues. *Courtesy National Archives, Record Group 65.*

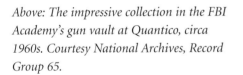

Above: The impressive collection in the FBI Academy's gun vault at Quantico, circa 1960s. Courtesy National Archives, Record Group 65.

Above: Bank heists aren't always this bloodless in real life. Here newly commissioned FBI special agents participate in a mock hold-up at their training academy at Quantico while studying bank robbery investigations. Courtesy National Archives, Record Group 65.

Left: FBI special agents fire tracer bullets from submachine guns on the FBI firing range at Quantico. The 1960s were unsettled—race riots, burgeoning crime, and a presidential assassination defined the period. These FBI agents would soon be combating new kinds of criminals using new criminal methods. An age of relative innocence was passing. Undated photo circa 1965, courtesy National Archives, Record Group 65.

CHAPTER VIII

THE FUTURE IS NOW

Good Morning Vietnam

Although Quantico did not suffer the same tumult and turbulence caused by the Vietnam War and the accompanying protest movements of the late 1960s and 1970s that rocked other areas of the United States, the war did affect Quantico in physical and psychological ways. In a physical sense, a little Vietnam came to the hillsides of Virginia in 1966. In order to accustom Marine officers to what they could expect in Vietnam, a replica Southeast Asian village was constructed at Camp Barrett in 1966. The composite village, named *Xa Viet Thang* ("Village of Vietnamese Victory"), included

Xa Viet Thang, or "Village of Vietnamese Victory," differed from the average straw-hut Vietnamese village: it was not in Vietnam. With America's increasing involvement in the war between the communist-run People's Republic of Vietnam and the Western-oriented Republic of Vietnam, Quantico began training Marines to fight in the tropics of Southeast Asia. Xa Viet Thang, built in 1966 by Marines in dense woods near Camp Barrett, served as an excellent Potemkin village. The Leatherneck, October 1971.

bamboo houses, mud huts, rice paddies, pagodas, pigs and chickens, and villagers themselves. All that was missing, noted the *Washington Post*, was the "searing heat" of the jungle and the "imminence of death." "Otherwise it is as real as the U.S. Marine Corps . . . could make it."[359] Every day ninety Marines would enter the village with the responsibility of ridding it of possible Vietcong by conducting a house-by-house search, all the while being careful to avoid the snipers and booby traps set for them. The scene was gruesome, but necessarily realistic, right down to the (mannequin) head of a village chieftain impaled on a stake for having resisted the Vietcong. In the more elaborate demonstrations then-Major William G. Leftwich's script would have:

> The helicopters—from Quantico's air station—whir overhead, scattering leaflets, loudspeakers booming a warning to the villagers to stand outside their homes and await the Marine assault without fear.
>
> A bonze (priest) is interrupted in his prayers. The village women stop their cooking. Children swarm excitedly into the square. And frantically, Vietcong soldiers race into the hidden tunnels.
>
> House by house, the Marines search the village as promised, and as they do, they encounter the VC tricks so deadly familiar in Vietnam. A medic treats the wounded.
>
> The tunnels are discovered. Gas and

These women Marines—no longer an oddity at Quantico, and thoroughly integrated into the force—raise the colors on a bright morning in May 1969. Their country was at war again, but unlike previous wars, the Vietnam conflict— while roiling the country tremendously—had less dramatic effects on Quantico, other than to herald the arrival of the modern era. Camelot had ended, and the future, however unsteady, had arrived. It was the dawn of a new day in more ways than one. Courtesy Defense Visual Information Center.

smoke are sent gushing into the entrances. Vietcong soldiers emerge and flee. There is a rifle crack, and one of them falls into the canal, its waters reddening with his blood. Another rifle crack and a sniper falls from a tree.

But amid the cacophony of make-believe battle, some Marines fall, too, as the sniper and the booby traps take their accustomed toll.[360]

It was a riveting drama for the Marine spectators in the stands, but it was also meant to sear images in their brains that one day might save their lives in real Vietnamese villages and against real Vietcong. By May 1967 more than three thousand students from The Basic School had been introduced to warfare at Xa Viet Thang.[361]

The addition of women and children, however, was a bit of last-minute inspiration by Major Leftwich, who recruited his own wife and children and those of other Marine families on base, to portray frightened villagers. Unfortunately, Lieutenant Colonel Leftwich himself would perish in a helicopter crash in Vietnam in November 1970.

In 1985, H. Ross Perot spoke at the dedication ceremony of a bronze statue of Leftwich that Perot had commissioned and funded in honor of his classmate at the U.S. Naval Academy. The Leftwich statue is located at The Basic School.[362]

Every war, regardless where it was fought, affected daily life around Quantico, and Vietnam was no exception. The Quantico Players cancelled the production of its new play in April 1967 when four of its cast and crew were mobilized for service in Vietnam. Although appreciative of past community support and the hard work of the company, the Players' president decided the quality of the show would suffer without the men involved. As the case of Lieutenant Colonel Leftwich proved, no matter how well trained were the Marines who went to Vietnam, not all of them would make it home. Like everywhere else in the nation, Quantico mourned its lost comrades, prompting officials to dedicate a memorial shrine in the base chapel in honor of those who gave their lives in Vietnam.[363]

Seeds of Discontent

While Quantico escaped much of the turmoil associated with the Vietnam War, it was not completely isolated from controversial issues facing the nation as a whole. Quantico Marines had access to an array of recreational and hard drugs, much like their peer group outside the military, and in 1970 a study of drug use at Quantico indicated that substance abuse was a "significant problem" on the base. The

This scene will be one remembered by generations of Marines training at Quantico—the building of esprit-de-corps, and of Marines. Courtesy base archive.

seriousness of the problem could not be avoided after Lance Corporal John Little died of a heroin overdose in the spring. The survey suggested that while drug use continued unabated at Quantico, the situation there was far from unique. "It's symptomatic of what is happening throughout society," the research team leader confirmed. Still, the gap between identifying a problem and finding a solution for it eluded the experts, and the commanders at Quantico. "They say we have a significant problem," observed Major Richard Evans of the Narcotics and Dangerous Drug Council, "but the thing that still escapes us, as with everyone is: What do you do? We need to teach the Marines what can happen both physically and punitively." By 1972 the statistics showed drug use on base had decreased, but largely due to fewer personnel being stationed at Quantico. Those who remained confirmed that any drugs desired could be obtained, albeit more discreetly than before. On Saturday nights "you'll see a lot of people high," a corporal suggested, "and it's not from the club." To address the problem, an

"Exemption" program encouraged addicts to come forward for treatment in exchange for amnesty from prosecution or dishonorable discharges.[364]

Given the nature of the duties performed by some Marines at Quantico, even the suspicion of drug use was enough reason to effect a transfer out of concern for national security. That thirteen enlisted men were transferred due to suspected marijuana use was not news. That five of the thirteen worked on the presidential helicopter fleet raised the alarm. While the suspicions remained just that—suspicions—even the idea that the men responsible for keeping presidential aircraft in good working order might have been under the influence of drugs was of tremendous concern. A spokesman for the Marines admitted that the incident confirmed that "there is drug use in the Marine Corps like there is in all other segments of society," but was quick to note that more than 90 percent of Marines followed the letter of the law with regard to drugs.[365]

In the era before President Bill Clinton's "don't ask, don't tell" policy with regard to homosexuals in the military, Quantico had already had to confront the issue. In 1958, five enlisted women from the Women Marine Detachment at Quantico faced accepting undesirable discharges or courts-martial stemming from homosexuality charges. The women decided to accept discharge papers rather than go on trial for lesbianism. Lance Corporal Jeffrey Dunbar hoped that the 1970s had brought with them an increased tolerance, but the nineteen-year-old received an undesirable discharge from the Marines in 1972 after authorities discovered evidence of his sexual orientation. While Dunbar admitted that he no longer wished to serve in the Marines because the airing of his preferences had made military life too difficult, he argued for an honorable discharge, explaining that "My sex life is my private affair. A less than honorable discharge will only stigmatize me for life." The American Civil Liberties Union took on Dunbar's case and a hearing at Quantico attracted a protest demonstration at Lejeune Hall by the Gay Activities Alliance. The case highlighted the polarized opinions held by many in the service on the issue of gays in the military. One honorably discharged gay Marine told the panel that homosexuality in the service was more widespread than they realized, and that many of the men who knew of his orientation accepted it with an "if that's your thing, fine" attitude. Another Marine observing the protest outside the building, on the other hand, expressed a wish for a grenade to lob "right in the middle of them." Dunbar lost his appeal for an honorable discharge. This demonstrated that Quantico would have to grapple with larger societal issues, just like the rest of the nation, and in the wake of the Civil Rights Movement, women's liberation, and assorted other protests over civil liberties, the status of gays in the military was one more issue Quantico would have to confront.[366]

Nor did Quantico escape racial tensions in the late 1960s and 1970s. Marine officials at Quantico frankly admitted concern in 1969 that escalating

Xa Viet Thang, built in a wooded Quantico valley as a mock-up of an actual Vietcong village, came complete with tunnels, propaganda, faux-Buddhist priests, and rice paddies. Courtesy base archive.

tensions between black and white Marines might lead to clashes, as had happened at Camp Lejeune and in Keneohe Bay, Hawaii. A small percentage of black Marines at Quantico considered themselves militants, while others sympathized with them, and finally there were "those who are just like society as a whole—they don't want to get involved." Ultimately Quantico escaped any serious racial violence, and many Marines chalked up isolated disturbances to the fact that "Marines are notorious for minor scraps," noting that prior to desegregation they would fight with each other "if there was no one from the Navy or Army around." Some officials at Quantico also pointed to liberal liberty policies and the proximity of Quantico town and Washington as outlets where Marines could blow off steam that might otherwise have manifested itself on base, as may have been the case at the geographically isolated Camp Lejeune.[367]

In the postdesegregation era at Quantico most racial tension did not reveal itself in open confrontation, but rather in charges of more subtle forms of discrimination. In 1971 several black Marines at Quantico testified before the

Schools Demonstration Troops at Xa Viet Thang act out a scenario, searching "dead enemy guerrillas" who "fired" on a Marine Civic Action Patrol in the faux–Southeast Asian village. The Leatherneck, October 1971..

Congressional Black Caucus of difficulties in securing adequate military housing, and that those who sought housing off base encountered resistance on the part of rental agents to show black tenants higher priced properties. The president of the Virginia chapter of the Southern Christian Leadership Conference complained in 1983 that the Marine Corps suffered from a "gross underutilization of blacks and women" as civilian workers on base, a significant statement considering that Quantico is one of the largest employers in Prince William County. Quantico officials denied this charge, countering that the base was "in full compliance" with government employment regulations. The SCLC's accusation did highlight that most black civilians on base worked in manual and service positions, rather than in professional jobs held primarily by whites, which echoed charges frequently leveled at large civilian employers nationally. Additionally, only 5 percent of the officers at Quantico were black. A decade later, the Marine Corps conceded confusion at statistics showing that minority servicemen dropped out of officer training programs at a higher rate than whites. Since Quantico produced 75 percent of Corps officers, its programs were a natural target of investigation, particularly after complaints from a Japanese-American officer candidate who the Corps acknowledged was "subjected to ethnic insensitivity" during his time at Officer Candidates School at Quantico.[368]

As the rest of the nation has witnessed people from all walks of life reach the pinnacles of their respective professions, Quantico has welcomed minority leaders whose talents transcended their gender, ethnicity, or skin color. Lieutenant General Frank E. Petersen came to Quantico in 1986 to head the Marine Corps Development and Education Command, after having earned distinction as the Corps' first black pilot and first black general. After tours in Korea and Vietnam, four thousand hours logged on fighter and attack aircraft, and a Purple

Tongue lolling, this determined young Marine meets the challenge over hill and dale at Quantico. Courtesy base archive.

Heart, Petersen found new challenges and excitement in administration at Quantico, which he called "the heart and pulse of the Marine Corps." A decade later Colonel Al Davis could be found at the helm of the Officer Candidates School at Quantico, the first African American to hold the position. While certainly a role model for minority students under his command, Davis' outlook on his job applied to all the men trained at OCS. "The joy you get out of this," he explained, "is impacting positively on people's lives." Brigadier General Gail M. Reals became the base commander at Quantico in 1988, a position she held until 1990. General Reals was the first woman to command a Marine base, a position for which she felt "very proud," while at the same time recognizing the "awesome responsibility" the milestone carried with it.[369]

Unfortunately the dawn of the twenty-first century did not bring with it complete elimination of racial and ethnic insensitivity, but Quantico's commanders continue to treat seriously negative influences on the morale and security of the military and civilian employees on base. "Obviously, there's not room for racism or discrimination of any kind at Quantico or anywhere in the military," confirmed base spokesman Major Timothy Keefe during an investigation conducted in 2001.[370]

"The Art of Warfighting"

Education and the training of officers was Quantico's single most important mission in the Vietnam and postwar era, and it remains so today. Some of the core schools, like The Basic School and Officer Candidates School, have been a constant presence at Quantico. Other courses of instruction came and went, or stayed, as global circumstances and the needs of the Marine Corps changed. But whatever the course, all training conditions would be helped along by the four seasons at

Quantico: "too hot, too cold, too wet and too dry."[371]

Officer Candidates School (OCS) functions as the Marines' "University for Officers" where officer candidates go through another "boot camp" experience at Quantico. The candidates are put through a grueling regimen of physical, mental, and leadership training, and the school operates under the philosophy that "before an officer can learn to give orders, he must learn to take them." Upon completion of the ten-week OCS program, the commissioned officers receive the gold bars of a second lieutenant. Women's companies were added to the men's full field training in 1977, although there were still legacies from the "powder puff" days of a separate women's OCS. Women, for example, still received a "beauty box" of cosmetics as part of their standard issue, to "keep them looking pretty" in the field. The times they were a 'changing, though, and the women often rejected concessions to their gender in order to bring them more in line with their male colleagues.[372]

Families—and wives—have historically been less numerous at Quantico than at other stateside military bases. But they have always been valued, as this tour of the base for Marine wives in 1966 demonstrates. Courtesy base archive.

From OCS, officers then transfer to The Basic School; something of a "finishing school" for officers. TBS's commander in 1989, Colonel Terry Ebbert, summed up the role of TBS: "The objective is to teach each lieutenant to be a thinking leader with the ability to make good judgments and to ensure that each is skilled in the warfighting techniques needed to lead an infantry platoon in combat—regardless of future military occupational specialty (MOS) assignment." Beyond that, Ebbert acknowledged, TBS courses would always be something of "a moving target," dependent upon the needs of the Corps. On one day, however, wives took over for their men. Beginning in the 1970s, wives of TBS students participated in "Jane Wayne Days" to

Historic Waller Hall on Rising Hill, the former Quantico Hotel—first occupied by the Marines in 1918—was razed as a safety hazard in 1968. Its role was assumed by the new Harry Lee Hall, new home of the Commissioned Officers Open Mess, which sported the best of 1960s chic interior design. Quantico Sentry, *October 18, 1968.*

get a feel for the kind of training their husbands underwent, and as an icebreaker for military wives who appreciated the opportunity to form social networks among themselves. "Now, when the husband comes in at the end of the day, there is an empathy, an understanding, a relating to a typical day at TBS," offered the wife of TBS's commanding officer.[373]

The Vietnam years did teach the Corps to take a closer look at itself and the men it recruited, and determined to accept only recruits who met a higher standard of professionalism. With this in mind, the Corps established the Staff NCO Academy at Quantico in 1971, designed to "educate the Staff Non-Commissioned Officer in the high standards of professional knowledge, *esprit de corps* and leadership traditional in the Marine Corps." Or, as *The Leatherneck* summed it up, "a six-week cram course in the 'how-to's' of being a SNCO." In the pre-Vietnam era, when promotions took longer, SNCOs had years of experience under their belts, and understood the hows and whys of certain functions. When the ranks of the Marine Corps expanded in the late 1960s and early 1970s, rapid promotions shaved an average of five years off the experience of a SNCO. The need for professionally trained SNCOs remained in the postwar era as the Corps looked to refashion itself as an ever-ready military force. By 1982 formal SNCO academies had also been established at Camp Lejeune and El Toro, California, although senior SNCOs completed specialized training at Quantico.[374]

In 1978 the Marine Corps Sniper Instructor School (later the Scout-Sniper School) got underway at Quantico. While the Marines had been utilizing snipers since World War II, the manufacture of an advanced rifle (the M40A1) and a renewed interest in sniper and stalking techniques, as well as intelligence gathering and observation skills after Vietnam, prompted the creation of the "Super Sneakers" course. Beginning in 1979, Quantico also trained classes of Marine Security Guards (MSG)

Above: Commissaries, so important to Marines and their families over the years, are products of their times, and this one opened at Quantico in 1973 with room enough for all the goods and displays modern Marine consumers were demanding. Courtesy base archive.

Quality of life for Quantico's families was promised by these metal homes, designed by the Lustron Corporation. Built in pastel colors, Lustrons were intended to be cheap and durable. Quantico had several in its Geiger Ridge and Argonne Hills housing districts—now the highest concentration of the spunky little houses anywhere. There was talk in the 1970s, 1980s, and 1990s of dismantling them, but an increasing sense of historic preservation has delayed what once seemed inevitable. Courtesy base archive.

Left: However far-fetched it may now seem, this Lustron Corporation advertisement extolled the ease of living in a Lustron home, such as those at Quantico. A well-clad 1960s housewife (in heels, no less) is seen hosing down her pastel-blue home. Via the Internet.

who would receive assignments all over the world. While guarding American embassy personnel and property might sound like light duty, consider all the occasions in which American embassies abroad have been attacked by terrorists or stormed by anti-American militants. Among the fifty-two hostages held captive in Iran for over four hundred days in 1979–1980 were nine Marines from the security detail. To further this training, the Corps added Marshall Hall to the base, a mock-up embassy in which instructors could run students through the basics, and incorporate practicum based on lessons learned from Tehran. In addition to the course at Quantico, MSGs were also taught by State

Department instructors, and subjected to frequent physical fitness and appearance tests. "Because our Marines will be representing our country at these overseas assignments, we want nothing but the best," explained one battalion commander. The only catch for candidates at the level of sergeant or below was being single, due to the possibility of serving in some of the more remote parts of the world.[375]

The Communication Officers School was also based at Quantico, and the forty-three-week course introduced students to the full range of communication tools, from satellite terminals to hand-crank telephones, as well as the logistical know-how to run a communications system. The Amphibious

Homes of a much less comfortable kind were the sort on offer at Combat Town, a concrete block settlement of faux homes, stores, and other buildings. Like its predecessor, Combat Village, FBI agents occasionally trained here too. The Leatherneck, *April 1985.*

Warfare School took a step back in time (or at least as far back as Smedley Butler), however, by including study of Civil War battles as part of the curriculum of military history courses. Like their predecessors in the 1920s, AWS students in the 1980s took field trips to prominent battlefields on the East Coast, studied the battles, and then in small groups planned operations over the same fields against a Soviet enemy.[376] What is "past is prologue," after all.

One of the most significant additions to Quantico's educational arsenal was the establishment of the Marine Corps University in 1989. Many familiar names were grouped under the university umbrella, including multiple noncommissioned schools and academies, TBS, OCS, AWS, the Command and Staff College, and the correspondence courses offered through the Marine Corps Institute. The reorganization signaled changes in curriculum as "FMFM-1, the Marine Corps' new philosophy on war, will be at the heart of every course. It is the study of the art of war that the University exists to promote." The university planned ultimately to offer master's degrees for

graduates of the Command and Staff College, receive accreditation for all its schools, and add to the faculty military and civilian experts in the field of military studies.[377]

Such an ambitious educational undertaking required an equally ambitious library and research facility to support the university's mission and its students. Ground was broken in 1991 for the 100,500-square-foot Marine Corps Research Center, designed not only to hold library and research materials, but also to serve as a conference facility. The planned center, according to then-Commandant General Alfred M. Gray "will serve as the hub of the Marine Corps University (MCU) and will dramatically improve the ability of the Marine Corps to collect, store, retrieve, and disseminate information related to the art of warfighting." Because not all Marine students would be physically located at Quantico, the research center also needed to offer an array of online resources and telecommunications technology to reach students at remote locations. In addition to housing the collection of James Carson Breckinridge University Library and the university research archives, the research center also offers leisure reading material for adults and a children's section for families. The research center opened in May 1993, and in recognition of his unfailing support of the library's mission, the center was renamed the "General Alfred M. Gray Marine Corps Research Center" in 2001. Although the library and archives collect materials from a variety of sources, the name of one particular donor would be recognized far outside of Corps circles. Movie actor Tom Berenger donated over one hundred military books from his personal collection to the center. Berenger has portrayed several historical military figures in his career, including Teddy Roosevelt and James Longstreet, and had amassed his collection while researching these roles.[378]

Complementary to its educational role, Quantico continues to lead the Corps in developing and testing new equipment supporting the art of war. In 1994 new NBC (Nuclear, Biological, and Chemical) equipment underwent trials at Quantico, and were deemed an improvement over the old gear. Forward Observer/Forward Air Controller System equipment was also developed at Quantico, and the technology reminded a *Leatherneck* contributor of the binoculars used by Luke Skywalker in *Star Wars*, only with a global positioning system, a computer, and a radio added. The GPS and computer technology allowed the FO/FAC equipment to locate enemy targets in a fraction of the time and with more accuracy than could be achieved by troops armed only with maps and binoculars. The Marine Corps Systems Command at Quantico was also responsible for developing a Chemical Area Monitor that would alert operators to the presence

of chemical agents. Quantico's Air Facility was also the first Marine station to link up with the Doppler Weather Surveillance Radar technology that is now standard in the aviation and meteorological communities. Not surprisingly, Quantico began hosting the Modern Day Marine Expositions in 1995, and provided the venue for a variety of other forums interested in new technology or the operation of the Marine Corps.[379]

While the schools for Marines flourished at Quantico, the base schools for Marine children were threatened with closure in 1981. And again in 2003. About every twenty years or so, whatever government agency then in charge of running post schools considers closing the schools on base and transferring the students to public facilities as a cost-cutting measure. Just as predictably, parents rally to the defense of their children's education, arguing that the high transfer rate of military children would make transitioning into public schools too disruptive, whereas the post schools dealt with student turnover rates on a regular basis. Local school districts express equal concern over their ability to

A Marine officer candidate receiving his first regulation haircut. The experience was often quietly traumatic as candidates watched their trademark locks fall to the floor. Rapunzel never had it so bad. The Leatherneck, *September 1990.*

Other joys awaited aspiring officer candidates after the first haircut was administered. In the exercise shown here, candidates are taught the value of teamwork: only through coordination could logs be lifted. The Leatherneck, *September 1990.*

Moving over and under objects silently while traipsing through water was taught to officer candidates in the Quigley, a stream emptying into the deeper Chopawamsic Creek. The Leatherneck, *September 1990.*

absorb Quantico children. The Defense Department usually backs down, and the post schools remain open. Even under the best circumstances, military children find it hard to make long-term friendships, and creating an atmosphere of school spirit is challenging, but parents and educators all agree that base schools provide a measure of security and flexibility lacking in public schools. "Our children benefit from being in an environment where people understand them," explained one parent. The students concurred, and recognized the benefit of being with other "military brats." "You get to grow a lot more here," one high school student commented. "Everyone gets to be a star here."[380]

The "West Point of Law Enforcement"

By 1965 the Federal Bureau of Investigation Academy at Quantico had expanded along with the national crime rate, and had outgrown its single building on Barnett Avenue. Rising crime statistics accompanying urbanization and civil unrest in America prompted President Lyndon Johnson and the FBI to request that Congress appropriate nearly $15 million to build a new FBI Academy at Quantico. Attorney General Nicholas Katzenbach

estimated that a larger academy could produce twelve hundred graduates annually, compared with two hundred at the smaller facility. Not only would more officers be on the streets, but they would be better trained to deal with the citizens they encountered, be they hardened criminals or civil rights protestors. "The better trained the officer," Katzenbach offered, "the more likely he will be to understand and respect the constitutional rights of the individuals." FBI director J. Edgar Hoover saw the academy developing into the "West Point of law enforcement" as the bureau incorporated new techniques and technologies into its training regimen. Armed with the president's support, the FBI had already received the appropriate acreage on the Quantico base from the Navy before it even approached Congress for funding. Not only would the new facility include residential space, classrooms, an auditorium and a library, but by relocating to the Guadalcanal Area of Quantico, FBI students would be considerably closer to the firing ranges at which they trained. The FBI did receive funding for the Quantico facility, but at the expense of requests for additional money to build a new FBI headquarters on Pennsylvania Avenue in Washington, D.C.

"It was felt the GSA shouldn't be building two FBI buildings at the same time," explained Representative Joe Evins. Aesthetics, in addition to budget constraints, may have delayed funding for the FBI headquarters since critics had charged "that it looks somewhat like a fort," which is what many Washingtonians have been saying in the years since its construction. The Secret Service also lost money on the Quantico deal, since the appropriations committee felt that the service could use the new FBI facility at Quantico for its training purposes, and did not need a separate center.[381]

By the time the new academy debuted at Quantico in 1972, its price tag had ballooned to $25 million. But the bureau was abundantly proud of its new facility and even detractors allowed that "students who go there should be impressed."

Unfortunately, the sterile building styles favored in the early 1970s failed to excite architectural critics or women. "The buildings suggest what the Mayans might have built in the jungles of Central America," the *Washington Post* observed, "if they'd had plate glass." Female reporters instead noticed that recruiting brochures ignored women by welcoming candidates regardless of "race, creed, color or national origin," and that the women's restroom facilities only offered bathtubs, not showers. Even worse, the general décor was described as "simple and masculine."[382]

If the FBI Academy was not fully prepared for fall-out from the sexual revolution, it was certainly prepared for the spectrum of criminal elements its graduates would face on the streets. On one end of the spectrum, the academy created something of a

Speed was of the essence for these Marine officer candidates engaging in the 3.2-mile log race, ever so conveniently routed over the roughest terrain available. The Leatherneck, *September 1990.*

"Las Vegas on the Potomac" by re-creating a casino environment to train agents in the recognition and apprehension of gamblers. In a casino environment, stocked with a roulette wheel, slot machines, and blackjack and craps tables (all of which had been confiscated from illegal gambling operations), agents learned how the games were played, and often rigged.[383]

Gambling rackets, however, looked tame in comparison with trying to get inside the mind of a killer. FBI agents at the Behavioral Science Unit at Quantico pioneered the use of computer technology to create psychological profiles of "the criminal mind" as a diagnostic tool for local police. In collecting the comparative data necessary to make their program work, Agents Bob Ressler and John Douglas interviewed "the country's most notorious mass murderers and assassins to find similarities between the personality of the offender and the offense." Included in the roster of interviewees were Charles Manson, Sirhan Sirhan, and "Son of Sam" killer David Berkowitz. The team's profiles proved remarkably accurate and helped further the use of psychological profiling in law enforcement. By 1984 the FBI had opened the National Center for the Analysis of Violent Crime (NCAVC) at the Quantico academy, devoted to applying "sophisticated behavioral science techniques" and computer technology to identifying serial killers and other criminal deviants. Out of NCAVC sprang the Violent Criminal Apprehension Program (ViCAP), which operates as something of a "nationwide clearinghouse" of information on patterns of violent crimes, which law enforcement officials can consult when try-ing to solve unsolved crimes in their own jurisdictions. Supporting the law enforcement community is the FBI laboratory, considered "one of the top forensic analysis centers in the world." In 2003 the FBI opened a new five-hundred-thousand-square-foot laboratory in Quantico, relocating FBI scientists out of their previous cramped quarters at FBI headquarters in Washington. For the first time in its history, the FBI laboratory would be housed in a facility specifically designed for scientific research, helping to maintain the purity and security of analyses of DNA samples, firearms, and other pieces of evidence.[384]

While psychological profile databases and state-of-the-art laboratories often garner the limelight, law enforcement still relies heavily on professional fieldwork, and for this reason Hogan's Alley still produces skilled graduates on a regular basis. Hogan's Alley took its name from a Richard Outcault cartoon first published in the 1890s called "The Yellow Kid," the protagonist of which lived in a New York slum called "Hogan's Alley."[385] The most recent incarnation of Hogan's Alley at

Officer candidates cheering for their platoon-mate (not shown) during pugil stick training. The Leatherneck, *September 1990.*

Maneuvers of a more general variety are also on tap at Quantico. Courtesy base archive.

Quantico was built in the 1980s. On the surface, Quantico's Hogan's Alley resembles nothing more than small-town America, with a bank, drugstore, and post office. But given that the bank is robbed on a regular basis, the comparison to a turn-of-the-century slum is not so far-fetched. "This is the most crime-ridden town in the world," joked Jim Pledger, the "mayor" of Hogan's Alley. Visitors to Hogan's Alley may also note that the Biograph Theatre in town perpetually shows "Manhattan Melodrama," the last picture gangster John Dillinger watched before being gunned down by G-men outside the real Biograph Theatre in Chicago in 1934. Inside jokes aside, Hogan's Alley has for years played a very serious role in training FBI and other law enforcement agents how to react to a variety of scenarios played out on the streets of America every day. The bureau's Practical Applications Unit at Quantico pits rookie agents against trained role-players to simulate real criminal activities that allow the rookies to put their training to the test, and to learn from their mistakes in a safe and constructive environment, rather than in the field. "The arrests never seem to happen the way you plan them," admitted Agent Emily of Syracuse, "but part of the preparation is planning for contingencies."[386]

Not only is Hogan's Alley good training for the agents, it allows ordinary folks to play criminal for the day. One woman, the wife of a Quantico Marine in real life, enjoyed her stint as a role-player. "I'm basically a housewife," she confessed, "but over here I get to carry drugs and wear a mink coat." An off-duty fireman echoed her sentiments. "It's a healthy way to be deviant."[387]

Over the years the reputation of the FBI Academy has so pervaded the national consciousness through the media that "Quantico" has become synonymous with excellence in law enforcement. Mystery writer Patricia Cornwell's forensic pathologist "Kay Scarpetta" regularly consults at Quantico, and makes use of ViCAP technology. "Clarice Starling," whose daring in playing cat-and-mouse with "Dr. Hannibal Lechter" in Thomas Harris' *The Silence of the Lambs* nets her a serial killer, is first seen while on her way from Hogan's Alley to the Behavioral Science Unit at Quantico. Viewers of the blockbuster movie version of this novel will recognize several real academy buildings in the background. Even soap operas have played on the Quantico name-brand to establish their characters' history. In 2003 the ABC soap "One Life to Live" introduced a serial-killer storyline, and established the brilliance of Agent John McBain by mentioning that "a couple times a year the bureau brings him to Quantico to actually teach the teachers."[388]

Beginning in 1985, the FBI ceased to be the only federal law enforcement agency to train at Quantico. In that year the training of agents for the Drug

Recreation and sport—however exotic—is essential to quality of life and development of a healthy Marine. The view at nine thousand feet looked good to these fifteen Marines, as they prepared to accept another into their ring. These men belonged to Quantico's skydiving team, formed in 1975. On this jump in 1978 they managed to assimilate eighteen skydivers into a formation known as the snowflake at five thousand feet, after jumping from a CH-53 Sea Stallion helicopter—truly thrilling stuff. Courtesy Defense Visual Information Center.

Enforcement Administration moved from Georgia to the FBI Academy at Quantico. At the time the move was viewed as evidence of a projected merger of the FBI and DEA, ultimately a false assumption. The two agencies shared training facilities until it was clear that their different functions required specialized spaces, and construction began on a DEA facility in 1997. The new DEA Training Academy, also located on MCB Quantico property, opened in 1999, and like the FBI compound, offered residential, classroom, and administrative spaces. The FBI and DEA do continue to share common facilities, such as the swimming pool and gymnasium.[389]

Little Pink Houses

When constructed in the late 1940s, the Lustron houses at Quantico were revolutionary, space-age, and addressed a serious housing shortage. By the 1960s the glow had begun to fade on the "lustrous enamel-on-steel" ramblers, literally. Although the enamel on the steel panels apparently never needed painting, decades of wear had taken its toll on the houses' vibrancy and durability. In 1983–84 the

Lustrons underwent a major renovation process involving the replacing of bathrooms, resealing of roofs, kitchen renovations, and repainting of interior and exterior surfaces with special paint designed to adhere to enamel surfaces. Fred Sullivan, Quantico's housing director, remembered that "the Lustron Homes were in really good shape" considering their age, and confirmed that they had required minimal maintenance over the years. He did concede that the Lustron lifestyle was a bit "like living in a filing cabinet," however.[390]

By the 2000s, though, Quantico found itself in a dilemma. Now over fifty years old, the Lustron houses no longer completely satisfied the needs of Marine families occupying base housing. The unusual construction materials of the Lustrons also meant that replacement parts were not available and prohibited compatible structural additions. For the Corps, demolition in favor of new housing seemed the best solution, but by now the Lustrons had become historic properties of interest to preservationists and people seeking hypo-allergenic housing alternatives. Backed by the government-sponsored

Hunting and fishing are readily available on Quantico's lakes and in its forests and fields. These fishermen are shown trying their luck on Lunga Reservoir, which also provides drinking water. The Leatherneck, *June 1963.*

Sometimes Quantico's teeming wildlife teems a bit too energetically. Here Staff Sergeant Clarence E. Wright inspects a beaver dam flooding an access road necessary for firefighting. The Leatherneck, *August 1971.*

Reconstruction Finance Corporation, the Lustron Company never made a profit and declared bankruptcy in 1950. Given that the company only produced twenty-five hundred units, the approximately sixty Quantico Lustrons form the largest collection of Lustrons in existence.[391]

But housing at Quantico entered a new phase in the 2000s as older facilities throughout the base are being demolished both for structural concerns and space issues. Duplexes at Thomason Park, for example, have been removed for newer housing that both suits the needs of modern Marine families, and explores public-private partnership efforts aimed at reducing the expense incurred by the military. Few former Thomason Park residents will miss their old quarters, apparently. On a recent visit to Quantico, Commandant Michael Hagee, who lived there during Basic, offered to help with the demolition. "I would not be opposed to coming down here with the bulldozer and taking that facility out," he offered. While certain buildings, like the commanding general's house, will be spared the wrecking ball in deference to their historic value, for housing directors at Quantico "the bottom line is our Marines are getting decent housing in a much faster

time" through new construction, rather than remodeling. As part of this new wave of residential construction at Quantico, in April 2002 the Corps dedicated two new Georgian-style brick barracks on base, honoring Corporal John H. Pruitt and Private John J. Kelly, two Quantico Marines who served in World War I.[392]

And the fate of the Lustron houses at Quantico? As of early in the year 2004, the housing authority on base plans to retain two of the houses in recognition of their historic value as examples of post–World War II residential architecture, and their contribution to base housing. Officials are hopeful that the market for Lustron houses will allow the rest to be sold to buyers interested in reassembling and rehabilitating the houses elsewhere. Those Lustrons not preserved at Quantico or sold to private parties are slated for demolition.[393]

Goodbye to the Old, Hello to the New

While the Lustron story has a happy ending, in October 1968 Quantico bid adieu to an old friend,

Waller Hall. Formerly, the Quantico Hotel, it predated the base, a vestige of Quantico's time as a resort. Concerns about the building's structural integrity caused it to be closed and demolished, but not before the Marines hosted a party to celebrate Waller Hall's fifty years of service to officers at Quantico. Harry Lee Hall took over the club functions, although no one was quite sure if the ghost of Waller Hall caretaker Booker T. Butler would stay with his beloved hotel, or would transfer with the officers that had been under his charge.[394] To this day, the site previously occupied by Waller Hall on Rising Hill remains empty.

Over the years maps of mainside would include new structures at the base. The Marine Corps Association moved into its new quarters on Broadway in 1986. The Staff NCO Club opened for business on the lower level of Daly Hall in 1990. The club boasted "modern and stylish furniture, a separate bar and lounge, and plenty of space to enjoy good times with friends." By 1995, however, this club had joined with officers' and enlisted clubs to form "The Clubs at Quantico," which were served by a central kitchen and support staff within a single building. Although the clubs remained separated by rank, merging them into one facility allowed them all to operate more efficiently. The new club facility also featured an outdoor garden area and banquet hall. With a play on Quantico's nickname as "Crossroads of the Marine Corps," the Crossroads Inn opened on mainside in 1997, replacing the old Hostess House as the recommended temporary

Left: The success of the FBI's small training academy on Barnett Avenue prompted the bureau to construct this palatial successor elsewhere on base. Although appearing verdant and lushly landscaped in this architect's conceptual rendering, the complex, when built, proved somewhat different—sterile and antiseptic concrete plazas, the abiding characteristic of 1970s urban design. Courtesy National Archives, Record Group 65.

Above: Computers take over the world in many a science fiction thriller. While that hasn't yet happened, they are now ubiquitous, and their importance caused Quantico to construct this Automated Data Systems facility in 1981. The building was designed to be environmentally friendly, with rooftop solar panels and planted earthen berms. Courtesy Defense Visual Information Center.

lodging facility on base. The Inn offers single rooms and suites, and is conveniently located near the clubs, swimming pool, and Exchange. In recognition of the phenomenal popularity of the annual Marine Corps Marathon, dubbed "The People's Marathon," the marathon's administrative headquarters received approval for its own building at Quantico in 2003, although the organization is paying for the structure itself. The marathon's headquarters will house the staff and will also store supplies for the race, which in 2002 used 21,500 space blankets, 130 pounds of Vaseline, and 116,000 safety pins![395]

Sports and Recreation

For those less inclined to run a marathon, the new fifty-eight-thousand-square-foot Colonel William

E. Barber Physical Activities Center opened at Quantico in 2003 at the corner of Barnett Avenue and Henderson Road. Unlike Larson Gymnasium, which was really a converted airplane hangar, the Barber Center was designed specifically for modern athletics, and offers the services of dieticians, classes in healthy cooking practices, and programs aimed at helping Marines to "stop smoking, manage stress, deal with diabetes and handle cholesterol." This was all instituted in the name of Quantico's "Semper Fit" program established in 1984 and aimed at promoting healthy lifestyles. But the Barber Center is not a complete break with tradition: free weights, basketball courts, and treadmills abound.[396]

Physical fitness has always been part of the Marines' mission to keep their troops in fighting trim. Established in 1967, the Physical Fitness Academy moved to Building 2001 in the year 1973. Like other academies on base, the PFA trained Marines to be instructors themselves, and imparting leadership strategies was as crucial in this course as any other. Students also took academic courses in physiology, nutrition, and first aid, all in support of their ability to "sell physical fitness" throughout the Corps. The academy suffered a tragic setback in 1968, though, when a routine training exercise in the Potomac led to the drowning deaths of eight Marines and a sailor attached to the academy after their twenty-five-foot "war canoe" overturned in the icy river. Because it was thought that the men had recently completed water survival training and should have had the skills to right their canoe after it capsized, a board of inquiry was established to investigate the incident. While the board did not reach any definitive conclusions in its month-long investigation, the limited amount of training time the men had received on the water, and the frigid temperature of the Potomac likely contributed to their inability to make it to shore.[397]

Recognizing the competitive streak among Marines, Quantico experimented with a "Survival of the Fittest" competition in 1982 as a way to get more Marines at the post interested in fitness activities and competing as units. The men and women competed in "military-type events" such as an OCS obstacle course, swim relay, boat race, and weapons firing demonstration. The event proved a success not just in encouraging physical fitness, but in showing the competitors that often technique and mental focus were more important than brute strength. While the Corps promotes teamwork in the field, the talent

of some Quantico athletes marks them for special recognition. Gunnery Sergeant Greg Gibson of Quantico won a silver medal in Greco-Roman wrestling at the 1984 Summer Olympics in Los Angeles, and triathlete First Sergeant Douglas Marocco of Quantico appeared on the cover of Cheerios boxes in 2003 as part of a cooperative effort between General Mills and Armed Forces Sports to promote military athletes.[398]

The year 1972 did see the end of a sports era at Quantico, when the football program, started in 1919, was discontinued after the commandant decreed that "continued personnel and financial support for football could not be justified." Coach Ron Eckert thought the decision shortsighted in comparison with the public relations and recruiting benefits the program accrued to Quantico, but resigned himself to dismantling the program since "an order is an order." Observers hoped the team

If commissaries are products of their times, the times are changing. Quantico received its newest commissary—at least its fifth since 1917, each bigger than the last—in 1997. Burgeoning availability of varieties and brands caused the need for more space. General Frances C. Wilson is shown presiding over opening day ceremonies. Courtesy Defense Visual Information Center.

Women officer candidates observe during physical training in 1980. Women have made great strides in winning acceptance in the Marines since the close of World War II. Courtesy Defense Visual Information Center.

would play the game of its life on November 18, but instead "performed today as if it were already entombed in Arlington Cemetery." Repeated fumbles and interceptions belied the emotions the team felt as it staged its last, unsuccessful campaign in Butler Stadium. Luckily, Quantico continued to field excellent marksmen in top shooting competitions, if Quantico fans sought another winning team to follow.[399]

With I-95 and destinations beyond so close to MCB Quantico, with so many Marines having their own cars and motorcycles and freedom of movement, with the proliferation of television, cable and the Internet, and with so many venues for recreation on base and in Q-Town, Quantico Marines in the late twentieth and early twenty-first centuries could find an abundance of recreational options at their disposal. As such, fewer and fewer blockbuster shows came along to entertain the troops, as had been the case during World War II. Modern USO shows focused on overseas outposts, where the men were craving reminders of home. But Quantico was not totally forgotten in the tour schedule, and in December 2001 Hootie and the Blowfish blew into town as part of the first "in-country" USO tour. In recognition of the domestic war on terrorism, the USO launched a Homeland Heroes tour, and took over a hangar at Marine Air Corps Facility, Quantico, to entertain the troops. By 2001 Hootie was no longer one of the hottest bands in the country, but the fact that they donated their time to the USO tour said quite a bit to the Marines who came out to listen. "I think this is a spectacular thing to do," said one Marine. "It lets Marines know they're right in our back pocket with us."[400]

. . . and a Little Stargazing

Quantico has always been good for a little stargazing, and not necessarily of the celestial variety. United States presidents visited frequently for a little rest and relaxation, and occasionally a celebrity

The manner and method of exercise is different, but, like the Marines from World War I pictured earlier, these officer candidates in 1980 continue the time-honored tradition of physically fit, physically competitive Marines. Courtesy Defense Visual Information Center.

recruit, like Tyrone Power, came through the ranks. Little changed in the Vietnam and postwar period. In this era, several of the celebrities on base came to witness their children enter the Corps. When Lewis B. Puller, Jr. enlisted in the Marine Corps and began his training at MCS Quantico, his father, the famed "Chesty" Puller, witnessed his son's enlistment. Actor Jimmy Stewart's stepson Ronald McLean did not follow in his father's famous footsteps and join the Air Force Reserves, but instead enrolled in the Officer Candidates School, bringing his father to Quantico to witness his induction as well. Unfortunately, neither story had a happy ending. First Lieutenant McLean was killed in Vietnam in 1969. Lewis Puller, Jr. was seriously wounded in Vietnam, losing both legs and parts of both hands in a land mine accident in 1968. He committed suicide in 1994, after having written a Pulitzer-Prize-winning autobiography about his ordeal.[401]

Celebrities of the presidential type continued to visit Quantico. Showing his Western background,

President Reagan went horseback riding in 1982. The first President Bush made a quick tour of Quantico in 1990, but still managed to hit the links while he was there. Their politics may have been different, but Presidents Bush and Clinton shared at least one thing: an enjoyment of golf. President Clinton took advantage of golf privileges at Quantico in June 1993, and his foursome included General Mundy, Commandant of the Marine Corps. The First Ladies, on the other hand, seemed to come to Quantico with more lofty goals in mind. Barbara Bush made the rounds of military bases during the 1991 Gulf War to show her support for the families of the men overseas, and included Quantico on her itinerary. After having written a book confirming that "it takes a village" to raise a child, First Lady Hillary Rodham Clinton was particularly interested in the childcare facilities on base during her 1997 visit to Quantico. Ignoring the media crews at her heels, Clinton took time to praise the children's arts-and-crafts projects and join them in making bead necklaces. Lynne Cheney, the wife of Vice President Dick Cheney, came to Quantico in October 2003 to promote the study of United States history.[402]

Conserving the Natural Environment

As far back as the 1920s, Quantico's planners recognized the value of the natural environment around the base and tried to incorporate ideas for the enhancement and conservation of the area's scenic splendor. Marines and civilians alike have always found Quantico a haven of outdoor recreation and abundant natural resources. Quantico's position at the confluence of Quantico Creek and the Potomac River ensured that the area would attract fishermen, and avid sportsmen contributed to enhancing Quantico's fishing and hunting resources. During

the 1950s, for example, the Rod and Gun Club undertook an enhancement program after surveying the Guadalcanal Area and discovering that the streams naturally flowing through the area were not suitable for stocking fish. Enter the beaver. The Interior Department's Fish and Wildlife Service introduced six pairs of "nature's greatest engineers," who quickly constructed dams which complemented man-made structures intended to control the water course. The erection of an additional dam on Beaver Dam Run resulted in the formation of Lunga Reservoir, which provided both recreational opportunities and a reliable supply of drinking water for the surrounding communities. Once the streams were cleared of debris, trails created to reach interior sites, the reservoir and streams stocked with fish, and picnic facilities installed, the resulting recre-

Physically competitive Marine Corporal Ken Owens of Quantico is shown here besting Nuri Zengin of the Turkish Armed Forces at the World Military Wrestling Championship in 2000. Courtesy Defense Visual Information Center.

Quantico's excellent sports record notwithstanding, it is hard to be more competitive than Sergeant Greg Gibson, who represented the United States in heavyweight Greco-Roman wrestling at the 1984 Summer Olympics. Gibson won the silver medal for his performance, thrilling the country—and his Quantico teammates. Courtesy Defense Visual Information Service.

ation area provided local residents with a "paradise" in which to enjoy boating, fishing, hunting, hiking, picnicking, and an array of outdoor activities.[403]

The ecosystem and wildlife management programs instituted at Quantico aspired to a happy balance between maintaining a stable animal population and meeting the needs of hunters. By the 1970s wildlife managers at Quantico had brought the white-tailed deer population back from the brink of extinction by monitoring hunting on the base and introducing agricultural areas aimed at providing year-round vegetation for deer and other forest creatures. But since the ideal deer herd at Quantico was estimated to be four to five thousand animals, recreational hunters served a useful purpose by ensuring that the herds would not go above this number and overpopulate the available conservation space. While poaching and dog packs still threatened the wildlife on the fifty thousand acres of open space, the conservation and wildlife programs

at Quantico rightfully earned high praise. As the Washington metropolitan area and suburban sprawl continued to inch ever southward, the natural areas maintained by Quantico and the neighboring Prince William Forest Park and Leesylvania State Park provided animal and human residents in the community with a welcome oasis from the urban jungle. "Between us and the parks," one Quantico natural resource officer concluded, "we're the only big green islands left."[404]

As a military post, however, the conservation areas at Quantico face unusual challenges in comparison with other parklands. Since the base's prime function is training, military maneuvers occasionally disrupt the natural wildlife habits in the area. "When the first round drops, the deer move out over the ridge," Wildlife Manager Bill Windsor explained in 1978, but "when it's over they move back in." Windsor also observed that the deer developed a sensitivity to the scent of ammunition shells, and tended to avoid those they found on base. But human hunters lacked the same acute sense of smell, and had to be aware that their hunting grounds contained unexploded ammunition dating back at least as far as World War II, if not earlier. In fact, as recently as the year 2001, Captain Milton Clausen came home to find an unexploded Civil War artillery round sitting on his deck. His children had found it while they were playing in the woods around Quantico and carried it home as a souvenir.[405]

On the other hand, the fires sometimes ignited by exploding ammunition in impact zones contribute to the ecosystem by adding plant nutrients and other trace minerals into the soil, eliminating

Nineteen eighty-four silver medal winner Sergeant Greg Gibson of Quantico, on podium at left, during the Romanian national anthem, played in honor of gold medalist Vasile Andrei. Courtesy Defense Visual Information Service.

underbrush, and encouraging the growth of herbaceous vegetation in its place, in much the same manner that Native Americans had done hundreds of years before. Even unexploded shells helped protect the environment by discouraging use of proving grounds for development, allowing birds, wildlife, and vegetation to flourish in relatively protected areas.[406]

Of course, as that old chestnut goes, you can't please all of the people all of the time, and Quantico has been no exception. In the 1970s thoughts of completing an official transfer of land from Prince William Park to the Marine base generated a little controversy. The five thousand acres in question had been part of the park, but used by the Marine Corps since World War II. The National Park Service was to have deeded the land to the Corps, but the deal was to have included the purchase of fifteen hundred acres of neighboring private property for the park. Congress never appropriated the

money, so the Marines simply used the land until an attempt was made to complete the transfer in the 1970s. Conservationists, however, protested the transfer saying that the park should keep the land for the benefit of all residents. They feared that since the Marines could eliminate public access to the property at any time, the Park Service would be a better custodian. Sportsmen countered this argument by claiming that the Marine Corps had instituted an excellent game management program, and should keep the property as hunting grounds. The Corps apparently kept the land under its control, since a letter to the editor of the *Washington Post* more than two decades later advocated revoking the Corps' land-use permit for the parkland. While these complaints did not fault the Marines for their stewardship of the land, others would. In 1993 the Environmental Protection Agency cited the base for violating clean air acts by releasing unacceptable levels of chlorofluorocarbons damaging to the ozone layer. The EPA and National Capital Planning Commission in 1996 protested that a new personnel building and parking lot proposed at Quantico would impact old-growth forest and was located too

Quantico's role in national affairs is demonstrated by this photo taken during the inauguration of President-elect Bill Clinton in 1993. Gunnery Sergeant Paul A. Avila of Quantico is shown controlling access to the Pentagon staging area. Marines from Quantico assist in inaugurations and other events. Courtesy Defense Visual Information Center.

Once inaugurated, President Bill Clinton fairly quickly—only four months later—discovered the delights of Quantico's spacious golf course. Clinton, being driven by Marine Corps Commandant C. Mundy, is by no means the only commander-in-chief to frequent Quantico's course. Courtesy Defense Visual Information Center.

First Lady Hillary Rodham Clinton is shown here visiting Quantico's child development center in 1997—perhaps during one of her husband's trips to the base golf course. Mrs. Clinton was known for her hard work and activism, reshaping the role of first lady. Courtesy Defense Visual Information Center.

near established wetlands. Despite objections, the project complied with all federal guidelines regarding environmental issues and continued apace.[407]

Quantico National Cemetery

Another sea of green was added to the map of the Quantico area in 1978: Quantico National Cemetery. As it became increasingly clear that Arlington National Cemetery would not be able to accommodate the thousands of aging veterans living in the Washington area, not to mention their families, the government began searching for a suitable alternative for those men and women who would not meet Arlington's stringent interment restrictions. A House of Representatives subcommittee investigated several possible sites, including Quantico, Lorton, Fort Belvoir, and a Civil War battlefield at Manassas. The historical import of the battlefield site quickly precluded it from consideration, while the proposed site at Quantico impressed the visiting delegation. A tract comprising more than seven hundred acres adjacent to Interstate 95 was chosen in 1976 for the cemetery at Quantico,

contingent on a transfer of the land from the Navy to the Veterans Administration, and Congress overwhelmingly supported legislation to officially create the cemetery. The Veterans Administration approved cemetery construction in 1978.[408]

Work on the cemetery was planned to be completed in phases over the next thirty years, and the first phase began in May 1983. As planned, the cemetery could accommodate over three hundred thousand burials. Quantico National Cemetery proved so popular a military burial site that by 1997 Prince William County and Veterans Administration officials, as well as veterans groups, were urging the county board of supervisors to consider widening Joplin Road to alleviate traffic congestion resulting from frequent funeral processions. With so much land available for burials, the national service director of AMVETS predicted in 1998 that Quantico National Cemetery could conceivably become "the largest of all the national cemeteries." By the end of fiscal year 2002 over seventeen hundred interments had taken place, including those of noted author and former Marine Leon M. Uris, and

Colonel William Higgins, who was taken hostage by terrorists in Beirut in 1988 and killed in 1990.[409]

The only potential drawback of the bucolic conditions at Quantico National Cemetery? Being adjacent to the Marine Base, Locust Shade Park, and Prince William Forest Park means that roaming deer have a tendency to take up residence in the cemetery and "graze on fresh flowers" they see as appetizers.[410]

The "Civilian Needle in a Military Haystack"

In many respects the town of Quantico is much like any other small town in America. Two main streets, Potomac Avenue and Broadway, help define its downtown shopping district. Residents often know each other by name, and descendants of the founding families still operate businesses in town and are active in local politics. It occasionally has disputes with adjoining jurisdictions, but generally coexists peacefully with its neighbors. It boasts a bank, post office, town hall, community center, real estate agents, laundromats and dry cleaners, restaurants, a train station, and a barber shop or two. Okay, more like five or six barber shops, which might be a visitor's first clue that there is something different about this town of over six hundred residents. An epidemic of overactive hair follicles among the population, or evidence of Rogaine in the drinking water, perhaps? No, just confirmation that the town of Quantico is next door to MCB Quantico, where the thousands of men stationed there routinely maintain their "high and tight" haircuts by visiting the barber shops in town on a weekly basis.[411]

A visitor's first clue to Quantico's unusual status probably would be passing a sentry gate on the way into town. By car, Quantico Town, or "Q-Town" as the Marines refer to it, can only be reached by Fuller or Russell Roads, linking to Barnett Avenue, all of which are part of and controlled by Marine Corps Base Quantico, thereby making automobile

access to Quantico Town dependent on the goodwill of the Marine Corps. Only transportation by train or boat links Quantico Town directly to the outside world. The town is surrounded on three sides by the Marine base, and on the fourth side by the Potomac River, which gave rise to Quantico's nickname as "the town that cannot grow," forever limited to its 42.7-acre boundaries. The town was once *completely* surrounded by the Marine Corps, which owned a sliver of the waterfront separating the town from the Potomac. The Marines transferred this land to the town in 1985.[412]

Not surprisingly, the presence of the Marine Corps dominates the town, leading one *Washington Post* reporter to describe Quantico as a "civilian

Quantico's proximity to Washington has ensured, over the years, a steady stream of members of Congress, such as Representative Beverly B. Byron of Maryland, a member of the House Armed Services Committee, seen here preparing to brave a demonstration flight in a Marine Corps TAV-8B Harrier aircraft. Undated photo, courtesy Defense Visual Information Center.

Quantico's launch of its Marine Corps University was already a success when Dr. Henry A. Kissinger, who was President Richard Nixon's national security adviser, visited as a guest speaker in 1998. Courtesy Defense Visual Information Center.

needle in a military haystack." The vast majority of the town's businesses rely on Marine customers, and during periods of military downsizing, troop deployments, or the institution of regulations on base affecting Marine access to Quantico Town, merchants suffer the consequences. "Ninety-eight percent of our business is Marines," confirmed Jack Scott, who owned two barber shops in town. "Without the Marine Corps, you could close this town down." Even something as simple as a change in dress regulations affected Quantico business owners enormously. In 1984, Quantico's commanding general Major General David Twomey lifted a three-year ban on Marines wearing camouflage ("cammies") in town between the hours of 6:30 a.m. and 6:30 p.m. During the ban, which merchants suspected had been instituted to prevent long lunches and beer breaks in town, Marines were required to change into formal uniforms or civilian clothes before entering town, which made running errands inconvenient. As a result, many men would stay in their cammies and shop and eat on base. Quantico businessmen lobbied Quantico officials to change the policy, and after the ban was lifted, merchants saw a 33 percent increase in their daytime trade. Town residents helped enforce the new regulations by warning camouflaged Marines of the approaching 6:30 p.m. deadline. Back in 1968, the town's dependence on the Marine Corps helped win it an exemption from a recent state law. The General

Assembly had passed the Alcoholic Mixed Beverage Law, barring towns of under twenty-five hundred residents from serving "mixed alcoholic beverages" within town limits. The population requirement immediately included Quantico within the regulation, but the prohibition on serving mixed drinks would have adversely affected restaurant and bar owners in Quantico who catered to Marines who patronized their establishments. Quantico businesses protested, which resulted in a bill that exempted from the previous code "any town within the State which is entirely surrounded by a base of the United States Armed Forces." A little creative legislation later, and the situation was well in hand for the town that could not grow![413]

Its economic resemblance to a company town aside, the town of Quantico has faced issues and

Mere men and women arrive at Quantico; Marine officers leave. The Officer Candidates School grounds, shown here in 1986, provide the location for the transformation—both physical and spiritual. Courtesy Defense Visual Information Center.

challenges apart from the Marine Corps. Like many other independent communities, local politics attracted the attention of interested residents, and ballots often included familiar family names like Bolognese, Pandazides, Giannopoulos, Raftelis, Abel, and Gasser. As the surnames suggest, many of the children of Quantico's founders remained in town, and many entered the political realm. "We conduct Town Council meetings in English," said Angelina Pandazides in 1967, "but we holler in Greek and Italian." But being a small town, sometimes political debate and elections were resolved in a "homespun" manner. When Howard Bolognese and Angelina Pandazides scored the same number of votes for mayor in 1969, town election commissioners merely picked a name out of a box rather than resort to a runoff election. (Bolognese won through the luck of the draw.) Mitchel Raftelis did not even have to mount

a campaign to be elected mayor in 1998, since no one opposed his candidacy. A Quantico native, Raftelis had served on the Town Council since 1967, but declined to run for mayor as long as his wife Georgia served as treasurer, which he thought might pose a conflict of interest. When Georgia Raftelis announced her retirement, her husband finally ran for the job he had unofficially been credited with having for years. As of the year 2004, Mitchel Raftelis is still ably serving as the mayor of his hometown.[414]

The presence of the Marine Corps has not eliminated crime in the hamlet next door, so Quantico provides its own police force. Military police did come to the town's aid when bandits robbed the Virginia National Bank in Quantico in 1970, took hostages, and led police and FBI agents on a car chase through Northern Virginia. Mitchel Raftelis remembered a time when some ne'er-do-wells

A lasting memory in the process of being created in 1999, during a low crawl competition held by India Company of the Officer Candidates School to settle a grudge. Courtesy Defense Visual Information Center.

were trapped by officials who tripped all the stoplights, causing a traffic jam on the one route out of town. By the late 1980s drug trafficking in the town and on base prompted Quantico town to supplement its three-officer force with ten extra reserve officers to combat the problem, and an undercover operation led to the arrest of ten Quantico residents on cocaine distribution charges. Quantico has also experienced some vandalism over the years, prompting the Town Council to institute a curfew for minors in 1990. Even one of Quantico's own law enforcement agents found himself in hot water in 1982. That spring Sergeant Leo Rodriguez was involved in an altercation in Quantico with a youth from Woodbridge, which led to the police officer's arrest on assault and battery charges, and being named in a civil rights lawsuit filed by the boy. Rodriguez pled guilty and received probation. Despite protests from some Quantico residents, he did retain his position as Quantico's police sergeant.[415]

Like its Marine Corps neighbors, the Town of Quantico is always looking forward for ways to improve the community, including bringing visitors to its doorstep. Ever since the RF&P Railroad extended its service to Quantico in the 1870s, the town has encouraged train service in the area. Falling ridership figures caused Amtrak to threaten discontinuation of service to the Quantico station in 1975, a threat which worried both the town and the Marine base serviced by Amtrak. A group of area residents formed the Save the Quantico Train Committee to lobby on behalf of the train stop. Fortunately, changes in train schedules and increased ridership allowed Amtrak to continue servicing Quantico, although passenger service would be severely limited and sometimes nonexistent until the Virginia Railway Express (VRE) began servicing Quantico in the early 1990s.[416]

But one thing has not changed since the 1970s: the train station at Quantico remains shuttered and passengers must wait on the platform for their trains. VRE and local train enthusiasts, however, are hoping that situation will change soon, and have begun the process of funding the remodeling of the Quantico train station. Members of the Prince

The stuff of nightmares in the Atomic Age, this photo captures a tremendous night-time explosion, but of a decidedly nonnuclear variety, during a 1987 live fire exercise. Courtesy Defense Visual Information Center.

Basic School students wearing field protective masks make their way through tall grass on Quantico's ample ranges. Warfare has grown more deadly, not less so, and protective gear is now considered standard kit. Courtesy Defense Visual Information Center.

Chemical/biological warfare is among the deadliest forms of warfare available, for both civilians and the armed forces. In this 2002 exercise, Operation Cold Dawn, Staff Sergeant Jamall Davis of the public safety team instructs Lance Corporals Nathan Reese and Juan Davila during a simulated biological attack on Quantico. Courtesy Defense Visual Information Center.

William Model Railroad Club will be largely responsible for remodeling the station, and in return will receive space in the station for meetings and model railroad displays. The first phase of the project has already removed asbestos from the building, while the next steps in renovation include updating restroom facilities, constructing display spaces, and adding a concession area for passengers and other visitors to the station. Local businesses hope that the reopening of the Quantico station will attract additional VRE riders, who will take the opportunity to shop in Quantico before or after their commute. Quantico officials also expect that the opening of the National Museum of the Marine Corps and Heritage Center will increase the traffic at the Quantico train station.[417]

Another proposal for creative transportation options to Quantico harks back to the town's days as Potomac, when trains were ferried down the Potomac for rail connections and passengers sailed to the area for recreation. For several years, regional transportation officials have been looking into establishing high-speed ferry services on the Potomac River between Quantico and Washington as a way of alleviating some of the congestion commuters experience on regional roadways every day. Thus far no concrete plans have been implemented, but Quantico town officials are still hopeful that the pier at Quantico will once again welcome commuters.[418]

Quantico already is looking to develop the potential of its waterfront, and plans are underway to beautify both the waterfront and the town itself. After the Marine Corps transferred four acres along the waterfront to the town in 1985, Quantico Municipal Park came into being. Town officials hope to someday build a picnic pavilion and new marina near the park, which would encourage recreational boaters to stop off in town. In the meantime, a new basketball court is planned for the park. The town has received a federal transportation grant to develop the Quantico Potomac Transportation Trail, a pedestrian and bicycle path starting at the train station and following the waterfront at the municipal park. The first phase of this system will concentrate on building the trail itself, while future phases may include other capital improvements, restoration of the seawall, and perhaps the long-awaited concert pavilion. In 1998, Quantico had hoped that a proposed twenty-mile scenic parkway connecting the town with Occoquan to the north would not only provide Quantico with another entrance into the town, but also lure tourists attracted to the small town charm of Occoquan. Between funding concerns and environmental impact issues, however, the controversial road never got off the ground.[419]

Beautification programs are also planned for revitalizing the business district, both to attract new visitors and business, and for the benefit of current Quantico residents. Joint efforts with local jurisdictions and the Marine Corps resulted in a grant providing Potomac Avenue with kousa dogwoods and seasonal plantings. The town's Streetscape and Revitalization Project hopes to fund new lighting and sidewalk projects, add new signage and store awnings, undertake building façade renovations, and perhaps even add sidewalk cafés.[420]

The town of Quantico is "rediscovered" every few years, and reporters invariably comment on Quantico's "Mayberry" and Main Street USA charm. The storefront signage might change over the years, but the storefronts themselves have remained remarkably consistent since the 1940s. For some visitors and returning Marines this feeling of nostalgia provides much of Quantico's appeal. There are, in addition, Quantico residents for whom change is not welcome. "They are not progressive in their thinking," Mayor Raftelis told the *Washington Post* in 1998. "They're not thinking ahead." But the Quantico of the 2000s hopes to be a community on the brink of change. Already an Internet café has arrived in the form of General Java's, and restaurants serving Japanese and Korean cuisine now compete with the pizza joints in town, although no one disputes the likelihood that the Marines will continue to be the primary economic influence in the area. Unfortunately, dreams cost money, which Quantico tends to receive in only small amounts in the form of federal funds and grants. "There's a lot more to it than just dreaming," Raftelis explains. Only time will tell if the Quantico of the twenty-

Marine Corps birthdays are important at Quantico. Here hundreds of Marines salute during a birthday ceremony at Butler Stadium. Courtesy Defense Visual Information Center.

first century will be able to strike a balance between maintaining its small town appeal, catering to the Marines, and attracting a more diverse group of visitors to its shores.[421]

September 11 and Security

Unless Q-Town becomes accessible by some undiscovered route, any development of the town will have to take into account heightened security concerns on base. America now lives in a post–September 11 world, with security in the forefront. Terrorism and security issues were certainly not new concerns to Quantico, and the base had a proven record of tightening security in times of societal turmoil. In spring 1971, for the first time since World War II, the base adopted a stricter security policy out of concern for drug activity, Weatherman bombings, and possible actions by

This photo shows two Quantico-area features: the Possum Point Power Station, which occupies the skyline north of Quantico town, and train service. This train is shown crossing the railroad's Quantico Creek bridge southbound from Possum Point during a rainy afternoon in 2000. Courtesy Rail Nutter News.

other militant groups. The base planned to channel civilian traffic through the main gate off Route 1, close shortcut roads, install new sentry boxes, and require visitors to obtain passes to travel on base. While these security policies also affected traffic in and out of Quantico Town, at first most people seemed to understand the rationale behind them. As Colonel George Babe put it, "We don't want to say tomorrow we wish we had done this today." When the base instituted random searches of cars entering at the main gate, then the protests began. "I felt like a fool getting out of my car and opening the trunk with all those men standing around," exclaimed seventy-two-year-old Elva Cornwell. "They didn't have to hassle an old, gray-haired lady like that." The Marines countered that the random searches had slowed the drug traffic on base, but still allowed civilians to traverse Fuller Road, which a district court had ruled a public thoroughfare in 1948. With all the focus on the main gate, however, the Stafford County entrance was somewhat ignored until 1999. At that time concerns about increased terrorism threats prompted officials to install a security gate at the unmanned entrance.[422]

Terrorist attacks on the World Trade Center and the Pentagon on September 11, 2001, changed the way all Americans thought of domestic security, and nowhere was that more true than in Washington and on military bases around the nation. Quantico went on "high alert." Captain Dan O'Connor, Quantico's antiterrorism force protection officer, began implementing security plans that had only been theoretical policies the day before. "It was high stress," he recalled later. "It was for real and it was uncharted waters." Vehicles were relocated from in front of buildings to avoid providing concealment for bombs of any kind. The Marine Band, the members of which are required to maintain physical and combat-related fitness, was called in for guard duty to protect the top Marine authorities on base. Over- and underpasses were examined for anything unusual, and visitors claiming to be going to Q-Town or the VRE trains were monitored more closely. Security agents immediately installed concrete barriers at both entrances to the base, added bomb-sniffing dogs to the security detail, and instituted stricter identification checks on everyone entering the base. The long waits at sentry positions inspired some employees to arrange staggered arrival times to ease delays. Some local authorities also met with officials from MCB Quantico, the FBI Academy, and VRE to coordinate their security efforts, especially with regard to vulnerable utilities, water treatment plants, schools, and transportation networks in the Quantico area.[423]

In the months after September 11, security concerns remained at issue, and authorities looked anew at their emergency procedures and prepared-

Architect's rendering of Quantico's spacious new national cemetery, as it was projected in 1977 to appear. A formal but subdued architectural style was used. Courtesy Veterans Administration.

The main gate of Quantico's new national cemetery. Although published in 1977, this rendering shows automobiles dating from the early 1970s, including one painted in avocado green, a color unique to that time. Courtesy Veterans Administration.

The Drug Enforcement Agency training academy, long hosted by the FBI, built itself spacious new quarters at Quantico in 1998. The DEA and FBI still share facilities, although not as many as before. Courtesy Drug Enforcement Agency and Federal Bureau of Investigation.

ness. On February 21, 2002, for example, selected VRE passengers, the Marines, fire and rescue workers, and area hospitals participated in a disaster drill on the railroad tracks next to MCB Quantico to practice response procedures in the event of a chemical or biological attack. While the rescue efforts did not unfold flawlessly and one participant found it hard not to laugh when the some of the "victim" Marines "were really hamming it up," it was clear the participating organizations had developed a workable plan for real emergencies. Likewise, Hogan's Alley at the FBI Academy now offers its share of terrorists to apprehend, in addition to the run-of-the-mill bank robbers, as the FBI seeks to refine its skills at counter-insurgency techniques.[424]

Although concrete Jersey walls still guide automobiles to sentry posts at the main gate on Fuller Road, civilians present identification while announcing their destination on base or in town, and heightened security measures are evident, Quantico has rebounded from September 11 and the subsequent military activity. The base and the town still convey an open atmosphere, and visitors are made to feel welcome in both locations, living proof that both move "always forward."

"Through the Eyes of Marines"

For the Marine Corps moving always forward requires also honoring where it has gone before. Quantico continued to honor notable figures from the Corps by naming buildings and installing statuary recognizing their contributions. One of the first dedications during the Vietnam era was something of a rededication. The original John A. Minnis Bridge at Quantico had been a wooden trestle bridge spanning Chopawamsic Creek, and had been dedicated in 1922 in the memory of an early Marine pilot killed in an accident at Quantico in 1921. The first Minnis Bridge was torn down in 1933, but replaced by another wooden span. By 1966 the "new" Minnis Bridge had so deteriorated that it collapsed under the weight of ice cover in November. Yet another, more sturdy Minnis Bridge was constructed in its place and rededicated in 1968. In a nice blending of past and present, three Marines had returned the original Minnis Bridge plaque to Quantico several years before. The men had found the bronze memorial plaque on a pile of lumber after the first Minnis Bridge had been demolished, and they had been passing it back and forth to one another for thirty years. They returned the plaque to

This new Navy Hospital, shown in 2000, replaced the grand old facility on Shipping Point, still in use. This building is a departure from tradition at Quantico, where most structures have long been curiously undistinguished—function over form. Courtesy base archive.

Centerpiece of the new Marine Corps University is this new research center, hosting a fine library collection and archive with many study areas. A university is only as good as its library, after all. The center is named for Alfred M. Gray, thirty-first commandant of the Marine Corps. Courtesy base archive.

the base for installation on the second Minnis Bridge, and in photographs of the dedication ceremony for the third bridge, the original plaque can be seen front and center.[425]

Anderson Hall was dedicated in 1970 to the memory of Private First Class James Anderson Jr., who posthumously received the Medal of Honor after being killed in Vietnam. Cox Hall at The Basic School, dedicated in 2000, took the unusual distinction of being named for an enlisted man, Sergeant Manuel A. Cox, who was killed in Beirut, Lebanon, in 1983. The Instructor Battalion wanted to honor Cox in order to recognize the role played by en-

listed Marines in training officers at TBS. A new fishing pier built at the Marine Corps Air Facility in 2002 took its name from Sergeant Joseph L. Fox Sr., a Purple Heart recipient wounded in Vietnam. The naming of the handicapped-accessible pier was particularly appropriate in light of Fox's service in the Paralyzed Veterans of America.[426]

Other plaques and statuary dedicated at MCB Quantico over the past three decades include well-known names and unsung heroes. In 2001, an admirer of General John A. Lejeune donated a life-size statue of the thirteenth commandant of the Marine Corps for display in front of Lejeune Hall in recognition of Lejeune's influence on the development of Quantico, Marine Corps education, and concentration on amphibious warfare. Women Marines were similarly honored with a "Molly Marine" statue placed in front of the new Gray Marine Corps Research Center in 2000. The statue, a replica of one dedicated in New Orleans in 1943, recognizes the contribution of all women to the Marine Corps, and its placement in front of the research center serves to remind students of the roles women continue to play in the Marine Corps University community.[427]

But not every worthy Marine has been a human, a fact not lost on those whose comrades were members of the animal kingdom. Born in 1935, Gracias served for thirty-three years as a training horse in the Quantico stables, occasionally substituted as a polo pony, and for the last few years of his life he provided leisurely horseback rides to Marines in search of a little recreation. When Lieutenant General Victor Krulak heard of Gracias' death in 1962, he recalled the affection his children had felt for the horse, and requested that Gracias be buried at his "old stomping grounds" near what is now the main exchange. It required the Maintenance Department and a front-end loader to do the job, but Gracias received a proper burial and his grave is now marked with a memorial plaque. In 2001, a

Efforts to improve the look of Quantico's Potomac Avenue are in the planning stages. Still after many years a healthy commercial corridor, the avenue should soon boast street trees, landscaping, and street furniture. It will be the first major change in appearance in many decades. To newcomers the town seems a throwback to a world gone by—where much that is good stayed that way. Courtesy Prince William County.

statue was dedicated in the lobby of the Marine Corps Research Center to the memory of war dogs. A replica of the Doberman pinscher statue erected in a World War II combat dog cemetery in Guam in 1994, the monument reminds human Marines of the valuable service dogs have given to the Corps in using their superior senses of smell and direction to locate enemy positions or warn of potential danger. "Far be it from me to advise the Marine Corps," one ceremony attendee remarked, "but before any Marine enters a cave, I hope he has a dog with him" for protection.[428]

Group achievement has also been the story of aviation museums at Quantico, which complemented the other museum facilities on base and at the Navy Yard in Washington. In 1966 retired Master Sergeant Clyde Gillespie received an assignment to create an aviation section of the Marine Corps Museum. A twenty-one-year veteran of Marine aviation, Gillespie was the perfect choice for heading an aviation restoration project at Quantico. Joined by his able assistant Leo Champion, the Aviation Section reassembled antiquated airplane engines, re-created space capsules and space suits, and displayed the helicopters which revolutionized the Corps. From these humble beginnings, the Marine Corps Aviation Museum was born at Quantico, and opened to the public in 1978. Like Gillespie and

Champion before them, the museum team often had to strip aircraft down to their component parts and completely rebuild them from the ground up. Such painstaking restoration not only showed the aircraft in all their original glory, but also made several of them operational. "Just as the Marine Corps has to be different and better to survive," said Colonel Tom D'Andrea, "the museum had to follow those lines. We decided to restore our planes not only to operational condition, but to combat readiness." Rather than stretching themselves too thin by covering the whole history of Marine aviation at one time, the museum team decided to focus first on World War II aircraft. Among the prized aircraft in the collection were examples of "Whistling Death" Vought F4U-4 Corsairs, one of the only surviving Grumman-built F4F-4 Wildcats, and one of the only Japanese Zeros thought to have participated in the bombing of Pearl Harbor. The aviation museum was later renamed the Marine Corps Air-Ground Museum in 1985 to encompass a broader scope of collections and displays, although like its predecessor it still called Brown Field its home, and in historic hangars no less. Among the "ground" acquisitions on display was a 1940 prototype Roebling Alligator, an early "amphibian tractor" which inspired the LVTs (Landing Vehicle Tracked) so integral to amphibious warfare. As of November 2002, the Air-Ground Museum closed to the public in preparation for moving to a new facility. The museum is scheduled to reopen in 2006.[429]

Of course, the most significant addition to the memorial landscape at Quantico will come with the

The FBI Academy campus at Quantico received a major new addition, in the form of a 500,000-square-foot laboratory built in a park-like setting. The facility opened in 2003. Courtesy Prince William County.

opening of the new National Museum of the Marine Corps and Heritage Center in 2006, which will bring together in one location the resources of the Marine Corps Air-Ground Museum and the Marine Corps Museum at the Washington Navy Yard.

Prince William County officials initially hoped that the Corps might consider a building site on the

Entrance plaza to the new National Museum of the Marine Corps. The soaring spire is meant to recall Marine aviation. Courtesy Marine Corps Heritage Foundation.

Cherry Hill peninsula just north of Quantico, arguing that locating the museum on the waterfront would allow for demonstration of landing craft and other amphibious activities. Land costs and accessibility factors, however, prompted planners to choose a site between Interstate 95 and Route 1, just outside the main gate of MCB Quantico. In 2001 Prince William County transferred 135 acres of Locust Shade Park to the Marine Corps for the purpose of building the Heritage Center. Plans for the Heritage Center ultimately call for a complex of buildings including the National Museum, History and Museums Division offices, artifact storage and restoration spaces, welcome center, conference and hotel facilities, a memorial park and chapel, parade grounds, hiking trails, and a large-screen format theater.[430]

This ambitious program has been a collaborative effort between the Marine Corps and the Marine Corps Heritage Foundation, the latter of which is raising the millions of dollars necessary to complete the first phase of museum construction. The Corps has funded the architectural and exhibit design phase, and will finance the cost of the exhibits themselves. The museum will ultimately be donated to the Marine Corps, while the Heritage Foundation will manage the revenue centers, such as gift shops and restaurants. The History and Museums Division will oversee the Heritage Center as whole.[431]

The architectural firm of Fentress Bradburn Architects, LTD, of Denver was chosen through a national competition. The firm is best known for designing the new Denver Broncos stadium and Denver International Airport. A 17,000-square-foot circular gallery anchors the museum space, above which is a 210-foot tilted glass and steel atrium. The modernistic design of the atrium's spire takes its inspiration from the World War II Iwo Jima flag-raising scene that has become so recognizable as the Marine Corps War Memorial, but also evokes visions of tilted howitzers, ascending aircraft, and a bayoneted rifle, all images associated with the Marine Corps. Exhibit halls can be accessed from this main gallery.[432]

Inside the galleries, the Corps' history can be followed in nine galleries devoted to particular eras. When the museum first opens, only three galleries covering the period 1940 to 1975 will have been completed; the rest will be completed in future phases. Visitors will also encounter "immersion experiences" in the era galleries which will tell the stories of Marine participation at Belleau Wood, Iwo Jima, Toktong Pass in Korea, and the Battle of Khe Sahn in Vietnam, all of which will support the museum's slogan, "Expect to Live It." A similar "Boot Camp Experience" is being developed to demonstrate to visitors who may have no prior association with the Marine Corps what boot camp is all about. Boston design firm Christopher Chadbourne and Associates is developing the exhibit galleries, work-

Interior hall of the new National Museum of the Marine Corps, featuring choice examples of the Marine Corps' excellent collection of airplanes. Courtesy Marine Corps Heritage Foundation.

ing in conjunction with the History and Museums Division. Since proponents of the Heritage Center hope the museum will attract families, the exhibit designers have had to find a balance between realistic depictions of all aspects of Marine Corps history and portrayals appropriate for children. As a compromise, "graphic displays will be camouflaged for the young."[433]

Planners anticipate that the Heritage Center will become a regional tourist destination, attracting as many as a half million visitors annually. While the museum has a natural audience in current and former Marines and their families, and those with a general interest in military history, the location of the museum also has geography in its favor for attracting visitors who might not seek out

Exterior of the new National Museum of the Marine Corps. The spire and its soaring atrium are the focal point of both the museum and the larger Heritage Center complex to be built around it. Courtesy Marine Corps Heritage Foundation.

the center on their own. Its proximity to Interstate 95 (the East Coast's primary north-south route) and Route 1, and Quantico's railroad facilities, will make the museum easily accessible by several transportation routes. The museum will also be located just a few minutes south of Potomac Mills shopping malls, currently one of Virginia's major tourist destinations.

Ground was broken on the Marines' site on September 27, 2003. Or rather, ground was broken near the site. Hurricane Isabel swept through the area on September 18, 2003, leaving in her wake damage and standing water at the museum site. Ever resourceful, the Marines simply transferred some dirt from the site to a drier parade field on base, allowing the groundbreaking to officially proceed as scheduled. The first phase of the Heritage Center is scheduled to open in late 2006.[434]

Proposed exhibit gallery in the new National Museum of the Marine Corps. This will be one of several galleries interpreting the rich history of the United States Marine Corps in war and peace. Courtesy Marine Corps Heritage Foundation.

BALLAD OF QUANTICO
(Tune: "My Country 'Tis of Thee")

My Quantico 'tis of thee,
With your quaint history
　Few can compare.
Midst your fair sylvan scenes
They find the ways and means
To train U.S. Marines
　Most everywhere.

Where the Potomac flows,
As on its way it goes,
　Built on its shore.
Post where Sea Soldiers came
Some woodlands to reclaim,
You'll bear an honored name
　For evermore.

Town where our nation's best
Trained in each grueling test
　To meet the foe.
Brave men without a sigh
Went forth to do or die,
Nor asked the reason why
　From Quantico![435]

Quantico means many things to many people. For some, Quantico is where the best and the brightest of the United States Marine Corps train as officers and for special duties at home and abroad. For others, Quantico is where FBI agents and associated law enforcement personnel hone their skills at solving crimes, and learn techniques to thwart lawbreaking before it occurs. For still others, Quantico is a quaint, if geographically confined little town that retains a yesteryear charm while catering to the needs of its Marine neighbors and its own year-round residents. Those with longer memories or an abiding interest in history may think of Quantico as part of a commerce route during the colonial days, as a port for Virginia's navy during the Revolutionary War, the site of formidable Confederate batteries at the beginning of the Civil War, or as a resort town and nascent industrial center at the end of the nineteenth century. Whatever connotation inspires each reader's initial interest in Quantico, all can agree that this place is more than the sum of its parts, and indeed boasts a rich and varied history with which "few can compare."

1. Carol Burke, "Marching to Vietnam," *Journal of American Folklore* 102 (October–December 1989): 426.

2. Charles A. Fleming, Robin L. Austin, and Charles A. Braley III, *Quantico: Crossroads of the Marine Corps* (Washington, D.C.: History and Museums Division, Headquarters, U.S. Marine Corps, 1978), p. 95. Hereafter Fleming, *Crossroads*.

3. Stephen R. Potter, *Commoners, Tribute and Chiefs: The Development of Algonquian Culture in the Potomac River Valley* (Charlottesville and London: University Press of Virginia, 1993), pp. 7–8.

4. Potter, *Commoners, Tribute and Chiefs*, pp. 1, 4, 9, 11; Fleming, *Crossroads*, p. 1.

5. Fairfax Harrison, *Landmarks of Old Prince William: A Study of Origins in Northern Virginia* (Richmond, Va.: Old Dominion Press, 1924; repr.: Baltimore, Md: Gateway Press, 1987), p. 19.

6. John Smith, *The General Historie of Virginia, New England and the Summer Isles. . . .* (London: I.D. and I.H. for Michael Sparks, 1624), pp. 20–40, 55–77; Helen C. Rountree, "Virginia Indians," *Encyclopedia of Southern Culture*, eds. Charles Reagan Wilson and William Ferris (Chapel Hill and London: University of North Carolina Press, 1989), p. 443.

7. Henry Fleet's writings as quoted in Fairfax Harrison, *Landmarks of Old Prince William*, pp. 143, 148.

8. Fleming, *Crossroads*, pp. 2–3; Virginia Writers' Project, *Prince William: The Story of its People and its Places. Originally Compiled in 1941 by Workers of the Writers Program of the Work Projects Administration in the State of Virginia* (Originally published, 1941; repr.: Manassas, Va.: The Bethlehem Good Housekeeping Club, 1988), p. 96; Henry J. Berkley, "The Port of Dumfries, Prince William Co., Va.," *William and Mary College Quarterly Historical Magazine*, second series, 4 (April 1924), p. 102.

9. R. Jackson Ratcliffe, *This Was Prince William* (Manassas: REF Typesetting and Publishing, 1978), p. 59; Fleming, *Crossroads*, p. 1; Berkley, "The Port of Dumfries," p. 99; Chester Horton Brent, *The Descendants of Collo. Giles Brent, Capt. George Brent, and Robert Brent, Gent., Immigrants to Maryland and Virginia* (Rutland, Vermont: Tuttle Publishing Company, 1946), pp. 50–51, 56–57, 63–64, 72–74 (quote on p. 73), 78.

10. Fleming, *Crossroads*, p. 3.

11. Eleanor Lee Templeman and Nan Netherton, *Northern Virginia Heritage* (privately published, 1966), p. 20; James R. Arnold, "Leesylvania State Park," *Northern Virginia Heritage* 7 (October 1985), available at www.historicprincewilliam.org/lee1.html (accessed January 2004).

12. Berkley, "The Port of Dumfries," pp. 101, 103–104.

13. Berkley, "The Port of Dumfries," pp. 104–106, 110, 113; Fleming, *Crossroads*, p. 4; Templeman and Netherton, *Northern Virginia Heritage*, p. 21; "The Henderson House," *Historic Dumfries, Virginia* website, http://www.geocities.com/TheTropics/Equator/ (accessed January 2004).

14. Emily J. Salmon and Edward D.C. Campbell, Jr., eds. *The Hornbook of Virginia History*, Fourth edition (Richmond, Va.: Library of Virginia, 1994), pp. 159, 164, 168, 170–171; Prince William County Historical Commission, *Prince William: A Past to Preserve* (Prince William, Va.: the Commission, 1982), p. 25.

15. Virginia Writers' Project, *Prince William*, p. 43.

16. Fleming, *Crossroads*, pp. 4–5; J. Devereux Weeks, *Dates of Origin of Virginia Counties & Municipalities* (Charlottesville, Va.: Institute of Government, 1967), pp. 4–5.

17. Virginia Writers' Project, *Prince William*, pp. 30–31; "Seven Years' War," *The Reader's Companion to American History*, eds. Eric Foner and John A. Garraty (Boston: Houghton Mifflin Company, 1991), pp. 984–985.

18. Richard L. Bushman, "Revolution," Foner and Garraty, *Reader's Companion*, pp. 936–939.

19. Fleming, *Crossroads*, pp. 5–6; "Dumfries Town Committee to Virginia Committee via Gentlemen in Fredericksburg," May 31, 1774, *Revolutionary Virginia: The Road to Independence, Volume II, The Committees and the Second Convention, 1773–1775, A Documentary Record*, William J. Van Schreeven and Robert L. Scribner, comps. (Charlottesville, Va.: University Press of Virginia, 1975), p. 92.

20. Virginia Writers' Project, *Prince William*, pp. 31–32.

21. Virginia Writers' Project, *Prince William*, pp. 33, 35.

22. Virginia Writers' Project, *Prince William*, p. 34; Fleming, Crossroads, p. 6.

23. *Leatherneck* (August 1933), p. 24; John E. Selby, *The Revolution in Virginia, 1775–1783* (Williamsburg, Va.: Colonial Williamsburg Foundation, 1988), pp. 126, 270; Arnold, "Leesylvania State Park."

24. Berkley, "The Port of Dumfries," pp. 115–116.

25. "Philadelphia Convention," Foner and Garraty, *Reader's Companion*, pp. 831–833; "Federalist Papers," *ibid.*, p. 387; "Ratification of the Constitution," *ibid.*, pp. 912–914; Virginia Writers' Project, *Prince William*, p. 37.

26. "William Grayson" and "Richard Henry Lee," *Biographical Directory of the United States Congress*, http://bioguide.congress.gov (accessed January 2004); Virginia Writers' Project, *Prince William*, p. 37; George Washington to William Grayson, January 22, 1785, *The Writings of George Washington from the Original Manuscript Sources, 1745–1799*, ed. John C. Fitzpatrick, available through the *George Washington Papers at the Library of Congress, 1741–1799*, http://memory.loc.gov (accessed January 2004).

27. Fleming, *Crossroads*, p. 4; L. C. Gottschalk, "Effects of Soil Erosion on Navigation in Upper Chesapeake Bay," *Geographical Review* 35 (April 1945), p. 231.

28. Ratcliffe, *This Was Prince William*, p. 57; Fleming, *Crossroads*, p. 7; Bishop Meade, quoted in Berkley, "The Port of Dumfries," p. 114; Virginia Writers' Project, *Prince William*, p. 37.

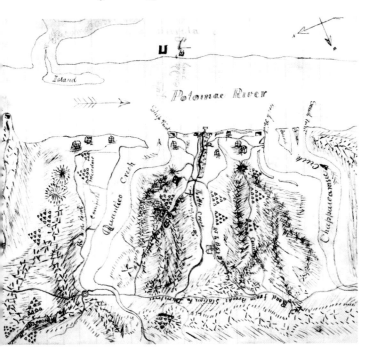

This map, drawn by a soldier of the 1st Arkansas Infantry— one of several regiments from across the southern states fortifying Quantico during the Civil War—shows a close-up view of the Confederates. Samuel Sidney Gause Papers, courtesy Dr. Edward L. Thackston, Nashville, Tennessee.

29. Virginia Writers' Project, *Prince William*, p. 42; Fleming, *Crossroads*, p. 7; Anthony S. Pitch, *The Burning of Washington: The British Invasion of 1814* (Annapolis, Md.: Naval Institute Press, 1998), pp. 39–40, 127–128, 172–173; *American State Papers*, Class V (Military Affairs), pp. 226, 568–569; Benson J. Lossing, *The Pictorial Field Book of the War of 1812* (New York: Harper and Bros., 1868), p. 919; Taylor Peck, *Round-Shot to Rockets: A History of the Washington Navy Yard and U.S. Naval Gun Factory* (Annapolis, Md.: United States Naval Institute, 1949), pp. 54, 56–65; Charles G. Muller, *The Darkest Day: 1814: The Washington-Baltimore Campaign* (Philadelphia: J. B. Lippincott, 1963), p. 139; Mordecai Booth, Report on September 10, 1814, Naval Records Collection of the Office of Naval Records and Library, Record Group 45, National Archives and Records Administration.

30. "War of 1812," Foner and Garraty, *Reader's Companion*, pp. 1129–1130.

31. University of Virginia Geospatial and Statistical Data Center. *United States Historical Census Data Browser*. ONLINE. 1998. University of Virginia. Available: http://fisher.lib.virginia.edu/census/. Accessed January 2004.

32. Samuel Sidney Gause, Jr., Co. G, 1st Arkansas Infantry, CSA, "Field Notes of Evansport and Vicinity," original manuscript in the possession of Edward L. Thackston, Nashville, Tennessee; Virginia Writers' Project, *Prince William*, p. 45.

33. Joseph Martin, *A New and Comprehensive Gazetteer of Virginia, and the District of Columbia* (Charlottesville, Va.: Moseley and Tompkins, 1835; repr. Westminster, Md.: Willow Bend Books, 2000), pp. 273–275.

34. Virginia Writers' Project, *Prince William*, p. 46; Angus James Johnston II, *Virginia Railroads in the Civil War* (Chapel Hill: University of North Carolina Press, 1961), p. 7.

35. Salmon and Campbell, *Hornbook of Virginia History*, pp. 45–46; Virginia Writers' Project, *Prince William*, p. 47.

36. Johnston, *Virginia Railroads in the Civil War*.

37. Evans, Samuel, Prince William County, Virginia, Eighth Census of the United States, 1860 (National Archives Microfilm Publication M653, reel 1373, p. 506), Records of the Bureau of the Census, Record Group 29, National Archives and Records Administration; Mitchel P. Raftelis, "Quantico History," draft of speech at Civ-Mil council meeting, September 20, 1995, courtesy of Mitchel P. Raftelis; interview with Mitchel P. Raftelis, February 18, 2004 (hereafter Raftelis interview); Maurice Evans Papers, 1837–1922, Mss1 Ev163a, Virginia Historical Society, Richmond, Virginia (hereafter Evans Papers).

38. Compiled military service record of Private Maurice Evans, Co. 1, 4th Virginia Cavalry, Compiled Service Records of Confederate Soldiers Who Served from Virginia (National Archives Microfilm Publication M-324, reel 40); Kenneth L. Stiles, *4th Virginia Cavalry. Virginia Regimental Histories Series* (Lynchburg, Va.: H. E. Howard, Inc., 1985), pp. 1, 109; Evans Papers, VHS; Magic Letter Express, Robert A. Siegel Auction Galleries, Inc., www.siegelauctions.com/enc/carriers/magic.htm (accessed January 2004).

39. P. G. T. Beauregard to W. B. Bate, June 17, 1861, in United States, War Department, *The War of the Rebellion: A Compilation of the Official Records of the Union and Confederate Armies*, ser. 1, vol. 2 (128 vols. Washington, D.C.: Government Printing Office, 1880–1901) (hereafter *OR*), pp. 932–933.

40. Mary Alice Wills, *Confederate Batteries Along the Potomac* (Prince William County Historical Commission, 1978; repr. 1983), pp. 9, 3; T. H. Holmes to George Deas, June 27, 1861, in United States, Naval War Records Office and Office of Naval Records and Library, *Official Records of the Union and Confederate Navies in the War of the Rebellion*, ser. 1, vol. 4 (30 vols., Washington, D.C.: Government Printing Office, 1894–1922) (hereafter *OR Navies*), p. 534; Fleming, *Crossroads*, p. 8.

41. J. C. Chaplin to S. C. Rowan, June 19, 1861, enclosure with Rowan to Gideon Welles, June 19, 1861, *OR Navies*, ser. 1, vol. 4, p. 525; Edward P. McCrea to Gideon Welles, September 24, 1861, *ibid.*, p. 686.

42. Beauregard to Bate, June 17, 1861, *OR*, ser. 1, vol. 2, p. 932; J. G. Barnard to George B. McClellan, September 28, 1861, *ibid.*, ser. 1, vol. 5, pp. 607–608; D. E. Sickles to S. Williams, September 30, 1861, *ibid.*, pp. 609–610; Jefferson Davis to Joseph E. Johnston, September 5 and September 8, 1861, *ibid.*, pp. 829–830, 834; J. Chaplin to S. C. Rowan, June 19, 1861, and T. H. Holmes to George Deas, June 27, 1861, *OR Navies*, ser. 1, vol. 4, pp. 525, 534; *New York Times* (hereafter *NYT*), October 9, 1861.

43. J. H. Ward to Gideon Welles, April 22, 1861, *OR Navies*, ser. 1, vol. 4, p. 420; Samuel L. Breese to Gideon Welles, May 12, 1861, *OR Navies*, ser. 1, vol. 4, p. 458; Eric Mills, *Chesapeake Bay in the Civil War* (Centreville, Md.: Tidewater Publishers, 1996), p. 41; Samuel L. Breese to Gideon Welles, May 17, 1861, *OR Navies*, ser. 1, vol. 4, p. 467.

44. Mills, *Chesapeake Bay in the Civil War*, pp. 47, 54–55; J. Russell Soley, "Early Operations on the Potomac River," *Battles and Leaders of the Civil War, Grant-Lee Edition, Volume II, part I* (New York: Century Co., 1887–1888; repr. Harrisburg, Penn.: Archive Society, 1991), p. 143

45. "Operations on the Potomac," *New York Herald*, October 14, 1861; A.D. Harrell to Thomas T. Craven, October 11, 1861, enclosure with Craven to Gideon Welles, October 11, 1861, *OR Navies*, ser.1, vol. 4, p. 710.

46. "Burning of a Rebel Schooner," *Saturday Evening Post*, November 16, 1861; A. D. Harrell to Thomas T. Craven, October 11, 1861, enclosure with Craven to Gideon Welles, October 11, 1861, *OR Navies*, ser. 1, vol. 4, p. 709; Welles to Harrell, October 12, 1861, *OR Navies*, ser. 1, vol. 4, p. 710.

47. Fleming, *Crossroads*, p. 9.

48. John P. Gillis to Gideon Welles, October 15, 1861, *OR Navies*, ser. 1, vol. 4, p. 719; Craven to Welles, October 15, 1861, *ibid.*, p. 718.

49. Gillis to Welles, October 15, 1861, *OR Navies*, ser. 1, vol. 4, p. 719.

50. Abstracts of log books of vessels serving in the Potomac Flotilla during the period from April to December 7, 1861, *OR Navies*, ser. 1, vol. 4, p. 762.

51. Craven to Welles, October 15, 1861, *OR Navies*, ser. 1, vol. 4, p. 718; *NYT*, December 8 and December 5, 1861.

52. Virginia Writers' Project, *Prince William*, p. 49; Soley, "Early Operations on the Potomac River," p. 143; *NYT*, February 12, 1862.

53. *NYT*, November 1, 1861.

54. *New York Herald*, October 14, 1861.

55. *NYT*, November 2, 1861; *NYT*, July 13, 1861; Spencer C. Tucker, "Torpedoes," *Encyclopedia of the American Civil War*, eds. David S. Heidler and Jeanne T. Heidler (New York and London: W. W. Norton and Company, 2000), p. 1963.

56. *New York Herald*, October 31, 1861; *NYT*, November 2 and 13, December 8, 1861.

57. Craven to Welles, October 15, 1861, *OR Navies*, ser. 1, vol. 4, p. 718; Craven to Welles, October 17, 1861, *ibid.*, p. 722; J. A. Dahlgren to Welles, October 15, 1861, *ibid*, p. 721.

58. *NYT*, October 18, 1861.

59. *NYT*, October 25, 1861; entry for September 1, 1862, *The Diary of Gideon Welles, Volume I: 1861–March 30, 1864* (Boston and New York: Houghton Mifflin Company, 1911), pp. 102–103; Soley, "Early Operations on the Potomac River," p. 143.

60. George D. Wells to George H. Johnston, November 10, 1861, *OR,*, ser. 1, vol. 5, p. 648.

61. *Supplement to the OR*, vols. 1–2, 5–6, 27, 48, 66, 68–69, 72; Graham Daves, "Twenty-Second North Carolina Infantry," *Southern Historical Society Papers* XXIV (Richmond, Va.: Southern Historical Society), pp. 256–258; *NYT*, December 20, 1861.

62. Private Robert H. Gaston and unnamed chaplain, quoted in Fleming, *Crossroads*, pp. 13, 14.

63. *NYT*, December 5, 1861; Joseph Hooker to S. Williams, February 20, 1862, *OR*, ser. 1, vol. 5, pp. 724–725; *NYT*, November 13, 1862; W. Robert Beckman, "Sickles, Daniel Edgar," Heidler, eds. *Encyclopedia of the American Civil War*, pp. 1784–1786.

64. Fleming, *Crossroads*, pp. 11–13.

65. Joseph Hooker to S. Williams, January 27 and February 20, 1862, *OR*, ser. 1, vol. 5, pp. 709–710, 724–725; Jos. Dickinson to John P. Van Leer, March 14, 1862, *ibid.*, p. 756; Wm. T. Street to E. P. McCrea, February 15, 1862, *OR Navies*, ser. 1, vol. 5, p. 22; *New York Herald*, January 5 and 16, 1862; *NYT*, February 9, 12, and 16, 1862.

66. Stephen W. Sears, *To the Gates of Richmond: The Peninsula Campaign* (New York: Ticknor and Fields, 1992), pp. 12–14.

67. Sears, *To the Gates of Richmond*, p. 8.

68. Wyman to Welles, March 9, 1862, *OR*, ser. 1, vol., 5, p. 23.

69. *New York Herald?*

70. *New York Herald*, March 17, 1862; E. J. Allen (a.k.a. Allan Pinkerton) to George B. McClellan, March 13, 1862, reel 18, Papers of George B. McClellan, Sr., Manuscript Division, Library of Congress.

71. Wyman to Welles, March 11, 1862, *OR Navies*, ser. 1, vol. 5, p. 25; *New York Herald*, March 17, 1862; *NYT*, March 21, 1862. See also W. H. C. Whiting to Major General Holmes, March 21, 1862, *OR*, ser. 1, vol. 5, p. 529; R. H. Wyman to Gideon Welles, March 9, 1862, *OR Navies*, ser. 1, vol. 5, p. 23; Gideon Welles to Joseph Bryan, March 17, 1862, *ibid.*, p. 26; *New York Herald*, March 10, 13, 17, 29, and April 8, 1862; *NYT*, March 12, 17, 21, 28, and April 6, 8, 1862.

72. *NYT*, March 12, 1862, and April 6, 1862.

73. Soley, "Early Operations on the Potomac River," p. 143; Fleming, *Crossroads*, p. 17.

74. Mills, *Chesapeake Bay in the Civil War*, p. 123; Elisha Hunt Rhodes, quoted in Sears, *Gates of Richmond*, p. 23.

75. Mills, *Chesapeake Bay in the Civil War*, p. 140; Egbert L. Viele, "A Trip with Lincoln, Chase, and Stanton," *Scribners Monthly* 16 (October 1878), pp. 813–823.

76. J. E. B. Stuart to R. H. Chilton, February 15, 1864, *OR*, ser. 1, vol. 21, pp. 731–735; Virginia Writers' Project, *Prince William*, p. 51; Arnold D. Blumberg, "Stuart's Dumfries (Virginia) Raid," in Heidler and Heidler, eds. *Encyclopedia of the American Civil War*, pp. 1895–1896.

77. Edwin M. Stanton to Abraham Lincoln, [April 1863] Transcribed and annotated by the Lincoln Studies Center, Knox College, Galesburg, Illinois. Available at *Abraham Lincoln Papers at the Library of Congress*, Manuscript Division (Washington, D.C.: American Memory Project, [2000–01]), http://memory.loc.gov/ammem/alhtml/alhome.html, accessed January 2004.

78. Charles Candy to John W. Geary, December 28, 1862, *OR*, ser. 1, vol. 21, p. 725; reports of J. E. B. Stuart (February 15, 1864), Fitzhugh Lee (January 5, 1863), James Watts (January 3, 1863), T. L. Rosser (January 3, 1863), and William H. F. Lee (January 4, 1863), *ibid.*, pp. 731–32, 738, 740–42; Extracts from "Records of Events" on the sever al returns for January 1863, *ibid.*, p. 755; F. Sigel to Major General Parke, January 21, 1863, *ibid.*, 991; F. Sigel to Charles Candy, January 22, 1863, *ibid.*, p. 995; Charles Candy to Major General Slocum, March 9, 1863, *OR*. ser. 1, vol. 25, pt. 2, p. 133; John M. Corse to Max Woodhull, May 20, 1865, *OR.*, ser. 1, vol. 47, pt. 3 p. 541; Virginia Writers' Project, *Prince William*, p. 53.

79. University of Virginia Geospatial and Statistical Data Center. *United States Historical Census Data Browser*. ONLINE. 1998. University of Virginia. Available: http://fisher.lib.virginia.edu/census/. Accessed January 2004.

80. Finding aid for Records of the Bureau of Refugees, Freedmen and Abandoned Lands, Record Group 105, National Archives and Records Administration.

81. Virginia Writers' Project, *Prince William*, p. 54.

82. "History of the Town of Quantico," courtesy of Mitchel P. Raftelis; John B. Mordecai, *A Brief History of the Richmond, Fredericksburg and Potomac Railroad* (self-published, 1940), p. 43–44. Mordecai indicates the road was the Alexandria and Fredericksburg Railway, rather than Alexandria and Washington, which reached Quantico in 1872. These two lines were both owned by the Pennsylvania Railroads at this time.

83. *Prince William Advocate*, reprinted in the *Alexandria Gazette*, August 1870?; *Alexandria Gazette*, July 22, 1871.

84. *State Journal*, quoted in *Alexandria Gazette*, April 23, 1872; Fleming, *Crossroads*, pp. 17–18; Virginia Writers' Project, *Prince William*, p. 55; Stuart W. Connock to Percy A. Brown, November 1, 1963, courtesy of Mitchel P. Raftelis.

85. *Washington Post* (hereafter *WP*), October 10, 1880.

86. Fleming, *Crossroads*, p. 18; "Work of the U.S. Fish Commission," *Scientific American*, June 10, 1882; *Letter from the Secretary of War, transmitting a letter from the Chief of Engineers, submitting copies of reports from Mr. S. T. Abert, United States Civil Engineer, of results and surveys of certain creeks and rivers in Virginia and North Carolina*, Senate Ex. Doc. 64, 48th Cong., 1st sess., 1884.

87. *Letter from the Secretary of War*.

88. *WP*, August 5, 1890.

89. Advertisement, *Forest and Stream* 36 (May 7, 1891), p. 323.

90. *Alexandria Gazette*, April 12, 1871; *WP*, October 10, 1892; *WP*, July 18, 1893; *WP*, March 30, 1899; *WP*, June 5, 1910.

91. *WP*, August 3, 1900; *WP*, January 16, 1901; *WP*, April 7, 1910; *WP*, July 30, 1896.

92. *WP*, October 13 and 14, 1894; *NYT*, October 14, 1894; Mordecai, *A Brief History of the Richmond, Fredericksburg and Potomac Railroad*, p. 53; *Alexandria Gazette*, November 12, 1894.

93. *WP*, January 29, 30, February 3, 8, 9, 24, 25, and March 1, 1896.

94. *WP*, November 24, 25, December 27, 1901; *NYT*, December 31, 1901.

95. *WP*, November 24, 25, 1901, and January 12, 1902.

96. *McClure's Magazine*, June 1897, pages unknown; *Scientific American*, December 22, 1894; *WP*, October 27, 1901; address of Alexander Graham Bell presenting the Langley Medal to Gustave Eiffel and Glenn Curtis, *Smithsonian Publication 2233*, 1913.

97. *WP*, September 18, 1912.

98. *Leatherneck* (February 1961), p. 26.

99. *WP*, February 22, 1916.

100. *WP*, April 16 and 23, 1916.

101. *Quantico Times*, July 14, 1916, copy in possession of Mitchel P. Raftelis; *WP*, May 21, 1916.

102. Woodrow Wilson, address, April 2, 1917, quoted in the *Columbia World of Quotations*, 1996.

103. Fleming, *Crossroads*, pp. 20–22.

104. Fleming, *Crossroads*, p. 22.

105. Fleming, *Crossroads*, pp. 22, 24.

106. Fleming, *Crossroads*, p. 24.

107. *WP*, May 2, 1917; Fleming, pp. 24–25.

108. *NYT*, October 14, 1917; *WP*, September 30, 1917; Fleming, *Crossroads*, p. 28.

109. *WP*, September 30, 1917; Robert F. Zissa, "Quantico," *Leatherneck* (November 1973), p. 46; John A. Lejeune, *Reminiscences of a Marine* (Philadelphia: Dorrance and Co., 1930), pp. 244–245; *WP*, March 14, 1918.

110. Fleming, *Crossroads*, p. 28.

111. *WP*, July 2, 1917; George B. Clark, *Devil Dogs: Fighting Marines of World War I* (Novato, Cal.: Presidio Press, 1999), p. 18.

112. Fleming, *Crossroads*, p. 26; Clark, *Devil Dogs*, p. 8.

113. *WP*, July 2, 1917; Fleming, *Crossroads*, p. 28; *WP*, September 30, 1917; *NYT*, October 14, 1917.

114. Lejeune, *Reminiscences*, p. 246.

115. *NYT*, October 14, 1917; *WP*, September 30, 1917.

116. Tim Travers, "Trench Warfare," in *The Oxford Companion to American Military History*, John Whiteclay Chambers, II, ed. (Oxford and New York: Oxford University Press, 1999), p. 734; *NYT*, October 14, 1917; James M. Sellers, quoted in Clark, *Devil Dogs*, p. 7.

117. *NYT*, October 14, 1917.

118. *WP*, September 30, 1917; *NYT*, October 14, 1917.

119. *NYT*, October 14, 1917.

120. Clark, *Devil Dogs*, p. 16.

121. Clark, *Devil Dogs*, pp. 16–17, 113.

122. Sellers, quoted in Clark, *Devil Dogs*, p. 7.

123. Frank F. Zissa, quoted in Zissa, "Quantico," pp. 44–45.

124. Zissa, "Quantico," p. 45.

125. Soldier quoted in Clark, *Devil Dogs*, p. 17.

126. Zissa, "Quantico," p. 45; *Leatherneck*, November 1975.

127. Captain John H. Craige, quoted in *Quantico Sentry*, November 7, 1941.

128. "The Duckboard," *Leatherneck* (November 1978), p. 23.

129. *Leatherneck* (October 1967), p. 69.

130. Lejeune, *Reminiscences*, pp. 244–245; *Quantico Sentry*, May 12, 1967; Craige, *Quantico Sentry*, November 7, 1941.

131. Fleming, *Crossroads*, p. 28; Marlene Gatewood to Kathleen Krowl, Vista, California, 2003.

132. Lejeune, *Reminiscences*, p. 244 (quote); John A. Lejeune to Augustine Lejeune, August 29, 1917, reel 2, Papers of John A. Lejeune, Manuscript Division, Library of Congress; Lejeune, *Reminiscences*, p. 460.

133. Zissa, "Quantico," p. 45.

134. *WP*, April 29, 1917.

135. *Leatherneck* (November 1967), p. 33; *WP*, May 13, 1918.

136. "The *Leatherneck* Legacy," *Leatherneck* website, http://www.mca-marines.org/Leatherneck/About.htm (accessed October 2003); *Leatherneck* (November 1967), p. 33; *Leatherneck* (November 1987), pp. 74–75.

137. *WP*, April 14, 1917; Fleming, *Crossroads*, p. 31.

138. *Purchase of Land for Marine Barracks, Quantico, Va.. Hearing before the Subcommittee of the Committee on Naval Affairs, United States Senate, Sixty-fifth Congress, Second Session, May 6, 1918* (Washington, D.C.: Government Printing Office, 1918); Fleming, *Crossroads*, p. 31.

139. Fleming, *Crossroads*, pp. 33–35.

140. *WP*, May 13, 1918; Zissa, "Quantico," p. 46.

141. *WP*, May 13 and April 1, 1918.

142. *WP*, April 7, 1918; Zissa, "Quantico," pp. 46–47.

143. Zissa, "Quantico," p. 46; *WP*, June 21, 1918.

144. *WP*, May 11, 1918.

145. D. Adallis, "The Grecians of Quantico, Va.," in *Fredericksburg Greek Colony, 1908–1933* (Fredericksburg, Va.: by Cooperation of the Leading Members of Fredericksburg Greek-American Colony, 1933), p. 27; Raftelis interview; Craige, *Quantico Sentry*, November 7, 1941; *WP*, December 27, 2003.

146. "Navy Women: An Early History," National Museum of American Jewish Military History website, http://www.nmajmh.org/supplies/wom-cat15.html (accessed January 2004).

147. *Leatherneck* (August 1993), p. 15.

148. *Leatherneck* (August 1993), p. 15.

149. Dr. Alfred Crosby, interview transcript, "The Film and More," *Influenza 1918*, American Experience series website, http://www.pbs.org/wgbh/amex/influenza/film-more/reference/interview/drcrosby1.html (accessed January 17, 2004).

150. *Influenza, 1918*, American Experience series, PBS documentary, 1998.

151. Fleming, *Crossroads*, p. 29. Fleming, et al., claim that the influenza outbreak at Quantico occurred in 1917, one year before the national epidemic. The current authors have found no corroborating evidence that the Quantico influenza incident happened in 1917, rather than 1918, and feel that Fleming, et al., are mistaken in their identification of the year. Unfortunately, the citation Fleming, et al., provided for this infomation is also incorrect, thus Fleming's source could not be checked on this matter.

152. *Influenza, 1918.*

153. Fleming, *Crossroads*, pp. 27–28; *WP*, September 25, October 25, 31, 1918; *NYT*, October 8, 1918; *Influenza, 1918*; "The Influenza Pandemic of 1918," http://www.stanford.edugroup/virus/uda/ (accessed January 2004).

154. Fleming, *Crossroads*, p. 36.

155. Fleming, *Crossroads*, p. 37.

156. *Leatherneck* (November 1975), p. 81.

157. Susan Canedy, "Demobilization," in *Oxford Companion to American Military History*, p. 209.

158. John Lejeune to Augustine Lejeune, November 2 and 9, 1919, reel 2, Lejeune Papers.

159. Fleming, *Crossroads*, p. 39.

160. Lejeune, "Address delivered to officers of Marine Corps School at Marine Barracks, Quantico, Va. On May 31st 1939," reel 10, Lejeune Papers.

161. Fleming, *Crossroads*, pp. 40–41.

162. Lejeune, quoted in Fleming, *Crossroads*, p. 39.

163. Fleming, *Crossroads*, p. 39; *Army and Navy Journal*, January 24, 1920, reprinted in *United States Naval Institute Proceedings* (March 1920), p. 457; *NYT*, June 20, 1920.

164. Fleming, *Crossroads*, pp. 39–40.

165. Fleming, *Crossroads*, pp. 41–42; *Leatherneck* (July 1983), p. 38.

166. Butler, quoted in Fleming, *Crossroads*, p. 40; *Leatherneck* (July 1995), p. 14.

167. Fleming, *Crossroads*, p. 60.

168. Fleming, *Crossroads*, p. 46; Suzanne Borghei and Victor J. Croziat, "Ellis, 'Pete' Earl Hancock," in *The Oxford Companion to American Military History*, p. 246.

169. Fleming, *Crossroads*, p. 46.

170. Fleming, *Crossroads*, p. 49.

171. Fleming, *Crossroads*, p. 51.

172. Fleming, *Crossroads*, p. 67.

173. Fleming, *Crossroads*, pp. 67–68.

174. *Leatherneck* (June 1975), p. 48; *NYT*, January 30, 1931.

175. Alexander A.Vandegrift, *Once a Marine: The Memoirs of General A. A. Vandegrift, United States Marine Corps, as told to Robert B. Asprey* (New York: W. W. Norton and Company, Inc., 1964), p. 62.

176. Fleming, *Crossroads*, p. 43; Vandegrift, *Once a Marine*, p. 65.

177. Vandegrift, *Once a Marine*, p. 65; "Butler, Thomas Stalker," *Biographical Directory of the United States Congress* (accessed February 2004); Fleming, *Crossroads*, p. 43.

178. Vandegrift, *Once a Marine*, p. 65; *Leatherneck* (September 1932), pp. 39–40.

"Nova Virginiae Tabula," mapmakers Arnoldus Montanus and John Ogilby. Note the llama, goat and unicorn pictured on this 1671 map—all supposedly native to the New World. The Quantico region was verdant, but not that verdant. Ogilby, America: Being the Latest, Most Accurate Description of the New World.

179. *WP*, March 27, 1927.

180. Vandegrift, *Once a Marine*, p. 62 (quote); *NYT*, August 13, 1922.

181. Fleming, *Crossroads*, p. 43; *NYT*, August 13 and November 2, 1922; *Quantico Sentry*, May 12, 1967.

182. Vandegrift, *Once a Marine*, pp. 62–63.

183. Vandegrift, *Once a Marine*, p. 62.

184. *Leatherneck* (June 1975), p. 48; Fleming, *Crossroads*, p. 44.

185. Lowell J. Thomas, *Old Gimlet Eye: The Adventures of Smedley D. Butler, As Told to Lowell Thomas* (New York: Farrar and Rinehart, Inc., 1933), pp. 259–260.

186. *WP*, January 16, 1927; "Sergeant Major Jiggs," Scuttlebutt and Small Chow website, http://www.scuttlebuttsmallchow.com/masjiggs.html (accessed February 2004); *NYT*, August 1, 1926.

187. *NYT*, August 1, 1926; *WP*, July 26 and 27, 1926.

188. *WP*, January 10, 1927.

189. *WP*, January 10 and 11, 1927; *NYT*, January 10, 1927.

190. *WP*, March 31, 1937; *Leatherneck* (May 1937), pp. 46, 51.

191. Fleming, *Crossroads*, p. 57.

192. *WP*, March 31, 1937.

193. *NYT*, June 19 and July 1, 1927.

194. *Leatherneck* (June 1928), p. 40.

195. *Leatherneck* (January 1938), pp. 32–33.

196. *WP*, August 11, 1941.

197. *Quantico Sentry*, January 22, 1943; Fleming, *Crossroads*, p. 58.

198. *WP*, September 26, 1921.

199. Thomas, *Old Gimlet Eye*, pp. 260–262.

200. *Marine Corps Gazette* (June 1988), p. 28; *WP*, August 7, 2001; "Ellwood Manor," Fredericksburg and Spotsylvania National Military Park, National Park Service, www.nps.gov/frsp/ellwood.htm (accessed February 2004).

201. *WP*, June 4, 1922.

202. "Detailed Instructions for Troops," Marine Corps Expeditionary Force, August 9, 1923, Virginia miscellaneous papers, ca. 1748–1942, Thornton Tayloe Perry Papers, Mss P4299 h77-89, Virginia Historical Society; *Leatherneck* (September 1, 1923).

203. Vandegrift, *Once a Marine*, pp. 63–64.

204. Fleming, *Crossroads*, p. 49.

205. Fleming, *Crossroads*, p. 66; *NYT*, April 25, 1937.

206. *NYT*, November 13, 1921; Fleming, pp. 47, 52.

207. *Quantico Sentry*, May 14, 1937.

208. *Leatherneck* (November 1989), pp. 36–39; *NYT*, May 7, 1940.

209. Fleming, *Crossroads*, pp. 50, 52; *WP*, March 31, 1927.

210. *Leatherneck* (March 1933), p. 26; Fleming, *Crossroads* p. 52; *NYT*, August 22, 1921; *WP*, September 27, 1926.

211. Fleming, *Crossroads*, p. 51; *NYT*, December 12, 1935; *New York Times*, January 14, 1938.

212. *WP*, January 15, 1939; *WP*, January 29, 1939.

213. *Leatherneck* (March 1933), p. 26.

214. *WP*, March 31, 1927; *Leatherneck* (March 1933), p. 26; *Leatherneck*, March 21, 1925.

215. *Leatherneck* (November 1969), pp. 66–71; "Amphibious Warfare: First World War," sponsor organization unknown, http://www.exwar.org/Htm/8000PopC7.htm (accessed February 2004).

216. Fleming, *Crossroads*, p. 48.

217. *Leatherneck* (August 30, 1924), p. 2.

218. *Annual Report of the Major General Commandant of the United States Marine Corps to the Secretary of the Navy, 1924*, quoted in Fleming, p. 55.

219. "Lejeune Deplores Quantico Buildings," *Washington Post*, December 16, 1925; *WP*, May 16, 1928.

220. Glenn Brown, "The Proposed Marine Barracks at Quantico, Va.," *Architectural Record* 57 (June 1925), pp. 511–516.

221. "The Memorial Room at Quantico, Va., to Captain Phillips Brooks Robinson," *Architectural Record* L (September 1921), pp. 235–240.

222. *WP*, February 6, 1927.

223. *NYT*, February 8, 1927; *WP*, June 21, 1926; *WP*, October 16, 1927; Fleming, *Crossroads*, p. 55.

224. *WP*, January 1, 1928; *WP*, June 16, 1929; Fleming, *Crossroads*, pp. 55, 69; *Quantico Sentry*, March 3, 1944; *Leatherneck* (June 1929), p. 13; *WP*, June 16, 1929.

225. *Leatherneck* (August 1929), p. 28.

226. *Leatherneck* (August 1929), p. 28.

227. Fleming, *Crossroads*, pp. 68–69; *WP*, August 4, 1938; *WP*, January 9, 1937; *Leatherneck* (November 1938), p. 38.

228. Fleming, *Crossroads*, p. 55; *NYT*, January 2, 1936; *WP*, May 16, 1938.

229. Fleming, *Crossroads*, p. 70.

230. Fleming, *Crossroads*, pp. 38, 44; *NYT*, May 28, 1922; *NYT*, April 20, 1923; *NYT*, July 11, 1923.

231. Fleming, *Crossroads*, p. 44; *NYT*, April 16, 1925.

232. Fleming, *Crossroads*, p. 59.

233. *WP*, May 6, 1928.

234. General Edward C. Dyer, quoted in Fleming, *Crossroads*, p. 60.

235. Fleming, *Crossroads*, p. 66.

236. *Leatherneck* (May 1982), pp. 18–23.

237. *WP*, July 2, 1926.

238. *WP*, February 15, 1936.

239. *WP*, June 10, 1921; Fleming, pp. 43, 44, 47; *NYT*, September 25, 1921.

240. *WP*, April 18, 1922; *NYT*, September 24, 1922; *WP*, June 11, 1924; Jess C. Barrow, *WWII: Marine Fighting Squadron Nine (VF-9M)*, *Modern Aviation* series (Blue Ridge Summit, Penn.: Tab Books Inc., 1981), pp. 36–37; *NYT*, November 21, 1936; *WP*, September 27, 1938.

241. Barrow, *WWII: Marine Fighting Squadron Nine*, pp. 61–63; *WP*, June 17, 1936; Fleming, *Crossroads*, p. 66.

242. *Leatherneck* (February 1961), p. 24; Fleming, *Crossroads*, p. 54.

243. *WP*, December 16, 1927.

244. *WP*, January 24, 1923; *WP*, December 27, 1923; *Leatherneck* (January 4, 1924), p. 1.

245. Norman H. Clark, "Prohibition and Temperance," Foner and Garraty, *Reader's Companion to American History*, pp. 871–874.

246. Thomas, *Old Gimlet Eye*, p. 299.

247. *NYT*, September 20, 1929.

248. *WP*, September 18, 1929; *NYT*, September 19, 1929.

249. *NYT*, September 20, 1929; *WP*, September 20, 1929.

250. *WP*, September 26, 1929.

251. *WP*, September 19, 26, and December 4, 1929.

252. Ronald L. Heinemann, *Depression and New Deal in Virginia: The Enduring Dominion* (Charlottesville: University Press of Virginia, 1983), pp. ix, x, 8–9, 46, 72, 80, 172–177.

253. *NYT*, May 25, 1935; *WP*, October 13, 1938; Heinemann, *Depression and New Deal in Virginia*, p. 17; *NYT*, August 1, 1930.

254. Heinemann, *Depression and New Deal in Virginia*, pp. 64–65.

255. *Dixie Yankee*, scattered issues between 1936 and 1938.

256. History of Prince William Forest Park, "'Bridging the Watershed': A 'National Parks Lab' Partnership between Potomac Area and National Parks and Schools," http://www.bridgingthewatershed.org/pwfphistory.html (accessed February 2004).

257. *Leatherneck* (November 26, 1921), p. 5.

258. *Leatherneck* (March 25, 1922), p. 2; *Leatherneck* (November 26, 1921), p. 5; *Leatherneck* (March 4, 1922), p. 2; "Leatherneck, November 26, 1921; Raftelis interview.

259. *Leatherneck* (May 1935), pp. 12–13.

260. "War of the Worlds Radio Broadcast Causes Panic," What You Need to Know About. . . . website, http://history1900s.about.com/library/weekly/aa072701a.htm (accessed January 2004).

261. *WP*, November 1, 1938.

262. *WP*, November 2, 1938; *WP*, November 10, 1938.

263. *Leatherneck* (March 4, 1922), p. 2; *WP*, March 6, 1932; *WP*, October 9, 1932; *WP* February 19, 1933; *Leatherneck* (March 1933), p. 25.

264. Fleming, *Crossroads*, p. 66; *Leatherneck* (November 1985), pp. 64–68; *WP*, July 3, 1944; "Miss Marine," *The American Magazine* (June 1942), p. 77.

265. *WP*, August 28, 1922; *WP*, April 14, 1924; *NYC*, April 14, 1924; *NYT*, December 22, 1924.

266. *WP*, May 28, 1933; *NYT*, May 28, 1933; "History of the Town of Quantico," courtesy of Mitchel P. Raftelis.

267. *NYT*, July 15, 1933; *WP*, September 5, 1933.

268. *NYT*, September 10, 1933; *NYT*, October 7, 1934; *NYT*, May 19, 1935; *NYT*, May 23, 1937.

269. Fleming, *Crossroads*, p. 70; "USA, Marine Corps," "USA," in *The Oxford Companion to World War II*, gen. ed. I. C. B. Dear (Oxford, England: Oxford University Press, 2001), p. 937.

270. *WP*, August 19, 1941; *NYT*, November 2, 1941.

271. "Naval Dispatch form the Commander in Chief Pacific (CINC PAC) Announcing the Japanese Attack on Pearl Harbor, 7 December 1941," in Papers of John J. Ballentine, Manuscript Division, Library of Congress. Available through *Words and Deed in American History: Selected Documents Celebrating the Manuscript Division's First 100 Years*, American Memory website, http://memory.loc.gov (accessed February 2004); Knox, quoted in Doris Kearns Goodwin, *No Ordinary Time: Franklin and Eleanor Roosevelt: The Home Front in World War II* (New York: Simon and Schuster, 1994), p. 289.

272. Goodwin, *No Ordinary Time*, p. 295; Franklin Delano Roosevelt, "A Date Which Will Live in Infamy," December 8, 1941, transcript available through U.S. Historical Documents Archive, http://ushda.org/infamy.shtml (accessed February 2004).

273. Grey, quoted in Goodwin, *No Ordinary Time*, p. 291.

274. *Quantico Sentry*, December 12, 1941; Fleming, *Crossroads*, p. 75.

275. *Quantico Sentry*, December 12, 1941.

276. *Quantico Sentry*, December 26, 1941.

277. *Quantico Sentry*, June 12, 1942.

278. Fleming, *Crossroads*, p. 74.

279. Fleming, *Crossroads*, p. 75; *Quantico Sentry*, May 12, 1967.

280. Fleming, *Crossroads*, p. 75.

281. Fleming, *Crossroads*, p. 75.

282. *Quantico Sentry*, April 30, 1943.

283. Fleming, *Crossroads*, p. 77.

284. Fleming, *Crossroads*, pp. 77–78.

285. Fleming, *Crossroads*, p. 80.

286. *Quantico Sentry*, April 7, 1944.

287. *Leatherneck* (February 1944), p. 33.

288. "The Quantico Post School," *Education for Victory*, official biweek ly of the U.S. Office of Education, Federal Security Agency, vol. 3 (March 20, 1945), p. 11.

289. Fleming, *Crossroads*, pp. 71–72, 73.

290. Fleming, *Crossroads*, p. 73.

291. Fleming, *Crossroads*, p. 78.

292. Fleming, *Crossroads*, pp. 73–74.

293. *Leatherneck* (May 1944), pp. 34–35; *Quantico Sentry*, November 2, 1944.

294. Fleming, *Crossroads*, pp. 76–78.

295. *WP*, October 7, 1942; *WP*, October 10, 2002.

296. *NYT*, December 29, 1940; *WP*, December 29, 1940; *NYT*, January 1, 1941.

297. *WP*, November 10, 1941.

298. *Quantico Sentry*, April 7 and 28, 1944.

299. *Quantico Sentry*, May 28, 1943.

300. *Quantico Sentry*, September 10, 1943.

301. Fleming, *Crossroads*, pp. 78–79; *Quantico Sentry* 1944.

302. Transcript of "This Nation at War: Banks in the War," July 13, 1943, courtesy of Mitchel P. Raftelis, Quantico, Virginia; *NYT*, January 7, 1943.

303. *Quantico Sentry*, April 5, 1945.

304. *Quantico Sentry*, April 23, 1943; the USDA guidebook appeared in the same issue of the paper.

305. *Quantico Sentry*, September 3, 1943; *ibid.*, March 12, 1943; *ibid.*, October 2, 1942.

306. *Quantico Sentry*, March 27, 1942; *Quantico Sentry*, March 5, 1943.

307. *Quantico Sentry*, November 16 and 30, 1944; *NYT*, April 5, 1943.

308. *WP*, July 1941; *Leatherneck* (March 1944), pp. 30–32; *WP*, August 22, 1942; *ibid.*, September 25, 1942; *Quantico Sentry*, March 31, 1944.

309. *Quantico Sentry*, June 26, 1942; *ibid.*, January 28, 1944.

310. *Quantico Sentry*, September 3, 1943; *ibid.*, February 1, 1945.

311. *Quantico Sentry*, October 8, December 3, 1943.

312. Roosevelt, quoted in Goodwin, *No Ordinary Time*, p. 602; Richard Overy, "Hitler as War Leader," in *Oxford Companion to World War II*, p. 424.

313. Robert Dallek, "Truman, Harry S," in *The Oxford Companion to World War II*, pp. 877–878.

314. *Quantico Sentry*, August 16, 1945.

315. Fleming, *Crossroads*, p. 81.

316. Thomas W. Miller Jr. *The Iwo Jima Memorial & the Myth of the 13th Hand*, second edition (Arlington, Va.: T. W. Miller, 2001); *WP*, November 11, 1951; Fleming, *Crossroads*, p. 82.

317. *WP*, November 16, 1945; *NYT*, August 6, 1949.

318. *Leatherneck* (July 1948), p. 41; Fleming, *Crossroads*, p. 93; *Leatherneck* (December 1962), pp. 48–51.

319. Fleming, *Crossroads*, p. 81.

320. Vandegrift, quoted in Fleming, *Crossroads*, p. 84.

321. *NYT*, February 18, 1947; Vandegrift, quoted in Fleming, *Crossroads*, p. 84.

322. *WP*, May 10, 1949; Fleming, *Crossroads*, pp. 84–85.

323. Fleming, *Crossroads*, pp. 85–86; *Leatherneck* (October 1948), pp. 8, 53; *Leatherneck* (September 1949), pp. 8–11.

324. Fleming, *Crossroads*, p. 86.

325. Fleming, *Crossroads*, p. 91; Cindy Fisher, "From Experimental to Presidential," available through MarineCorps.com (accessed February 2004).

326. Fisher, "From Experimental to Presidential," MarineCorps.com; *Leatherneck* (September 1997), p. 32.

327. *WP*, December 22, 1961; *Leatherneck* (September 1997), p. 32.

328. *Leatherneck* (September 1997), pp. 32–33.

329. Fleming, *Crossroads*, p. 82; *NYT*, November 15, 1959.

330. Fleming, *Crossroads*, pp. 87–88, 93.

331. Fleming, *Crossroads*, pp. 82, 87, 89–90, 92; *WP*, October 10, 2002; *Leatherneck* (April 1946), p. 35; *Quantico Sentry*, May 5, 1967.

332. Fleming, *Crossroads*, p. 87; *Marine Corps Gazette* (September 1979), p. 4.

333. Fleming, *Crossroads*, p. 88.

334. Fleming, *Crossroads*, pp. 83, 93; *WP*, July 14, 1957.

335. *WP*, September 30, 1960.

336. *NYT*, January 24, 1951; *WP*, February 2, 1954.

337. *WP*, February 26, 1955; *NYT*, February 26, 1955; *WP*, March 2 and 11, 1955.

338. *WP*, November 28,1948; *ibid.*, December 5, 1948; *Leatherneck* (July 1949); "Quantico Marine Corps Base, Lustron District," *Buildings of Virginia: Tidewater and Piedmont*, Richard Guy Wilson, ed. (Oxford and New York: Oxford University Press, 2002), p. 77; Mike Sajna, "Unusual Ceramic Houses Result in Off-Beat Study for UPB Professor," University of Pittsburgh *University Times* 28 (July 1996), available at http://www.pitt.edu/utimes/issues/28/71896/11.html (accessed February 2004); *WP*, June 30, 1988; *Leatherneck* (May 1973), p. 21.

339. *WP*, February 3, 7, and 8, 1950.

340. *WP*, February 6, 1950.

341. *WP*, March 16, 22, May 10, and August 20, 1950; *ibid.*, July 14, 1954.

342. *WP*, September 1, 1951; January 19, 1952; August 1, 1953; December 16, 1953; March 26, 1960.

343. Fleming, *Crossroads*, p. 92.

344. *WP*, September 13, 1953; October 18, 1953; August 13, 1960.

345. *NYT*, January 1 and 2, 1946.

346. *WP*, February 24, 1946; *NYT*, February 24, 1946; "History of the Town of Quantico," courtesy of Mitchel P. Raftelis.

347. *NYT*, April 27, 1946; July 31, 1948; September 18, 1949.

348. *NYT*, June 16, 1950; *WP*, June 16, 1950. The *Times* and *Post* reprinted slightly different versions of Truman's remark to the pho tographers, and the version used here has been transcribed from the *Post*.

349. *WP*, July 26, 1953; *NYT*, July 26, 1953; *NYT*, September 6, 1960.

350. *NYT*, January 5, 1954.

351. *WP*, August 3, 1946; November 28, 1946; December 23, 1948; September 4, 1953; September 9, 1953; March 17, 1972.

352. *Leatherneck* (January 1948), pp. 13–15; *Leatherneck* (December 1948), pp. 30–34.

353. *Leatherneck* (January 1948), p. 14.

354. *Leatherneck* (July 1963), pp. 58–61.

355. *WP*, October 28, 1956; *Leatherneck* (December 1963), pp. 32–35; *Leatherneck* (August 1948), pp. 46– 47; *WP*, December 11, 1955.

356. *WP*, May 11, 12, July 10, 1957; October 30, 1958; May 21, 1960.

357. Fleming, *Crossroads*, p. 91; *WP*, November 4, 1961; Glenn, quoted in *Quantico Sentry*, April 6, 1990.

358. *NYT*, May 7, 1955.

359. *WP*, July 1, 1966.

360. *WP*, July 1, 1966.

361. *Quantico Sentry*, May 12, 1967.

362. Captions for photos DMST8608628 and DMST8608625, dated 18 November 1985, available through the Defense Visual Information Center website, www.dodmedia.osd.mil/dvic (accessed February 2004).

363. *Quantico Sentry*, April 14, 1967; *WP*, October 16, 1965.

364. *WP*, June 24, 1970; January 4, 1972.

365. *WP*, September 13, 1979.

366. *WP*, October 30, 1958; March 22, 1972; June 2, 1972.

367. *WP*, August 18, 28, 1969.

368. *WP*, January 4, 1972; *ibid.*, November 16, 1971; *ibid.*, August 29, 1998; *ibid.*, November 3, 1983; *NYT*, November 20, 1992.

369. "Top Man at Quantico," *Ebony* 42 (December 1986), pp. 140, 144, 146; Sonya Stinson, "Colonel Al Davis USMC, Commanding Officer, Officer Candidates School," *Black Collegian* 26 (February 1996), p. 61; *WP*, July 10, 1988; *WP*, March 29, 1990.

370. *Free Lance-Star* (hereafter *FL-S* , Fredericksburg, Va., June 9, 2001.

371. *Leatherneck* (November 1977), p. 38.

372. *Leatherneck* (February 1969), pp. 35–36; *Leatherneck* (April 1978), pp. 20–21.

373. *Leatherneck* (February 1969), p. 95; *Marine Corps Gazette* (March 1989), p. 50; *Leatherneck* (May 1984), pp. 46–49; *Quantico Sentry*, April 20, 1990.

374. *Leatherneck* (July 1971), p. 31; *ibid.* (June 1980), pp. 41–43; *ibid.* (June 1982), p. 42.

375. *Leatherneck* (January 1979), pp. 27–31; *ibid.* (March 1984), p. 34; *ibid.* (April 1984), pp. 16, 20; *WP*, February 28, 1981; *Leatherneck* (September 1979), pp. 17–21; *ibid.* (February 1992), p. 22.

376. *Leatherneck* (August 1986), pp. 46–47; *Marine Corps Gazette* (June 1988), p. 27.

377. *Marine Corps Gazette* (October 1989), pp. 11–12; *Leatherneck* (July 1994), p. 40.

378. *Leatherneck* (September 1991), p. 45; "General Alfred M. Gray Marine Corps Research Center," www.mcu.usmc.mil/MCRCweb/index.html; *Leatherneck* (July 1993), p. 43; *ibid.* (January 2002), pp. 50–51.

379. "New NBC Gear Put To Use at Quantico," *Marines* 23 (March 1994), p. 3; *Leatherneck* (October 1995), p. 45, 47; *ibid.* (March 1992), p. 31; *ibid.* (January 1995), pp. 34–39; *ibid.* (January 1996), p. 43; *ibid.* (December 2000), pp. 48–49; *FL-S* , September 20, 2002; *ibid.*, May 7, 2003.

380. *WP*, July 2, 1981; December 19, 2003; July 17, 2002.

381. *WP*, May 27, 1965; October 13, 1965; July 9, 1965; October 13, 1965; May 6, 1966.

382. *WP*, July 8, 1972.

383. *NYT*, December 8, 1974.

384. *WP*, November 29, 1980; *ibid.*, July 11, 1984; Eric W. Witzig, "The New ViCAP More User-Friendly and Used by More Agencies," *FBI Law Enforcement Bulletin* 72 (June 2003), available at www.fbi.gov/publications/leb/2003/june2003/june03leb.htm (accessed February 2004); *WP*, April 25, 2003; *FL-S* , April 25, 2003; *ibid.*, April 26, 2003.

385. Ben Proctor, *William Randolph Hearst: The Early Years, 1863–1910* (New York and Oxford: Oxford University Press, 1998), p. 101.

386. *NYT,* November 26, 1989; Kristin McMurran, "In Hogan's Alley, the Pseudo-town Where F.B.I. Rookies Go to School, the Gunplay's the Thing," *People* 33 (May 1990), pp. 91; "FBI Part II: Elaborate FBI Drills Polish Agents' Skills, *Pittsburgh Post-Gazette,* March 9, 1998; "FBI Agents Endure Hard Training," Associated Press article, reprint ed in the *Daily Beacon,* University of Tennessee, available at http://dailybeacon.utk.edu/article.php/2821 (accessed February 2004).

387. McMurran, "In Hogan's Alley," *People,* p. 92.

388. "One Life to Live Recap for Wednesday, November 12, 2003," What You Need to Know About website, available at http://onelifetolive.about.com/cs/recaps/a/111203recap_p.htm (accessed February 2004).

389. *WP,* May 25, 1985; *NYT,* May 26, 1985; "DEA Training Academy," U.S. Drug Enforcement Administration, available at www.usdoj.gov/dea/programs/training/part4.html (accessed November 2003).

390. *WP,* June 30, 1988; February 23, 2002.

391. Eric Hunting, "Shelter: Documenting a Personal Quest for Non-toxic Housing," available at http://radio.weblogs.com/0119080/stories/2003/03/04/galleryLustronMania.html (accessed February 2004); *WP,* February 23, 2002; Wilson, *Buildings of Virginia,* p. 77; Mike Sajna, "Unusual Ceramic Houses Result in Off-Beat Study for UPB Professor," University of Pittsburgh *University Times* 28 (July 1996), available at http://www.pitt.edu/utimes/issues/28/71896/11.html (accessed February 2004).

392. "Frequently Asked Questions" Public Private Ventures (PPV), available at http://www.quantico.usmc.mil/quanticoppv/faq.htm (accessed February 2004); *FL-S ,* October 28, 2003; *ibid.,* March 31, 2002; *ibid.,* April 30, 2002.

393. Telephone interview with Public Affairs Office representative, MCB Quantico, February 27, 2004.

394. *Quantico Sentry,* October 18, 1968; Fleming, *Crossroads,* p. 96.

395. *Leatherneck* (December 1986), p. 17; *Quantico Sentry,* June 1, 1990; *Leatherneck* (October 1995), p. 43; *ibid.,* (August 1997), p. 48; *FL-S ,* July 15, 2003.

396. *FL-S ,* June 26, 2003; "Getting Semper Fit," *Parks and Recreation* 34 (December 1999), p. 62.

397. Fleming, *Crossroads,* p. 95; *Leatherneck* (April 1973), pp. 30, 33–34; *WP,* March 8, 11, and 26, 1968. For more details of the investigation of drowning deaths, see coverage in the *Washington Post* during the month of March 1968.

398. *Leatherneck* (January 1983), pp. 49–51; *FL-S ,* August 19, 2003.

399. *WP,* November 16 and 19, 1972; *Leatherneck* (January 1972), pp. 71–73; *ibid.* (September 1979), pp. 25–29; *ibid.* (March 1984), pp. 20–25; *ibid.* (December 1993), p. 48.

400. *FL-S ,* December 1 and 5, 2001.

401. *Leatherneck* (January 1968), pp. 64–65; "Lewis B. Puller, Jr.," Arlington National Cemetery website, www.arlingtoncemetery.net.puller.htm (accessed February 2004).

402. *NYT,* April 22, 1982; *Quantico Sentry,* April 6, 1990; photos MDSC9401814-9401816, Defense Visual Information Center website, www.dodmedia.osd.mil/dvic (accessed February 2004); *WP,* February 27, 1991; *WP,* October 4, 1997; *NYT,* October 2, 1997; *FL-S,* October 23, 2003.

403. *Leatherneck* (June 1962), pp. 40–43.

404. *Leatherneck* (February 1977), pp. 47–49; *WP,* July 9, 1967; *WP,* September 11, 1978; Arnold, "Leesylvania State Park"; *WP,* November 9, 1998.

405. *WP,* September 11, 1978; *FL-S ,* May 23, 2001.

406. *WP,* November 9, 1998; telephone interview with George L. Krowl, February 27, 2004.

407. *WP,* January 14, 1971; *ibid.,* February 21, 1971; *ibid.,* April 25, 1993; "EPA Cites CFC Violations at Quantico Marine Base," *FDCH Regulatory Intelligence Database,* October 12, 1999; *WP,* December 7, 1996.

408. *WP,* December 6, 1975; January 27, 1976; April 6, 1976; May 29, 1976; July 1, 1976; June 10, 1978.

409. *WP,* January 15, 1997; "Statement of Chuck Burns, AMVETS National Service Director before the House Veterans Affairs Committee on the VA Budget Fiscal Year 1999," February 12, 1998, House Committee on Veterans' Affairs, available at www.house.gov/va/hearings/schedule105/feb98/hearing2-12-98/amvets2-12.htm (accessed February 2004); Quantico National Cemetery interments, www.findagrave.com (accessed February 2004); Quantico National Cemetery, www.cem.va.gov.nchp/quantico.htm#gi (accessed February 2004).

410. Quantico National Cemetery, www.cem.va.gov.nchp/quantico.htm#gi (accessed February 2004).

411. *WP,* February 22, 1998.

412. "Town of Quantico: A Community Profile" brochure, published by Virginia Power, 1996; *WP,* October 25, 1985.

413. *WP,* November 1, 1998; *ibid.,* February 22, 1998; *ibid.,* November 28, 1984; *ibid.,* December 13, 1984; House Bill No. 935, February 12, 1968, adding section 4-98.12:1; Mitchel P. Raftelis, "Quantico History," draft of speech at Civ-Mil council meeting, September 20, 1995, courtesy of Mitchel P. Raftelis; Raftelis interview.

414. *WP,* December 14, 1967; June 13, 1969; January 3, 1979; May 3, 1998; June 13, 1998.

415. *NYT,* June 12, 1970; Raftelis interview, February 18, 2004; *WP,* June 1, 1989; *ibid.,* June 10, 1989; *ibid.,* September 15, 1990; *ibid.,* September 23, 1990; *ibid.,* April 28, 1982; *ibid.,* May 5, 1982; *ibid.,* June 23, 1982; *ibid.,* September 22, 1982; *ibid.,* June 27, 1983.

416. *WP,* August 9, 1975; September 11, 1975; June 10, 1976; September 30, 1998.

417. *WP,* August 24, 1997; *ibid.,* September 30, 1998; Raftelis interview.

418. *WP,* October 27, 1998; Raftelis interview.

419. *WP,* October 25, 1985; *ibid.,* November 7, 1985; Raftelis interview; Mitchel P. Raftelis, "Community Cooperation: Town of Quantico Beautification," *The Dumfries Community,* website of Maureen S. Caddigan, Dumfries Magisterial District Supervisor, Prince William County, Virginia, www.dumfries.com/community.asp?article=845 (accessed February 2004); *WP,* August 23, 1998; *ibid.,* September 2, 1998; *ibid.,* December 27, 1998.

420. Raftelis, "Community Cooperation," *The Dumfries Community*; "Quantico," Planning Office, Prince William County Government, Virginia website, www.co.princewilliam.va.us/planning/Quantico/quantico.html (accessed October 2003).

421. *WP,* November 6, 1994; *ibid.,* November 1, 1998; *ibid.,* December 27, 1998; Raftelis interview.

422. *WP,* March 10, 1971; March 23, 1971; October 13, 1982; March 31, 1999.

423. *FL-S ,* October 15, 2001; "MCB Quantico G-3, Band, www.quantico.usmc.mil/g3/band/index.htm (accessed February 2004); *FL-S ,*September 12, 2001; *WP,* September 13, 2001; *FL-S,* September 18, 2001; "At FBI's Behest, Authorities Take Precautions," *Free Lance-Star,* October 10, 2001.

424. *FL-S,* March 3, 2002; *Philadelphia Inquirer,* May 20, 2002.

425. *Quantico Sentry,* April 5, 1968; *Leatherneck* (September 1962), p. 63.

426. *Leatherneck* (April 1970), p. 66; *ibid.* (October 2000), pp. 60–61; *FL-S,* May 22, 2002.

427. *FL-S,* December 5, 2001; *Leatherneck* (November 2000), pp. 82–83; "Molly Marine Statue Unveiled at Quantico," *Marines* 29 (October–December 2000), p. 11.

428. *Quantico Sentry,* June 22, 1990; *FL-S,* November 2, 2001.

429. *Leatherneck* (May 1973), pp. 30–35; *ibid.* (July 1978), p. 26; *ibid.* (May 1979), pp. 36–37; *ibid.* (September 1977), p. 54; *ibid.* (May 1986), pp. 55–59.

430. *WP,* September 19, 1998; *Leatherneck* (November 2001), p. 58.

431. *Leatherneck* (March 2003), p. 47.

432. *Leatherneck* (March 2003), pp. 47–48; The Building, National Museum of the Marine Corps and Heritage Center, www.usmcmuseum.org/build.htm (accessed February 2004); *Leatherneck* (November 2001), p. 59; Press Room, National Museum of the Marine Corps and Heritage Center, www.usmcmuseum.net/pr3.htm (accessed February 2004).

433. *Leatherneck* (March 2003), pp. 46, 48, 49–50; Press Room, National Museum of the Marine Corps and Heritage Center.

434. *WP,* November 6, 2003; *Leatherneck* (March 2003), p. 50.

435. "Our Corps, by Old-Timer," *Quantico Sentry,* March 3, 1944.

BIBLIOGRAPHY

PRIMARY SOURCES

Manuscript and Photographic Collections

Personal Papers Collections, Manuscript Division, Library of Congress
John J. Ballentine
Alexander Graham Bell
John A. Lejeune
Abraham Lincoln
George B. McClellan Sr.
George Washington

National Archives and Records Administration
Records of the U.S. Army Air Forces, Record Group (RG) 18.
Records of the Bureau of the Census, RG 29.
Naval Records Collection of the Office of Naval Records and Library, RG 45
Records of the Federal Bureau of Investigation, RG 65.
Records of the Bureau of Yards and Docks, RG 71.
War Department Collection of Confederate Records, RG 109 (Compiled Service Records of Confederate Soldiers Who Served from Virginia, National Archives Microfilm Publication M-324)
Records of the United States Marine Corps, RG 127.

Virginia Historical Society, Richmond, Virginia
Barbour Family Papers, Mssl B2346a.
Maurice Evans Papers, 1837–1922, Mss1 Ev163a.
Thornton Tayloe Perry Papers, Mss P4299 h77-89.

Other Repositories and Private Collections
Defense Visual Information Center, March Air Reserve Base, Moreno Valley, California.
Gause, Samuel Sidney Jr., Co. G, 1st Arkansas Infantry, CSA, "Field Notes of Evansport and Vicinity." Original manuscript in the possession of Dr. Edward L. Thackston, Nashville, Tennessee.
Colonial-era Continental Army recruitment poster, George Washington's Office Museum, Winchester, Virginia.
Etching of George Mason, Gunston Hall Plantation, Lorton, Virginia.
Marine Corps University Research Archives, General Alfred M. Gray Marine Corps Research Center, Quantico, Virginia.
Marine Corps Historical Center, Washington Navy Yard, Washington, D.C.
District of Columbia boundary marker, Mary Riley Styles Public Library, Falls Church, Virginia.
Houdoun bust of Washington, Mount Vernon Ladies Association, Alexandria, Virginia.
Prints and Photographs Division, Library of Congress.
Prince William County Public Library, Manassas, Virginia.

Newspapers, Journals and Magazines

Alexandria Gazette. Alexandria, Va.
Architectural Record
Dixie Yankee, scattered issues between 1936–1938, Joplin, Va.
Free Lance-Star. Fredericksburg, Va. (abbreviated here as: *FL-S*)
Illustrated London News. London, England.
Leatherneck. Quantico, Va.
Marine Corps Gazette.
New York Herald. New York, N.Y.
New York Times. New York, N.Y. (abbreviated here as: *NYT*)
Prince William Advocate. Manassas, Va.
Quantico Sentry. Quantico, Va.
Saturday Evening Post. New York, N.Y.
Washington Post. Washington, D.C. (abbreviated here as: *WP*)

Books, Articles, and Reports

Army and Navy Journal, January 24, 1920, reprinted in United States Naval Institute Proceedings, March 1920.
Brown, Glenn. "The Proposed Marine Barracks at Quantico, Va.," *Architectural Record* 57 (June 1925): 511–516.
"DEA Training Academy," U.S. Drug Enforcement Administration, available at www.usdoj.gov/dea/programs/training/part4.html (accessed November 2003).
"Potomac Riverfront Park," Dewberry and Davis in cooperation with the Northern Virginia Planning District Commission. Fairfax, Va.: Dewberry and Davis, 1989.
Guernsey, Alfred H. and Henry M. Alden. *Harper's Pictorial History of the Civil War.* New York: Gramercy Books, 1866.
Guernsey, Alfred H. and Henry M. Alden. *Harper's Pictorial History of the Great Rebellion.* New York: Gramercy Books, 1868.
Lejeune, John A. *Reminiscences of a Marine.* Philadelphia: Dorrance and Co., 1930.
Letter from the Secretary of War, transmitting a letter from the Chief of Engineers, submitting copies of reports from Mr. S. T. Abert, United States Civil Engineer, of results and surveys of certain creeks and rivers in Virginia and North Carolina, Senate Ex. Doc. 64, 48th Cong., 1st sess., 1884.
Martin, Joseph. *A New and Comprehensive Gazetteer of Virginia, and the District of Columbia.* Charlottesville, Va.: Moseley & Tompkins, 1835. Reprint Westminster, Md.: Willow Bend Books, 2000.
"The Memorial Room at Quantico, Va., to Captain Phillips Brooks Robinson," *Architectural Record* L (September 1921): 235–240.
"Miss Marine," *The American Magazine* (June 1942): 77.
Murray, Hamilton Stanislaus, ed. *Letters to Washington and Accompanying Papers.* Boston: Houghton, Mifflin & Co., 1898.
National Museum of the Marine Corps and Heritage Center, www.usmcmuseum.org/
Ogilby, John. *America: Being the Latest, and Most Accurate Description of the New World. . . .* London: the Author, 1671.
Purchase of Land for Marine Barracks, Quantico, Va.. Hearing before the Subcommittee of the Committee on Naval Affairs, United States Senate, Sixty-fifth Congress, Second Session, May 6, 1918. Washington, D.C.: Government Printing Office, 1918.
"Quantico," Planning Office, Prince William County Government, Virginia website, www.co.princewilliam.va.us/planning/Quantico/quantico.html (accessed October 2003).
Quantico National Cemetery, www.cem.va.gov/nchp/quantico.htm#gi (accessed February 2004).
"The Quantico Post School," *Education for Victory,* official biweekly of the U.S. Office of Education, Federal Security Agency 3 (March 20, 1945): 11-12.
Raftelis, Mitchel P. "Community Cooperation: Town of Quantico Beautification," *The Dumfries Community,* website of Maureen S. Caddigan, Dumfries Magisterial District Supervisor, Prince William County, Virginia, www.dumfries.com/community.asp?article=845 (accessed February 2004).
Smith, John. *The General Historie of Virginia, New England and the Summer Isles. . . .* London: I.D. and I.H. for Michael Sparks, 1624.
Smith, John. *The True Travels, Adventures and Observations . . . in Europe, Asia, Africke, and America.* 1st American reprint. Richmond: Franklin Press, 1819.

Color scenes of Quantico's Hostess House, 1936 (above); main gate, circa 1940 (right); and Daly Hall, the enlisted men's club, circa 1950 (above right). Courtesy base archive.

Soley, J. Russell. "Early Operations on the Potomac River," *Battles and Leaders of the Civil War, Grant-Lee Edition, Volume II, part I.* New York: Century Co., 1887–1888; reprint: Harrisburg, Penn.: Archive Society, 1991.

"Statement of Chuck Burns, AMVETS National Service Director before the House Veterans Affairs Committee on the VA Budget Fiscal Year 1999," February 12, 1998, House Committee on Veterans' Affairs, available at www.house.gov/va/hearings/schedule105/feb98/hearing2-12-98/amvets2-12.htm (accessed February 2004).

Thomas, Lowell J. *Old Gimlet Eye: The Adventures of Smedley D. Butler as Told to Lowell Thomas.* New York: Farrar and Rinehart, 1933.

United States. War Department. *The War of the Rebellion: A Compilation of the Official Records of the Union and Confederate Armies.* Ser. 1–4. Washington, D.C.: Government Printing Office, 1880–1901.

United States. Naval War Records Office and Office of Naval Records and Library. *Official Records of the Union and Confederate Navies in the War of the Rebellion.* Washington, D.C.: Government Printing Office, 1894–1922.

Vandegrift, Alexander A. *Once a Marine: The Memoirs of General A. A. Vandegrift, United States Marine Corps, as told to Robert B. Asprey* (New York: W. W. Norton and Company, Inc., 1964.

Viele, Egbert L. "A Trip with Lincoln, Chase, and Stanton," *Scribners Monthly* 16 (October 1878): 813–823.

Welles, Gideon. *The Diary of Gideon Welles, Volume I: 1861–March 30, 1864.* Boston and New York: Houghton Mifflin Company, 1911.

"Work of the U.S. Fish Commission," *Scientific American,* June 10, 1882.

Zissa, Frank F., quoted in Robert F. Zissa, "Quantico," *Leatherneck* (November 1973): 44-47.

SECONDARY SOURCES

Adallis, D. "The Grecians of Quantico, Va.," in *Fredericksburg Greek Colony, 1908–1933.* Fredericksburg, Va.: by Cooperation of the Leading Members of Fredericksburg Greek-American Colony, 1933.

Arnold, James R. "Leesylvania State Park," *Northern Virginia Heritage* 7 (October 1985), available at www.historicprincewilliam.org/lee1.html (accessed January 2004).

Barrow, Jess C. *WWII: Marine Fighting Squadron Nine.* Blue Ridge Summit, Pa.: Tab Books, Inc., 1981.

Berkley, Henry J. "The Port of Dumfries, Prince William Co., Va.," *William and Mary College Quarterly Historical Magazine,* second series, 4 (April 1924): 99–116.

Biographical Directory of the United States Congress, http://bioguide.congress.gov.

Blumenthal, Mark. *Quantico. Images of America* series. Charleston, S.C.: Arcadia Publishing, 2003.

Brent, Chester Horton. *The Descendants of Collo. Giles Brent, Capt. George Brent, and Robert Brent, Gent., Immigrants to Maryland and Virginia* (Rutland, Vermont: Tuttle Publishing Company, 1946.

Burke, Carol. "Marching to Vietnam," *Journal of American Folklore* 102 (October–December 1989): 424–427.

Chambers, John Whiteclay, II, ed. *The Oxford Companion to American Military History.* Oxford and New York: Oxford University Press, 1999.

Clark, George B. *Devil Dogs: Fighting Marines of World War I.* Novato, Calif.: Presidio Press, 1999.

"EPA Cites CFC Violations at Quantico Marine Base," *FDCH Regulatory Intelligence Database,* October 12, 1999.

Fleming, Charles A., Robin L. Austin and Charles A. Braley III. *Quantico: Crossroads of the Marine Corps.* Washington, D.C.: History and Museums Division, Headquarters, U.S. Marine Corps, 1978.

Fisher, Cindy. "From Experimental to Presidential," available through MarineCorps.com (accessed February 2004).

Foner, Eric and John A. Garraty. *The Reader's Companion to American History.* Boston: Houghton Mifflin Company, 1991.

Goodwin, Doris Kearns. *No Ordinary Time: Franklin and Eleanor Roosevelt: The Home Front in World War II.* New York: Simon and Schuster, 1994.

Gottschalk, L. C. "Effects of Soil Erosion on Navigation in Upper Chesapeake Bay," *Geographical Review* 35 (April 1945): 219–238.

Harrison, Fairfax. *Landmarks of Old Prince William: A Study of Origins in Northern Virginia.* Richmond, Va.: Old Dominion Press, 1924. Reprint Baltimore, Md: Gateway Press, 1987.

Heidler, David S. and Jeanne T. Heidler, eds. *Encyclopedia of the American Civil War.* New York and London: W. W. Norton and Company, 2000.

Heinemann, Ronald L. *Depression and New Deal in Virginia: The Enduring Dominion.* Charlottesville: University Press of Virginia, 1983.

History of Prince William Forest Park, "'Bridging the Watershed': A 'National Parks Lab' Partnership between Potomac Area and National Parks and Schools," http://www.bridgingthewatershed.org/pwfphistory.html (accessed February 2004)

"History of the Town of Quantico," courtesy of Mitchel P. Raftelis, Quantico, Virginia.

Influenza, 1918, American Experience series, PBS documentary, copyright 1998.

Johnston, Angus James II. *Virginia Railroads in the Civil War.* Chapel Hill: University of North Carolina Press, 1961.

Johnson, Rossiter. *Campfire and Battlefield: An Illustrated History of the Campaigns and Conflicts of the Great Civil War.* New York: Bryan, Taylor and Co., 1894, reprint 1999.

Leslie, Frank and Rossiter Johnson. *The American Soldier in the Civil War.* New York: Bryan, Taylor and Co., 1895.

Lossing, Benson J. *Our Country: A Household History of the United States for All Readers. . . .* New York: Johnson and Bailey, 1894.

Lossing, Benson J. *The Pictorial Field Book of the Revolution.* New York: Harper and Bros., 1851.

Lossing, Benson J. *The Pictorial Field Book of the War of 1812.* New York: Harper and Bros., 1868.

McMurran, Kristin. "In Hogan's Alley, the Pseudo-town Where F.B.I. Rookies Go to School, the Gunplay's the Thing," *People* 33 (May 1990): 91–94.

Miller, Thomas W., Jr. *The Iwo Jima Memorial & the Myth of the 13th Hand.* Second edition. Arlington, Va.: T. W. Miller, 2001.

Millett, Allan R. *Semper Fidelis: History of the United States Marine Corps.* New York: Macmillan, 1980.

Mills, Eric. *Chesapeake Bay in the Civil War.* Centreville, Md.: Tidewater Publishers, 1996.

Mordecai, John B. *A Brief History of the Richmond, Fredericksburg and Potomac Railroad.* Self-published, 1940.

Moskin, J. Robert. *The U.S. Marine Corps Story.* Boston: Little, Brown and Co., 1992.

Muller, Charles G. *The Darkest Day: 1814: The Washington-Baltimore Campaign.* Philadelphia: J. B. Lippincott, 1963.

Peck, Taylor. *Round-Shot to Rockets: A History of the Washington Navy Yard and U.S. Naval Gun Factory.* Annapolis, Md.: United States Naval Institute, 1949.

Pitch, Anthony S. *The Burning of Washington: The British Invasion of 1814.* Annapolis, Md.: Naval Institute Press, 1998.

Potter, Stephen R. *Commoners, Tribute and Chiefs: The Development of Algonquian Culture in the Potomac River Valley.* Charlottesville and London: University Press of Virginia, 1993.

Prince William County Historical Commission. *Prince William: A Past to Preserve.* Prince William, Va.: the Commission, 1982.

Ratcliffe, R. Jackson. *This Was Prince William.* Manassas, Va.: REF Typesetting and Publishing, 1978.

Salmon, Emily J. and Edward D.C. Campbell Jr., eds. *The Hornbook of Virginia History.* Fourth edition. Richmond, Va.: Library of Virginia, 1994.

Sears, Stephen W. *To the Gates of Richmond: The Peninsula Campaign.* New York: Ticknor and Fields, 1992.

"Sergeant Major Jiggs," Scuttlebutt and Small Chow website, http://www.scuttlebuttsmallchow.com/masjiggs.html (accessed February 2004).

Simmons, Edwin Howard. *The United States Marines: A History.* Annapolis: Naval Institute Press, 1998.

Smithsonian Institution. Address of Alexander Graham Bell presenting the Langley Medal to Gustave Eiffel and Glenn Curtis. *Smithsonian Publication 2233.* Washington: the Institution, n.d.

Stephenson, Richard W. and Marianne M. McKee, eds. *Virginia in Maps: Four Centuries of Settlement, Growth, and Development.* Richmond: The Library of Virginia, 2000.

Stiles, Kenneth L. *4th Virginia Cavalry. Virginia Regimental Histories Series.* Lynchburg, Va.: H. E. Howard, Inc., 1985.

Stinson, Sonya "Colonel Al Davis USMC, Commanding Officer, Officer Candidates School," *Black Collegian* 26 (February 1996): 61.

Templeman, Eleanor Lee and Nan Netherton. *Northern Virginia Heritage.* Privately published, 1966.

"Top Man at Quantico," *Ebony* XLII (December 1986): 140, 144, 146.

University of Virginia Geospatial and Statistical Data Center. *United States Historical Census Data Browser.* ONLINE. 1998. University of Virginia. Available: http://fisher.lib.virginia.edu/census/. Accessed January 2004.

Van Schreeven, William J. and Robert L. Scribner, comps. *Revolutionary Virginia: The Road to Independence, Volume II, The Committees and the Second Convention, 1773–1775, A Documentary Record* Charlottesville, Va.: University Press of Virginia, 1975.

Virginia Writers' Project. *Prince William: The Story of its People and its Places. Originally Compiled in 1941 by Workers of the Writers Program of the Work Projects Administration in the State of Virginia.* Originally published, 1941. Reprint: Manassas, Va.: The Bethlehem Good Housekeeping Club, 1988.

Weeks, J. Devereux. *Dates of Origin of Virginia Counties & Municipalities.* Charlottesville, Va.: Institute of Government, 1967.

Wills, Mary Alice. *Confederate Batteries Along the Potomac.* Prince William County Historical Commission, 1978; reprint 1983.

Wilson, Charles Reagan and William Ferris, eds. *Encyclopedia of Southern Culture.* Chapel Hill and London: University of North Carolina Press, 1989.

Wilson, Richard Guy, ed. *Buildings of Virginia: Tidewater and Piedmont.* Oxford and New York: Oxford University Press, 2002.

Witzig, Eric W. "The New ViCAP More User-Friendly and Used by More Agencies," *FBI Law Enforcement Bulletin* 72 (June 2003), available at www.fbi.gov/publications/leb/2003/june2003/june03leb.htm (accessed February 2004).

Wright, Marcus Joseph, Benjamin La Bree, and James Penny Boyd. *Official and Illustrated War Record.* Washington, D.C.: [publisher undetermined], 1898.

Italicized numbers indicate subject is included in an illustration or caption, in some cases in addition to the text itself.

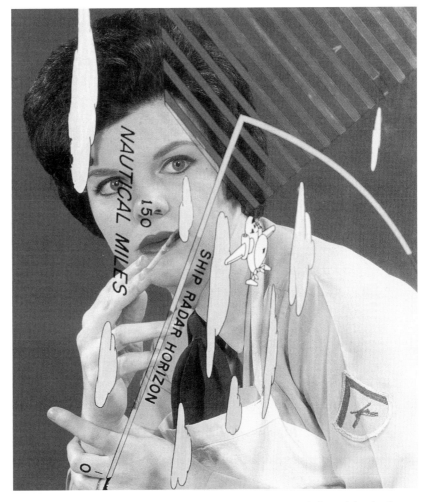

A lance corporal works on a position chart in 1969. Quantico's position in the national military firmament hardly needs charting—its contributions cannot be numbered. Courtesy Defense Visual Information Center.

ABOUT THE AUTHORS

Bradley E. Gernand

Bradley E. Gernand is a native of Antlers, Oklahoma, located in the beautiful and verdant Kiamichi Mountains. Antlers is downriver from Tuskahoma ("Place of the Warrior"), the historic and now judicial capital of the Choctaw Nation. Gernand's childhood spent among the Indians began a lifelong interest in history. He graduated from the University of Oklahoma with both a B.A. and M.A. in journalism, and worked for two years toward his Ph.D. in American Indian history. Gernand is also a Navy reserve officer, serving for several years in the fleet's information command in the Pentagon. He continues to hold a military commission.

Gernand has served as an archivist in the National Archives, and for ten years was a senior archivist in the Library of Congress. He now oversees library and information services for two government think tanks—the Institute for Defense Analyses, serving the Secretary of Defense, Joint Chiefs of Staff, and the unified commands; and the Science and Technology Policy Institute, serving the Executive Office of the President and, more particularly, the president's science advisor. This is Gernand's third book.

Michelle A. Krowl

A native of Vista, California, Michelle A. Krowl grew up in the shadow of Camp Pendleton, but her passion for Virginia and Civil War history pulled her into the orbit of Quantico. Dr. Krowl completed her undergraduate training at the University of California, Riverside, and graduate work at the University of California, Berkeley, earning her Ph.D. in history in 1998. She is currently an independent scholar, a research assistant for historian Doris Kearns Goodwin, and is embarking on a teaching career. She also serves on the board of directors of Cherry Hill Farmhouse in Falls Church, Virginia.

Dr. Krowl would like to dedicate her work on this book to the memory of the late Captain Thomas W. Turner of Vista, a beloved neighbor who passed away while this project was still in progress. Tom shared Michelle's love of history, and she hopes the career Marine would have been pleased with the results of her foray into Corps history.